A GOD'S GREENHOUSE BOOK

SANCTIFICATION

HOW GOD CREATES
SAINTS OUT OF SINNERS

TOM SWARTZWELDER

SAGE

WORDS

Pedro, Ohio

Sanctification: How God Creates Saints out of Sinners
A New Creation View of Biblical Sanctification

Visit Tom Swartzwelder's website: godsgreenhouse.net.

Many scripture quotations are the author's own translation or paraphrase.

Cover Design: Paula Wiseman

Other God's Greenhouse Books by Tom Swartzwelder

God's Greenhouse: How to Grow People God's Way
15 Spiritual Laws to Grow People

To the many voices
(of the "One Above All")
crying in today's wilderness:

Keep sowing Jesus!

CONTENTS

OVERVIEW OF GOD'S GREENHOUSE SERIES

This book represents the third resource in the *God's Greenhouse* series. Whereas each book has value as a stand-alone book, each book also represents a much-needed piece in the puzzle of how to develop Great Commission Christians that can truly change the world for Jesus Christ. More purpose-driven books have been written in the last twenty years than have been written in the entire history of Christianity. However, there have been few efforts to create a cohesive yet complete overview of the entire subject. This humble effort is a contribution to that endeavor.

The first book *God's Greenhouse: How to Grow People God's Way* develops the child of God into a *leader* with a Great Commission mindset. The book can be used for individual development, leadership training, or, most importantly, training the entire church body in Great Commission philosophy. *The latter possibility makes this book much different than other leadership books.*

Perhaps you are from the old school, and you remember the flannelgraph. The flannelgraph provided children with a *visual* of the spoken lesson. Its use was in line with the adage, "If I can see it, I can understand it."

God's Greenhouse presents a visual for adults because it includes the construction of a small greenhouse in the auditorium. This how-to-do text walks the entire congregation through God's Great Commission plan for each local church and each believer. ***It is purposely designed to help people see the church as a spiritual greenhouse***—that the church exists for the primary purpose of *growing people spiritually into Great Commission Christians*. Its goal is to transform the way people, especially leaders, think about the entire church experience.

The book includes numerous skits, handouts, and easy-to-use teaching material. Email me at pdcpastort@gmail.com for an editable copy.

The second book, *15 Spiritual Laws to Grow People,* focuses on the role of the *sower.* "Behold, a sower went forth to sow!" Whereas the first book defines "who we are and what we do," the second book develops "how to *keep* doing it." *15 Spiritual Laws* develops the psyche of God's sower. The sower may be a preacher, deacon, teacher, department leader, Gideon, missionary, children's worker, or a member. This how-to-do book helps the sower think through his entire ministry—to realize his most basic calling is that of sowing his Christlike life in the lives of others. These pages provide an understanding of the principles associated with ministry . . . principles that are critical to a prosperous long-term walk with God.

This book, *Sanctification: How God Creates Saints out of Sinners,* focuses on the believer as a *saint.* What does God intend to do with me both now and in the future? How does a believer grow in the grace and knowledge of our Lord and Savior? This book provides a thorough overview of the believer's sanctification from the two vantage points of biblical doctrine *and* practical application. The theological (some might prefer the word "theoretical") meets the experiential in this volume. That combination makes this a very rare book indeed.

The next book will focus on the believer as an *infant* ("babe in Christ") in need of everything. He may be a new believer, or he may be a longtime believer that has not grown much in his Christian life. *The Growing Up Book* develops Paul's *milk* principles in 1 Corinthians. Paul writes, "I wanted to feed you solid meat, but I had to stay with milk. Why? You have not grown very much in your Christian life." This book will be very beneficial for those Christians who are still in the childhood stage spiritually. It can be used for individual study or small group study. If God permits, *The Growing Up Book* will be available in 2021. It should be presented to every new convert!

With God's help, more pieces will be added to the puzzle over the next decade. The God's Greenhouse books and GodsGreenhouse.net belong to God and to Him alone. Making disciples or growing people spiritually has been my goal for more than forty years. I believe with all of my heart that God's Greenhouse provides a significant contribution to that goal.

INTRODUCTION

The news is timely, but the truth is timeless." Today's news will soon become yesterday's news and, in most cases, forgotten. But truth remains today, tomorrow, the day after tomorrow, and on and on not only throughout the centuries of time but also throughout eternity.

This book is about truth. *God's* truth. We know it is truth because it is taught in the Word of God. The emphatic statement, "Thy Word is truth" (John 17:17), sets the Bible apart from every other book in the history of the world. God's truth is the same regardless of the century, the setting, the level of one's education, or one's attitude. God's truth is indeed timeless. God's truth forms the basis for the entire *God's Greenhouse* series of books plus the *GodsGreenhouse.net* website.

More specifically, this book is about *transforming* truth. One cannot read the Bible without realizing that God's truth changes people. It may be a builder named Noah, a nomad named Abraham, a prostitute named Rahab, a shepherd named David, a young betrothed couple named Joseph and Mary, a son of thunder named John, a murderous sheriff named Saul of Tarsus, or just an ordinary young man named John Mark. In each case, God's truth transformed them from something they were not into something special of God's own design.

The end product of their lives became a work wholly of God's grace and without any help from their sinful flesh. In no case was it an instantaneous transformation, but, in every case, it was a gradual transformation. The business world would say, "They moved over time from the lower-left corner (quadrant) to the upper-right corner (quadrant)." The direction was up . . . again, not instantaneous but gradual as in a trendline. Some trendlines were more gradual, whereas other trendlines were steeper, but there was a discernible trend.

This biblical truth is expressed in terms of "growing in grace" (2 Peter 3:18). It is a truth I have experienced in my own life. The best way to frame the discussion is to say, "My life is different because of Jesus." Likewise, it is a truth you are currently experiencing in your own life; otherwise, you would not be reading a book which deals with the spiritual life.

"Growing in grace" is the very distinct lifestyle of growing into someone more special than you; that someone more special is our Lord and Savior Jesus Christ.

Consider these next few verses in terms of an opening act to where our journey will eventually lead us.

"And we all, with unveiled face, beholding the glory of the Lord, are being transformed into the same image from one degree of glory to another. For this comes from the Lord who is the Spirit" (2 Corinthians 3:18, ESV).

"Do not be conformed to this world, but be transformed by the renewal of your mind, that by testing you may discern what is the will of God, what is good and acceptable and perfect" (Romans 12:2, ESV).

"And we know that for those who love God all things work together for good, for those who are called according to his purpose. For those whom he foreknew he also predestined to be conformed to the image of his Son, in order that he might be the firstborn among many brothers" (Romans 8:28-29, ESV).

God's ultimate goal is *sainthood* for every single one of His children. Complete sainthood. Ultimate sainthood. Perfect sainthood. Unblemished sainthood. Faultless sainthood. Sinless, holy, Christlike sainthood 100% of our eternal existence. Yes!

How will God perform this transformation in our lives? Rest assured, God's process comes both *at* us and *to* us from multiple directions. We will delve deeply into many of those directions. It is my prayer that these pages will help you gain a better understanding of what God is doing in your life . . . and how God is conforming you more and more into the image of His dear Son.

Let's begin with what turned out to be a most interesting enigma: How should one title this book? One would not ordinarily consider that question to be an enigma, but it became one for reasons you will soon understand.

"Growing in grace" actually falls into a subcategory in the theological field known as sanctification. More specifically, it falls into the subcategory known as *"progressive sanctification."* Thus, it made sense to begin the title with the word "Sanctification" since that word clearly identifies the subject material to any reviewer. But it then became much harder to develop the rest of the title.

Here are some possibilities, along with the reasons those possibilities were rejected. First, let's explore the title *How God **Grows** Saints out of Sinners.* That's a catchy title, but, based upon God's truth, it is inaccurate. Such a title suggests a process of reformation, such as "turning over a new leaf," is indeed a possible means to sainthood.

If that were true, this world would be a much better world. For example, people make more resolutions on New Years' Eve than any other day of the year. But those resolutions do not seem to last very many days. (It is estimated that 80% of New Years' resolutions fail by early February.) Such a reformation approach to life falls far short of the Bible's insistence that the sinner must be born again. Jesus told Nicodemus, "Do not be surprised at this teaching that a man must— absolutely must—be born again" (John 3:7). God's truth states that *a new life must be created rather than an old life reformed.* Hence, the first title must be rejected.

A second possible title is *How God **Turns** Sinners into Saints.* Once again, though, we begin with the same (shall we be so bold as to say) rotten raw material. The Bible presents *and* solves the dilemma in this fashion: "Can the Cushite change his skin, or a leopard his spots? If so,

7

you might be able to do what is good, you who are instructed in evil" (Jeremiah 13:23, CSB). Obviously, the Cushite (often rendered Ethiopian) and the leopard are what they are . . . and will *remain* what they are. Likewise, the apostle Paul confirmed, "For I know that nothing good lives in me, that is, in my flesh" (Romans 7:18, CSB). Thus, God doesn't take the corrupt sin nature and somehow mold it into an incorruptible, sinless nature. God instead *adds or creates* a new nature called the born-again nature, a nature also described as, "Christ lives in me" (Galatians 2:20).

The Bible states, "If any man be *in Christ* (saved through the power of regeneration) he is a *new creation* or a new man" (2 Corinthians 5:17). Ephesians 4:22-24 mentions taking off "the old man" and putting on "the new man." Clearly, the Bible differentiates between the old man and the new man. God is not working on the old man; He is instead *starting over* with a new man. Thus, this title was also rejected.

What, though, about this title? *How God **Creates** Saints out of Sinners: A New Creation View of Biblical Sanctification.* It may not be a picturesque title, but it is consistent with biblical teaching as well as the purpose of this book.

First, this book is a "how" book. It describes a past, present, and future process known as sanctification in a step-by-step fashion.

Second, this book emphasizes that God and God alone can do what needs to be done. "The arm of the flesh is weak and will fail you; you dare not trust your own strength!" "Nothing in my hands I bring, simply to Thy cross I cling!"

Third, we will learn through the scriptures that salvation is a born-again, *creative* process that includes the placing or depositing of a totally new life called "Christ in me" in the life of the believer.

Fourth, God's ultimate, eternal goal for the believer is complete, thorough sainthood, or complete sanctification. The Bible says, "Without holiness no man shall see the Lord" (Hebrews 12:14). That holiness, though, can never be my own because of the sinfulness of the old man.

Therefore, what holiness can it be but the holiness of God's own nature in the believer?

Fifth, this work is done by God on behalf of sinners like you and me. It is not done for the sinful angels, but it is done for sinful humanity. It is done for all of the wretches like me.

As a result of God's *complete* sanctification, I shall someday be like Christ! "Dear friends, we are God's children now, and what we will be has not yet been revealed. We know that when He appears, we will be like Him because we will see Him as He is" (1 John 3:2, CSB). In other words, I have a glorious future because I myself will someday be glorified just like my Savior has already been glorified!

In that future, heavenly day, no one will find a single fault in me, nor in you! God's goal for us will be finally accomplished. He will make us saints in every sense of the word—so much so, the Bible promises, "God Himself shall be with them and be their God" (Revelation 21:3). The God who is so holy that He cannot look upon evil (Habakkuk 1:13) will not lower His holy standards even one iota, but *He will raise us to meet those same holy standards!*

"Blessed and *holy* is he that has part in the first resurrection" (Revelation 20:6). Imagine someday being 100% holy or saintly! It will someday be real to all of us who know Jesus Christ as our personal Lord and Savior!

Question: How will God perform this incredible work in your life and mine? How will God make us like Christ?

Let's begin.

OUR MAIN TEXT

"Be constantly growing in the grace and knowledge of our Lord and Savior Jesus Christ. To Him be the glory both now and throughout eternity."

(2 Peter 3:18)

Above all, never, never, never stop growing in Him!

SECTION ONE

THE THEOLOGY OF
SANCTIFICATION

1

GROWING UP SPIRITUALLY

From a Friend of Long Ago

"Grow—make that keep growing—in the grace and knowledge of our Lord Jesus Christ." Grow today, grow tomorrow, grow the day after tomorrow, and the day after the day after tomorrow and keep on doing it. Eventually, you will experience a lifetime of growth. And you will look back and realize that growth did indeed happen. As a matter of fact, you will realize how much you have grown . . . and that your life is worth sharing with others.

Near the end of my life I wrote two books that became part of God's holy Word. My books include many, many items that pertain to your spiritual life, but I also included some personal experiences. Why? *I believe my life, dear reader, will serve as an example to you about how many times one can fail and yet, in the end, over time, grow up spiritually to achieve God's purpose for his life.*

Perhaps it is best to go back to the very beginning to place things in perspective. My spiritual journey, let's call it a spiritual transformation, began with a roughly clothed preacher by the name of John the Baptist. At that time, our country was not very religious. The religion of our day was very ritualistic. In those days, I was not sure why we did what we did! Quite honestly, most of us were simply going through the motions. There had been talk about a messiah, but such talk had been around for a long, long time. Talk is cheap. It did not interest me.

But then word came of a so-called prophet of God named John the Baptist. This John was different, even much different than the conventional, establishment preachers. He had no official certification from the councils of the Pharisees or Sadducees. He was just out there on his own in the wilderness of Judaea. Some people talked about his strange clothing; they said he wore clothing made from camel's hair instead of a typical rabbinical robe.

But it was this man's preaching that seemed to have the most impact. The people said that he spoke as if he was a prophet from God.

I was naturally skeptical about these claims, but I decided to see for myself. And what then happened was the most important event in my entire life.

I heard John preach. It was not the best-delivered message I have ever heard, but it was a message which somehow penetrated the very depths of my heart. John declared in a loud, bold voice, "I have been sent to prepare the way of the Lord! The Messiah is coming! The King and His kingdom are on the doorstep! Confess your sins, and prepare your hearts for the coming Messiah! If you agree with my message, join me in the waters of this Jordan River and I will baptize you."

For the first time in my life, I passed from a religious experience to a true spiritual experience. My blindness was gone; I could see with my heart that John was somehow right. I did not know *how,* but I still knew! And I believed . . . one moment I did not believe, and the next moment, I did believe. It was a blindness to "now I see" experience. I did not understand at the time that this transformation was brought about by God the Holy Spirit. But I knew things were somehow different. I believed!

I obeyed John's instructions and was immediately baptized. Some people later mocked me for being one of John's followers. Their message was clear: What kind of fool would follow a man dressed in camel's hair—a man who also lacked a rabbinical degree or certification?

I stayed, listened, and learned from this God-anointed man. Day after day, he proclaimed "the good news of the kingdom." That message was food to my soul. Everyone in Israel yearned for the day that some called "the consolation, or deliverance of Israel from its foreign oppressors." I wondered, could our long-awaited deliverance be about to take place?

Then one day, He was suddenly among us. He was later described as "meek and lowly" rather than "arrogant and mighty," and that was my first impression, too. John pointed to Him and announced, "Here is the Lamb who will take away the sin of the world." My sin! And your sin, too, dear reader!

Did I understand how it would happen? By no means. But I somehow believed. I believed enough that I was *convinced* God would somehow work out all the details.

Looking back on it now, I realize that I was living by faith, just like Father Abraham in the old days. I had found John, whom I believed to be a prophet of God. I had also found the Messiah, whose name was Jesus.

I was also there for one of the most tremendous days in all of history. John Mark later recorded my words, "In those days Jesus came from Nazareth in Galilee and was baptized by John in the Jordan. Immediately coming up out of the water, He saw the heavens opening, and the Spirit like a dove descending upon Him; and a voice came out of the heavens: 'You are My beloved Son, in You I am well-pleased'" (Mark 1:9-11, NASB).

I wish you, dear reader, had been there to see it, but then again, I wish you had been with us to see a lot of things. That baptism was THE baptism of all baptisms. Even my later experience at Pentecost paled in significance to this one baptism.

By now, my life had become much different. I now had a holy purpose for living: That I might know the Messiah, learn from Him, imitate Him in all His ways, and be committed to His purpose rather than my own purpose.

That is why I immediately responded when He called, "Come, follow me." I left my fishing nets (I failed to mention earlier that my trade was that of a fisherman) and went to follow Him. I am happy to say that, except for only a few days, I have followed Him for the rest of my life. I am also pleased to write that, as time passed, *I became much less occupied with the Messiah's kingdom and much more consumed with the Messiah Himself.*

I agree (and you would also agree if you had been here with me) with my brother John's assessment, "And there are also many other things which Jesus did, which if they were written in detail, I suppose that even the world itself would not contain the books that would be written" (John 21:25, NASB).

Many years have passed. Indeed, more than thirty years have now passed. I just recently wrote my own contribution to the Bible. I pray that you will be able to glean my deep, profound enthusiasm for Jesus, my Messiah. He is beyond remarkable, beyond wonderful, beyond any earthly description. He is truly above all; He is the awesomely perfect Son of God.

At the same time, I hope you will be able to glean my failures in these pages. I suspect many future sermons will be preached about my failures. Truth be told, there were times when I soared in Christian success. Unfortunately, there were other times when I plummeted in fleshly failure.

I believe all of those up-and-down experiences can be helpful to you in your Christian journey. I have learned the Christian life is not one of 100% successful triumphs, but it also has more than its share of miserable failures. But I never allowed those failures to stop me for long.

And I urge you not to allow your failures to stop you for long, either. If I could keep going, so can you!

For example, my second book shares my memory about being on the Mount of Transfiguration with our Lord. What an event that was! I have experienced many thrilling events, but this particular event belongs in the Top Ten.

Elijah and Moses met with our Lord, and our Lord's appearance was changed, or transfigured, into that of a glorified being . . . like God Himself. But wouldn't you know it? I terribly messed up that Top Ten event. I became so caught up in my emotions that I suggested we commemorate the place by building three booths in honor of the Messiah, Moses, and Elijah. My mess-up was so bad that the Father of our Lord and Savior Jesus Christ *vocally* rebuked me. I doubt if you have ever been rebuked in the same manner. Hardly had I uttered my foolish suggestion about building three booths than the Father said, "This is My beloved Son! I am well pleased with Him! Listen to Him!" Well, I learned to listen to Him!

Do you remember some of my other words? "The devil is on the prowl like a roaring lion seeking whom he may devour." There are occasions in life when all of God's children are sifted like wheat by the devil. Tests come, trials come, temptations come. As for me personally, I was so strong at times, only to be so weak at other times. I was so willing to die for my Lord in the Garden that I used a sword to defend my Messiah. I swung the sword at someone's head but, sad to say, I only got his ear. Then, just minutes later, I went fleeing for my life.

Before the breaking of the next dawn, I denied not just once, not just twice but *three* times that I even knew the Lord. And the lion then roared the loudest roar you have ever heard. And I then went out and wept bitterly. That's why I write about, "the proving of your faith . . . being tested by fire." Pardon the pun, but in my case, it was a literal fire in the courtyard, for I was warming myself by the devil's fire while Jesus was on trial.

One of the other apostles often chided me, "Brother, the only time you open your mouth is to change feet." There has been a lot of truth in that statement.

My lack of faith often plagued me, too. That's why I mention faith seven times in my books. I specifically recall the time I saw the Lord walking upon the sea. I asked Him to let me share in that experience, too. And He said, "Come on!" I courageously left the boat (I remember no one else followed me) and walked toward Him. I realized more than ever before that anything is possible with God! I was actually walking on the water like Jesus!

But I soon became conscious of the raging sea, my faith turned to fear, and I took my eyes off my Messiah. I immediately began to sink into the water, and, in my despair, I cried out like a drowning man. My gracious Messiah reached down, took my hand, and delivered me from my despair. Then He admonished me, "You have so little faith. Why did you doubt?" I must admit it wasn't just Thomas who doubted in those days.

I must sadly admit, too, that my lack of consistency has been a lingering issue for me even as I have become an older apostle. I will be credited forever with being strong enough to refute centuries of traditionalism/legalism, open the door of God's grace to the Gentiles (the first Gentile's name was Cornelius), and present a strong, irrefutable case for admitting the Gentiles into God's church.

However, a few years later, I bowed beneath the same religious pressure and disassociated myself from the same Gentiles. *I learned even the best of men is still nothing but a man at his best.* Thankfully, the apostle Paul was stronger than I was, and he rebuked me for my inconsistency. But the hurt of that moment still lingers.

Let my life be a warning that these failures can happen to you, too! But at the same time, please allow the successes of my life, and there have been many successes, to also be an encouragement to you.

I have experienced something remarkable, even miraculous, called "growing in grace." ***If grace can do a maturing, sanctifying work in*** *me, grace can also do a maturing, sanctifying work in you!* There have been many times when I thought I was hopeless, but God's grace has continued to transform me into someone whom God could use to His own glory and honor.

There were many additional items I considered for my two books. But my time was limited . . . and my parchment was limited, too! Besides, the main purpose was to write about what you *needed* to know. After all, I'd much rather that you become more like Jesus than me. In addition, my personal stories, including my lapses in spiritual growth, have been adequately recorded in the four gospels, Acts, and Paul's writings.

I leave you with these simple words of encouragement. These words also represent the very last words I wrote in the Bible. In many ways, they may be the most important words of all because they are based upon my own experiences.

"Grow and keep growing—be constantly growing—in the grace and knowledge of our Lord and Savior Jesus Christ." If I were writing the same passage today, I might phrase it like this, "Grow and *never* stop growing . . . *never* stop becoming more and more like Jesus."

In so doing, you will be greatly blessed, and you will become an even greater blessing to others.

Yours truly,
Simon Peter

2

LET THERE FIRST BE LIFE!

The United States is recognized throughout the world as a *Christian* nation. As a matter of fact, one recent poll revealed that more than half of all Americans claim to be Christians. Unfortunately, the poll did not provide a specific definition for the term "Christian." Thus, everyone was at liberty to define the term in their own words. As a result, some people defined the term "Christian" as simply anyone who believes in God, whatever God happens to be to that particular person. But is that a biblical definition? And wouldn't we agree the only definition which really matters is a biblical definition?

A Christian couple placed an advertisement in the newspaper which read, "Free room in exchange for services by a Christian lady." The couple expected a sweet, motherly Christian woman to live in their house and assist them with the children.

Several women immediately applied for the position. The couple's first question never varied. They always asked, "Are you a Christian?"

The answers were often strange and far-fetched. But the strangest answer of all came from a woman who replied, "In your opinion, what is a Christian?"

The man of the house said, "I will give you my answer after you first give me your answer."

The woman said curtly, "A Christian is anybody who is not a Jew or an Asian."

Is that woman right? Is that all there is to be properly classified as a Christian? If the answer is no, then what exactly is a Christian? How does one become a Christian? Can one know for certain that he or she is a Christian?

The main text for *Sanctification: How God Creates Saints out of Sinners* is 2 Peter 3:18, which states, "Be constantly growing in the grace and knowledge of our Lord and Savior Jesus Christ. To Him be the glory both now and throughout eternity. Amen." It is the concluding verse for both the book of 2 Peter as well as Peter's ministry. In many ways, it describes the way Peter wants to be remembered in our present day.

This little book of 2 Peter is a very important book because it deals with three erroneous ideas regarding the Christian religion. (Indeed, Peter uses the word "error" in 2 Peter 2:18 and 3:17.) These erroneous ideas are displayed by the attitude which declares, "A Christian is anybody who is not a Jew or an Asian."

Let's consider the three errors in reverse order. *The third error is the world's belief that judgment day will never come.* The world mockingly asks, "Where are the signs of God's coming? Everything continues as it has since the beginning of time" (2 Peter 3:4). The next verse, though, contradicts the world's attitude with the words, "But they *willfully* ignore the judgment associated with Noah's flood—the flood proves that everything has *not* continued since the beginning of time."

The rest of the chapter contains phrases like, "The Day of the Lord, the universe passing out of existence with a loud noise, the elements burning and even melting, everything on earth shall be destroyed."

Therefore, we can be confident that judgment day is indeed coming—it is coming, though, on God's schedule. It has not been delayed. We must accept that concept as a reality. All of us will someday stand before God. That means I myself must be ready to stand before God. Above all, I must know the correct definition of a true Christian!

The second error is the belief that "all the paths in the pasture lead back to the barn." In other words, no religion is superior to any other religion. The Muslims, Hindus, Catholics, Christians, Buddhists, Mormons, and other religious people are on an *equal* path which will deliver all of us to our blessed heaven, nirvana, or whatever is out there.

Peter insists that such teaching is utterly and totally false. Peter refers in his second chapter to such beliefs as false teaching, damnable or destructive heresies, depraved ways, maligning/distorting the way of truth, irrational animals, spots and blemishes, delighting in their deceptions while they feast with you, and gone astray from the way of truth.

Peter is not quietly disagreeing with other beliefs, but he is hotly contesting their genuineness. Either Peter is right, or he is badly wrong. If he is right, our souls hang in the balance as to what we do with his teaching. The Old Testament cautions us, "There is a way which seems right to a man but the end of that way is the way of death" (Proverbs 14:12).

What, though, is the *first* error? It is the reason for writing this Greenhouse book's opening chapter. *The first error is that of assuming one possesses salvation when the biblical evidence suggests otherwise.* Peter warns the members of his Christian community to make certain— absolutely, 100% certain—of their own salvation.

Please do not treat this subject lightly. "Therefore, brothers and sisters, make every effort to confirm your calling and election, because if you do these things you will never stumble" (2 Peter 1:10, CSB). "These things" include the various Christian graces outlined in the preceding verses. Peter considers "these things" to be *evidence* of genuine salvation. From Peter's viewpoint, "these things" are a good way to *confirm* that you are a genuine Christian rather than a look-alike Christian.

Vance Havner says, "If you are what you've always been, you are not a Christian. A Christian is a new creation."

During my teenage years, someone concocted a way to frame this discussion so that everyone could understand. On one occasion, we turned the church auditorium into a courtroom. Several people were put on trial for their Christian faith. The prosecutor asked, "Is there enough evidence to identify you as a genuine believer and to convict you as a genuine Christian?"

Those words stirred the consciousness of many. Why? It was customary for people to answer, "I was saved when I was a child. I was baptized when I was a child. Let me show you my baptismal certificate."

But for many people, that experience happened more than one generation ago! *Surely, we have confirming evidence in how we are living today* . . . and yesterday . . . and the day before. Surely, we can talk about the preciousness of our Lord, how we are following the Lord in our daily life, and how He has become our very best friend. But, strangely, some in the Christian community cannot do so!

Peter is calling every single one of us to look for *confirming evidence* in our lives. He is not calling us to discuss an event of thirty years ago which has apparently made little difference in how we live. He is calling us to look at our current lives and to identify the specific evidence that we have been born again.

The apostle Paul issues a similar call: "Examine yourselves to see if you are legitimately *in* the Christian faith. *Put yourself to the test.* Do you not know that the life-changing Jesus Christ indwells you? That is true unless you have failed the test" (2 Corinthians 13:5).

Sadly, many people will stand before God and defend themselves by saying, "My name is on the church roll. Or I made a profession of faith. Or I was baptized. Or I sang in the choir. Or I attended church. Or I gave a sizable contribution."

However, many people will learn that their religious experience was *not* a legitimate born-again experience. Do you remember the words of Jesus?

> *Not everyone who says to me, 'Lord, Lord,' will enter the kingdom of heaven, but only the one who does the will of my Father in heaven. On that day many will say to me, 'Lord, Lord, didn't we prophesy in your name, drive out demons in your name, and do many miracles in your name?' Then I will announce to them, 'I never knew you. Depart from me, you lawbreakers!'* (Matthew 7:21-23, CSB).

Herbert Lockyer writes,

> Paul writes of those who had a form of godliness, but who were destitute of its power (2 Timothy 3:5). They pretend a holiness they do not possess. They have a dazzling profession, but are lamps without oil. A true holiness (Ephesians 4:24) implies there is a feigned brand. Clouds are without rain (Jude 12). A pretended sanctification is a statue without life. Behind holy habits there must be a holy heart. (*All the Doctrines of the Bible*, p. 217)

I cannot state the next sentence strongly enough. *It is critical that you, dear reader, understand the born-again experience and can confirm its existence in your own life.* That is the reason for this chapter. It is also the reason why a similar chapter appears in all of my books. Hell will be full of church members; I do not want you to be in their midst.

1. THE NEW BIRTH PRECEDES GROWTH

What does the new birth have to do with growing? Everything!

Let's take a trip to the cemetery. Most cemeteries have a *large* population. (The size is important because, in most cases, a larger sample size should provide more reliable results.) Let's hire an instructor to educate the cemetery's entire population for eight hours a day for an entire year. What kind of results should we expect from such an effort? How much will our instructor accomplish? Will any of the inhabitants become better in any area of life?

The answer to every question will be negative. The results will be the same as if we had exerted no effort at all. The reason for the instructor's failure is quite simple: The population is dead and beyond help. There is no life in any member of the cemetery's population. Each and every member is dead and unable to receive even the simplest instruction.

They cannot hear, communicate, sense, comprehend, touch, laugh or cry, grow or change because they are dead . . . 100% totally dead. Beyond hope. Beyond help.

Their state of deadness prevents growth of any kind from occurring. This same principle carries over into our current discussion.

Spiritual deadness prevents spiritual growth from occurring.

Spiritual growth can only develop *out* of spiritual life; that spiritual life can only happen *out* of a heaven-sent, born-again experience.

That is why 2 Peter 3:18 says, "Be constantly growing *in* the grace and knowledge of our Lord and Savior Jesus Christ." Spiritual growth occurs *in* a spiritual greenhouse (some suggest the word "sphere") named "Grace and Knowledge." This same spiritual greenhouse is also expressed as "In Christ" in the writings of the apostle Paul.

The point is that spiritual growth does not occur where death exists but only where life exists. No one can **grow** spiritually unless he or she first **exists** spiritually. *Spiritual life must exist before spiritual growth can develop.*

What is the title of this chapter? *"Let There First Be Life!"*

One cannot **grow** *as a Christian until he or she first* **becomes** *a Christian.* No one grows into salvation. Salvation is not a gradual process where one evolves into salvation. Nor is salvation the result of associating with other Christians until their Christianity rubs off on you, and you gradually become a Christian.

No one in any century, any race, or any education has the ability to put himself into God's spiritual greenhouse known as "Grace and Knowledge." This greenhouse is the position or sphere of privilege which God grants to every true believer in His Son, Jesus Christ.

*It cannot be emphasized too much that everyone must be spiritually born again **before** they can grow spiritually.* The admonition to "be constantly growing" can only apply to those who know Jesus Christ as their Lord and Savior. If one tries to grow without being born again, his life may indeed be the life which is described in 2 Peter chapter two—a life of religion without the real God.

Remember this: Chapter two pictures the failure of reformation or religion—such man-made efforts fall far short of being remade in the image of Jesus Christ.

2. WHAT IS THE NEW BIRTH?

Jesus said to Nicodemus, "Do not be surprised when I say to even a religious man like you, 'You must be born again! Except a man be born again, he cannot see the kingdom of God'" (John 3). "Born again" is the Bible's way of expressing "the new birth."

Charles Haddon Spurgeon explains,

> I was staying one day at an inn in one of the valleys of northern Italy where the floor was dreadfully dirty. I had it in my mind to advise the landlady to scrub it. But when I perceived that it was made of mud, I reflected that the more she scrubbed it, the worse it would be. The man who knows his own heart soon perceives that his corrupt nature admits of no improvement. There must be a new nature implanted or the man will only be 'washed' to deeper stains. God declares, 'Ye must be born again.' Ours is not a case for mending but for making new.

29

Why should you or I be made new? I stated earlier that it is impossible to grow that which is dead. I used the cemetery as an illustration, but at that time, I did not prove why the cemetery is a good analogy. It is now time, though, to see why the Bible describes the soul of man as being fit for the cemetery.

And you were dead in your trespasses and sins in which you previously lived according to the ways of this world, according to the ruler of the power of the air, the spirit now working in the disobedient. We too all previously lived among them in our fleshly desires, carrying out the inclinations of our flesh and thoughts, and we were by nature children under wrath as the others were also. But God, who is rich in mercy, because of his great love that he had for us, made us alive with Christ even though we were dead in trespasses. You are saved by grace! (Ephesians 2:1-4, CSB).

Paul begins by stating that man is spiritually dead in "sin" or a sinful condition. He then describes the lifestyle of a spiritually dead person as being in accordance with the "ways of this world" or "the drumbeat of this world." Paul finishes the passage by stating a second time that people are "dead in trespasses." Dead, dead, dead. You can't get any deader than dead!

Contrary to what some imagine, it is not a case that the spirit of man is dead because man is essentially a spirit living in a human body (Genesis 2:7, Daniel 7:15). The scriptures, though, indicate that man's spirit has become deadened *toward* God. It is not my purpose to do a full explanation on the subject of human depravity, but, suffice it to say, Adam's sin (see Genesis 3 and Romans 5) created a separation between man and God, a separation so wide that only the cross of Jesus Christ can bridge it.

Lewis Sperry Chafer writes, "The first sin of Adam caused him to be transformed downward into a different kind of being from that which God had created."

All of man's being (will, intellect, spirit/soul, flesh) became deadened toward God. It is as if man turned his back upon God so he could no longer *see* God, deafened his ears so he could no longer *hear* God, removed all of his nerves so he could no longer *feel* God, damaged his taste buds so he could no longer *taste* God, even plugged his nose so he could no longer *smell* God. Based on Adam's sin, all of mankind has been born into a condition that is deadened toward God.

That leads you to a reasonable conclusion, which is also a biblical conclusion. What do you do with a dead man? You must resurrect him!

The spiritually deadened man needs a *resurrection* to spiritual life, to a life that allows him to know, comprehend, and experience his God and Creator. Man needs a capacity to know God! *That's exactly what the new birth does.*

The above passage states that God has "made us alive" by imparting to us the life of the resurrected Christ. The Bible says, "Just as Christ was raised from the dead by the glory of the Father, so we too may walk in newness of life. For if we have been united with him in the likeness of his death, we will certainly also be in the likeness of his resurrection" (Romans 6:4-5, CSB). "Newness of life" expresses a resurrection.

"So, you too consider yourselves dead to sin and alive to God in Christ Jesus" (Romans 6:11, CSB). *Once again, we are viewed as possessing a life which did not previously exist.*

The story is told of an old Roman who tried to make a corpse stand upon its own feet. He finally gave up and said, "Something is lacking inside." He thought for a moment longer then said, "This corpse doesn't need props. It needs new life!" Amen!

". . . [Y]ou have been born again, not of perishable seed but of imperishable, through the living and abiding word of God" (1 Peter 1:23, ESV). What we are by *physical birth* will someday perish because we are the product of perishable seed. But what we are by *spiritual birth* will never perish because we are the product of imperishable seed.

"So if you have been raised with Christ, seek the things above, where Christ is, seated at the right hand of God. Set your minds on things above, not on earthly things. For you died, and your life is hidden with Christ in God. When Christ, who is your life, appears, then you also will appear with him in glory" (Colossians 3:1-4, CSB). Again, note the concept of "raised" or "resurrected" with Christ. Also, this new life is described as "Christ, who is your life."

Colossians 1:27 further defines this life as being, "Christ in you, the hope of glory."

"And when you were dead in trespasses and in the uncircumcision of your flesh, he made you alive with him and forgave us all our trespasses" (Colossians 2:13, CSB).

There is a law in nature which states that water will not rise above its own level or flow uphill. Likewise, the old nature cannot rise to the portals of Glory to look upon the face of a holy God. There absolutely must be a new nature!

That is why the Bible says, "Have no confidence in the flesh" (Philippians 3:3). "Not that we are sufficient in ourselves to claim anything as coming from us, but our sufficiency is from God, who has made us sufficient to be ministers of a new covenant, not of the letter but of the Spirit. For the letter kills, but the Spirit gives life" (2 Corinthians 3:5-6, ESV).

Through the new birth, God provides a new nature, which is often described as the born-again nature. This new nature is not a re-design or recharacterization of the first nature given to us at physical birth. For all intents and purposes, God has chosen to by-pass the first nature as if it is irreparable . . . which it is. "Can the Ethiopian change his skin or the leopard his spots? Then you also can do good who are accustomed to doing evil" (Jeremiah 13:23, NASB).

Once more, it cannot be emphasized too much that the new birth or "being born again" is the impartation of a new nature patterned according to God's own likeness. "Blessed be the God and Father of our Lord Jesus Christ. Because of his great mercy he has given us new birth into a living hope through the resurrection of Jesus Christ from the dead" (1 Peter 1:3, CSB).

"No one born of God makes a practice of sinning, for God's seed abides in him; and he cannot keep on sinning, because he has been born of God. By this it is evident who are the children of God, and who are the children of the devil: whoever does not practice righteousness is not of God, nor is the one who does not love his brother" (1 John 3:9-10, ESV). The one who is born of God has God's seed abiding in him!

Paul urges us, "to put on the new self, the one created according to God's likeness in righteousness and purity of the truth" (Ephesians 4:24, CSB). "Created" is indeed the right word because, "if any man is in Christ, he has become a new creation; old things have passed away and all things have become new" (2 Corinthians 5:17).

How much clearer can it be that God requires a born-again experience from all of us?

3. HOW IS A PERSON BORN AGAIN?

". . . [B]orn again—not of perishable seed but of imperishable— through the living and enduring word of God" (1 Peter 1:23, CSB).

It is common today to treat the expression "born again" as synonymous with reformation or "turning over a new leaf." But such a definition falls far short of what God requires. The Bible teaches that a genuine born-again experience results in the creation of an entirely new person called "Christ in you!"

Quite honestly, religion is often more of a hindrance than a help, because, unfortunately, religion tends to be very ritualistic. And genuine, biblical Christianity is not about rituals but about having a relationship with a Person: the Lord Jesus Christ!

Someone asked, "Why is there so much emphasis upon rituals in religion?" The answer is very simple. The flesh can understand and relate to rituals, but the flesh cannot understand and relate to the Spirit of God.

John MacArthur led a man to the Lord after a Sunday night church service. This man had attended a Roman Catholic church earlier in the day in order to confess his sins to a priest. The priest said, "My son, you've earned forgiveness. Now go and pray fifty Hail Marys with these prayer beads."

The young man went to the altar and started through the Hail Marys. He suddenly jumped up, threw the beads across the church, and shouted, "This is ridiculous! This isn't doing anything for my sin." He then ran out of the church.

Several hours later, he attended MacArthur's church, heard an explanation of salvation, and accepted Jesus Christ as his personal Lord and Savior. In so doing, he was genuinely forgiven of his sins and born again into God's family.

Arthur Pink writes in his excellent book, *The Doctrine of Sanctification* (p. 46), "It is a common error of those that are unregenerate to seek to reform their conduct without any realization that their state must be changed before their lives can possibly be changed from sin to righteousness. The tree itself must be made good before its fruit can possibly be good."

Thank God, when God saved us, "He saved us—not by works of righteousness that we had done, but according to his mercy—through the washing of regeneration and renewal by the Holy Spirit" (Titus 3:5, CSB).

How can I have, or experience, this washing of regeneration and renewal by the Holy Spirit?

Above all, we must understand that the new birth *does not come through any ritualistic means.* A ritual is normally viewed as a religious ceremony that includes step one, step two, step three, etc. *The process is often emphasized even more than the result.* If one is not careful, he has fooled himself into placing more faith in the ritual than in the desired outcome.

The great preacher H. A. Ironside was about to broadcast a gospel message from a large radio station in Cleveland. He patiently waited to begin his message. Suddenly he heard the announcer do a commercial. The advertiser said, "If you need anything in watch repair, go to such-and-such a firm."

An employee looked over at Ironside and muttered, "I need no watch repairing. What I need is a new watch."

Rituals tend to be a Band-Aid when you actually need something brand new.

What is the biblical goal of this chapter? It is to make certain that you are born again. *No ritual, though, can produce that goal, because rituals do not possess the power to bring about the new birth.*

Jesus told Nicodemus, "You must be born again." The word "again" is translated from the Greek word *anothen*. It is commonly known that *anothen* has two possible translations. The first translation is "again" as in a second time. The second translation is "from above." Indeed, the Holman Christian Standard Bible includes a note on its translation of John 3:3, which says, "The same Gk word can mean *again* or *from above* (also in v. 7)." (The American Standard Version, English Standard Version, New American Standard Bible, New International Version, New King James Version, and New Living Translation have a similar note.)

(Note: *Anothen* is translated "from above" in John 3:31, Matthew 27:51, and James 1:17.)

We often sing,

> "There's not a single blessing
> Which we receive on earth
> That does not come from heaven,
> **The source of our new birth.**"

> Barney E. Warren

The message of, "Ye must be born again" apparently sailed over poor Nicodemus' head. Nicodemus responded by asking, "Can a man return to his mother's womb and be born a second time?"

Jesus rebuked his foolish thinking by saying, "The fleshly birth is of the flesh, but the spiritual birth is of the Spirit." (Note: Where does the Spirit come from? He comes from above! Poor Nicodemus never bothered looking up!)

One common ritual that is often emphasized in evangelical churches is repeating a sinner's prayer. The seeker is told, "If you would like to be born again, repeat the following words after me." The soul winner then leads the seeker through a prayer which includes the ABC's of Admit you are a sinner, Believe in Jesus, and Confess Jesus as your Savior.

I often do a similar sinner's prayer with those whom I counsel *provided* they have a good understanding of their own sinfulness, Jesus' substitutionary death on the cross as payment for their sins, *and* Jesus' resurrection from the grave to be the one and only Savior. In other words, they must have a good understanding of the good news known as the gospel!

However, and this is a monstrously big however, praying a formula prayer or even praying an un-formula prayer can be very ritualistic and fall far short of a genuine born-again experience. Why? It is because the person may be putting his faith in a prayer or in a ritual rather than in the Person of the Lord Jesus Christ. Sadly, the person may not even know who Jesus really is!

The next statement may seem difficult, but it is accurate. The sinner's prayer is not the way *to* faith, but it is an expression of an *already existing* faith. "'Whoever will call on the name of the Lord will be saved.' How then will they call on Him in whom they have not believed? How will they believe in Him whom they have not heard? And how will they hear without a preacher?" (Romans 10:13-14, NASB).

We could paraphrase Paul's words like this: "How will they pray to Him unless they have already believed in Him?" Genuine belief or faith *precedes* the genuine praying or the genuine calling! You don't call unless you already believe He will both hear and save!

Let me cite my own salvation as an example. I was raised in a church where sinners customarily came forward in a sermon-ending invitation (Billy Graham style) to receive Christ as Savior. Sinners would kneel at an altar and pray to receive Christ.

In my case, I had been under the conviction of the Holy Spirit for more than a year. I was only nine years of age, but I knew I was lost, hell-bound, without hope, and did not have God in my life. I also knew Jesus Christ, God the Son, had died on the cross to pay the penalty for my sins. The final step was for me to receive Him as my Lord and Savior—to commit my life, my soul, my sins, my all to Him in an act of faith or belief. In essence, to believe in Him instead of anything else. I needed to place myself in His hands . . . and I did!

During a revival meeting on Thursday, January 14, 1965, at 9:00 p.m., I left my third-row seat and came to the altar to receive Christ. I prayed, I cried, and I left the altar happy.

But when was I actually born again? In my case, I was born again when I took my *first* step toward that altar because that was when I exercised faith in Him to receive a sinner like me. *My heart had already beaten my feet to the altar!* I was not coming to the altar for further counseling, but I was coming because I had already committed in my heart to receive Christ as my Savior. I did not fully understand every step in the process, but I was firmly convinced that Jesus would keep my soul, which I was committing to His care (2 Timothy 2:12).

I write this because I want you to know it was *not the ritual* that saved me. The altar was a nice piece of wood, but it did not have anything to do with my salvation. The prayer was a contrite prayer from the heart of a nine-year-old boy, but it had nothing to do with my salvation. The people around the altar . . . many came forward to pray with me, but that had nothing to do with my salvation. I experienced a wide range of emotions, too, but those emotions had nothing to do with my salvation . . . nor will emotions have anything to do with your salvation, either.

What happened? In my heart (on the third row) I said, *"I will arise* and go to Jesus, He will embrace me in His arms. In the arms of my dear Savior, O, there are 10,000 charms." And, in faith, I arose, and He received me!

"For by God's grace are you *saved through faith and faith alone,* and that not of yourselves; it is God's gift. Salvation is not of works lest any man should boast" (Ephesians 2:8-9).

"But as many nine-year-old boys as *receive* Jesus, to them God gives the right to become children of God" (John 1:12).

> *For God so loved the world, that He gave His only begotten Son, that whoever believes in Him shall not perish, but have eternal life. For God did not send the Son into the world to judge the world, but that the world might be saved through Him. He who believes in Him is not judged; he who does not believe has been judged already, because he has not believed in the name of the only begotten Son of God (John 3:16-18, NASB).*

"But these have been written so that you may believe that Jesus is the Christ, the Son of God; and that believing you may have life in His name" (John 20:31, NASB).

The ritualistic sinner's prayer may help you to *express* your faith, but it will never ever be a substitute for real faith!

Above all, don't rely on a ritual!

Let's imagine you die ten seconds from now and arrive at the pearly gates. The angel asks, "Why should I admit you into God's heaven?"

How would you respond? Would you say, "I completed the ritual of 10,000 Hail Marys on the earth"? Would you say, "I was baptized twenty times—ten by immersion, five by pouring, and five by sprinkling"? Would you say, "I went to church thirty years without missing a Sunday"? Would you say, "I prayed the sinner's prayer when I was a child"? Or would you say, "I plead the blood of my Savior, Jesus Christ. He died for me on the cross of Calvary as a sacrifice and substitute for my sin"?

We are called and required to believe in Him . . . in Him and Him alone . . . not in a ritual, not in a church, not in a personal accomplishment but solely in Him.

If you believe in **Him**, you have passed from death unto life, and you have been born again. But if you believe in *anything other than Him,* you have not yet passed from death unto life, and you have not yet been born again. "Received **Him**" (John 1:12). "Whoever believes in **Him**"

(John 3:15). "Whoever believes in **Him**" (John 3:16). "The one believing on **Him** is not condemned but the one believing not is condemned already because he has not believed in the name (the name represents the person) of the only begotten Son of God" (John 3:18). "He that believes on the **Son** has everlasting life but he that believes not the Son shall not see life" (John 3:36). "He that believes on **Me** has everlasting life" (John 6:47). "Whoever believes in **Me**" (John 11:26). It's all about Him, and there is no Savior without Him!

One evening a Catholic woman disagreed with evangelist B. R. Lakin about the way of salvation. She said, "I am going to heaven by virtue of Saint Peter because he holds the keys to the door!"

Lakin replied, "I am going to heaven by virtue of Jesus Christ because He Himself is the door!" (John 10:9)

Charles Haddon Spurgeon writes,

> "My hope lives not because I am not a sinner, but because I am a sinner for whom Christ died; my trust is not that I am holy, but that being unholy, He is my righteousness. My faith rests not upon what I am or shall be or feel or know, but in what Christ is, in what He has done, and in what He is now doing for me. Hallelujah!"

I say, "Hallelujah!" too. Can you say the same?

A student came to a Scottish preacher and asked how long he might safely put off committing his soul to Jesus Christ. The Scottish preacher gave a strange reply. He said, "Until the day before your death."

The student said, "But I cannot tell you when I shall die."

The preacher said, "Then decide now."

Now is the acceptable time. Now is the day of salvation.

Be sure you have been born again. Write down the date of your salvation in the margin of this page. If the date is unknown, write down the general date such as the season and year or time of your life. Then thank God that you know—you truly know—you have been born again.

"I write these things to you who believe in the name of the Son of God, that you may know that you have eternal life" (1 John 5:13, ESV). Thank God, you can know!

First, there must be life.

Then it is time to grow.

3

WHAT IS GOD DOING WITH ME?

A beautiful little girl lived in the slums of a large eastern city. God touched the hearts of some Christians in that little girl's neighborhood. Those Christians opened a little gospel mission which the girl attended. She won her way into the hearts of these Christian workers. She became the object of their love and care.

Easter came. A generous florist sent some beautiful white lilies to the mission to be distributed among the less fortunate people of the slums. The mission workers gave the most beautiful lily of all to this little girl. They waited to see her reaction because she had never seen a flower as beautiful as this one. She smiled, laughed, then broke into tears and began to cry.

The workers were dismayed. They asked, "Why are you crying? Don't you like that lily? Don't you think it is beautiful?"

She said, "Oh, yes, I like it . . . I surely do. It is so beautiful and white. But I didn't know how dirty I was until I saw how white this lily is. That's why I am crying."

In its simplest form, the doctrine of sanctification is God's process of turning dirty, even filthy sinners into the purest of saints. Sound impossible? It is for us, but not for our God.

Based upon our acceptance of the previous chapter, we know that we have been born again by receiving Jesus Christ as our Lord and Savior.

We know by experience what the little boy meant when he received Christ, then exhaled the loudest exhale ever heard by mortal man and said, "At last, that's settled!" The burden had been lifted, and peace with God was now his.

I know I am born again, but now what? What does God intend to do with me in the years ahead *before* I enter heaven? And, also, *when* I enter heaven? Plus, what will I be like *in* heaven? According to the Bible, God intends to do an abundance of life-changing items with each one of us!

Many of God's intentions are fulfilled through this big Bible word called *sanctification*. Sanctification is both a big-picture concept as well as a smaller, very specific, even detailed process. *This particular chapter will present the big picture.* The next chapter will deal with the timing of these events.

1. THE BIG PICTURE: THE MEANING OF SANCTIFICATION

Arthur W. Pink frames the discussion quite well:

> But how shall men be sanctified so as to be suited unto the presence of an infinitely pure God? By nature they are utterly without holiness: they are 'corrupt, filthy, an unclean thing.' They have no more power to make themselves holy than they have to create a world. We could tame a tiger from the jungle far more easily than we could our lusts. We might empty the ocean more quickly than we could banish pride from our souls. We might melt marble more readily than our hard hearts. We might purge the sea of salt more easily than we could our beings of sin. (*The Doctrine of Sanctification*, p. 51)

Ah, what a problem man has! "Even if you wash with lye and use a great amount of soap, the stain of your sin is still in front of Me. This is the Lord God's declaration" (Jeremiah 2:22, HCSB).

Adam's sin had two important consequences. Why? Adam was our representative or, as scholars like to say, our Federal Head. Lewis Sperry Chafer writes, "As a limitless forest of oak trees may be embraced in one acorn, so a race was contained in Adam. The Biblical principle which proceeds on the basis that unborn generations do act in their fathers, or share in that responsibility which their fathers bear, is declared in Hebrews 7:9-10." (*Systematic Theology Volume VII*, p. 113)

The passage states, "One might even say that Levi himself, who receives tithes, paid tithes through Abraham, for he was still in the loins of his ancestor when Melchizedek met him" (Hebrews 7:9-10, ESV).

Chafer concludes, "Here Levi, who lived by tithes being paid to him and who was a great-grandson of Abraham, paid tithes, although being then only in the loins of his great-grandfather, Abraham."

Similarly, our president is the Federal Head of the United States. For example, he has the power to begin a war that has the potential to end with the death of every American. In such matters, he speaks for all of us. No election is held to ratify such a decision, but, as our representative, he decides for all of us . . . and all of us bear the consequences of his decision.

Likewise, the weight of the entire world, including humanity, creation, and all earthly created beings, rested upon Adam's shoulders. Adam foolishly chose to rebel against God. Adam's horrendous decision set many awful things in motion.

Above all, Adam's one sin caused God to place a curse upon *all* of creation. That is why the Bible says, "Many died because of the offense or trespass of the one man, Adam . . . because of one man's sin, death now reigns through that one man, Adam . . . therefore, *one* sin—just *one* sin—led to the condemnation of *all* men" (Romans 5:15-18).

First, Adam's guilt was imputed or charged to our account. Though yet unborn, we shared in his sin. We were equally condemned with him.

Second, and of equal importance, Adam's fallen, sinful nature was communicated to us. The first consequence declares in God's courtroom that we are sinners in need of salvation; the second consequence results in our daily lifestyle being a sinful lifestyle.

Chafer writes, "No other human being than Adam has ever become a sinner by sinning. All others were born sinners." (Eve, of course, shared in the consequences of Adam's sin.)

But along comes God and *God commences a process called sanctification* which, in its final stage, will result in God's people becoming 100% pure, holy, and Christlike throughout the eons of eternity. Sound too good to be true? That's why it is called grace!

The word "sanctify" appears more than one hundred times in the Old Testament and at least thirty times in the New Testament. The word is translated from the Hebrew word *qodesh* and the Greek word *hagiazo*.

Thiessen's *Introductory Lectures in Systematic Theology* is a classic text for either the beginner or the scholar. (Note: I prefer the first edition.) Thiessen comments on page 377, "Both the Hebrew *qodesh* and the Greek *hagiazo* mean essentially to separate."

The Greek scholar Kenneth Wuest specifies that *hagiazo* means "to consecrate, for instance, altars, sacrifices, to set apart for the gods, to present, to offer." It does not mean, "merely 'to set apart,' but in the case of the pagan word, 'to set apart for the gods,' and in the case of the Christian word 'to set apart for God.'" (*Studies in the Vocabulary of the Greek New Testament*, p. 30)

The New Testament word "sanctify" is usually derived from the Greek verb *hagiazo*. It is translated hallowed ("Hallowed be Thy name"), sanctify, and holy. The related noun *hagiasmos* is translated sanctification and holiness. A similar word, *hagion*, is translated sanctuary and holy place. A fourth word, *hagios*, is, most notably, translated holy as in the title "Holy Spirit," but it is also translated saint in Paul's writings.

With that in mind, let us look first at the most basic meaning of "to set apart."

Many years ago, a house guest asked his hostess if he could borrow one of those newfangled writing instruments called a fountain pen. The hostess brought several to the guest. He chose one and prepared to write. But the hostess immediately identified the pen and stopped him from writing.

She said, "Excuse me. I did not notice this pen was among the others. Would you mind using another pen? This is my *special* pen. I've noticed that it doesn't write smoothly after someone else has used it."

In other words, that hostess had a "sanctified" pen. She had "set apart" one pen from the others. In the same way, *God sets people apart from other people.* That action is called "sanctification."

Herbert Lockyer writes in his usual excellent way, "Its root meaning suggests a setting apart from that which is common and unclean. The Old Testament uses the term, generally speaking, to describe *things*, while the New Testament employs it to denote *persons*." (*All the Doctrines of the Bible*, p. 217)

Henry Thiessen adds these comments:

> Usually we have simply the positive idea of separation or dedication to God. In this sense the tabernacle and the temple were sanctified with all their furniture and vessels (Ex. 40:10, 11; Num. 7:1; 2 Chron. 7:16). In this sense also a man might sanctify his house or a part of his field (Lev. 27:14, 16). In this sense the Lord sanctified Israel's firstborn to Himself (Ex. 13:2, Num. 3:13, Neh. 8:17). In this sense also the Father sanctified the Son (John 10:36) and the Son sanctified Himself (John 17:19). In this sense, finally, Christians are sanctified at the time of their conversion (1 Cor. 1:1, 2; 1 Pet. 1:1, 2; Heb. 10:14). Jeremiah was sanctified before he was born (Jer. 1:5), and Paul speaks of being separated from his mother's womb (Gal. 1:15). (*Introductory Lectures in Systematic Theology*, p. 378)

It's time to dig a little deeper into the definition and, at the same time, issue a warning to one and all. As noted above, the word sanctification means "set apart to be holy" or "set apart for God's holy use" in its normal Bible usage. *I urge the reader, though, to always look closely at* the context before extrapolating a definition beyond the "set apart" format.

For example, Jesus prayed in John 17:19, "And for their sakes I sanctify Myself." *It is clear that Jesus, the Holy One of God, could not become holier than He already was.* (Thus, in this case, the definition cannot mean "to become holy.") This verse teaches that Jesus *set Himself apart* for a holy task! He set Himself apart from the everyday tasks of life to the Father's monumental assignment of dying for the sins of the world. In other words, "I have reached a new stage in My ministry. The climax of My ministry has come. It is now time to fulfill My primary mission. In accordance with the Father's will, I now set Myself apart to give My life as a ransom for many."

This testimony of Jesus also expresses the primary focus of this entire book. In the same manner, God is <u>setting us apart</u> to know <u>Him</u>, serve <u>Him</u>, imitate <u>Him</u>, and someday be with <u>Him</u>!

Through the process of sanctification, God is creating saints out of sinners! Many people, though, have an incorrect view of sainthood. As a result, our culture classifies some Christians as saints but classifies other believers as being inferior to the saints.

W. A. Criswell explains the world's false view of sainthood in this manner:

> To us the word 'saint' is a human designation. It refers to a technical human achievement. God is subordinate. All God does in our modern definition of saint is to receive the dedication of these human efforts. A saint to us is somebody who is striving to be good or striving to serve or striving to be consecrated or striving to get nearer to the Lord. That is a saint. But in the Bible, a saint is somebody whom God's grace has set aside and chosen and dedicated to Himself.

This truth makes all the difference in the world. My salvation and any dedication that I have and any call that I might know come from God and not from me. (*Great Doctrines of the Bible Volume VI*, p. 27)

Salvation has two directions—it is *from* hell and *to* heaven. Sanctification sets us apart *from* those on the broad road to a devil's hell and establishes our new direction *with* those on the narrow road to God's heaven. My eternal home is not "where the fire is never quenched and the worm dieth not" but my eternal home is where God dwells. I even have the promise that "God Himself shall be with them and be their God." It can't and won't get any better than that.

2. THE BIG PICTURE: THE PURPOSE OF SANCTIFICATION

The big picture regarding the purpose of sanctification is as broad as the universe and yet also as narrow as a tiny crack in the sidewalk. If we are not careful, we will step over the smallest details and totally miss what God is doing with our lives. Sanctified or "set apart" affects practically every single detail of our lives, including our very innermost being.

More specifically, the purpose of sanctification is to set us apart:

- From hell to heaven,
- from sinfulness to holiness,
- from works to grace,
- from darkness to light,
- from an old creation to a new creation,
- from corruption to incorruption,
- from a worldly purpose to a heavenly purpose,
- from carnality to spirituality,
- from a temporal goal to an eternal goal,
- from outside Christ to inside Christ, and
- from dishonor to ultimate glory!

Thank God, I've been set apart *from* all of the first items in that list and set apart *to* all of the second items on that list! In other words, God has a big agenda for me . . . and for you, too.

Herbert Lockyer says, "Election is the *cause* of salvation, but sanctification is the *evidence* of it!"

Perhaps Revelation 20:6 is the best verse to explain the big picture of sanctification. "Blessed and holy is the one who participates in the first resurrection!" A cursory review of every commentary in my study indicated that, without exception, every commentator's attention was drawn to the part about the "first resurrection." I will agree with the commentators that prophecy is an important study, but, speaking for myself, I am much more interested in what God intends to do with me.

This phrase "blessed and holy" describes my final, ultimate state of being . . . in other words, what I will be throughout eternity, world without end!

Practically every translation uses the same three words to begin verse six. The term "blessed" means happy or joy-filled; the primary reason for our joy is that our faith has now become sight! The people described in verse six are no longer imagining eternity, but they are experiencing it.

Verse six also explains that we have now been translated into a state or condition of perfect holiness. We know it is complete holiness because there is no such thing as 99% holiness. When God identifies Himself as being holy, He means exactly what He says: 100% holy.

Conclusion: Our final destiny is perfect holiness. To be honest, in my current state, I cannot conceive what such a condition will be like. But I'm sure I will like it! Most Christians are preoccupied with such heavenly items as walking on golden streets, shaking hands with Abraham, kneeling at the feet of Jesus, and being free of aches and pains. *But the final destination of perfect holiness is the first item that God stresses* . . . and, indeed, it is the foundational principle and condition for living in that heavenly place.

God's church (the body of Christ) has a similar destiny, too, because His corporate church consists of individual believers like us. "Husbands, love your wives, as Christ loved the church and gave himself up for her, that he might sanctify her, having cleansed her by the washing of water with the word, so that he might present the church to himself in splendor, without spot or wrinkle or any such thing, that she might be holy and without blemish" (Ephesians 5:25-27, ESV).

The ultimate destiny of the bride of Christ is to be "holy and without blemish." Can you imagine such a time when you are "holy, even without blemish" *and* you are surrounded by all of your born-again friends who are also "holy, even without blemish"? All of us will be above criticism in that day.

Plus, our goal will become a holy goal, too! The Westminster Larger Catechism poses its first question, "What is the chief and highest end of man?"

The answer is, "Man's chief and highest end is to glorify God, and to enjoy him forever."

Through sanctification, we will finally accomplish our created purpose. *We were created for Him!* With that in mind, Peter tells us to "sanctify Christ as Lord in your hearts, always *being* ready to make a defense to everyone who asks you to give an account for the hope that is in you, yet with gentleness and reverence" (1 Peter 3:15, NASB).

Isaiah testified in chapter six of his amazing book that he, a sinful man, saw the Lord Jehovah sitting upon a throne, high and lifted up in heaven. That vision had to be spectacular. But perhaps even more important was that Isaiah *internalized* the vision. He sanctified, or exalted, the Lord *in his heart* above all other people or things. The results are very evident in the remaining sixty chapters of Isaiah's prophecy.

3. THE BIG PICTURE: THE TRINITY'S ROLE IN SANCTIFICATION

All of the following had their origin with the Being known as God: the universe, angels, animal life and human life, heaven and hell, salvation, the Bible, the nation of Israel, and the church. Thus, no one should be surprised in the least that the believer's sanctification begins with God, too.

"For it is God who works in the believer both to will (desire) and to do whatever pleases Him" (Philippians 2:13). It is God who takes the initiative and not we ourselves.

The Bible makes it abundantly clear that all three members of the Godhead (Father, Son, and Holy Spirit) are deeply involved in our sanctification.

Thiessen writes,

> God the Father sanctifies the believer in that He reckons the holiness of Christ to him (1 Cor. 1:30), works in him that which is well-pleasing in His sight (Heb. 13:21), and disciplines him (Heb 12:9, 10; 1 Pet. 5:10). Christ sanctifies the believer by laying down His life for him (Heb. 10:10; 13:12; Eph. 5:25-27) and in producing holiness in him by the Spirit (Heb. 2:11). The Holy Spirit sanctifies the believer in that he frees him from the carnal nature (Rom. 8:2), strives against the manifestation of it (Gal. 5:17), puts to death the old nature as the believer yields it to Him for crucifixion (Rom. 8:13), and produces the 'fruit of the Spirit' (Gal. 5:22, 23). Thus, there is a definite function for each of the trinity in our sanctification. (*Introductory Lectures in Systematic Theology*, p. 384)

4. THE BIG PICTURE: THE BELIEVER'S ROLE IN SANCTIFICATION

Based on the above discussion, we should not be surprised to learn that God's sanctifying graces are designed to work holiness into our lives in the here and now. One can even think of such graces as a little touch of heaven in this present evil day!

Once again, I wish to quote from Arthur Pink's *The Doctrine of Sanctification*. He writes on page 76, "It is greatly to be regretted that so many when thinking or speaking of the 'salvation' which Christ has purchased for His people, attach to it no further idea than deliverance from condemnation. They seem to forget that deliverance from *sin*—the cause of condemnation—is an equally important blessing comprehended in it."

The adage is biblically true: Christ has not purchased security IN sin but FROM sin. That is done through sanctification.

Once again, let's look to the Word of God.

"I will consecrate the tent of meeting and the altar; I will also consecrate Aaron and his sons to minister as priests to Me" (Exodus 29:44, NASB).

"You shall know the truth and the truth shall set you free" (John 8:32).

"Likewise, reckon, or count, yourselves to be dead unto sin as your master, but alive unto God through Jesus Christ, our Lord. Do not ever again allow sin to reign as king in your lives" (Romans 6:11-12).

"For the love of Christ compels us, since we have reached this conclusion: If one died for all, then all died. And he died for all so that those who live should no longer live for themselves, but for the one who died for them and was raised" (2 Corinthians 5:14-15, CSB).

"Who gave Himself for us to redeem us from every lawless deed, and to purify for Himself a people for His own possession, zealous for good deeds" (Titus 2:14, NASB).

"For if the blood of goats and bulls and the ashes of a young cow, sprinkling those who are defiled, sanctify for the purification of the flesh, how much more will the blood of Christ, who through the eternal Spirit offered himself without blemish to God, cleanse our consciences from dead works so that we can serve the living God?" (Hebrews 9:13-14, CSB).

"He Himself bore our sins in His body on the cross, so that we might die to sin and live to righteousness" (1 Peter 2:24, NASB).

Each verse clearly states that the believer has been "set apart for God's holy use." Based upon comparing the Old and New Testaments, it can be fairly stated that *the New Testament gospel is no less holy than*

51

the Old Testament law—in other words, the holiness required in the New Testament is equal to the holiness required in the Old Testament.

E. M. Bounds writes,

> Under the Jewish dispensation the high priest had inscribed in jeweled letters on a golden frontlet: 'Holiness to the Lord.' So every preacher in Christ's ministry must be molded into and mastered by this same holy motto. It is a crying shame for the Christian ministry to fall lower in holiness of character and holiness of aim than the Jewish priesthood. Jonathan Edwards said: 'I went on with my eager pursuit after more holiness and conformity to Christ. The heaven I desired was a heaven of holiness.' (*Power Through Prayer*, p. 9)

Robert Murray M'Cheyne instructs us to, "Study universal holiness of life. Your whole usefulness depends on this for your sermons last but an hour or two; your life preaches all the week."

Harold Sightler declares, "We don't talk like the world and we don't act like the world. We have doors open to anyone who believes what we believe."

God's call to you and me is the same as God's call to those in the Old Testament: "I will also consecrate or sanctify Aaron and his sons to minister as priests to Me. The nation's duty is to set them apart for My purpose. *It is the duty of Aaron and his sons to set themselves apart for My purpose*" (Exodus 29:44, Leviticus 8).

One can imagine God saying the same thing about you and me. "I will also consecrate _____ (write your name) to minister to Me."

The calling is a holy calling, and it must be answered by holy people. The calling originates with God, but the answer must originate within us. "It is their duty to set themselves apart for My purpose."

This challenge aptly describes our role in sanctification, for we have truly been set apart for His holy purpose. How, though, will we respond? With diligence or resignation? With enthusiasm or reluctance? By

saying, "Yes, all to Jesus, I surrender" or saying, "No, let me first go do
_____"?

One pastor illustrated the level of required commitment by pointing out, "Even something as simple as church attendance does not happen by proxy. It must be done by you. You must get out of your chair at the house. You must get dressed. You must walk to the car. You must drive the car to the church. You must get out of the car and walk into the church. No one can do this but you. You and you alone are the one responsible for your spiritual growth. Lazy Christians do not grow. *Disciplined* Christians grow. That's why they're called *disciples*!"

> "Is your all on the altar of sacrifice laid?
> Your heart does the Spirit control?
> You can only be blest,
> And have peace and sweet rest,
> As you yield Him your body and soul."

> E. A. Hoffman

4

THE MAJOR STAGES OF SANCTIFICATION

The subject of sanctification generates many questions for both the Calvinist and Arminian. Arthur W. Pink provides an excellent summary of such questions in the introduction of his classic book *The Doctrine of Sanctification.*

> But what is 'sanctification': is it a quality or position? Is sanctification a legal thing or an experiential? That is to say, Is it something the believer has in Christ or is it in himself? Is it absolute or relative? By which we mean, Does it admit of degree or no? Is it unchanging or progressive? Are we sanctified at the time we are justified, or is sanctification a later blessing? How is this blessing obtained? By something which is done for us or by us or both? How may one be assured he has been sanctified: what are the characteristics, the evidences, the fruits?

From my humble perspective, the best way to get your arms around this subject is to categorize the scriptures. I have been in the ministry for more than forty years. I have seen an abundance of material oriented to sanctification. In many cases, the material is good, but it is not good for the reader, especially the beginner or the Sunday School teacher, because it is not presented in an organized manner. Quite often, the reader feels whipsawed instead of illuminated.

I do not recall seeing any author categorize/organize the scriptures in the following format. Perhaps there is a good reason for that, but, in my case, I sometimes must see something in my mind before I can grasp it. (I have often said I could fully understand life if it was only an Excel spreadsheet.) From my perspective, a picture, or visualization, is worth more than a thousand words!

That leads me to the next paragraph, which is very important. Please read it *twice* before you move further into the book.

Harry Ironside, pastor of Moody Church, was asked by a stranger if he was saved. The famous pastor replied, "Yes, I have been, I am being, and I shall be." What did he mean? **Properly viewed, God's salvation has past, present, and future components!**

"I have been saved, I am being saved, and I shall be saved." That is true of me. That is true of you. That is true of everyone who has been born again.

Such a statement may be new to you, but it is still true. It is difficult to present such a statement in a sermon or lesson because it requires a person to mentally think through the *entire* statement. That normally takes time. It even takes time to contemplate how to put it into writing.

"I have been saved, I am being saved, and I shall be saved." Pause for a moment to consider that the statement consists of three verb tenses: past, present, and future. God's sanctification of the believer occurs in *all three* verb tenses, also. The past tense indicates there are scriptures that discuss that God has sanctified me at the very moment I was born again. (I will refer to those scriptures as *positional* sanctification.) In this stage, the believer is saved from the **penalty of sin**.

The present tense indicates there are scriptures that discuss God sanctifying me in my present-day life—my life *following* my born-again experience and terminating at my death or the Rapture. (I will refer to those scriptures as *progressive* sanctification.) In this stage, the believer is being saved from the **power of sin**.

Finally, the future tense indicates there are scriptures that discuss God sanctifying me in the future resurrection and glorification of God's saints. (I will refer to those scriptures as *perfect* sanctification because that stage wonderfully results in my perfection in every sense of the word.) In this stage, the believer is finally saved from the **presence of sin**.

Through God's three-fold process of sanctification, the believer is saved from the penalty of sin, the power of sin, and the presence of sin!

It should be noted that practically all of the sanctification verses will fit in only one of these three stages or categories, whereas a few may be categorized in two stages.

STAGE ONE: POSITIONAL SANCTIFICATION

Scholars use the term "positional" to indicate truths that have happened to the believer solely because of his position or location *in the mind of God.* It is similar to being in a grocery store where one finds all kinds of blessings. At that particular time, each person in the world falls into one of two categories: Each person is either inside the grocery store, or he is outside the grocery store. The same principle carries over into theology. Every human being is either "in Adam" or "in Christ." He is either in the "First Adam" from Garden of Eden fame or in the "Second Adam" who is Christ, the Savior (1 Corinthians 15:45).

The same principle exists in what we call "positional sanctification" for lack of a more descriptive term. The easiest way to grasp positional sanctification is to think of it as *this is how God currently sees the believer*. In God's heavenly courtroom, God has ruled the believer to be both justified (righteous) and sanctified (set apart for Himself).

Ephesians 1:1-3 says,

> *Paul, an apostle of Christ Jesus by the will of God, To the saints who are at Ephesus and who are faithful in*

> *Christ Jesus: Grace to you and peace from God our*
> *Father and the Lord Jesus Christ. Blessed be the God*
> *and Father of our Lord Jesus Christ, who has blessed us*
> *with every spiritual blessing in the heavenly places in*
> *Christ (NASB).*

Paul makes it plain in verse one that the Ephesian letter is addressed to the saints. Paul does not describe them as transitioning into saints or someday becoming saints but as *already being* saints or sanctified ones.

The term applies to all of the born-again people in Ephesus . . . to those who are currently filled with the Spirit as well as those who are not filled with the Spirit . . . to all regardless of their current submission to the Holy Spirit.

We must, therefore, conclude that this action happened in the same past event for everyone since it includes all genuine Christians. No genuine Christians are excluded; therefore, it must have happened at the same time in *all* of our lives, namely, the time when we trusted Jesus Christ for salvation.

Furthermore, notice *how* they have been sanctified, separated, or set apart. Paul addresses them as saints because they are "*in* Christ Jesus." They have been set apart from their old position "in Adam" and are now seen by God as being "in Christ Jesus." They have been set apart or sanctified positionally! Moved from being "in Adam" to being "in Christ."

Charles C. Ryrie teaches, "In Christ is the redeemed man's new environment in the sphere of resurrection life." Ryrie quotes Stewart saying about the believer, "He has been transplanted into a new soil and a new climate, and both soil and climate are Christ." (*Biblical Theology of the New Testament*, p. 204)

To use my own analogy, the believer is now in God's Greenhouse. The believer has been separated from the wilderness and is now in resurrection life, new soil, and a new climate.

Thiessen writes on page 378, "Believers are called 'saints' in the New Testament irrespective of their spiritual attainments (1 Cor. 1:2, Eph. 1:1, Col. 1:2, Heb. 10:10, Jude 1, 3)."

"I chose you before I formed you in the womb; I set you apart before you were born. I appointed you a prophet to the nations" (Jeremiah 1:5, CSB). Travis Agnew asked, "When does God appoint? He appointed Jeremiah the prophet within the womb. That means that his calling preceded his résumé. It helps me remember that God's calling is more secure than my abilities."

Likewise, the apostle Paul testifies, "But when God, who from my mother's womb set me apart and called me by his grace" (Galatians 1:15, CSB). Obviously, neither Jeremiah nor Paul had done anything to warrant the "setting apart." Such action pre-dated even their births. Their "setting apart" *in the mind of God* undoubtedly affected their adult here-and-now, but it, nevertheless, preceded their adult here-and-now, even their conception.

"Wherefore, holy brethren, partakers of the heavenly calling, consider the Apostle and High Priest of our profession, Christ Jesus" (Hebrews 3:1, KJV). "Holy brethren" describes us as God's people. It does not describe only a few of God's people but is an identifier for all of God's people. Through the process of positional sanctification, we are regarded as holy by God even though we often live unholy lives. The unholy are deemed holy because of our sanctified, set-apart position in the Holy Son of God.

"And such were some of you. But you were washed, you were sanctified, you were justified in the name of the Lord Jesus Christ and by the Spirit of our God" (1 Corinthians 6:11, ESV). The verbs washed, sanctified, and justified are in the past tense in our translations. This past tense translation agrees with the aorist tense in the Greek text. The apostle Paul normally uses the aorist tense to indicate the action was completed in the past and is not ongoing in the present. It would be appropriate to define the aorist tense in this particular verse as meaning "once-for-all."

When was the person justified? At his salvation. When was the person washed or regenerated or born again? At his salvation. And when was the person sanctified or set apart? Obviously, at his salvation. *It is clear that all of these events occurred simultaneously.*

Interestingly, this verse also teaches that *all* of the Corinthians were considered as sanctified, even though many of them were still living in a carnal state (1 Corinthians 3:1). Clearly, *how one lives does not change one's position* of being washed, justified, and sanctified. The position is fixed even though the lifestyle may vary from day to day.

(Note: The above verse also indicates that God justifies the believer at the moment of regeneration. The word "justify" means "to declare righteous." The believer is justified or declared righteous by the Judge at the moment he accepts Christ as his personal Lord and Savior (Romans 5:1). The believer can never be *more* justified in the future than he is at the moment of salvation. Justification is a once-for-all completed action on the part of God to which nothing can ever be added, diminished, or removed. The court of heaven has issued its ruling, and there is no higher court to overrule God's court! *Although sanctification includes three stages, justification includes only one stage.)*

"Paul and Timothy, bond-servants of Christ Jesus, To all the saints in Christ Jesus who are in Philippi, including the overseers and deacons" (Philippians 1:1, NASB). Other translations use the words "holy people" in place of "saints." As in the case of the Ephesian epistle, the Philippian letter is not addressed to the saintly saints but to the saints. The saints are the people who have been saint-ified or sanctified (set apart) in Christ. Please note they are saints solely for the reason of their position: set apart in Christ. We could even translate the verse, "To all of those who have been set apart in Christ Jesus." This verse provides another example of positional truth.

It has been said that the entire ministry of the apostle Paul could be wrapped up in these two words "in Christ." As a matter of fact, Paul writes entire chapters about who we are and what we can now do based solely upon our position in Jesus Christ. The truth is no one yet has plumbed the deepest depths of what it means to be "in Christ."

Think about it like this. When Noah went inside the ark, God shut the door. The flood then came, but Noah was safe. He lived for 371 days inside the ark. During that time, God met every single one of Noah's needs because Noah was *inside* the ark of safety.

That is exactly what happens when we believe in Jesus Christ. God immediately sets us apart *inside* the ark of safety; that ark of safety is His Son, Jesus Christ. It is *in* the greater ark of His own Son that God has promised to meet every single one of our needs.

That is why Paul makes such a big deal of these two little words "in Christ." Always remember this: Being in Noah's ark in the Old Testament is a picture of being "in Christ" in the New Testament.

(Note: The believer's position "in Christ" is established by another positional teaching known as the baptism of the Holy Spirit. "For by one Spirit we were all baptized into one body, whether Jews or Greeks, whether slaves or free, and we were all made to drink of one Spirit" (1 Corinthians 12:13, NASB). Some quibble over whether the Greek preposition *en* should be translated "in," "by," or "of," but, from my point of view, the difference is immaterial. The end result is the same. The Holy Spirit unites the believer with Christ, the Anointed One, at the time of salvation (1 Corinthians 6:17). In so doing, the believer becomes joined to Christ in His crucifixion, burial, and resurrection to new life (Romans 6:3-8). Water baptism pictures our union with Christ. *Water baptism is the ritual, whereas Spirit baptism is the reality.* For further study, please see Romans 6:3-5, 2 Corinthians 1:21, Galatians 3:27, Ephesians 2:10 and 4:5, Colossians 2:12.)

"Jude, the servant of Jesus Christ, and brother of James, to them that are sanctified by God the Father, and preserved in Jesus Christ, and called" (Jude 1, KJV). (Note: The Nestle text substitutes *agape* for *hagios*, thereby rendering the verse "divinely loved by God the Father" instead of "sanctified by God the Father.")

"For the one who sanctifies and those who are sanctified all have one Father. That is why Jesus is not ashamed to call them brothers and sisters" (Hebrews 2:11, CSB). Once again, the verb "sanctified" is in the past tense, thus indicating it is a finished deed for all of us who believe. Since it has been done to all, it must, therefore, have occurred when all believed in Jesus.

"By this will, we have been sanctified through the offering of the body of Jesus Christ once for all" (Hebrews 10:10, NASB). The writer offers this statement as proof of the New Covenant's superiority over the Old Covenant. Sacrifices were repeatedly offered for the believer's sins in the Old Testament. However, Jesus offered Himself only once! His sacrifice was of such high quality that He only needed to offer Himself once. That one offering satisfied God the Father to such a degree that the one offering has once-for-all sanctified us. God now views us as acceptable or separated to Him.

"For we know that our old self was crucified with Him in order that sin's dominion over the body may be abolished, so that we may no longer be enslaved to sin, since a person who has died is freed from sin's claims" (Romans 6:6-7, HCSB). This passage will be explained as part of a different discussion in the next chapter. Suffice it to say, this passage covers two tenses of the believer's life: his past salvation experience and his current life. We could paraphrase the verse like this: "For we know that at salvation our old self was once-for-all positionally crucified with Him . . . with the result that in the here and now, we can live free from the dominion of sin." The here-and-now part is based upon the once-for-all part.

"But we should always give thanks to God for you, brethren beloved by the Lord, because God has chosen you from the beginning for salvation through sanctification by the Spirit and faith in the truth" (2 Thessalonians 2:13, NASB). There are levels in this verse that are beyond human comprehension. J. Vernon McGee, no slouch when it comes to knowing the Bible, writes,

That looks back to the past. All I know is what it says, and I believe it. Do you mean to tell me that God chose us before we even got here? Spurgeon used to put it something like this: 'I am glad God chose me before I got here because if He waited until I got here He never would have chosen me.' It simply means you do not surprise God when you trust Christ . . . You are sanctified both as to position and to practice. When you accept Jesus Christ as your Savior, you are in Christ—that is positional sanctification; that is the past tense of salvation. Then there is also the practical side of sanctification which concerns your life. Through the Spirit of God you are to grow in grace. (*Thru the Bible with J. Vernon McGee Volume V*, p. 417)

We should also point out the order of events that appear in this verse. Three of the events happen before our birth, but that does not suggest the fourth event is unimportant. The four events are loved by God, chosen by God, sanctified or set apart for salvation by God, and man's faith in the truth.

Are the first three events causative of the fourth event as some suggest or merely the order as others suggest? But if they are causative, why isn't the second event caused by the first event, etc.? Let us always remember the will of one party does not, by itself, change the will of a second party. Needless to say, all four events will happen in the life of a believer, but in a general sense, only the first event will happen in the life of a non-believer (John 3:16).

The apostle Peter expresses the same concept in practically the same words, "according to the foreknowledge of God the Father, in the sanctification of the Spirit, for obedience to Jesus Christ and for sprinkling with his blood" (1 Peter 1:2, ESV). Peter establishes a clear order of events as well as the grouping of those events. Regarding the latter, the first group (foreknowledge and sanctification) *precedes* regeneration while the second group (obedience/faith and sprinkling/application of the blood) occurs *at* regeneration. Each activity is mentioned in proper chronological order!

However, in what sense can even an unbeliever be sanctified? (Note: Paul uses "sanctification" in the same sense in 1 Corinthians 7:14.) Our personal salvation experience answers that very question. Every sinner knows there was a time when he was not interested in God. But then God called, and we became interested! "Common grace" opened our hearts to an understanding of sin, righteousness, and judgment to come. We were drawn, even dragged, into the glorious light of the gospel, whereas another sinner in the same pew may not have experienced the same enlightenment. He may have been yawning and counting down the minutes, whereas we were listening very intently! We had been set apart to the Spirit's call.

Thiessen describes this pre-salvation event as one in which "God graciously restores to all men sufficient ability to make a choice in the matter of submission to Him. This is the salvation-bringing grace of God that has appeared to all men" (*Introductory Lectures in Systematic Theology*, p. 345).

On the other hand, Wuest, a stronger Calvinist, believes, "God the Father chose the sinner out from among mankind to be the recipient of the setting-apart work of the Spirit, in which work the Holy Spirit sets the sinner apart from his unbelief to the act of faith in the Lord Jesus." (*First Peter in the Greek New Testament*, p. 16)

Suffice it to say, no one is in heaven by accident, no one gets saved by accident, and no one gets saved without exercising faith. (I suggest we leave the God-side to God and work on the man-side of discipling men to the point of belief.)

Based upon 2 Thessalonians 2:13, 1 Peter 1:2, Romans 8:29-30, and the Majority Text rendering of Jude 1, we can properly conclude that logically in God's mind as well as in systematic theology, positional sanctification precedes justification and regeneration. But chronologically in the believer's life, all three occur *at the same time* as a sinner exercising faith in Jesus Christ. That is the beauty of the union between Common Grace and Efficacious Grace.

"For in Him all the fullness of Deity dwells in bodily form, and in Him you have been made complete, and He is the head over all rule and authority" (Colossians 2:9-10, NASB). Neither the word sanctify nor any of its derivatives appear in this passage, but the impact of sanctification can be clearly seen. The believer is identified as being "in Him," and, as we have already learned, that does not happen without the work of the Holy Spirit. As a result, Paul states the believer is now complete or filled with no room for anything to be added.

How, though, can we define the level of completeness that is found in Colossians 2:10? Paul's own words define it to the Corinthians. "No one can boast in His presence. But it is from Him that you are in Christ Jesus, who became God-given wisdom for us—our righteousness, sanctification, and redemption, in order that, as it is written: The one who boasts must boast in the Lord" (1 Corinthians 1:29-31, HCSB).

Pink explains,

> If we are considered as what we are in ourselves, not as we stand in Christ (as one with Him), then a thousand things may be 'laid to our charge.' It may be laid to our charge that we are woefully ignorant of many parts of the Divine will: but the sufficient answer is, Christ is our Wisdom. It may be laid to our charge that all our righteousnesses are as filthy rags: but the sufficient answer is, that Christ is our Righteousness. It may be laid to our charge that we do many things and fail to do many others which unfit us for the presence of a holy God: but the sufficient answer is, that Christ is our Sanctification. It may be laid to our charge that we are largely in bondage to the flesh: but the sufficient answer is, Christ is our Redemption. 1 Corinthians 1:30 then is a unit. (*The Doctrine of Sanctification,* p. 109)

It is a unit of positional truth. It is indeed our spiritual position because we are "in Him" or "in Christ."

R. A. Torrey eloquently states:

> When Jesus died, he died as my representative, and I died in him; when he arose, he arose as my representative, and I arose in him; when he ascended up on high and took his place at the right hand of the Father in glory, he ascended as my representative and I ascended in him, and today I am seated in Christ with God in the heavenlies. I look at the cross of Christ, and I know that atonement has been made for my sins; I look at the open

sepulcher and the risen and ascended Lord, and I know the atonement has been accepted. There no longer remains a single sin on me, no matter how many or how great my sins may have been. (*The Bible and Its Christ*, p. 107)

Just before his death, the English preacher Rowland Hill (age 84) attended a Sunday night service. The service eventually ended, and the lights in the auditorium were extinguished. It was dark, but Hill was still rejoicing in the dark auditorium. The people in the foyer heard him singing,

"When I am to die, receive me I'll cry,
For Jesus has loved me, I cannot tell why;
But this I do find, we two are so joined,
He'll not be in heaven and leave me behind!"

Thank God, I, too, am one with Him! "Holy Spirit crucified with Him, buried with Him, risen with Him, joined to Him, baptized into Him!" One with Him!

Stage 1 Summary: Positional Sanctification is an act . . . a single act.

STAGE 2: PROGRESSIVE SANCTIFICATION

The *everyday* experience of "growing in grace and knowledge of our Lord and Savior Jesus Christ" occurs in Stage 2. But, never forget, it cannot occur without the foundation of positional sanctification, because progressive sanctification is built upon positional sanctification.

Charles Stanley says, "The process of perfection began with sanctification—being set apart—and continues until the end of our lives. *It is the period of progression between these two events that requires our full attention.*"

Theologians use several terms to describe this stage of sanctification. For example, Pink employs the term "practical sanctification." Others use the expression, "experiential sanctification." Both terms describe what is happening in the believer's everyday *experience* or his *daily life/walk.*

Perhaps Paul's statement, though, is the best definition of all. He captured the entire meaning in six simple words: "For me to live is Christ" (Philippians 1:21). Those words are quite true because the sanctified life is truly the Christlike life.

Pink writes,

> At regeneration a principle of holiness is communicated to us; practical sanctification is the *exercise of* that principle in living unto God. In regeneration the Spirit imparts saving grace; in His work of sanctification, He *strengthens and develops* the same. (*The Doctrine of Sanctification*, p. 88)

God's purpose is not only to *declare* His people holy through positional sanctification but also to *make* us holy through progressive sanctification.

Progressive sanctification should be thought of as the "growth" phase of the Christian life. (The "growth" phase occupies Section Two of this book.) Not only are we *already* sanctified (past tense—see positional sanctification above), but we are also in a state or condition of *being* sanctified. "Being sanctified" is an ongoing, daily process. It is progressive rather than punctiliar. Therefore, we refer to it as progressive sanctification.

James P. Boyce, founder and president of Southern Baptist Theological Seminary, writes:

> It is not a certain degree of attainment, possessed by all alike, and remaining always in this life the same; it is a growth from the seed planted in regeneration, which is constantly bringing forth new leaves, and new fruit; it grows with increased intellectual knowledge of God's truth, with a clearer perception of human sinfulness and corruption, with stronger faith and brighter hope, and more confident assurance of personal acceptance with God, with a more heartfelt conception of the sacrificing love of Christ, and with a more realizing belief in his constant presence and knowledge of what we do. (*Abstract of Systematic Theology*, p. 414)

Many years ago, I either authored or copied this definition of progressive sanctification: *"The work of God in the believer through the Spirit and the Word which changes him into the image of Christ progressively and reaches perfection at Christ's second coming."*

In many ways, our progressive sanctification is the result of the Holy Spirit impressing His own holiness/sanctity upon our lives.

"Therefore we do not lose heart, but though our outer man is decaying, yet our inner man is being renewed day by day" (2 Corinthians 4:16, NASB). The inner man is the born-again nature in the believer. Whereas the outer man draws on the energy of this godless world, the inner man draws on the energy of God above. This "renewal" never exhausts the energy of our God. It will be sufficient for the struggles in everyday life.

"Therefore, having these promises, beloved, let us cleanse ourselves from all defilement of flesh and spirit, perfecting holiness in the fear of God" (2 Corinthians 7:1, NASB). Paul encourages the believer to separate himself from the pollution of this world to both experience and express God's holiness in holy living and holy standards. The believer, though, must commit himself to this goal. It does not happen automatically.

"And He gave some *as* apostles, and some *as* prophets, and some *as* evangelists, and some *as* pastors and teachers, for the equipping of the saints for the work of service, to the building up of the body of Christ" (Ephesians 4:11-12, NASB). Obviously, Paul views the saints as a work in progress!

"Walk . . . as becometh saints" (Ephesians 5:2-3). This passage shows we are saints regardless of how we live. However, saints should live like saints or practice sainthood in their lives. We may hit the ball out of the ballpark on some days yet on other days . . .

How are you progressing in your saintly walk? Perfectly or progressively? There is a good reason we refer to this stage as "progressive."

"How blessed is the man who does not walk in the counsel of the wicked, Nor stand in the path of sinners, Nor sit in the seat of scoffers! But his delight is in the law of the Lord, And in His law he meditates day and night" (Psalm 1:1-3, NASB). This man has not arrived at perfection. But he is not standing still either!

"This book of the law shall not depart from your mouth, but you shall meditate on it day and night, so that you may be careful to do according to all that is written in it; for then you will make your way prosperous, and then you will have success" (Joshua 1:8, NASB). The more we know, the better we can act, and the more successful we will be!

"For this is God's will, your sanctification: that you abstain from sexual immorality, so that each of you knows how to control his own body in sanctification and honor, not with lustful desires, like the Gentiles who don't know God" (1 Thessalonians 4:3-5, HCSB). God desires that the believer set apart his body for God's use rather than fleshly, immoral use. This command applies for the rest of our lives and, therefore, must be addressed every day of our lives.

" Now may the God of peace Himself sanctify you entirely; and may your spirit and soul and body be preserved complete, without blame at the coming of our Lord Jesus Christ. Faithful is He who calls you, and He also will bring it to pass" (1 Thessalonians 5:23-24, NASB). We need to get our arms around the word "entirely." Adam's sin affected the entire person. It had the effect of "depraving every part of our being." Thus, we should not be surprised that God's sanctification also affects the entire person.

Progressive sanctification has the effect of "delivering every part of our being" and bringing the "entire person" into conformity with God's righteous standards. Let us never forget the physical body has now become the temple of the Holy Spirit. It is hard to imagine my body being more of a temple than a church building, cathedral, or the Old Testament tabernacle. But it is!

Not that I have already obtained it or have already become perfect, but I press on so that I may lay hold of

> *that for which also I was laid hold of by Christ Jesus.*
> *Brethren, I do not regard myself as having laid hold of it*
> *yet; but one thing I do: forgetting what lies behind and*
> *reaching forward to what lies ahead, I press on toward*
> *the goal for the prize of the upward call of God in Christ*
> *Jesus (Philippians 3:12-14, NASB).*

One can sense Paul's yearning to be even better than he is. He writes this passage nearer the end of his ministry than its beginning. But his direction is still progressively upward!

"Blessed are those who continually hunger and continually thirst after God's righteousness, for they shall be filled" (Matthew 5:6). The use of the present tense in the Greek text indicates the Christian life is one of growing or increasing in knowing God.

> *For the grace of God has appeared, bringing salvation*
> *to all men, instructing us to deny ungodliness and*
> *worldly desires and to live sensibly, righteously and*
> *godly in the present age, looking for the blessed hope*
> *and the appearing of the glory of our great God and*
> *Savior, Christ Jesus, who gave Himself for us to redeem*
> *us from every lawless deed, and to purify for Himself a*
> *people for His own possession, zealous for good deeds*
> *(Titus 1:12-14, NASB).*

Throughout the Bible, we are taught that being born again does not result in a complete deliverance from the sinful nature. However, that does not mean the believer is destined for a defeated lifestyle. Instead, through the power and enablement of the sanctifying Holy Spirit, the obedient Christian is able to deny ungodliness and worldly desires; at the same time, he is now enabled to live sensibly, righteously, and godly. Again, it is a progressive work.

We need to remind ourselves that, in salvation, God does not plant weeds in a person but rather the seed that produces flowers of holiness! But we need to purge the weeds for the flowers to grow.

"Nevertheless, God's solid foundation stands firm, bearing this inscription: The Lord knows those who are his, and let everyone who calls on the name of the Lord turn away from wickedness" (2 Timothy 2:19, CSB). Herbert Lockyer adds the thought, "It is one thing to be a saint—all the saved are saints—but a different thing to be a sanctified saint."

"As a deer longs for streams of water, so I long for You, God. I thirst for God, the living God. When can I come and appear before God?" Psalm 42:1-2, HCSB). King David had his ups and downs. This psalm records one of his progressively up experiences. You can sense his hunger for the Lord, but we must also temper that knowledge by remembering his lust for Bathsheba. The same man experienced both hungers!

Are we any different than David? No. Abraham, Samson, Jonah, and the apostle Peter were up and down, too. So is the best Christian I know.

We may ask ourselves, "Am I as sanctified as brother so-and-so?" The answer is yes in *positional* sanctification, but the answer may be yes, no, or even more so, in *progressive* sanctification. There is much difference between believers in our current experience.

In many ways, our daily life is similar to a marathon race. Everyone begins at the same point of being born again, but each person progresses throughout the journey at his own rate. Indeed, God's people have a bad tendency to become strung out over a long distance as in a marathon race. We will examine this subject in great detail in chapter six ("In Which Stage Am I?").

"Sanctify them in the truth; Your word is truth. As You sent Me into the world, I also have sent them into the world. For their sakes I sanctify Myself, that they themselves also may be sanctified in truth" (John 17:17-19, NASB). The first five words indicate the apostles still had room to grow—to progress in their Christian lives.

"Dear friends, we are God's children now, and what we will be has not yet been revealed. We know that when He appears, we will be like Him because we will see Him as He is. And everyone who has this hope in Him purifies himself just as He is pure" (1 John 3:2-3, CSB). The word "purifies" is another present tense verb indicating the believer is being called to continuing action or progressive action in the here-and-now.

"No one born of God makes a practice of sinning, for God's seed abides in him; and he cannot keep on sinning, because he has been born of God" (1 John 3:9, ESV). John uses an abundance of present tense verbs in his writings to emphasize continuing or repetitive action. Most translations appropriately use the word "practice" in verse nine because "practice" conveys an ongoing action.

"As obedient children, do not be conformed to the former lusts which were yours in your ignorance, but like the Holy One who called you, be holy yourselves also in all your behavior; because it is written, 'You shall be holy, for I am holy'" (1 Peter 1:14-16, NASB). "Be holy" is a daily mandate from our Lord.

> *For this reason also, since the day we heard this, we haven't stopped praying for you. We are asking that you may be filled with the knowledge of His will in all wisdom and spiritual understanding, so that you may walk worthy of the Lord, fully pleasing to Him: bearing fruit in every good work and growing in the knowledge of God (Colossians 1:9-10, CSB).*

This entire passage is about growing into what God designed us to be! Yes, we are designed to be like Him!

In addition to the above scriptures, there are a few scriptures that *combine* the two ideas of positional sanctification and progressive sanctification.

"So if you have been raised with Christ, seek the things above, where Christ is, seated at the right hand of God. Set your minds on things above, not on earthly things" (Colossians 3:1-2, HCSB). This verse combines the believer's position of "raised" with the expected practice of "seeking" and "setting." No Christian should be satisfied with just being saved; he or she should seek to live out his or her salvation in progressive fashion.

"I have been crucified with Christ (positional sanctification), nevertheless I still live but the life I now live is the life of Christ living in me (progressive sanctification)" (Galatians 2:20). Notice that the order is first, union with Christ then, second, the manifestation of that life. It corresponds with Colossians 3:1-2.

"For by a single offering he has perfected for all time those who are being sanctified" (Hebrews 10:14, ESV). We often use this verse to indicate that the one whom God saves is saved forever. It is impossible for a perfected person to lose his salvation.

"Perfected" comes from the Greek word *teleioo,* which has the idea of having attained a state of completeness. That completeness applies to the believer because the sacrifice of Jesus fully satisfied God's wrath against the believer's imperfections. Nothing more can be added to Christ's sacrifice. The set-apart ones have been perfected for all time.

"Being sanctified" is a present passive participle. Passive signifies the sanctification is not being done by us in our own strength but is being displayed through us from another person's strength: the Holy Spirit. The present tense again indicates the sanctification is ongoing in the believer's life.

Thiessen writes regarding the apostle Paul, "In Thessalonians he affirms that his readers are already 'sanctified,' and then he prays for their sanctification (2 Thess. 2:13, 1 Thess. 5:23-24)." What a combination! It easily shows the relationship *and* the distinction between positional sanctification and progressive sanctification (p. 380).

"He that has been completely bathed (positional sanctification or cleansing) with the present result that he is still bathed (the Greek perfect tense indicates a completed action in the past which is still in effect in the present) now only needs to wash (progressive sanctification) his feet" (John 13:10). This passage shows the relationship between the complete bathing forgiveness received at salvation, which covers all sins (past, present, and future), and the everyday "forgive us of today's sins," which preserves our fellowship and communion with our Friend.

Stage 2 Summary: Progressive Sanctification is a process, an every day, continuing process.

STAGE 3: PERFECT SANCTIFICATION

Perfect sanctification will finally provide us with the reality of our perfect position in Christ. "We are not yet what we shall be," but those eight words represent only a temporary condition! The Bible promises, "That which is in part shall be replaced by that which is perfect. Today we see through a glass darkly or in a mirror but on that future day we shall see face to face and be known even as we are now known" (1 Corinthians 13).

Based on the Word of God, this event will happen when Jesus comes again!

> *For if we believe that Jesus died and rose again, in the same way, through Jesus, God will bring with him those who have fallen asleep. For we say this to you by a word from the Lord: We who are still alive at the Lord's coming will certainly not precede those who have fallen asleep. For the Lord himself will descend from heaven with a shout, with the archangel's voice, and with the trumpet of God, and the dead in Christ will rise first. Then we who are still alive, who are left, will be caught up together with them in the clouds to meet the Lord in the air, and so we will always be with the Lord. Therefore encourage one another with these words (1 Thessalonians 4:14-18, CSB).*

"And just as we have borne the image of the man of dust, we will also bear the image of the man of heaven" (1 Corinthians 15:49, CSB).

"So it is with the resurrection of the dead: Sown in corruption, raised in incorruption; sown in dishonor, raised in glory; sown in weakness, raised in power; sown a natural body, raised a spiritual body" (1 Corinthians 15:42-44, CSB).

> *What I am saying, brothers and sisters, is this: Flesh*
> *and blood cannot inherit the kingdom of God, nor can*
> *corruption inherit incorruption. Listen, I am telling you*
> *a mystery: We will not all fall asleep, but we will all be*
> *changed, in a moment, in the twinkling of an eye, at the*
> *last trumpet. For the trumpet will sound, and the dead*
> *will be raised incorruptible, and we will be changed.*
> *For this corruptible body must be clothed with*
> *incorruptibility, and this mortal body must be clothed*
> *with immortality (1 Corinthians 15:50-53, CSB).*

We shall be changed! We shall be perfected!

Some people use the term "entire sanctification" to describe this stage. That is a good term because the born-again child of God is *entirely* sanctified in this stage. He will never again sing, "Prone to wander, Lord, I feel it, Prone to leave the God I love." He will never again miss or fall short of the will of God. He will never again have sins to confess.

The child of God has been a saint in positional sanctification since the day of his salvation, has been progressing along in his holiness journey for many years, but that journey is past, and he has now finally arrived at his destination of complete sainthood in body, soul, spirit, will, speech, attitude, etc.

"For those whom he foreknew he also predestined to be conformed to the image of his Son" (Romans 8:29, ESV). The word "conformed" deserves special attention. Kenneth Wuest explains,

> The word 'conformed' is *summorphoo*, 'to bring to the same form with' some other person or thing, 'to render like.' The noun *morphe* refers to the outward expression of an inward essence or nature. Thus, in the process of sanctification, the saint is transformed in his inner heart life to resemble the Lord Jesus, which inner change results in a change of outward expression that reflects the beauty of the Lord Jesus. (*Romans*, p. 145)

Romans 8:29 conclusively demonstrates that the believer will be thoroughly changed and brought into alignment or conformity with the resurrected, glorified Son of God. God's purpose will be done!

We usually think of "no more death, no more crying, no more sorrow," and rightfully so, but God thinks more about "no more sin." "For the sinful things have all passed away, too."

"These whom He predestined, He also called; and these whom He called, He also justified; and these whom He justified, He also glorified" (Romans 8:30, NASB). The entire process will be completed at our glorification. Jesus was raised from the dead with a glorified body, which is also somehow viewed by Paul as a spiritual body—a body not restricted to earthly limitations. Everything about us will be glorified or perfected. Come quickly, Lord Jesus!

"But you have come to Mount Zion and to the city of the living God, the heavenly Jerusalem, and to myriads of angels, to the general assembly and church of the firstborn who are enrolled in heaven, and to God, the Judge of all, and to the spirits of *the* righteous made perfect" (Hebrews 12:22-23, NASB). The sin nature will finally be removed; only the righteous, born-again nature will remain. Thus, we are left with the "spirits of the righteous made perfect."

"Beloved, now we are children of God, and it has not appeared as yet what we will be. We know that when He appears, we will be like Him, because we will see Him just as He is" (1 John 3:2, NASB). Like Him who has never sinned or had even one sinful thought! The partial has now become the perfect!

"May He make your hearts blameless in holiness before our God and Father at the coming of our Lord Jesus with all His saints. Amen" (1 Thessalonians 3:13, CSB).

> "When all my labors and trials are o'er,
> And I am safe on that beautiful shore,
> Just to be near the dear Lord I adore,
> Will through the ages be glory for me.
> When, by the gift of His infinite grace,
> I am accorded in heaven a place,

Just to be there and to look on His face,
Will through the ages be glory for me."

Charles Gabriel

Stage 3 Summary: Perfect Sanctification is an act, a single act that does not need to be repeated.

Let's compare the three stages in a simple chart.

STAGE	NAME	RATE	RESULT
1	Positional	Once	Set apart in Christ, ruled/declared a saint
2	Progressive	Daily	Daily growing more like Christ
3	Perfect	Once	100% of our being is glorified, no more curse!

Sanctification Stage 1 is a single, unrepeated act on the part of God setting apart the believer. Sanctification Stage 2 is a continuing, repeated process from the day of salvation to the day of our going to be with the Lord. Sanctification Stage 3 is a single, unrepeated act when God, once and for all, eradicates the sin nature, glorifies the fleshly body, and allows the new nature to assume total control. (Note: There will be a period of time between God eradicating the sin nature at death, and God glorifying the body at the resurrection. This subject is explored in detail in chapter twenty-two. However, each of these steps is done only once.) What a day that will be for the child of God because it will be the day of complete deliverance!

On that day, will I be as sanctified as brother so-and-so? Yes! In perfect sanctification, there will be *no difference* between believers. All of us will be completely, 100% sanctified in Christ Jesus both on the outside *and* on the inside. None of us will ever sin again. None of us will ever fall again from a state of holiness. Nor will we ever again experience any consequences of the curse associated with Adam's original sin.

The Bible assures us, "Blessed and holy is the person who has a part in the first resurrection" (Revelation 20:6). May I suggest that you underline the word holy? Finally, everything about us will be holy. 100% holy.

Pink reminds us regarding God, "Holiness is the perfection of all His glorious attributes: His power is holy power, His mercy is holy mercy, His wisdom is holy wisdom." Let's continue the thought. His decrees are holy, His goodness is holy, His patience is holy, His love is holy, His wrath is holy, His gospel is holy!

Holiness is the very foundation of God's throne. Miracle of miracles, in that day, my mind will be holy, my flesh will be holy, my tongue will be holy, my heart will be holy, my attitude will be holy, and my thoughts will be holy. Plus anything else of me for *all of me* will be totally holy!

I, along with you, will be fully delivered from the body of this death (Romans 7:24-25). No wonder we are described as "blessed!"

Will you join me in praying, "Even so, come, Lord Jesus"? Perhaps our glorification will happen today!

5

CONFUSING ISSUES, BIBLICAL ANSWERS

When personalized license plates were first introduced, one state's Department of Motor Vehicles received over a thousand requests for the number "1." Someone had to decide who would receive the only plate displaying the number "1." The state official in charge of the decision said, "I'm not about to assign it to someone and disappoint a thousand people." What was his solution? He assigned the number to himself.

Through God's process called sanctification, we are being converted from "self-hood" to "saint-hood." The previous chapter walked us through the general process of positional sanctification, progressive sanctification, and perfect sanctification.

But the previous chapter did not resolve several important issues. These issues are not linked except in the sense that they pertain to the overall subject of sanctification. However, if not properly understood, they can become obstacles to our growing in grace and knowledge of our

Lord and Savior Jesus Christ. Therefore, each of the following eight issues, though confusing, deserves our careful deliberations.

1. FLESHLY MORALITY

Sanctification is not the same as fleshly morality. Our own experience tells us there are many good moral people in the world in the sense that the world defines good morality. However, the world's standard falls far short of God's holy standard. The Bible's standard is God's standard, and God's standard is 100% holiness or righteousness.

The Bible says, "For whosoever shall keep the whole law, and yet offend in one point, he is guilty of all" (James 2:10). "For all have sinned and come short of the glory of God" (Romans 3:23). "There is not one single person who continually does good, no, not one" (Romans 3:12).

Chafer approvingly quotes Shedd as saying, "Total depravity means the entire absence of holiness, not the highest intensity of sin. A totally depraved man is not as bad as he can be, but he has no holiness." (*Systematic Theology Volume II*, p. 219)

Fleshly morality, despite being encouraged as a means to improve our world, will always fall short of God's holy standard.

2. RELIGIOUS TRADITIONS AND RITUALS

Sanctification is not the same as observing religious traditions or rituals. The problem is they much too often become a work of the human flesh with little thought to the spiritual meaning associated with those same traditions and rituals.

Some people view such traditions/values as expressed in the Golden Rule ("do unto others as you would have them do unto you") as achieving God's standard. However, as noted in James 2:10, Romans 3, and Matthew 5:48, there is more to life and God's requirements than just the Golden Rule.

It is true that God instituted many traditions or rituals in the Old Testament, such as the festivals, sacrifices, health regulations, and even dietary laws. The New Testament includes the traditions known as believer's baptism and the Lord's Supper.

But most religious traditions or rituals in our current day are man-made, that is, made of the flesh. Such traditions and rituals fall far short of biblical sanctification. According to Lockyer, sanctification is "not merely an external covering as dew wets grass, but as sap in a root. We do not become holy by adopting clean habits. Holiness must be inwrought by God. Sanctimoniousness is not Biblical sanctification." (*All the Doctrines of the Bible*, p. 218)

For example, Roman Catholicism has its seven sacraments. But based upon what? Loraine Boettner's excellent *Roman Catholicism* includes the following argument on page 189:

> What was the purpose of the Church of Rome in appointing seven sacraments? Probably in order that it might have complete control over the lives of its people from the cradle to the grave. This sacramental system is designed to give the priest control at the most important events of human life. From baptism as soon as possible after birth to the shadow of approaching death the laity is kept dependent on and under the control of the priest.

In addition, where is the scripture authorizing anyone to pray to Mary or another saint? Pardon me, but don't pray to Saint Swartzwelder because I am very limited in my abilities! Or what about extreme unction, including the priest, serving as the dying person's proxy, forgiving the sins of the dying sinner? Or the horrible, totally unbiblical tradition of purgatory? (See twenty-two in this book.) Thank God, Jesus once and for all purged our sins on the cross of Calvary (Hebrews 1:3).

Jesus' biggest conflict was with the traditionalists or ritualists (Pharisees) of His day. Jesus warned them,

Woe to you, scribes and Pharisees, hypocrites! You pay a tenth of mint, dill, and cumin, and yet you have neglected the more important matters of the law— justice, mercy, and faithfulness. These things should have been done without neglecting the others. Blind guides! You strain out a gnat, but gulp down a camel! Woe to you, scribes and Pharisees, hypocrites! You clean the outside of the cup and dish, but inside they are full of greed and self-indulgence. Blind Pharisee! First clean the inside of the cup, so that the outside of it may also become clean. Woe to you, scribes and Pharisees, hypocrites! You are like whitewashed tombs, which appear beautiful on the outside, but inside are full of the bones of the dead and every kind of impurity. In the same way, on the outside you seem righteous to people, but inside you are full of hypocrisy and lawlessness (Matthew 23:23-28, CSB).

We should always be ready to accept God's traditions; however, we should be wary of man's traditions, because man's traditions are only skin deep! *Man's traditions don't go deep enough!* After all, man needs a change of heart, and such a change is more than skin deep.

3. TWO NATURES BUT ONE PERSON

The most complicated person in today's world is the one who believes in Jesus Christ as Lord and Savior. That is so because the believer is biblically described as *two people in one body*. Peter writes that God has made us "partakers of the divine nature, having escaped from the corruption that is in the world because of sinful desire" (2 Peter 1:4, ESV). Jesus said to Nicodemus twice, "You must be born again . . . born anew . . . or born from above." The apostle Paul writes about "putting off the old man and putting on the new man" as well as being a "new creation" or a "new man." John writes about a believer's life becoming more holy because "God's seed is in the believer."

In a nutshell, everyone is born into this physical world with one nature: the sin nature which is patterned after our Federal Head or first father, Adam. But everyone in God's family has been born again into the spiritual world (the kingdom of God) with a *second* nature: a holy nature which is patterned after our Heavenly Head or second Father. The second nature is an *additional* nature. In this case, one nature plus one nature equals two natures. Two natures in one person! What a combination! That's why the Christian is the most complicated person in today's world. He has both a worldly longing *and* a heavenly longing!

Renald E. Showers writes in *The New Nature* (p. 55), "Peter is saying that Christians partake of the divine nature in the sense that they receive a disposition which is an expression of the holy nature of God." (Showers employs the term "disposition" in the same way that I employ the word "nature." Others have suggested the word "capacity" or Paul's "new man/new creation.") The point is, the believer has received something new which he did not formerly possess. That "something new" is of a spiritual nature and delights in a spiritual lifestyle rather than the Adamic nature's worldly lifestyle.

Romans chapter seven pictures the struggle between these two contrasting natures.

> *Now if I do what I do not want, I am no longer the one that does it, but it is the sin that lives in me. So I discover this law: When I want to do what is good, evil is present with me. For in my inner self I delight in God's law, but I see a different law in the parts of my body, waging war against the law of my mind and taking me prisoner to the law of sin in the parts of my body. What a wretched man I am! Who will rescue me from this body of death? Thanks be to God through Jesus Christ our Lord! So then, with my mind I myself am serving the law of God, but with my flesh, the law of sin" (Romans 7:20-25, CSB).*

Could this comparison be a reasonable analogy to our dilemma? Jesus is recognized as the unique God-man, 100% God at the same time that He was 100% man. In a similar but not fully identical fashion, *the believer is the unique sinner-saint,* 100% sinner at the same time that he is 100% saint.

Regarding the believer, neither nature controls nor dominates the other. Both natures co-exist in the same body/mind/heart. Both wish to rule. Hence, we read Paul's words in Galatians 5:17 that "the flesh *wills* against the Spirit and the Spirit *wills* against the flesh." Neither one will surrender to the will of the other. Both could be described as hard-headed, stubborn, and refusing to yield!

As believers we are two natures but somehow one person. Not two people but one. As if both natures have been fused together but are still separate. This one person is accountable to God as to which nature is allowed to rule in the person's life. How can that be? The answer is unknown, even unfathomable, but yet it is!

Arthur Pink explains,

> The Old and New Testament alike insist it is the person who sins— 'against Thee . . . have I sinned' (Psalm 51). Paul himself concludes Romans 7 by saying, 'O wretched man that I am!' This reminds us of an incident wherein a 'Bishop' was guilty of blasphemy in the House of Lords (where all 'Bishops' have seats). Being rebuked by his manservant, he replied, 'It is the 'lord' and not the 'bishop' who cursed.' His servant responded, 'When the Devil gets the 'lord'' where will the 'bishop' be?' Beware, my reader of seeking to clear yourself by throwing the blame upon your 'nature.' (*The Doctrine of Sanctification,* p. 59)

4. ERADICATION (REMOVAL) OF THE SIN NATURE

In my early days (before the ATM days), I worked three years as a motor bank teller in Portsmouth, Ohio. One of my customers was a wonderful Pentecostal man. One night he came to the window to cash a check. I gave him the money, then he asked me a question I had never heard before. He asked, "Have you received the second blessing?" I had never heard of the second blessing. I did not know how to respond.

I went home and told my father (a Baptist pastor) about our conversation. I said, "Dad, he asked me if I had received the second blessing, and I did not know what to say."

Dad said, "If he asks you again, just tell him that you have received the second blessing and the third blessing and the fourth blessing and the fifth blessing and the sixth blessing and the seventh blessing and all the other blessings, too, but you received all of them at the moment you were saved, and God sealed you in the Anointed One!"

The Bible says every born-again child of God automatically receives the same Holy Spirit along with **all** of the blessings that are connected to the Holy Spirit. Romans 8:9 says, "If any man claims to be saved but does not have the Holy Spirit that man is none of Christ's—he has never been saved." Ephesians 1:3 states, "We (all of God's people) have been blessed with *every spiritual blessing* in Christ Jesus." Peter elaborates on this theme by declaring, "His divine power has given us everything required for life and godliness through the knowledge of him who called us by his own glory and goodness" (2 Peter 1:3, CSB).

From the moment of salvation to the moment of our homegoing, the believer does not need to receive *more* of the Holy Spirit. He already has *all* of the Holy Spirit that he needs. The issue is no longer one of the believer getting more of Him but of *Him getting more of the believer!*

My bank customer's question was my introduction to the false belief known as the eradication or removal of the old, Adamic nature. Let me begin with common ground for all sides on this important issue. With very few exceptions, all sides agree that Adam's sin affected all of us. All sides agree that man is born with a diseased nature inherited from father Adam. All sides also agree this diseased nature is an anti-God nature that intentionally draws a man away from God. All sides agree that this nature is so diseased that no human being can earn his way to heaven based upon his good works. Therefore, we all agree that man needs a Savior other than himself and that Savior is Jesus Christ!

Thus, we call the sinner to repent of his sin and be born again. In so doing, he will receive a new nature from heaven patterned after God's own nature (see the above study "Two Natures But One Person"). *This brings us to our disagreement.* The non-eradication arm of Christianity (consisting of Calvinists, Biblicists, Baptists, and even some Arminians) believes the old, Adamic nature is with the believer until the day he or she goes to be with the Lord.

However, the eradication arm of Christianity (Holiness, Pentecostals, Assembly of God, Church of the Nazarene, Wesleyan Methodists) believes it is possible for the believer to experience a *second* work of grace in which God *removes* the sin nature from the believer's life. This second work of grace (also known as the second blessing, complete sanctification, or eradication of the sin nature) sets the believer free from sinful acts because he is now free from sinful temptations. According to this view, the devil no longer has a foothold in the believer. *From this point forward, the believer will never sin again.*

The Methodist John Wesley is most credited with popularizing this teaching. Wesley, though, recognized the believer may still fail even after this so-called second blessing, but he referred to those failures as *mistakes* rather than *sins.* His teaching is a classic example of a person taking a position only then to have to explain away the scriptures that disprove his position. We'll explore this contradiction further in just a moment.

The Methodist Adam Clarke writes in his article, "Entire Sanctification," "What then is this complete sanctification? It is the cleansing by the blood of that which has not been cleansed; it is washing the soul of the true believer from the remains of sin." In other words, Clarke believes there is such an experience as a post-salvation experience, also known as the eradication of the sin nature or the second blessing.

D. Shelby Corlett, an entire sanctification advocate in the Church of the Nazarene, declares in his book *The Meaning of Holiness*:

> This work of entire sanctification is a definite experience, a mighty work of grace, wrought by God in the life of the Christian in response to his faith. It is an experience that marks a

definite second crisis in the spiritual life, purifying the heart, filling the life with the Holy Spirit, bringing a spiritual wholeness to life and the heart into full devotedness to God. (Note: Corlett's entire book is available on the internet in a free pdf version.)

However, the Bible evidence shows that growing in grace is an *everyday growing* process. The present tense (2 Peter 3:18) indicates it is a continually growing experience, not a once-and-done experience that places us on higher ground, which can become no higher or lower in the future.

Let me cite three statements from the eradication proponent John Wesley. In a 1774 correspondence with Miss Jane Hilton, he writes, "It is exceeding certain that God did give you the second blessing, properly so called. He delivered you from the root of bitterness, from inbred as well as actual sin."

Second, in his *Plain Account of Christian Perfection* Wesley writes, "We do not know a single instance, in any place, of a person's receiving, in one and the same moment, remission of sins, the abiding witness of the Spirit, and a new, a clean heart."

The third citation originated in a 1759 Methodist conference. During an open forum, someone asked, "If two perfect (the sin nature has been eradicated) Christians had children, how could the child be born in sin since there was none in the parents?"

Wesley responded, "It is possible but not a probable case. I doubt whether it ever was or ever will be."

I agree with the words of many, "If one's view of sin were only shallow enough, sinless perfection would not be an impossible attainment." To be honest, the only proper view is God's view; God's view is not shallow by any means.

Herbert Lockyer, though, counters the eradication approach with the more Calvinistic argument, "Sin does not die within the believer, he dies to sin. When Paul declared 'I die daily' he meant that he had acquired the habit of reckoning himself dead unto sin. There is a difference between sin being in us against our will, and reigning in us with our permission (Romans 6:12). A person who claims he is so sanctified that he cannot sin, actually sins by such an assertion." (*All the Doctrines of the Bible*, p. 218) (Note: In this paragraph, Lockyer uses the word "sin" in reference not to specific acts of sin but to the sin nature itself.)

Arthur Pink, a strong Calvinist, further counters the entire sanctification argument by writing, "Scriptural sanctification is neither the eradication of sin, the purification of the sin nature, nor even the partial putting to sleep of the 'flesh'" (*The Doctrine of Sanctification*, p. 43).

Let's look first at how the Bible solves this dilemma, then look second at why the Arminians miss the Bible solution.

Many passages contradict the theory of eradication. Paul testified, "For the good that I want, I do not do, but I practice the very evil that I do not want. But if I am doing the very thing I do not want, I am no longer the one doing it, but sin which dwells in me. I find then the principle that evil is present in me, the one who wants to do good" (Romans 7:19-21, NASB). Though born again and even writing books under the inspiration of the Holy Spirit, Paul writes about "sin which dwells in me" and "evil is present in me." It is clear that Paul *never* *experienced* the eradication that was taught by Wesley. Based on Paul's experience, I think we can reasonably conclude that Wesley did not experience it either.

John teaches, "If we say we have no sin nature, we deceive only ourselves" (1 John 1:8). The Greek scholar Kenneth Wuest explains in his book *In These Last Days* (p. 103), "'Sin' here is singular in number and is used without the definite article, all pointing to the fact that the nature is referred to, not acts of sin. Here we have the denial of the indwelling, totally depraved nature passed down the race from Adam."

Based upon that verse, it appears some people believed the eradication argument even in John's day. They contended they no longer possessed a sin nature. John countered, "They deceive, even fool themselves but fool no one else!" Indeed, the greatest testimony against a "sinless" husband is an honest wife! She knows differently! It is true some people are holier-than-thou, but unfortunately, that is only true in their own eyes.

Furthermore, the entirety of Romans chapter six refutes the total eradication theory. Paul says the believer should "reckon" or "consider" that sin can now be defeated through the power of the cross. More will be said about Romans chapter six in a later section. But it should be pointed out that the "reckoning" in chapter six did not eliminate the conflict which arose in chapter seven.

In addition, let's consider the spiritual testimony of the apostle Paul. All sides would agree that Paul's lifestyle was definitely worthy of imitation (1 Corinthians 4:16). Yet who can forget Paul's wretched cry, "Who shall deliver me from the body of this death?" Paul describes himself three additional times in the biblical record. Let's view those three times in their chronological order (the earliest date is provided first).

- Written in A.D. 56: "For I am the least of the apostles, and not fit to be called an apostle, because I persecuted the church of God" (1 Corinthians 15:9, NASB).
- Written in A.D. 60: "Unto me, who am less than the least of all saints, is this grace given, that I should preach among the Gentiles the unsearchable riches of Christ" (Ephesians 3:8, KJV).
- Written in A.D. 64: "This saying is trustworthy and deserving of full acceptance: 'Christ Jesus came into the world to save sinners'—and I am the worst of them" (1 Timothy 1:15, HCSB).

Certainly, Paul's view of himself does not support the theory of the eradication of the sin nature. If such a condition is indeed possible, Paul missed it! As a matter of fact, Paul writes the last verse only three years before his death. He does not say, "I *was* the worst of them," but, based upon his own inward look, he writes, "I *am* (currently) the worst of them." It seems clear that Paul would have agreed with the old saying, *"They who fain would serve Thee best are conscious most of wrong within."*

One searches in vain throughout Paul's writings for his own "second blessing experience." It should be noted, though, that Paul writes about everything else! Surely, he would have mentioned such an experience as well as the means for us likewise to attain it if it were a valid spiritual experience.

Why, though, are the above evidences missed, overlooked, or rejected by the Arminians? My personal copy of Pink's *The Doctrine of Sanctification* was previously owned by an Arminian who clearly believed in the eradication of the sin nature. On page sixty-seven, Pink points out the sin nature is not eradicated from the believer until he leaves this world. The previous owner, though, disagrees and inserts the following words, "A. W. Pink missing again. Way out!" He then references Pink's list of scriptures as "Scriptures on perfection."

Where, though, did the Arminian err? *He took scriptures that are oriented to either positional or perfect sanctification and misinterpreted them as pertaining to progressive sanctification.* As a result, he came to a false conclusion about the meaning of the scriptures. Sadly, he also came to a false view of himself. For the record, let's remember Paul's view (including his view of himself) went in the exact opposite direction.

5. WHEN PERFECT DOESN'T MEAN PERFECT

Genesis 6:9 says, "Noah was a just man and perfect in his generations, and Noah walked with God" (KJV). The key word for this particular discussion is the word "perfect" (the Hebrew word is *tamim*). More modern translations use the word "blameless" or "man of integrity." Some people insist that Noah attained a level of sinless perfection because of the KJV translation "perfect." In their eyes, this translation surely implies that the sin nature has been totally removed because Noah is clearly identified as a man who lived above sin. After all, perfect means perfect, and Noah attained a level of perfection.

Wilson's Old Testament Word Studies (p. 307) provides this definition of the Hebrew word in question: "Complete, to make full, perfect, or entire, to finish . . . the proper notion is that of simplicity, sincerity, absence from guilt or evil intention: implying completeness of parts rather than of degrees . . . integrity."

The Hebrew word *could* mean perfect as in the sense of absolute perfection, or it could mean perfect as in the sense of maturity or integrity, that something has reached its goal. Wilson makes it clear that the focus is not on the degree of perfection but the completeness of the product. Is the product whole and ready to use? We might define the word perfect in terms of fully assembled.

How can we know if Noah was absolutely perfect? As usually happens, one can read the surrounding scriptures and find the answer. We read three chapters later (Genesis 9:20-27) that "perfect" Noah was guilty of multiple, heinous sins. He became drunk and, in his drunkenness, exposed his nakedness to his son, who immediately told everyone in the community. Noah responded by placing a curse upon someone who was not even involved: his grandson! Noah's testimony was probably ruined by his sinfulness.

Do those actions sound like a man who is no longer able to sin? The answer is no.

The same interpretation is likely in the case of Job. Job's "perfection" (Job 1:1) was shown to be horribly lacking when God thundered His wisdom in Job chapter thirty-eight. Job then concludes his writings by "abhorring himself and *repenting* in dust and ashes" (Job 42:6). It should go without saying (but I need to go on the record and say it) that a perfect man does not need to repent! Job fell short of absolute perfection.

One dear brother believed, though, that perfect always means perfect. One day he went to visit a good Christian neighbor. The two of them began to discuss this very subject. The neighbor asked, "Can you point to a single perfect man or woman in the Bible?"

The first man said, "Yes. Turn to Luke 1:6, and you will read about two named Elizabeth and Zacharias who walked in all the commandments and ordinances of the Lord *blameless*."

The neighbor said, "Then you consider yourself blameless like Zacharias?"

The first man said, "Yes, I do."

The neighbor said, "I thought you might believe that, but we read only a few verses further on that Zacharias was struck dumb for his unbelief." Zacharias was unable to speak because of his lack of faith. We can say with certainty that Zacharias did not qualify as a perfect or blameless man.

Thus, we may conclude the Bible usually has one of two meanings when it uses the word perfect. It may mean high integrity as in the sense of Christian maturity. Or it may mean absolute perfection as in the sense that God Himself is perfect. (The goal of Matthew 5:48 is no less perfect than the perfection required by the Old Testament law.) In the latter case, the believer's perfection exists, not because of the believer's own accomplishments, but because the believer is positioned in the perfect Son of God and, therefore, partakes of His perfections (1 Corinthians 1:30-31).

It is always best to look at the context to determine which meaning is in view.

6. HEBREWS 12:14

"Strive for peace with everyone, and for the holiness without which no one will see the Lord" (Hebrews 12:14, ESV). Some elements in the Holiness movement emphasize the believer must achieve absolute holiness in *this present life,* or the believer will fall short of eternal salvation. The movement constantly reminds us, and rightfully so, that, "without holiness no one shall see the Lord." But who among them ever achieves such a level of absolute holiness in his or her personal life? The answer is "none, no not one."

The movement views its interpretation as achievable because of the word "strive." The Greek verb *dioko* translated "strive", "pursue", "follow" or "do your best" is an imperative, present tense verb meaning it is to be done immediately and continually. Such a level of perfection is deemed as being within the capability of all believers. But, as we have noted many times in these pages, even the greatest of God's saints fall short of attaining absolute holiness in his daily life. If we are truly honest, we must acknowledge with the apostle Paul that we remain the "chiefest or worst of sinners" (1 Timothy 1:15).

Thiessen offers,

> "This Scripture does not so much stress the realization of absolute holiness in this life, as the pursuit of it . . . He who believes in Christ is sanctified positionally, for Christ is at that moment made unto him sanctification (1 Cor. 1:30). Next must come the pursuit after holiness. He who does not follow after the 'sanctification' shall not see God." (*Introductory Lectures in Systematic Theology*, p. 377)

It is my humble opinion that Hebrews 12:14 includes *both* positional and progressive sanctification *but in reverse order.* "Strive for holiness" is quite obviously an experiential pursuit (progressive sanctification) of a holy lifestyle. But "without which no man shall see God" is a positional (and ultimately perfect) concept because it emphasizes that absolute holiness is a requirement to being accepted by God. Such holiness can only be viewed on this side of the grave as imputed (positional) holiness. But on the other side, it will be *glorified* holiness which will then, for the first time, also be *realized* holiness. (See Section Three.)

Thus, the chronological order becomes: First, the sinner is made aware that he *must* be holy if he is to ever stand in God's presence. Of course, this problem is solved at one's salvation when God imputes the perfect holiness of Christ to the believer's account (1 Corinthians 1:30, Romans 4:5). Second, on the basis of his new position and new holy nature, the believer is motivated to live a holy life in progressive sanctification. In other words, Hebrews 12:14 shows the proper linkage of positional sanctification to progressive sanctification. The first creates the motive to do the second.

This interpretation lines up nicely with John's writings.

> *"This is the message we have heard from him and declare to you: God is light, and there is absolutely no darkness in him. If we walk in the light as he himself is in the light, we have fellowship with one another, and the blood of Jesus his Son cleanses us from all sin" (1 John 1:5, 7, CSB).*

One's position in the light both predates and provides the daily cleansing experience.

John adds, "My little children, these things write I unto you, that ye sin not. And if any man sin, we have an advocate with the Father, Jesus Christ the righteous" (1 John 2:1, KJV). Please notice John does not view sin like we often preach! He does not say, "*When* a man sins," but, "*If* a man sins." From John's viewpoint, sin is not a continual transgression but an *occasional* transgression.

That is why John writes, "Whoever is born of God does not practice sin" (1 John 3:9). Also, "whoever practices righteousness is righteous" (1 John 3:7) or, as I prefer to say it, *"the righteous one practices righteousness."* One does not become righteous because of what he does, but, rather, he does righteousness because he is already righteous. In so doing, his born again, holy nature is "striving for that holiness without which no man will see the Lord."

7. CHRISTIAN LEGALISM

Modern-day Christian legalism places an *excessive* emphasis upon *outward* separation as grounds for both personal and church fellowship. In so doing, legalists often become more recognized for their greater emphasis on "what we're against" than "what we're for."

During my lifetime God's people have been *branded by others of God's people* for everything imaginable including their style of worship music, their choice of a Bible translation, their favorite television preacher, their choice of appearance as in the case of a woman wearing slacks or makeup, even the length of a man's hair or length of a woman's hair. (The length of my hair failed a Baptist school's examination because a few hairs *barely* touched my ear.) On and on the list goes. It is a case of man, unlike God, looking on the outside rather than the heart.

As a little boy, I recall one visiting preacher being criticized for wearing colored socks! One pastor said of such critics, "They would have a hissy fit if they could see the color of my underwear!"

I recently had a discussion with a well-known, very successful evangelist. His doctrine and lifestyle are very sound, but, even so, he faced opposition from some within his own denomination. He admitted, "I am too fundamental for that group but not fundamental enough for that other group." We referred to such groups as cliques in high school; I guess we should call them bigger cliques in Christianity!

The apostle Paul writes these words to the legalists of all centuries, "I only want to learn this from you: Did you receive the Spirit by the works of the law or by believing what you heard? Are you so foolish? After beginning by the Spirit, are you now finishing by the flesh?" (Galatians 3:2-3, CSB).

Unfortunately, people often become identified with every evil associated with a movement/denomination regardless of their own beliefs.

Far too often, we forget that biblical sanctification is not only separation *from* worldliness, but it is also separation *to* God. As a matter of fact, separation from worldliness is *secondary* to the primary goal of separation to God and His use. A legalist (I've known many) will always look spit-and-polished on the outside, but he may be empty of the Holy Spirit on the inside. Such a person has not yet completed the step of sanctification *to* Christ. He is still more preoccupied with rules than with Him!

Chafer writes, "True spirituality does not consist in what one does *not* do, it is rather what one *does*. It is not suppression: it is expression. It is not holding in self: it is living out Christ . . . It is not a pious pose. It is not a 'Thou shalt *not*': it is 'Thou *shalt*.'" (*He That Is Spiritual*, p. 60)

The bottom line is we desperately need the working of the Holy Spirit in our lives, or else our living is in vain.

8. DEAD TO SIN

One of the most peculiar expressions in the Bible is "dead to sin" or its companion "died to sin." One believer said, "I believe that 'self' ought to be judged as dead. I know that it is only in the place of death that blessing comes, but *my 'self' is not dead, and it won't die.*" Wonder why? Perhaps it is because of a misinterpretation of scripture.

A lady once said to the Scottish scholar John Cumming, "I don't find anything like this death in my own experience. I have worried and fretted over the lack of death to self. I have done everything I could to *kill* self, but self seems more active than ever." Wonder why? Once again, perhaps it is because of a misinterpretation of scripture.

F. B. Meyer's statement puts the entire issue in perspective: "On this platform (a reference to the Keswick Bible Conference) we never say self is dead; were we to do so, self would be laughing at us around the corner."

This concept "dead to sin" appears extensively in Paul's doctrinal sections. For example, "What should we say then? Should we continue in sin so that grace may multiply? Absolutely not! How can we who died to sin still live in it?" (Romans 6:1-2, CSB). "For we know that our old self was crucified with him so that the body ruled by sin might be rendered powerless so that we may no longer be enslaved to sin, since a person who has died is freed from sin" (Romans 6:6-7, CSB). "So, you too consider yourselves dead to sin and alive to God in Christ Jesus"

(Romans 6:11, CSB). "If you died with Christ to the elements of this world, why do you live as if you still belonged to the world? Why do you submit to regulations?" (Colossians 2:20, CSB). "For you have died, and your life is hidden with Christ in God" (Colossians 3:3, ESV). "I have been crucified and still am crucified (the Greek word is a perfect tense verb) with Christ!" (Galatians 2:20).

The apostle Peter uses the term only once in his writings. "We, being dead to sins, should live unto righteousness" (1 Peter 2:24, KJV).

None of the other New Testament writers mention this idea of being dead to sin.

Some believers erroneously think the term indicates that a believer has "died out" to sin in the sense that he can no longer sin or is even beyond the capability of sinning. This is a companion idea to the eradication of the sin nature, which has been previously discussed. Thiessen, though, provides an excellent explanation of what it means to be "dead to sin." He writes:

> It is clear that this is an objective experience in which the believer is identified with Christ. If this were an absolute experiential death, why then does Paul insist that we need yet to 'reckon' ourselves dead to sin and alive to God? One who is absolutely dead does not need to reckon himself dead; he simply is dead apart from any reckoning. In the 7th chapter of Romans Paul pictures his own condition, as an unsaved man in vss. 7-13 and as a saved man in vss. 14-24. He finds deliverance from a life of defeat, not in the eradication of the carnal nature, but in the Lord Jesus Christ (Rom. 7:25). Romans 8 shows that Christ makes this victory real by the Holy Spirit, Whom the believer has received. First, He delivers him from the 'law of sin and of death', i.e., the carnal nature; then the believer is able to 'walk after the Spirit' and to 'mind the things of the Spirit' (vss. 2-10). But deliverance from the 'law of sin and of death' does not mean the eradication of the fallen nature; for the Apostle insists that the believer needs still by the Spirit to 'put to death the deeds of the body' (vs. 13). The Greek verb used here (*thanatoute*) is in the present tense; this is something that has to be done

repeatedly, whenever the inclinations of the flesh rise up to tempt us.

But we must beware of concluding that the defeated life is the normal life. Someone has well said, that as 'sinless perfection' is an unscriptural doctrine, so also is 'sinful imperfection.'

The sin nature continues to exist in the believer, but the believer should no longer be controlled or dominated by it. (*Introductory Lectures in Systematic Theology*, p. 382)

My old notes include Joseph Rotherham's translation of Romans 6:6, "Of this taking note, that our old man was crucified together with Him, in order that the sinful body might be made powerless, that we should no longer be in servitude to sin . . . so ye also be reckoning yourselves to be dead unto sin."

Merrill Unger, the author of the fabulous *Unger's Bible Dictionary*, adds these words:

The basis of experiential sanctification, or actual holiness of life, is positional sanctification or what one is in Christ. Only those 'in Christ,' that is, regenerate and thus concomitantly sanctified, are candidates for experiential sanctification. This phase of sanctification is effected by faith which reckons upon one's position in Christ (Rom. 6:1-10). One's position is true whether or not he reckons or counts it to be true. But it becomes experientially real only in proportion as one reckons it to be true (Rom. 6:11). (*Unger's Bible Dictionary*, p. 966)

I suggest the reader place a checkmark next to these very important words: *"One's position is true whether or not he reckons or counts it to be true. But it becomes experientially real only in proportion as one reckons it to be true."*

Paul states the reality of our current situation in his instructions to a young preacher named Timothy: "Flee youthful lusts!"

Pink writes,

Were the carnal nature gone from the Christian, he would be quite unfitted for such duties as the confessing of sins (1 John

1:9), loathing himself for them (Job 40:4), praying earnestly for the pardon of them (Matt. 6:12), sorrowing over them with godly sorrow (2 Cor. 7:10), accepting the chastisement of them (Heb. 12:5-11), vindicating God for the same (Psa. 119:75), and offering Him the sacrifice of a broken and a contrite heart (Psa. 51:17). (*The Doctrine of Sanctification*, p. 67)

Yet, at the same time, Lockyer was surely right when he says, "We should be more afraid of Christian *imperfection* than Christian *perfection*." (*All the Doctrines of the Bible*, p. 218)

A. W. Tozer expresses the same thought, "If we are not *changed* by grace, then we are not *saved* by grace."

Why is this particular chapter necessary? Some reason, "Surely we can gloss over the differences in our doctrine." But no! This chapter is necessary because a *sincere* believer cannot help but notice that he still falls short of what God expects. *"They who fain would serve Thee best are conscious most of wrong within."* You can sense Paul's own groanings for a higher plane of living when he confessed, "I do not consider myself to have apprehended all that God wants me to be."

Paul recognized the weaknesses of his flesh. He did not treat those weaknesses as mere mistakes or errors of judgment, but, very late in life, he still recognized himself as the "chiefest of sinners" when he compared himself with the Holy Son of God.

Every Christian needs to understand, and, therefore, *not dismay or become defeated* to the point of resignation when he loses a battle to the sin nature. Some Christians look in the mirror, see their many blemishes, and say, "I must not be saved because a saved person would not have done that."

Such failures produce consternation of the heart that can be very immobilizing. Such failures can even destroy one's faith! I beg you: Don't let that happen to you!

That is why this book's opening chapter is about the many ups and downs of the apostle Peter. His life did not become noteworthy because of the "eradication of the sin nature" but because he was continually "growing in the grace and knowledge of our Lord and Savior Jesus Christ."

I recall sitting at the feet of my mentor, Pastor Carl Holderby, and hearing him preach about Peter denying our Lord. Carl said, "Never forget that a saved person can still commit practically every sin that an unsaved person can commit. The same flesh is still in you until you go to be with the Lord!"

I may wish it were not so, but it is so. Unfortunately, the Bible and my earthly experience confirm it to be so.

God, though, has a wonderful solution for when we sin. Thankfully, His solution works every single time. "If we confess our sins, He is faithful and righteous to forgive us our sins and to cleanse us from all unrighteousness. If we say that we have not sinned, we make Him a liar and His word is not in us" (1 John 1:9-10, NASB). The fact is we *will* sin; the fact is He *will* also forgive.

In 1964 Alan Redpath, former pastor of Moody Church in Chicago, suffered a serious stroke. He became very despondent. He reached the point of praying, "O Lord, deliver me from the devil's attack! Take me home right now!"

The Lord answered, "It is I, your Savior, who has brought this experience into your life to show you that this is the kind of person you will always be but for My grace—a person who still has sinful thoughts and sinful temptations even though you thought they were things of the past!"

Someday God will fully deliver us from our sinful thoughts and our sinful temptations. But someday is not yet today.

God help us to seek His holy face and to *sin less* even though we are not yet *sinless*.

6

THREE CLASSIFICATIONS OF HUMANITY

It happened at a tournament for college speakers. One of the young female contestants walked to the microphone only to find it was at least twelve inches above her head. She made several unsuccessful attempts to lower the microphone. She finally turned to the director of the tournament and said, "The mic's too high for me."

The director, whose sense of humor was well known, replied, "You have ten minutes! Grow!"

Life, at its root, is about growing. Colleges provide classes in such areas as physical development, psychological development, cognitive development, plus much more for us to facilitate the process known as personal growth. The Bible, though, is more occupied with sanctification because the focus is *spiritual* growth.

William Law's self-evaluation has stood the test of time. He noticed how the farmers would rise early and not waste time. Law then said, "Who am I to lie folded up in a bed late of a morning when farmers have already gone about their work and I am so far behind on my sanctification?"

Law's point is well taken: Spiritual growth requires work. Spiritual growth does not occur automatically, instantly, or easily. Spiritual growth cannot be inherited, such as in the case of a monetary inheritance. Instead, spiritual growth must be *earned.* The Smith Barney television commercial of the 1980s said, "We make money the old-fashioned way. We earn it!" But many people do not want to pay that price. Thus, many people fall far short of God's ideal.

According to the Bible, there are three and *only* three possible classifications for each one of Adam's seed. The apostle Paul's main discussion of these three classifications is addressed to the one church which manifested all three in abundance: the church at Corinth. Each classification is emphasized in bold print in the passage below.

> But the **natural** man receiveth not the things of the Spirit of God: for they are foolishness unto him: neither can he know them, because they are spiritually discerned. But he that is **spiritual** judgeth all things, yet he himself is judged of no man. For who hath known the mind of the Lord, that he may instruct him? but we have the mind of Christ. And I, brethren, could not speak unto you as unto spiritual, but as unto **carnal**, even as unto babes in Christ. I have fed you with milk, and not with meat: for hitherto ye were not able to bear it, neither yet now are ye able. For ye are yet carnal: for whereas there is among you envying, and strife, and divisions, are ye not carnal, and walk as men? (1 Corinthians 2:14-3:3, KJV).

The New Scofield Reference Bible presents the standard interpretation of this passage. Its note on 1 Corinthians 2:14 is very helpful. It states:

Paul divides men into three classes: (1) *psuchikos*, meaning of the senses, sensuous, (Jas. 3:15, Jude 19), natural, i.e., the Adamic man, unrenewed through the new birth (Jn. 3:3,5); (2) *pneumatikos*, meaning spiritual, i.e., the renewed man as Spirit-filled and walking in the Spirit in full communion with God (Eph. 5:18-20); and (3) *sarkikos*, meaning carnal, fleshly, i.e., the renewed man who, walking 'after the flesh,' remains a babe in Christ (1 Cor. 3:1-4). The natural man may be learned, gentle, eloquent, fascinating, but the spiritual content of Scripture is absolutely hidden from him; and the fleshly or carnal Christian is able to comprehend only its simplest truths, 'milk' (1 Cor.3:2).

Thus, we are faced with three uniquely different classifications . . . but in which classification am I?

1. THE *PSUCHIKOS* OR NATURAL MAN

"But the **natural** man receiveth not the things of the Spirit of God: for they are foolishness unto him: neither can he know them, because they are spiritually discerned."

As noted above, the translation "natural" comes from the Greek word *psuchikos* (also appears in 1 Corinthians 15:44 and 46, James 3:15, Jude 10 and 19), meaning "of the senses, sensuous, natural, i.e., the Adamic man." The related noun *psukee* is predominantly translated "soul."

Psuchikos is translated in the New Testament as natural, sensual (of the senses rather than of the higher human spirit or Holy Spirit), unbeliever, not spiritual, unspiritual, self-centered, unspiritual nature, physical, instinct, worldly, worldly-minded, they think only about this life, men of the world.

Based upon the context, the CSB uses the phrase "the person without the Spirit" to translate *psuchikos* in 1 Corinthians 2:14. That translation captures Paul's meaning precisely.

In other words, *psuchikos* is focused on the nature of our being, specifically the lower part of our immaterial nature as in contrast to the higher part (spirit). The term describes man in his most basic unregenerate being. 2 Peter 2:12 is translated in the King James Version as "natural (*psuchikos*) brute beasts," thereby indicating an almost animalistic instinct to the *psuchikos* individual.

Jude 19 captures the essential thought that the *psuchikos* individual is devoid of God's Holy Spirit. What an awful condition! *To be soulish but not knowing the Holy Spirit!*

It is for this reason that Charles Haddon Spurgeon writes, "All men are negligent of their souls till grace gives them reason, then they leave their madness and behave and act like rational beings, but not till then." This behavior exists because man is limited by his own worldly nature.

Chafer explains depravity or man's limitation in this manner:

> If, as viewed by men, it is asserted that there is nothing good in man, the statement is untrue; for, as man is quick to declare, there is no human being so degraded that there is not some good in him. If, on the other hand, as viewed by God, it is claimed that man is without merit in His sight, the case is far different. Depravity as a doctrine does not stand or fall on the ground of man's estimation of himself; it rather reflects God's estimation of man. (*Systematic Theology Volume II*, p. 218)

(Note: Mankind is not pure evil in the sense of the Greek word *kakos*. We must always remember that man was created in the image of God. Adam's sin, though, marred or scarred the image of God into something much less than its original design. Perhaps that is the reason the Bible records that Adam fathered a child in *his* likeness in accordance with *his* image rather than the image of *God* (Genesis 5:3). The difference is similar to a defaced coin. The coin still retains value, but it has lost much of its beauty.)

Let's note some characteristics of the natural man. First and foremost, the natural man has a horizontal (earth-directed) plane of living but no vertical (heaven-directed) plane of living. Albert Brumley sings,

> "This world is not my home, I'm just a-passing through.
> My treasures are laid up somewhere beyond the blue.
> The angels beckon me from heaven's open door
> And I can't feel at home in this world anymore!"

Father Abraham could have written those very words, because "he looked for a city with foundations whose architect and builder is God"

(Hebrews 11:10). Abraham looked up because he lived *vertically.* "Up, up, and away!" "Looking unto Jesus!" "Look up for your redemption is drawing near." "Looking for the blessed hope and His appearing!" "I lift up my eyes!" "I feel heaven tugging on my soul!" "I saw the Lord, high and lifted up!" *But, no, not so with the natural man because he has only a horizontal plane of living.*

There is a re-occurring expression in the Revelation which illustrates this characteristic of the natural, *unheavenly,* earthbound man. The first appearance states, "Because you have kept my word about patient endurance, I will keep you from the hour of trial that is coming on the whole world, to try those who dwell on the earth" (Revelation 3:10, ESV). The Greek words translated "those who dwell on the earth" are repeated in almost the exact same way in 6:10, 11:10, 13:8, 13:14, 14:6, and 17:8. This oft-repeated phrase makes the point that God's judgment is directed against a group of people whom we might label or categorize as "earth dwellers."

In other words, their home is Planet Earth. Their lifestyle is Planet Earth. Their plans are Planet Earth. Their thoughts are Planet Earth. Everything about them is horizontal—they are a one-dimensional people because they have only a natural (Adamic) nature. That's why Paul says, "they walk according to the pattern, or drumbeat, or course of this world system" because this world system is their home. *It's the only home they know.* They would be out of place in my new home called heaven!

Second, the natural man may be religious or not religious. His immaterial being (consisting of a soul and spirit) recognizes an emptiness that man, in many cases, tries to fill with religion. Saint Augustine teaches, "Thou, God, hast made us for Thyself and our souls are restless until they find their rest in Thee." Both the Bible (Old Testament idolatry and New Testament philosophies) and history reveal man is a religious being, though some have made the deliberate choice to *will* God out of their thoughts. But, even so, religion falls far short of personally knowing God.

Third, the religious natural man tends to emphasize rituals over substance in his religion. Do you ever wonder why so much emphasis is placed upon religious rituals? Perhaps it is simply an issue of nature. *The psuchikos man can understand and relate to physical rituals, but the psuchikos man cannot understand and relate to the Spirit of God.*

For example, the Pharisees of Jesus' day were deeply religious but very vain in that same religion. The apostle Paul, a Pharisee himself, described his unregenerate state as being religious with a capital R in Philippians 3:6. "Regarding zeal, I intensely persecuted the church; I considered myself blameless regarding the righteousness based upon the Old Testament law." But he later learned he was so wrong!

Fourth, the *psuchikos* man is unable to understand the holy Scriptures.

> *Now we have received not the spirit of the world, but the Spirit who is from God, that we might understand the things freely given us by God. And we impart this in words not taught by human wisdom but taught by the Spirit, interpreting spiritual truths to those who are spiritual. The natural person does not accept the things of the Spirit of God, for they are folly to him, and he is not able to understand them because they are spiritually discerned (1 Corinthians 2:12-14, ESV).*

Speaking for myself, I am unable to comprehend many things in the scientific world, such as chemistry. My mind is unable to comprehend those facts, but yet I somehow have a daughter with a master's degree in chemistry. Similarly, the natural man is unable to comprehend the spiritual teachings of the Bible.

Jesus said to Nicodemus, "Do not be surprised at this truth, but you must be born again!" Nicodemus' response was the classic response of, "How? How can a grown man be born a second time from his mother's womb?"

Rest assured, his bewilderment, though, was not his alone. The same bewilderment is expressed by the natural man in every culture to the same words of Jesus. That's why Spurgeon says, "All men are negligent of their souls till grace gives them reason, then they leave their madness and behave and act like rational beings, *but not till then.*"

"O, to grace, how great a debtor
Daily I'm constrained to be."
Robert Robinson

"Years I spent in vanity and pride,
Caring not my Lord was crucified;
Knowing not it was for me He died on Calvary!"

William Newell

Fifth, the natural man rejects salvation by substitution. Adam and Eve sinned, but God sacrificed an animal as payment for their sin. Furthermore, God clothed them (a picture of imputed righteousness by substitution) with the skin of that substitute.

Then along came son number one: Cain. Cain's life is an accurate portrayal of the ordinary *psuchikos*. Genesis 4:3 says that Cain rejected salvation by a sacrificial substitute and instead approached God with the work of his own hands, perhaps just a sack of potatoes!

What does the New Testament say? "For the message of the cross is foolishness to those who are perishing, but it is God's power to us who are being saved" (1 Corinthians 1:18, HCSB). Thank God, I, for one, still believe in a hill called Mt. Calvary, how about you?

Sixth, the natural man still possesses a moral conscious or compass. This is true even though man has inherited Adam's sinful disposition. "They show that the work of the law is written on their hearts. Their consciences confirm this. Their competing thoughts either accuse or even excuse them" (Romans 2:15, CSB). Though Adam's depravity touches every part of the *psuchikos* man, he still retains an awareness of proper morality.

Seventh, the *psuchikos* produces the works of the flesh. The term "flesh" refers to the depraved nature which was received by us at birth. The phrase "sin nature" is another designation for the "flesh."

> *I say then, walk by the Spirit and you will certainly not carry out the desire of the flesh. For the flesh desires what is against the Spirit, and the Spirit desires what is against the flesh; these are opposed to each other, so that you don't do what you want. But if you are led by the Spirit, you are not under the law. Now the works of the flesh are obvious: sexual immorality, moral impurity, promiscuity, idolatry, sorcery, hatred, strife, jealousy, outbursts of anger, selfish ambitions, dissensions, factions, envy, drunkenness, carousing, and anything similar. I am warning you about these things— as I warned you before—that those who practice such things will not inherit the kingdom of God. (Galatians 5:16-21, CSB)*

Eighth, the natural man tends to humanize the Creator rather than treat Him as Sovereign.

> *For his invisible attributes, that is, his eternal power and divine nature, have been clearly seen since the creation of the world, being understood through what he has made. As a result, people are without excuse. For though they knew God, they did not glorify him as God or show gratitude. Instead, their thinking became worthless, and their senseless hearts were darkened. Claiming to be wise, they became fools and exchanged the glory of the immortal God for images resembling mortal man, birds, four-footed animals, and reptiles. (Romans 1:20-23, CSB)*

Ninth, the natural man views truth as variable rather than constant. By contrast, we believe that truth—all truth—begins with God. That includes scientific truth, mathematical truth, moral truth, religious truth, etc. Yet the natural man rejects that very premise. "For God's wrath is revealed from heaven against all godlessness and unrighteousness of people who by their unrighteousness suppress the truth" (Romans 1:18, CSB). The word "suppress" perfectly expresses the attitude of the *psuchikos*. "We know that God's judgment on those who do such things is based on the truth. Do you really think—anyone of you who judges those who do such things yet do the same—that you will escape God's judgment? Or do you despise the riches of his kindness, restraint, and patience, not recognizing that God's kindness is intended to lead you to repentance?" (Romans 2:2-4, CSB).

Amazingly, not even one of these nine characteristics is up for debate among serious Bible students. Truth be told, even more characteristics could be mentioned. The reality is very simple: Man is a sinner and needs to be saved through the mighty power of regeneration.

It is true that man may rise to great heights, but such achievements can never change man's basic nature. One such man, Alexander III of Macedon, became the most powerful man of his day by conquering all of the known world. He earned the title of Alexander the Great or The Great King. Alexander conquered everything there was to conquer, but he could not conquer his own sin nature. Alexander died at the young age of thirty-three in a drunken stupor.

The bottom line is sinful man needs to become a *new creation* through faith in Jesus Christ.

Thus, this particular teaching forms the basis of this book's title. *Sanctification: How God Creates Saints out of Sinners* is in total agreement with the inspired Bible teaching that man is a sinner with no hope except the hope of being born again!

2. THE *SARKIKOS* OR CARNAL MAN

The second classification of mankind introduces us to those who have moved beyond the *psuchikos* classification. It should be noted that the percentage of mankind in the *psuchikos* classification is much greater than the percentage of people in the remaining two categories (*sarkikos* and *pneumatikos*). As a result, the Bible teaches that "hell has enlarged itself . . . enlarged its throat to gobble up even more people and has widened its enormous jaws" (Isaiah 5:14).

Three facts need to be noted at this time. First, the *sarkikos* and *pneumatikos* categories describe born-again Christians. Second, the universe or scope of *sarkikos* and *pneumatikos* is *not* the same as the number of local church members since one can be a church member and not be born again. Third, the *sarkikos* and *pneumatikos* categories describe born-again Christians in two widely different stages of their spirituality. *Every* born-again Christian will be classified as either *sarkikos* or *pneumatikos*. There are no other options.

Based upon that foundation, let's first turn our attention to the *sarkikos* classification. Once again, 1 Corinthians 2:14-3:3 is the basis for our study. I am indebted to Charles Ryrie of Dallas Theological Seminary for his excellent thoughts.

> The Greek word *'sarkikos'* means 'fleshly' or 'of the flesh' with the idea of weakness; in v.3 fleshly has the overtone of willfulness. Fleshly Christians (brethren) are babes in Christ (i.e., undeveloped) who cannot understand the deeper truths of the Word of God (v.2) and who are characterized by strife (v. 3). (The Ryrie Study Bible, p. 1730)

That's more of a theological definition, so let me give you a common man's definition.

> A carnal Christian is a saved man who lives, in many ways, like an unsaved man . . . a man with a born-again nature who is instead dominated by his old, unsaved, Adamic nature given to him at physical conception. He has yet to grow into the overcoming life of both Holy Spirit enablement and evaluation capacity.

Lewis Sperry Chafer writes,

> A carnal Christian is as perfectly saved as the spiritual Christian: for no experience or merit of service can form any part of the grounds of salvation. Though but a baby, he is, nevertheless, in Christ (1 Cor. 3:1). His obligation toward God is not to exercise saving faith, but rather to adjust to the mind and will of God. It is of fundamental importance to understand that a normal Christian experience is realized only by those who are Spirit-filled. (*Major Bible Themes*, p. 214)

Sarkikos, in Chafer's view, "represents a living reality which includes in it a fallen nature with all its inherent forces and relationship—a fallen nature which knows no eradication, but continues with the believer as long as he is in the world and which is overcome only by a ceaseless appropriation of the power of the indwelling Spirit." (*Systematic Theology Volume III*, p. 359)

We must remember that the new birth is where growth *begins*. The new birth, though, is not the end. It is only the beginning of a process that leads the believer to his ultimate end: to be like Christ in every manner consistent with Christ's holy nature.

But the growth process has stalled in the life of the sarkikos *saint!* He is still living under the control of the *sarx*, commonly translated by our English word "flesh." It should be obvious to all that Paul uses the term *sarx* or flesh in contrast to the *pneumatikos* or spirit. The flesh, of course, is still tied to this world, while the new spirit man or new creation is tied to God's world and God's kingdom.

J. Allen Blair describes the carnal, fleshly *sarkikos* saint as, "Though they believe on Christ for salvation, they look to the world for satisfaction." In other words, the *sarkikos* saint has not yet made the transition from filling his soul with the world to filling his soul with God. Like the prodigal son (Luke 15), he is still feeding his soul with the pig's food when he could be feasting at his Heavenly Father's table!

The Scottish preacher Robert Murray M'Cheyne says, "Most of God's people are content to be saved from the hell that is *without*. They are not so anxious to be saved from the hell that is *within*."

Without a doubt, it does not require any effort to be a carnal Christian. That fact explains why there are so many of them. Indeed, the church at Corinth could have been renamed The First Carnal Church of Corinth! Carnality existed throughout the Corinthian membership.

(Note: We know the Corinthian church had a church membership roll because Paul commanded the church to exclude a member and to disassociate from that person (1 Corinthians 5). How can one be *excluded* unless he has first been *included*?)

But it does require effort to grow! "Do your best to show yourself approved unto God" (2 Timothy 2:15). "Give diligence to make your calling and election sure" (2 Peter 1:10). "Hold fast what you have" (Revelation 3:11). "Be faithful unto death" (Revelation 2:10). "Present your body as a living sacrifice to God" (Romans 12:1).

Solo comments in an on-line devotional (*The King's Corner*), "A carnal Christian is ruled by self-centeredness, self-glory, self-exultation, self-love, self-pity and self-importance, self-ambition and pride. Everything he does, he does for show and to gain something for himself, even if it's just the praise of men."

There are many identifying characteristics of a *sarkikos* or carnal Christian. The following list contains characteristics that may appear in some people but not appear in others. (We will look closer at the characteristics of the new believer in chapter seven).

First, the *sarkikos* saint places little value on personal or churchwide revival. A season of revival services can stir the heart of even the most spiritual saint to greater service for our Lord! Most of today's churches have abandoned the idea of a lengthy revival because *their own members will not attend.* I have often remarked that the favorite song of the carnal Christian is, "I shall not be moved!" Indeed, the carnal Christian has dug in his feet against spiritual progress!

Second, *sarkikos* saints are often recognized by a critical attitude. This attitude may be accompanied by another un-Christlike trait known as self-promotion. The carnal Christian tends to tear down people in the hope that he will be the only one left standing. Instead of climbing the ladder, he pulls others down the ladder! On the other hand, a forgiving spirit (see *God's Greenhouse: How to Grow People God's Way* for a multi-chapter discussion of forgiveness) appreciates and supports the effort to exalt Jesus.

Such a critical spirit reminds me of a church member whom my father met in one of his revivals. This church had once been known for its excellent children's ministry, including a summer camp for children. The man said, "I have some advice for you as a young preacher. The worst thing you can ever start in your church is a youth ministry." 99.99999% of us would disagree strongly with that man. Undoubtedly, that man was a problem for his church.

Third, the carnal Christian may display a rebellious spirit. As a general rule, the carnal Christian struggles with such songs as "Have Thine Own Way, Lord" and "I Surrender All." The inbred Adamic nature is all about King Self! It is true that King Self had to be overcome to be saved. But the will of King Self has reasserted itself in the carnal believer and is now fighting the call of God in a very powerful and victorious way.

Fourth, *sarkikos* saints tend to lose big-time in the battle against sin. Spurgeon says, "No man can have peace while he is at peace with any sin." God calls His people to overcome the flesh, the world, and the devil, but carnal Christians have instead been overcome by those foes. In so doing, the salt of the earth loses its savor and, in Jesus' own words, "is now fit for nothing except to be cast outside the house where it can be walked upon by people passing by."

Fifth, and this is a very dangerous characteristic, the *sarkikos* saint may be preoccupied with how much he knows versus how much he does. A doctorate in theology is indeed impressive, but it does not indicate the condition of the believer's heart. Far too many Christians can recite the facts, read Greek and Hebrew, quote the entire list of Israel's kings, but lack in the more important category called experiential knowledge. In their case, "the letter of the law" needs to be replaced by "the spirit of the law."

Sixth, the fleshly Christian often lacks a strong stand against sin. "Onward Christian soldiers, marching as to war" is not one of his slogans. One such believer said, "I will support alcohol in our community because I do not want my taxes to increase!" One can only wonder if his view would change if his child ever became an alcoholic . . . or if someone brought whiskey to the next church social!

Seventh, let's add that such a one is usually lazy regarding spiritual matters. Such a person may be active in the church, but he often lacks concerning the Great Commission—to the spiritual side of things. He may be busy (like the church at Laodicea) but busy about insignificant things. Someone commented to me about a very busy church member, "How busy she is in the church, but did you ever hear her say anything spiritual? Does she ever talk about her walk with the Lord?" Sadly, the answer was no. Perhaps she had nothing to talk about!

Eighth, inconsistency! The Old Testament character Lot is a great example of an inconsistent Christian. He saved the angels from the evil men of Sodom but offered his daughters to the same men (Genesis 19). He believed in God's judgment, but he had no testimony before others. In many ways, the carnal Christian's favorite saying is, "Do as I say, not as I do."

Ninth (and the list keeps growing), there is no hunger for the deeper Christian life, such as learning the Bible, seeking God's face in prayer, or winning the lost to Christ. But such a one may be very interested in the entertainment side of Christianity. An Assembly of God pastor in Orlando, Florida, moaned, "If we have a service focused on fasting and prayer, no one will come. But everyone will come if we have a healing service with the big-name television preacher."

Tenth, a sponge attitude. One church member told me, "The problem with our church is we have too many chiefs and not enough Indians." Guess what? The statement was made by someone who wanted to be the chief and let others do the work! In far too many cases, *sarkikos* people are content to be sponges . . . their sole reason for existence is to soak up the blessings and let others do the real work.

Eleventh, the *sarkikos* believer is not a happy person. Jesus defined biblical happiness in the Beatitudes (Matthew 5); interestingly, each beatitude is the exact opposite of a *sarkikos* lifestyle.

What word would best describe the *sarkikos* believer? How about defeated? Let's add words such as frustrated, confused, contradictory, and restless. Carnality is not a pleasant lifestyle. Indeed, such a person may be known more for a sandpaper personality!

The sarkikos *believer is caught between two competing worlds.* The old nature is reaching back (and down) while the new nature is reaching ahead (and up). It is not a pleasant time, but a contradictory time. This struggle is discussed at great length in chapter sixteen's "Growing through God's Discipline."

I knew of one church that became known in the community as "The Mad Church." Why? It consisted of members who became mad in their own church and joined this particular church. Of course, "The Mad Church" did not have any lasting success!

Based on the Word of God *and* my more than forty years in ministry, *I am convinced that a commitment to the Great Commission would handle 95% of our church problems!* A commitment to God's program will guarantee God's blessings and "where the Spirit of the Lord is, there is liberty or freedom also!"

Twelfth, *sarkikos* believers are easily divided. Paul mentions "envy and strife" as a prevailing characteristic of a *sarkikos* church. This is true because the focus is upon things rather than Jesus Christ. The prodigal's brother (Luke 15) pictures this condition. The brother was *in* the family but did not wish to be *with* the family!

Let's finish the list of *sarkikos* characteristics with something similar to a previous discussion but yet different. We identified earlier that the natural man has a horizontal (earth-directed) plane of living but no vertical (heaven-directed) plane of living. The *sarkikos* man, though, is different. The *sarkikos* man possesses a *more* horizontal (earthward) plane of living and *less* vertical (heavenward) plane of living. In other words, he is moving in two directions at the same time, but the earthward plane has more appeal than the heavenward plane.

He is like water choosing the path of least resistance and choosing to live on an earthly plane void of the Holy Spirit and spiritual emphasis. However, there are times (usually times of short duration) when he rises up and rallies to the cause of Christ. He may be as unpredictable as the weather in winter. As a pastor, I am usually surprised at this sudden, spontaneous revival of involvement, and I immediately pray that it will continue . . . and sometimes it does, and it is not long until the carnal Christian grows into a spiritual Christian.

It has been suggested that the spiritual or *pneumatikos* life is like taking a walk in the park . . . and having God as one's companion. But the carnal or *sarkikos* life is like taking a walk in a different park . . . Jurassic Park with the dinosaurs as one's companion!

Vance Havner says, "The average Christian is living so subnormal that if he ever lived normal, the world would think he is abnormal!" Havner could say that because Jesus says, "I have come in order for you to have life and have it more abundantly" (John 10:10). Likewise, Psalm 23 begins with the beautiful words, "The Lord Jehovah is my shepherd. What else do I need because I will never lack anything in His presence." The psalmist then proceeds to elaborate on what the normal Christian life is all about.

But that is not so with the *sarkikos* Christian. He is still trying to cling to the world, and his eyes are looking back and down instead of ahead and up!

Paul writes to the *sarkikos* believer, "I have no choice but to give you milk to drink. I cannot feed you solid food, because you are not yet ready or mature enough to consume it" (1 Corinthians 3:2). Why, though, aren't they ready? Paul goes on to say, "It is because you are still *sarkikos* or carnal! Controlled by the flesh! Your maturity pales in comparison to the maturity level of the *pneumatikos* or spiritual man."

What happens when carnal Christians make up the majority of the church membership and especially the leadership team? Nothing good! There will be no thirst for spiritual matters but rather a thirst for taking the easy road. There will be no desire for revival. Soul winning and the Great Commission will rarely be mentioned. The church will be inward focused rather than outward focused. A critical spirit will likely permeate the membership. Very few will take a strong stand against sin either inside or outside the church. There will be no hunger for deeper Bible study or prayer. And the sponges will far outnumber the servants.

Henry Foster writes in *A Homiletic Commentary on the Epistles of St. Paul the Apostle to the Corinthians,*

> The beauty of a baby is no beauty when it becomes permanent. Fifteen or fifty with the face and mind and powers of five years of age would be a calamity to the grown child, an agony to the parents, a subject of mockery, or of pity to outsiders. There are such in every church. Always learning to stand, to walk, to do; never accomplishing much at either; indeed, spiritually always learning to live. To them the church is hardly yet a school; certainly not a workshop; more truly a nursery.

Heaven forbid! A nursery for adults!

As a longtime pastor, I often find myself wondering, "How many church members get beyond the *sarkikos* stage? How many actually grow beyond the baby or nursery stage?"

I must confess there have been times during my more than four decades of ministry that I have run out of pacifiers. From a pastor's perspective it is exasperating trying to manage carnal Christians. We pastors haven't been called to manage day care centers but, far too often, our churches more resemble day care centers than Great Commission centers.

Are you a dedicated pastor, deacon, or teacher? If the answer is yes, you already recognize *the carnal Christian must be treated like a baby.* (It is not an accident that Paul compares the carnal Christian to a baby in verse one even though he may have been a Christian for many years.)

Sometimes I groan about having to ask a carnal Christian to do *anything,* but, then again, God has a tendency to offset that negative with the best Christians I could ever ask for—spiritual Christians whose motto is, "Whatever I can do is what I will do for my God! And if I've never done it before, I will still try!" Those people are such a blessing! They will never know what a blessing they are to God's pastor. Thank God, for His gifting them to us!

3. THE PNEUMATIKOS OR SPIRITUAL MAN

An old axiom says, "Weeds grow by themselves, but flowers are planted." The first requires no work, but the second requires much work. Chafer says,

> There are two great spiritual changes which are possible to human experience—the change from the 'natural' man to the saved man, and the change from the 'carnal' man to the 'spiritual' man. The former is divinely accomplished when there is a real faith in Christ; the latter is accomplished when there is a real adjustment to the Spirit. (*He That Is Spiritual*, p. 22)

The third classification of mankind is the highest classification of all—the *pneumatikos* or spiritual man.

> *"But he who is spiritual appraises all things, yet he himself is appraised by no one. For who has known the mind of the Lord, that he will instruct Him? But we have the mind of Christ. And I, brethren, could not speak to you as to spiritual men, but as to men of flesh, as to infants in Christ" (1 Corinthians 2:15-3:1, NASB).*

The word "spiritual" comes to us from the Greek word *pneumatikos*. *Vine's Expository Dictionary of New Testament Words* notes the Greek term does not appear in the Septuagint or the four Gospels, but my research shows that it appears twenty-eight times in the later writings.

W. E. Vine writes,

> According to the Scriptures, the 'spiritual' state of soul is normal for the believer, but to this state all believers do not attain, nor when it is attained is it always maintained. Thus the Apostle, in 1 Cor. 3:1-3, suggests a contrast between this spiritual state and that of the babe in Christ, i.e. of the man who because of immaturity and inexperience has not yet reached spirituality, and that of the man who by permitting jealousy, and the strife to which jealousy always leads, has lost it. The spiritual state is reached by diligence in the Word of God and in prayer; it is maintained by obedience and self-judgment. Such as

are led by the Spirit are spiritual, but, of course, spirituality is not a fixed or absolute condition, it admits of growth; indeed, growth in 'the grace and knowledge of our Lord and Savior Jesus Christ,' 2 Peter 3:18 is evidence of true spirituality. (*Vine's Expository Dictionary of New Testament Words*, p. 1088)

The term "spiritual" or *pneumatikos* describes one as being "controlled or dominated by the Holy *Pneuma* or Spirit." It is more than "being filled with the Holy Spirit" (Ephesians 5:18), an experience that happens immediately at salvation for the newborn child of God.

The term "spiritual" implies that one has become *seasoned* in the lifestyle of the Holy Spirit (Galatians 6:1). This lifestyle is not a one-day-a-week event like attending church on the Lord's Day, but it is a part of the believer's everyday life. It just continually happens in the same way the sun rises in the east. In other words, it is so automatic that it is considered a part of everyday life.

The difference between the *sarkikos* believer and the *pneumatikos* believer is like night and day. The *sarkikos* believer lives in the energy of the flesh or Adamic nature. But the *pneumatikos* believer lives in the energy of the Holy Spirit and the new nature. They are vastly different in terms of daily lifestyle, attitude, and goal.

To summarize, the carnal Christian is habitually controlled or dominated by the sinful flesh, but in the mature/spiritual stage, one is habitually controlled, or dominated, by the Holy Spirit. We might even say the Holy *Pneuma* is pneumatizing or spiritualizing the believer.

Chafer states,

> No manner of walk, however perfect, will even tend to preserve the child of God. He is secure by another provision altogether, namely, his place in the resurrected Christ. In the matter of a consistent life, which glorifies the One who saves him, the believer may claim all the supernatural power of the indwelling Spirit . . . It is possible for the Holy Spirit to defend the believer and deliver him from Satan's power on the ground of the fact that Satan has been judged by Christ in His death . . .

Like a criminal who has been sentenced to die and awaits the day of his execution, so Satan is already judged and awaits the day of the administration of His sentence. Though judged, Satan is a living, mighty power and is to be resisted by the believer's steadfast faith (1 Peter 5:8-9). (*Systematic Theology Volume III*, pp. 359-360)

Although cumbersome, the literal rendering of Philippians 3:12-14 is perhaps the finest biblical description of the *pneumatikos* saint.

Not that I already made acquisition or that I have now already been brought to that place of absolute spiritual maturity beyond which there is no progress, but I am pursuing onward if I may lay hold of that for which I have been laid hold of by Christ Jesus. Brethren, as for myself, as I look back upon my life and calmly draw a conclusion, I am not counting myself yet as one who has in an absolute and complete way laid hold (of that for which I have been laid hold of by Christ Jesus); but one thing: I, in fact, am forgetting completely the things that are behind, and am stretching forward to the things that are in front; bearing down upon the goal, I am pursuing on for the prize of the call from above of God which is in Christ Jesus. (Philippians 3:12-14, *The New Testament: An Expanded Translation* by Kenneth S. Wuest, p. 466)

We are commanded to grow! But it must be remembered that a tree grows automatically if the tree is healthy. Bless God, the believer can be so firmly rooted in the Holy Pneuma that he is able to throw out branches and increase his fruit-bearing potential.

Thiessen writes, "God has already set apart to Himself everyone who believes in Christ; now the believer is to set himself apart to God for His use."

What are the characteristics of a *pneumatikos* believer?

First, and this characteristic sets the stage for the other characteristics, the believer's core being is directed more vertical (heavenward) and less horizontal (earthward). He has not yet arrived at a perfectly vertical condition, but he is definitely looking up more than he is looking around.

Enoch walked with God. That's vertical living! So did Noah. So did Abraham. So did Peter, James, and John. So did Paul. And so does the *pneumatikos* saint. God is as real to him as anyone in his family. He knows God not only with his head but also with his heart. He has a walk with God, which is described in the Bible as a *gnosis* or experiential walk. He does not need you to tell him about God because he personally knows God!

Have you ever noticed that these people tend to stand out from the rest? It is because they do indeed have a different lifestyle.

Second, the *pneumatikos* saint is surrendered to the will of God.

> *Therefore, brothers and sisters, in view of the mercies of God, I urge you to present your bodies as a living sacrifice, holy and pleasing to God; this is your true worship. Do not be conformed to this age, but be transformed by the renewing of your mind, so that you may discern what is the good, pleasing, and perfect will of God. (Romans 12:1-2, CSB)*

Those verses are *real* to the *pneumatikos* saint. They are more than mere words on a page. Rick Warren cautions, "Worship is not a style of music, but living a lifestyle that is pleasing to God." The *pneumatikos* saint has moved beyond the music to a lifestyle!

"Then Jesus said to his disciples, 'If anyone wants to follow after me, let him deny himself, take up his cross, and follow me. For whoever wants to save his life will lose it, but whoever loses his life because of me will find it'" (Matthew 16:24-25, CSB). Some of us are in the "finding business."

This act of surrender is similar to some words which appear on the back cover of my first book, *God's Greenhouse: How to Grow People God's Way.* The first two lines on the back cover read, "It's who we are. It's what we do." The *pneumatikos* saint has willingly accepted his role as a servant of the Most High God; that act of the will defines what he now does.

Third, the *pneumatikos* believer routinely acknowledges and confesses his sin. By contrast, the carnal believer resists confessing his sin! One of the old-time preachers said, "Life will be much easier if you keep a short list with God." In his mind, that short list consisted of our sins. I agree with his logic, and, most importantly, God agrees. It's much easier to clean work clothes every day than to do so after the everyday grime has become ingrained.

Fourth, and this should be no surprise, the *pneumatikos* believer produces the fruit of the Holy Pneuma. The Christian life is designed to be a changed life. The *pneumatikos* believer demonstrates that change by allowing the Holy Pneuma to flow through him. *As the believer walks in the Spirit, the Spirit walks through him.*

This act of submission allows the Holy Spirit to produce His fruit in the believer's life.

> *But the fruit of the Spirit is love, joy, peace, patience, kindness, goodness, faithfulness, gentleness, and self-control. The law is not against such things. Now those who belong to Christ Jesus have crucified the flesh with its passions and desires. If we live by the Spirit, let us also keep in step with the Spirit (Galatians 5:22-25, CSB).*

"Keeping in step with the Holy Spirit" is a *pneumatikos* goal. Ryrie even goes so far as to suggest that the fruit of the Spirit is genuine sanctification!

How is such a level of living possible? Chafer states,

> The nine words which define Christian character . . . it will always be found (1) that they are always presented as being divine characteristics, though they sometimes have a shadow of their reality in the relationships and ideals of the world; (2) they are assuredly expected by God in the believer's life; and (3) they are always produced only by the Spirit of God. (*He That Is Spiritual*, p. 47)

Fifth, the *pneumatikos* saint is faithful. The simplest definition of faithful is "full of faith." Therefore, he *keeps* doing what he is doing because he believes, or trusts, or faiths, in the rightness of what he is doing. Demas quit on the apostle Paul, but Luke remained faithful!

Sixth, the mature saint is committed to the Holy Scriptures. Based upon Paul's declaration that "all or every single scripture, including jot and tittle, is inspired or God-breathed" (2 Timothy 3:16), the *pneumatikos* saint uses those same scriptures to become "thoroughly prepared to do the Lord's will."

Seventh, the *pneumatikos* believer has an ability to comprehend the spiritual teachings in the Bible. Though the *psuchikos* unbeliever can comprehend the historical teachings, he is completely baffled by the spiritual teachings. The *psuchikos* unbeliever Nicodemus could only scratch his head when Jesus said, "You must be born again." Nicodemus was totally out of his league!

The apostle Paul emphasizes, "The *pneumatikos* man discerns or evaluates all things" (1 Corinthians 2:15). What things? We can interpret it broadly or narrowly. The surrounding context, though, is clearly aligned with an understanding of the Bible. The context mentions deep, biblical truths which "eye has never seen nor ear heard, neither has any heart conceived . . . the deep things of God . . . revealed by the Spirit . . . that we might know the things which have been freely given to us by God . . . interpreting spiritual truths to those who are *pneumatikos* or spiritual."

Eighth, his approach to Christ is one of beauty and admiration. Before the believer's regeneration, there was "no beauty in Him that we should desire Him," but after regeneration, the same One has become "the fairest of ten thousand to our souls."

Ninth, the *pneumatikos* believer has aligned his values with those of the Great Commission. The Great Commission is repeated four times in the Gospels and one more time in Acts 1:8. The old song says, "Rescue the perishing, care for the dying, snatch them in pity from sin and the grave." The *pneumatikos* believer not only knows the song, but he also practices the song! He is involved in bringing people to know Jesus as Savior! "He that wins souls is wise" (Proverbs 11:30).

Tenth, the *pneumatikos* child of God is spiritually adept at handling sin and sinners. Galatians 6:1 says, "Brothers and sisters, if a man or woman becomes trapped in some sin, you who are at the *pneumatikos* level, restore that brother in the spirit of gentleness, always being watchful that you do not become trapped in the same sin." This activity is similar to rescuing a drowning man. If you aren't careful, the drowning man will drown both of you! But the *pneumatikos* believer knows how to protect both.

Eleventh, the *pneumatikos* saint views life with the mind of Christ. What happens when we grow the way we should grow? The apostle Paul teaches, "But he who is spiritual appraises all things, yet he himself is appraised by no one. For who has known the mind of the Lord, that he will instruct Him? But we have the mind of Christ" (1 Corinthians 2:15-16, NASB). *The "mind of Christ" means that one thinks biblically—to think biblically is to think like Jesus Christ.* As the believer increasingly thinks biblically, he tends to increasingly make the right spiritual decisions.

Ryrie writes, "The mature Christian who is led and taught by the Spirit appraises all things, i.e., he can scrutinize, sift, and thereby understand all things; but unbelievers and even carnally-minded Christians cannot appraise (understand) him." (*The Ryrie Study Bible*, p. 1730)

The mind of Christ is a learned mind, a learned behavior, and a learned viewpoint. It results in a discipled or disciplined mind, behavior, and viewpoint.

Charles Stanley says, "As your faith increases, your trust in Him will increase, and your life will show the evidence of maturity."

We might define the "mind of Christ" in terms of a Christian worldview. It's like wearing sunglasses. The tint of my sunglasses changes the way I view the world. Most sunglasses employ a gray tint while others possess a rose or brown tint. Each customer gets to make his own choice. But, oh, how that tint changes what I see!

Likewise, the tint known as "Mind of Christ Tint" changes the way I view the world. *I see the world much differently than others because I see it more from God's perspective.* God's perspective states, "The whole world persists under the devil's sway in wickedness or opposition to God" (1 John 5:19). That perspective is not a commonly held view in our culture.

But the *pneumatikos* believer is not a part of the world's culture. Thus, I think differently than the average American. This Christian worldview leads me to make different decisions than an unsaved co-worker, unsaved relative, or unsaved friend. We genuinely see life from a different perspective.

The mind of Christ helps me answer the following questions: What is right? What is wrong? Where did I come from? Why am I here? Where am I going? Is there a real devil? Is man's nature good or sinful? Does man need a Savior? Is there any such thing as absolute truth? Is there life after death, and, if yes, how should I live before death? Does God have a plan for my life, or am I here on my own?

Remember: If you are not thinking *right*, you must be thinking with the *wrong* mind! The right mind is the mind of Christ; the wrong mind is the mind of sinful Adam!

Kenneth Osbeck remarks, "An intimate fellowship with our Lord should produce at least three basic differences in our living: more humility, more happiness, more holiness."

"He who is spiritual correctly appraises or weighs all things." *This statement is critically important in choosing people for church leadership.* Paul mentions one of the qualifications for a pastor/bishop/elder is that he not be a new convert to Christ, lest he "become inflated with pride, conceited, puffed up, and fall into the same judgment of the devil" (1 Timothy 3:6). Undoubtedly, the same principle is in view in choosing the first deacons or servants. Acts 6:3 mentions the selected men were to be full of the Holy Spirit and wisdom—i.e., spiritually seasoned and able to "appraise or weigh all things."

You may not know this, but the apostle John became known as the apostle of *love* at the end of his ministry. But he was known as the son of *thunder* at the beginning of his ministry. What a difference! The gap between the son of thunder and the apostle of love became filled with the ingredient called spiritual growth. Over many years John grew past the too much fleshly and too little Spirit stage into the less fleshly and more Spirit stage.

This brings us to a very interesting question that is not emphasized enough by Bible writers or pastors.

How long should it take a believer to move from the newborn stage to the mature/spiritual stage?

We have *three clues* in Paul's experience with the Corinthians.

Clue #1: Paul established the church at Corinth during his second missionary journey (Acts 18). Acts 18:11 indicates that Paul ministered in Corinth for eighteen months. There is a general consensus among conservative Bible scholars that this ministry occurred in A.D. 50-52.

Clue #2: The date of A.D. 55-early 56 is commonly accepted for the writing of 1 Corinthians. That gives us a gap of no more than six years (most likely, three or four) between the first two clues.

Clue #3: Let's use a different translation for 1 Corinthians 3.

> *Brothers, I was not able to speak to you as spiritual people but as people of the flesh, as babies in Christ. I gave you milk to drink, not solid food, because you were not yet ready for it. In fact, you are still not ready, because you are still fleshly. For since there is envy and strife among you, are you not fleshly and living like unbelievers? For whenever someone says, 'I'm with Paul,' and another, 'I'm with Apollos,' are you not unspiritual people? (1 Corinthians 3:1-4, HCSB).*

Notice the two references to the word "still." One can also sense the word in other places, too. It is clear Paul is startled to learn the Corinthians, as a whole, have not yet made it to the spiritual stage. "You are **still** not ready" speaks volumes! Clearly, they should have arrived at that stage "by now."

What then does "by now" mean? It means the believers have received *more* than enough time to make the transition from babes to mature/spiritual. Some should have been well-qualified spiritual leaders by this time. That means some should have been mature, Spirit-seasoned pastors, teachers, deacons, soul winners, and on and on the list goes.

We can conclude from this text that it *does not take a lifetime* to become mature/spiritual like Jesus. Don't forget that Paul's words, "We have the mind of Christ," are a *present* reality rather than a future reality! This growth stage can occur in just a few short years if one is yielded to the Lord, grows in Bible teachings, and allows the Holy Spirit to rule in his heart.

The New Scofield Reference Bible adds, "Even though Paul had ministered in Thessalonica for less than a month, many great doctrines of the Christian faith are alluded to in this Epistle." The book of 1 Thessalonians includes teaching material on the Trinity, the Holy Spirit, Christ's second advent, the Day of the Lord, assurance, conversion, election, resurrection, sanctification, and Christian behavior. We might say, "That's a full and overflowing plate for a young church!" But it strongly suggests that Paul expected a sharp growth uptrend for these young believers.

God wants His children to grow quickly because He has a work for each one of us. People need what God can do through you.

On the other hand, achieving the mature/spiritual state does not mean one has "totally arrived" and has no more room to grow. The Bible makes it clear that no one should ever stop growing. There will always be more to learn.

James P. Boyce offers,

The process of sanctification is like the ascent of a mountain. One is always going forward, though not always upward, yet the final end of the progressive movement of every kind is the attainment of the summit. Sometimes, because of difficulties, the road itself descends, only more easily to ascend again. Sometimes certain attractions by the way cause a deviation from the route most suitable for ascent. Often it is feared that there has been no higher attainment, often that it has been but a continual descent, until, perchance, some point of view is gained from which to look down upon the plain whence the journey was begun and behold the height which has already been overcome. Often, with wearied feet, and desponding heart, the traveler is ready to despair, because of his own feebleness, and the difficulties which surround. But he earnestly presses forward and the journey is completed, the ascent is made, the end is attained. (*Abstract of Systematic Theology*, p. 415)

Let me share an example that starts bad but ends up good. I visited one of my wayward members in my days as a young minister. I remember standing in this member's backyard and specifically asking him if he still had beer in his refrigerator. (Hint: Every Christian's standards should be at least as high as those of Alcoholics Anonymous. If you have a different view, please read 1 Corinthians 8:13.) His answer was yes.

This man was making life difficult for his family in more ways than just alcohol. The family life was so bad that on one occasion, his wife brought the television remote control to the Sunday night service. She said, "He can stay home from church, but he can't watch the television!" Oh, times were bad!

This man was a *sarkikos* Christian. He confessed to me in his backyard that he was in rebellion against God. It was easy to see he was a modern-day Jonah running from God, but it was also clear that God had already run him down and was making life miserable for him. (Note: He was a good example of how God chastens His children. See Hebrews 12:5-11. This material is explained further in chapter sixteen.) Some months later, that man openly confessed his sin in a church service and returned to the Lord. What a wonderful change took place!

A few years later, God called that man to be a pastor. I am glad to report he became a really good pastor, too. Many were saved and baptized under his ministry.

His life was a fascinating study for me as a young pastor. In my early days with him, this believer was dominated by the sinful flesh. He was a *sarkikos* believer. Then he repented, did an about-face, and, in time, grew into the *pneumatikos*, or spiritual, stage. The words "mature, spiritual, and knowledgeable" accurately described him!

Three classifications: the natural (*psuchikos*) man, the carnal (*sarkikos*) man, as well as the spiritual (*pneumatikos*) man. One of those classifications describes you. Which one? And, most importantly, how long will it describe you?

7

HOW TO THINK ABOUT THE NEW BELIEVER

My father served the Lord for more than twenty-five years as a bi-vocational pastor and had the privilege of leading many, many people to the Lord.

One of Dad's most blessed moments actually occurred before he began preaching. Dad often told this story in his sermons, and it was indeed a story worth telling! I was not a witness to the event because I was very little, and I was already in bed. Eight p.m. was my bedtime in those days!

As I recall, it was probably January since that was when most of the area churches held their annual revival. One weeknight, sometime after 9:00 p.m., a car appeared in our driveway. The driver's door opened, a man jumped out and ran to our house. His name was Bill Winters. Bill entered our house, threw his arms around Dad, began crying, and said, "I just got saved."

It was one of the happiest experiences in my father's life. Bill and Dad were very close. Not only were they hunting buddies, but they even helped begin the local volunteer fire department. I can still see Dad crying as he shared the story of Bill's salvation with his churches. Dad's only regret was that he had not gone with Bill to that nearby church and seen the whole thing for himself!

Bill was soon baptized in the creek, began growing in the Lord, and in time he grew into one of the finest deacons I have ever known. Yes, a fine deacon but an even finer Christian!

Bill grew . . . but from what did he grow?

Paul (1 Corinthians 3:1), Peter (1 Peter 2:2), and John (1 John 2:12) describe the new believer as a "new babe" in Christ. The Greek word *teknion* carries with it the idea of "newly born" or "little born ones." This term agrees with the three writers' concept that salvation includes a born again experience. Salvation includes the birthing of something brand new: a new creation or a new babe.

If this pastor were presenting the classifications of spiritual growth in a series of messages, I would break it down into *four* sermons rather than three. The first three sermons are obvious: the natural man, the carnal man, and the spiritual man. The fourth sermon is less obvious but equally important regarding how the church as a whole must think about the new believer, or, as described elsewhere, "the babe in Christ."

Most theology books gloss over this fourth description. The theologian tends to see things from a purely theological perspective. (There is a reason why theologians don't *usually* make good pastors and vice versa. It is because they have different spiritual gifts.) As a result, the theologian, for organizational purposes, correctly groups the new believer in the carnal classification. But the discussion should not stop at that point.

Why not? The new believer in Christ is described as a "babe" because first, the new believer has distinct characteristics which are peculiar to him, and, second, the church needs to both understand these characteristics *and* plan a process to deal with these *distinct* characteristics. (Please remember my primary purpose in writing the *God's Greenhouse* series is not merely to present classroom theology for the sake of knowledge but to present experiential theology for the sake of growing people spiritually.)

Kevin Bloomfield, president of nearby Tri-State Bible College, succinctly states the problem: "There is a *high infant mortality rate* among babes in Christ. So many never seem to progress."

The church needs a fresh appreciation of this very concept. We older saints tend to take our spiritual life for granted; thus, we forget that everything in the spiritual life is new—brand new—to the babe in Christ. *The babe needs nurturing!*

For example, our new granddaughter is exactly that: new! Everything, and I do mean everything, is new to her. She is just now arriving at the "da-da" stage for "daddy." She's thrilled to be walking rather than crawling. She is even feeding herself, but she has yet to fill a bottle or prepare a meal or change a diaper.

Just last week, she climbed into her Fisher-Price car, lost her balance, and flipped the car over. But, based on her rate of growth, that failure will soon be a thing of the past. Quite simply, she is new to this world. We, as her family, have a great responsibility to educate her on how to live in this new world.

Similarly, one of the most important tasks for any church is to develop a process to grow new believers into mature believers. Does your church have such a process?

What does that include? Much more than most churches provide! It is sad to say, but spiritual growth in many churches is more the result of an *accident* than a *process!*

My first book, *God's Greenhouse: How to Grow People God's Way*, includes a chart on page 382 of specialized development (I prefer the word "development" rather than "discipleship") classes offered within specific denominations. For instance, only 36% of Baptist churches offer a class in the basics of Christianity. Only 49% of evangelical churches offer such a class. Only 23% of evangelical churches offer a class on the basics of the church's denominational perspectives. Fewer than a third offer classes in the area of spiritual gifts or spiritual ministries!

Based upon such a weak process, how is a new believer to grow?

Think about the incredibly unchristian background of the Corinthian believers.

> . . . *[B]rother goes to court against brother, and that before unbelievers! As it is, to have legal disputes against one another is already a defeat for you. Why not rather be wronged? Why not rather be cheated? Instead, you yourselves do wrong and cheat—and you do this to brothers and sisters! Don't you know that the unrighteous will not inherit God's kingdom? Do not be deceived: No sexually immoral people, idolaters, adulterers, or males who have sex with males, no thieves, greedy people, drunkards, verbally abusive people, or swindlers will inherit God's kingdom. And some of you used to be like this. But you were washed, you were sanctified, you were justified in the name of the Lord Jesus Christ and by the Spirit of our God. (1 Corinthians 6:6-11, CSB)*

The Corinthian believers came from a very unchristian lifestyle. Their sins were some of the most abominable of all. There was so much they needed to learn about this new life called "Christ in you." *Quite honestly, these new believers were a mission field in every sense of the word.*

Likewise, we should assume that *every new believer is a mission field.* The new believer has been conditioned for many years in how to think like an unbelieving, rebellious world where men "love darkness rather than light." But now this new believer is different. He has become a new creation, and he needs to be taught how to express that difference.

(Note: This issue is the primary reason for the next chapter, "Growing through God's Code of Conduct." New believers should be started on the basics; the Ten Commandments express the most basic principles of all.)

I was recently introduced to a young father who had received Christ as his Savior. This salvation experience supposedly happened two years ago. Well, a few months ago, he became the father of a child, but he is not the husband of the mother. They have never married. They are simply living together. The punishment for this horrendous sin in the Old Testament was death by stoning (Deuteronomy 22:24).

In many ways, that young man represents the new believers of our current day. He has no background in knowing right and wrong from a biblical viewpoint. He is like the Corinthians who have been saved from a background that might be described as debauchery of the worst kind. He is like the heathen on the mission field who needs to be taught about the most basic things. He needs a lot of nurturing.

We as believers need to step up to home plate and intentionally develop processes to grow the new believer, even if he is a heathen, into a spiritual child of the King! (Note: A process is more than providing a class because a process does not stop with the completion of a class.)

How, though, should we categorize the young father mentioned in the above story? He is not in a fourth classification, because there are only three available classifications: the natural man, the carnal man, and the spiritual man.

Based on the *assumption* this young man is a *true* believer in need of proper instruction, he would not be categorized as a natural man. Though he is a sinner with many needs, he is still a sinner saved by grace. That means he is viewed positionally as a saint even though experientially, he lives far from sainthood. The Holy Spirit lives in him; that means he has the potential for spiritual growth.

Perhaps it is best to pause for a moment and say that I am a firm believer in the teaching that "by their fruit you shall recognize them. A good tree brings forth good fruit but an evil tree brings forth evil fruit" (Matthew 7:16-17).

B. R. Lakin points out, "I am not the judge. I am only the fruit inspector. The kind of fruit on the tree reveals the identity of the tree!" Those words are true in both our natural world and our spiritual world.

But I am also a firm believer in God's maturing process—that saints aren't grown overnight. Salvation is like the measles; if you have it, it will eventually break out all over you. But, as happens in the gardening world, salvation often takes time for the roots to take hold and solidify the plant.

Therefore, we should not be hasty in declaring someone is only a professor of Christ and not a possessor of Christ! Such a judgment may be right, but then again, it may be wrong. To be honest, the only person I am absolutely sure about is me. Can you say the same?

On the other hand, should this young man be characterized as a spiritual man? No, not by any means. We noted in the previous chapter that *the spiritual man has attained a very specific level of Christian maturity and lifestyle.* May I repeat the words of Charles Ryrie? "The mature Christian who is led and taught by the Spirit appraises all things, i.e., he can scrutinize, sift, and thereby understand all things; but unbelievers and even carnally-minded Christians cannot appraise (understand) him."

This young man needs to be discipled. Unfortunately, he does not live in our area. I could only suggest that he find a Baptist (my denominational preference is Baptist) church in his community and begin the discipleship process. He has much to learn. I pray for the sake of the child, mother, and himself that he learns what he needs to learn and then practices what he learns.

The only classification which fits the young father is that of a *carnal* man or a flesh-controlled believer. My meeting with him consisted of little more than an introduction and word of encouragement. But it was evident in the service that he did not know the old hymns and was unacquainted with the routine of a church service.

The Bible records a similar issue. The apostle Paul was very upset with the slothfulness of the Corinthians. They were still struggling in infancy instead of marching forward in maturity! Let's take a slightly different look at 1 Corinthians 3:1.

> *Brothers and sisters, I could not address you as spiritual Christians . . . as saints who have the mind of Christ and think like Christ and behave like Christ . . . who are controlled by the Holy Spirit . . . but I had to address you as just recently born babes or new believers in Christ who are **still carnal, still fleshly** and **still controlled** by your fleshly, evil, sinful nature.*

A companion passage states:

> *We have a great deal to say about this, and it is difficult to explain, since you have become too lazy to understand. Although by this time you ought to be teachers, you need someone to teach you the basic principles of God's revelation again. You need milk, not solid food. Now everyone who lives on milk is inexperienced with the message about righteousness, because he is an infant. But solid food is for the mature—for those whose senses have been trained to distinguish between good and evil. (Hebrews 5:11-14, CSB)*

Let's list the phrases in both passages that would describe the young father. "Recently born babes . . . new believers in Christ . . . still carnal . . . still fleshly . . . need someone to teach you the basic principles . . . need milk, not solid food . . . everyone who lives on milk is inexperienced . . . he is an infant." Need we say more?

In simple terms, the babe has to emerge from his old pattern of living according to the flesh to one of living according to the Spirit of God. Such a transition is enormous in scope, especially for an adult. Thank God, the Holy Spirit assists the new believer in that growth to maturity. As growth occurs, the Holy Spirit will *gain* more and more control over the believer, while the flesh will *lose* more and more control. In time (and time is a necessary part of God's process), the Holy Spirit will grow the believer out of fleshly, worldly living and into spiritual, Christlike living.

The Holy Spirit's ministry in the new believer begins at the very moment of salvation (Romans 8:9). During his early months and years, the new believer may at times be Holy Spirit controlled, but he will need development to reach the level of Holy Spirit maturity (also known in Paul's writings as "spiritual" or having the "mind or thinking capacity/worldview of Christ").

John Walvoord, former President of Dallas Theological Seminary, teaches,

> While any Christian may be spiritual, may walk in the Spirit, and abide in Christ, even though a newborn saint, there is a gradual spiritual growth which issues in maturity and ultimate conformity to Christ when the body of flesh is cast aside in death or at the Lord's coming for His own. This gradual growth while conditioned to some extent upon the spirituality of the individual is nevertheless in the sovereign control of God . . .
>
> While it is impossible for any Christian to attain spiritual maturity apart from the gradual process which it entails, any Christian upon meeting the conditions may enter at once into all the blessedness of the fullness of the Spirit. The correspondence of spirituality and maturity to the health and growth of the physical body is obvious. A child may be immature as to stage of growth but at the same time be perfectly healthy. Growth of the body requires time and development, while health is an immediate state of the body which determines its present enjoyment and growth. Likewise, in the spiritual realm, a newborn saint may have the fullness of the Spirit, while being nevertheless quite immature, and in contrast a mature saint may lack the fullness of the Spirit . . . A saint will mature in the faith more rapidly when living in conscious fellowship with God in the fullness of the Spirit than if wandering in the realm of the flesh. A 'babe in Christ' is one who has had time to reach some maturity but whose development has been arrested by carnality. What physical health is to the growth of the physical body, the fullness of the Spirit is to spiritual growth. (*The Holy Spirit*, p. 191)

Read these two sentences again with me. "A child may be immature as to stage of growth, but at the same time, be perfectly healthy. Growth of the body requires time and development . . ."

"Time and development" require God's church to provide the necessary training to grow the newborn child of God into a full-grown child of God!

A chronic complainer stated, "Our church costs too much. I am getting sick and tired of it."

A dear saint said, "Yes, there is a high cost to what we do. But I want to tell you a story about my own life. Some time ago a baby boy came into my house and from the time he was born, he cost me something. I had to buy food, clothing, and medicine, and, after a while, toys and a puppy dog. When he started school, he cost me more and more. When he went to college, he cost me even more. Then he began to go out with the girls, and you know how much that costs. Then in his senior year, he suddenly died, and he has not cost me one penny more."

Yes, there is a high cost to growing people.

But isn't that what our calling is all about?

SECTION TWO

THE DAILY EXPERIENCE OF SANCTIFICATION

"After the merriness of a new baby wore off and living for the baby was not enough; I became miserable. Through all the fears and uncertainties of the future, I saw myself wretched, poor, blind, and in need of a Savior. I could not sleep anymore.

"One night, while I sat thinking about things in which I had no control, I turned my life over to the Lord. I knew I could not go on without Him. I began to search diligently for a church because I had the desire to be baptized. My husband was saved, and the Lord guided us into a Bible-teaching church where **we grew in the knowledge of the Lord and His mercies.**"

How, though, do we grow?

8

GROWING THROUGH GOD'S CODE OF CONDUCT

A pastor friend of mine often distributed an email which he called *Humor of the Day*. The first item in the email was called Today's Zinger. Today's Zinger not only caused you to laugh, but it also caused you to think.

Let me share one of those zingers. It is short, but it is powerful. Someone wrote, "I drive way too fast to worry about cholesterol."

Might you have written that? Hopefully not. What does that zinger mean? It means the person doesn't plan to live very long because he drives dangerously.

All of us are aware that driving too fast is dangerous for our health. This awareness means we need a policy about how fast we drive. Also, we know that high cholesterol can damage our health. Therefore, we need a policy about what we eat and how much we eat. Furthermore, we know that jumping from an airplane without a parachute is a very bad idea. So we don't do it!

Thus, we develop policies to guide us in practically everything we do. Those policies don't have to be a hundred pages in length or cover every subject imaginable. All of us, though, would agree that our policies need to be well-conceived and thoroughly evaluated. Our policies need to get us where we need to go from today's Point A to the end-of-life's Point Z.

We might think such an assignment would be overwhelming, but that is not so.

Quite honestly, our most basic policy for life can be as simple as ten rules that can guide us in every decision we make.

Life is not complicated if a person follows some very simple rules.

Do you know how one should think about God's Ten Commandments? The Ten Commandments form a *Code of Conduct* or a *Code of Ethics* for our personal life.

Many of today's businesses have a Code of Conduct to guide them in how they *treat their customers and their employees*. By contrast, the utility company Enron did not adhere to even a child's code of conduct. Enron's failure led to bankruptcy, lawsuits, and in a few cases, even prison sentences.

May I suggest that every person needs a Code of Conduct or a Code of Ethics to guide his or her daily life? That Code of Conduct should meet four conditions.

First, your Code should be written. Writing your Code will require you to give it careful thought. The old saying, "Writing makes an exact man," will apply in this situation. I wrote my Code of Conduct in 2006. I then placed it under a pane of glass on my desk. It has never been moved. That Code greets me every morning.

Second, your Code should describe <u>who</u> you want to be. We must remember that what we become in life is not an accident, but it is usually the result of our daily choices.

One day a distraught man saw a painting that portrayed a joyful man and said, "I want to be that man." He bought the painting and studied it every day. He longed so much to become the man in the painting! Time passed. Something strange happened. This man's facial features began to resemble those of the man in the painting. Why? His longing to be the man in the painting produced a change in his heart, and the changed heart produced a change in his facial features! *The unseen affected the seen!*

Similarly, you can use your Code as a goal for who you wish to become. I have not changed my Code since its original writing. It still works for who I want to be.

Third, your Code should fulfill the primary goal of putting God first. The Bible says, "Whatever you eat, drink, think, plan, buy, sell, or say— do everything, absolutely everything, to the glory of God" (1 Corinthians 10:31). Jesus says, "Seek first the kingdom of God and His righteousness; God will then take care of everything else" (Matthew 6:33).

My Code begins, "Since I am on mission for Jesus Christ, the King of Kings and Lord of Lords, I should reflect the image of Jesus Christ in my heart, family, church, and community." My Code even includes, "Commit all of my assets to God for His use." My wife and I have tried to do exactly that.

Fourth, your Code should encompass how you interact with everyone. That includes your family, neighbors, co-workers, church family, etc. Though dead, John Donne continues to teach, "No man is an island but every man is a piece of the continent." How do you wish to interact with the rest of the continent? Your interaction will largely determine how the continent remembers you.

I wrote in my Code, "Esteem my wife as my companion for life, my truest friend, and my best advisor. Edify my children by uplifting the value/image of each individual and making myself a part of their lives/activities. Be honest in all of my dealings." Plus more.

In other words, a Code of Conduct states the governing principles by which one chooses to live.

May I suggest a beginning point? The best Code of Conduct will *include* the Ten Commandments in Exodus chapter twenty. Why? *The Ten Commandments cover every major area of your life!* God's list is amazingly thorough; it will help you develop a policy for handling every major area of your life.

Do you want to live a good life? Do you want Christ to be reflected in your life? Then you need to make God's Code of Conduct your Code of Conduct for everything you do. Type it, print it, and place it where you can see it, even review it several times a week.

Let's look one by one at God's Code of Conduct; be sure to pick out the items that you need to really work on.

1. DO NOT HAVE ANY OTHER GODS BESIDES THE ONE, TRUE GOD OF HEAVEN.

The Ten Commandments cover every major area of your life. Do you know why? *It is because God's Code of Conduct goes in <u>two directions</u>.* The first four commandments go vertically and talk about our relationship with God. The last six commandments go horizontally and talk about our relationship with our fellow man.

Notice the order: First, I get right with God, and once that goal is accomplished, I can then be right with my fellow man. My fellow man may still be wrong with me, but I can be right with him in my heart!

God begins our Code with, "Do not have any other gods besides Me" (Exodus 20:3).

Why is that statement so significant? It is because God has created a God-sized hole in each of our hearts.

Who is bigger than God? No one. What is bigger than God? Nothing. Thus, if I have a God-sized hole in the center of my being, what can fill that hole except God? The answer, of course, is nothing.

Many people don't understand this. They try to fill the hole in their heart with everything *except* God.

For example, they buy a boat and go boating on Sunday while we are in church. They feel really good on Sunday but guess what? Monday (also known as "Back-to-Work Day") is coming. They need something to fill the hole in their hearts on Monday, but that boat is no longer available.

Everyone needs something to fill the hole in his heart on Sunday, Monday, Tuesday, Wednesday, etc. The only thing which can fill that emptiness is the living God of heaven.

Lehman Strauss writes in *The Eleven Commandments* (p. 26),

> We are convinced that enthroned in every man's heart is a god whom he worships. Doubtless, the god at the center of many lives is a false god. Nevertheless, there is something which every man worships. Luther says, 'That upon which you set your heart and put your trust is properly your God.'

How do you intend to fill the God-sized hole in your own heart?

May I say nothing else will work except God Himself—that includes money, romance, a new automobile, even retirement on an island in the Caribbean. Nothing else will work except God Himself.

How do I know? Because that is the way God designed us. God made us so we *would* never and *could* never be satisfied until we bow before Him and make Him our God!

J. I. Packer presents this argument in *Growing in Christ* (p. 239).

> What other gods could one 'have' beside the Lord? Plenty. For Israel there were the Canaanite Baals, those jolly-nature gods whose worship was a rampage of gluttony, drunkenness, and ritual prostitution. For us there are still the great gods Sex, Shekels, and Stomach (an unholy trinity constituting one god, self), and the other enslaving trio, Pleasure, Possessions, and

Positions, whose worship is described in 1 John 2:16 as 'the lust of the flesh and lust of the eyes and pride of life.' Football, the Firm, Freemasonry, the Family are also gods for some, and indeed the list of other gods is endless, for anything that anyone allows to run his life becomes his god.

One of the greatest basketball players of all time was Wilt Chamberlain. I recall, as a little boy, watching the Sunday afternoon contests between Wilt and the Boston Celtics' Bill Russell. Without fail, they were awesome games!

During those years, my Sunday School teacher Molly Jean Winters met Wilt and the rest of the Philadelphia 76ers on a plane. Molly told our class, "I shook hands with Wilt!"

We were so impressed that we shook hands with our teacher in the hope that some of Wilt would rub off. It didn't, but we tried! We didn't wash that hand for several days. It was a "WOW!" experience for some boys in little Deering, Ohio.

But it was during that same time I met Someone even bigger than seven-foot Wilt Chamberlain. I met Someone who towers over everyone and everything, including even the entire universe. That Someone has been able to fill the enormous hole in my heart. Quite honestly, He has made all the difference for me. I can say without fear of apology that He can make all the difference for you, too.

"Do not have any other gods besides Me." Thus, worship God and Him alone. Focus your heart and affections upon Him rather than people or things. Establish Him where He deserves to be: upon the throne of your heart. Let Him be your God and volunteer yourself to be His servant.

Such a commitment will revolutionize your entire life. It is for this reason that the first commandment deserves to be the *first* commandment.

2. RECOGNIZE GOD IS SPIRIT, AND I MUST WORSHIP HIM IN SPIRIT.

The second commandment says, "You shall not make for yourself an idol, or any likeness of what is in heaven above or on the earth beneath or in the water under the earth. You shall not worship them or serve them; for I, the Lord your God, am a jealous God" (Exodus 20:4-5, NASB).

A city fellow came to the proverbial fork in the road and did not know whether to take the left fork or the right fork. He saw an old farmer nearby and shouted, "Hey, Old Timer, I'm heading into the next town. Does it make any difference which road I take?'"

The old farmer answered, "Not to me, it doesn't."

The Bible has good news for all of us: It *does* make a difference to God which road we take. One of those roads is dedicated to how we worship Him. The first commandment is about *whom* we should worship. The second commandment is about *how* we should worship the triune God of heaven: God the Father, God the Son, and God the Holy Spirit.

In Bible times, many cultures worshiped physical idols, which one can see with his eyes and touch with his hands. The Hebrew word for "idol" is *pesel* and has the idea of something carved from wood or stone. *In other words, the people worshiped a god of their own carving or creation.* How foolish! Imagine worshipping a supposedly infinite god that we, finite human beings, personally created!

Such a thought is incredibly mind-boggling. The people, in their foolishness, manufactured a god, then knelt before that same idol god and prayed to it, sang to it, and offered sacrifices to it. Sometimes they even offered their own children to such a god!

But twenty-first-century America believes itself to be smarter than the people of old. Today's humanity has proudly, even brazenly risen to a level where it declares such idol worship is imbecilic. But, even so, America still worships false idols! And, like in primitive Old Testament cultures, America worships gods of its own making.

Today's America worships cars, money, houses, education, vacations, weekends, jobs, and even our bodies. As a matter of fact, many Americans would sell their soul for a job making $100,000 a year. To make matters worse, someday, man will worship THE MAN—the Antichrist of the next age (Revelation 13:8). Man, in the final days of human rule, will worship himself!

Interestingly, our word "worship" actually comes from the old English word "worthship." If we insert the two letters "th" in "worship", we get a much better sense of what worship is. What exactly do we worship? We worship something or someone that we believe to be *worthy*. We worship something or someone we consider to hold value— value which is so immense it consumes our thoughts and desires.

A counselor once told an audience that he could reveal the highest desires of their hearts. The people laughed in ridicule. Someone, though, was bothered enough to ask, "And how do you intend to do that?"

The counselor replied, "Bring me your checkbook and financial statements. *Those statements will reveal what you truly value.* How you spend your money tells me what you really believe is important." We might paraphrase his words in this manner, "Those financial statements will reveal what you truly worship because they are deemed worthy of your hard-earned money."

How do we express our worship? First, we express our worship in how we spend our time. For example, where does God fit into our schedule? Is God even a part of our schedule? Could it be that we have somehow compartmentalized God out of our lives?

Second, we express our worship in how we spend our money. Many Christians sing, "I Surrender All" on Sunday, but hold back their tithes and offerings for something else they worship more. God challenges that line of thinking by asking, "Will a man rob God? Yet you are robbing Me! But you say, 'How have we robbed You?' In tithes and offerings" (Malachi 3:8, NASB). Unfortunately, many of our Sunday morning attendees are thieves in God's sight!

We also express our worship in how we deal with this sinful world. God's people are called to be a shining light before a dark world. We are to be a godly influence like salt before a decaying society. But many prefer to be accepted by the crowd rather than to stand against the sin of the crowd.

Many people fail to understand that worship is the act of "assigning worth" to something. In some cases, they worship they know not what, but they do indeed worship something.

This failure even carries over into our so-called "worship service" on Sunday morning. Let me share how we sometimes do it. Some churches put an order of service in the bulletin. They publish the order of specific songs, the time of the offering and greeting, the sermon title, along with closing events. Everyone knows what is happening and when it will happen. There's nothing wrong with such an order of service. As a matter of fact, every church has an order of service—after all, the music always comes first!

Unfortunately, many people look at the order of service as if it is a scorecard of things to be done before we go home. They say, "We sang this song," and they check it off as done. They continue through the list one item at a time. Finally, they reach the last item: the benediction (a fancy name for the final prayer). They check off that item then say to themselves, *"We've completed the list. That means we've worshiped,"* and they walk out the door. But did they worship? Maybe. But, then again, maybe not.

We need to understand that worship isn't the act of following a pattern, nor is it in performing a religious activity; on the contrary, worship is the conscious act of giving or submitting your heart to the awesome God of heaven.

True worship is not occupied with things but with Him! It is not occupied with His saints or Mary but with Him! It is not occupied with crucifixes, altars, stained glass windows, the order of service, church business and committees, dress codes, visioning, furniture, rituals, choir robes, formal prayers, speaking in tongues, physical healing, the doxology, or even a particular translation but with Him! *There simply is no substitute for Him!*

That's why God says, "I am a *jealous* God! Truly jealous for your attention! I alone am worthy of your wor<u>th</u>ship. My worth is greater than all created things! Therefore, come and know Me! Come and experience Me!"

Do you remember what Jesus said to Martha? Martha was so busy with church *things* (the subject of her "worthship") that she missed the best part of all!

> *Now as they were traveling along, He entered a village; and a woman named Martha welcomed Him into her home. She had a sister called Mary, who was seated at the Lord's feet, listening to His word. But Martha was distracted with all her preparations; and she came up to Him and said, 'Lord, do You not care that my sister has left me to do all the serving alone? Then tell her to help me.' But the Lord answered and said to her, 'Martha, Martha, you are worried and bothered about so many things; but only one thing is necessary, for Mary has chosen the good part, which shall not be taken away from her.' (Luke 10:38-42, NASB)*

Henry Blackaby has provided one of the finest discipleship texts of all time: *Experiencing God.* I urge you to purchase a copy and read it at least once every five years. Blackaby writes on page nineteen:

> We are a 'doing' people. We always want to be doing something. The idea of doing God's will sounds fairly exciting. Once in a while someone will say, 'Don't just stand there; do something.' Sometimes individuals and churches are so busy doing things they think will help God accomplish His purpose, that He can't get their attention long enough to use them as servants to accomplish what He wants. We often wear ourselves out and accomplish very little of value to the kingdom.
>
> I think God is crying out and shouting to us, 'Don't just do something. Stand there! Enter into a love relationship with Me. Get to know Me. Adjust your life to Me. Let me love you and reveal Myself to you as I work through you.' A time will come when the doing will be called for, but we cannot skip the relationship. The relationship with God must come first.

Genuine worship, or worthship, produces a commitment of the soul as we sing the great consecration hymns of the faith!

> "Have thine own way, Lord,
> Thou art the potter, I am the clay,
> Mold me and make me, after Thy will,
> While I am waiting, yielded and still."
>
> Adelaide A. Pollard

> "All hail the power of Jesus name!
> Let angels prostrate fall;
> Bring forth the royal diadem
> And crown Him Lord of all!"
>
> Edward Perronet

True worship understands that God means what He says. The second commandment includes these words, " . . . for I, the LORD your God, am a jealous God, punishing the children for the fathers' iniquity, to the third and fourth generations of those who hate me" (Exodus 20:5, CSB). This scripture includes a warning which, to the best of my knowledge, has never been revoked. "God rewards the father's iniquity by not only punishing the father but his descendants as far as the fourth generation." That means you and I might be enduring a problem (physical, mental, social) because of something our great-grandfather did many years ago.

Could it be that this verse partially explains why certain illnesses seem to be genetic illnesses? Might depression be one of those illnesses? Some families have an alcoholic propensity for generations. On the other hand, some families seem to have God's blessings for generations!

But this verse also looks forward, too! This verse also means that I can have a great impact upon my great-grandchildren. What a shame it would be if my wayward life damaged their future! I must never forget that my God of love wants what is best (God always defines what is best) for me as well as what is best for my children and grandchildren. Having the best begins with putting God first.

Above all, I must be careful what I put at the top of my life because there is no substitute for the one true God of heaven!

3. RESPECT THE NAME OF THE LORD.

Let's add a third policy to our Code of Conduct or value system. It's verse seven. "Do not misuse the name of the Lord your God, because the Lord will not leave anyone unpunished who misuses His name" (Exodus 20:7, HCSB).

James O'Conner says that what we say and how we say it reflects who we are. God knows that truism better than any of us; that is why two of the Ten Commandments are about the use of our tongue. This commandment is about profanity: using God's name as a curse word *or* just a common expression. By contrast, the ninth commandment is about lying and saying things that are blatantly false.

It must be emphasized that how we use God's name reveals to others what we *really* think about God. The Bible says we should never use the name of God in our ordinary conversation unless we employ the name in *honor* of God!

The ancient Jewish scribes had tremendous reverence for the name of God. The scribes were responsible for copying the Bible manuscripts for perpetuity and distribution. When the scribes came to the Old Testament name of Jehovah, the scribe would stop, bathe himself thoroughly, select a writing instrument which had *never* been used and, only then would he write the holy name of Jehovah. He would then throw away the writing instrument because that pen was now deemed sacred—it was no longer proper to write a common, ordinary word with that pen.

Let us never forget that, "The degree of our respect is concealed in the heart but is revealed through the mouth."

Someone rightfully said, "What the telescope is to the scientist the Name of God is to His children."

> "Jesus, Jesus, Jesus, Sweetest name I know;
> Fills my every longing, Keeps me singing as I go!"

Luther B. Bridgers

May I beg you: Don't use God's name in your everyday conversation unless it is to honor Him!

4. TAKE CARE OF MY BODY.

Verse eight contains the fourth instruction for our Code of Conduct.

Remember the Sabbath day, to keep it holy. Six days you shall labor, and do all your work, but the seventh day is a Sabbath to the Lord your God. On it you shall not do any work, you, or your son, or your daughter, your male servant, or your female servant, or your livestock, or the sojourner who is within your gates. For in six days the Lord made heaven and earth, the sea, and all that is in them, and rested on the seventh day. Therefore, the Lord blessed the Sabbath day and made it holy. (Exodus 20:8-11, ESV)

Today's average American is on more medication than any generation before him. We are so wound up that we can't wind down! We do not know how to de-stress from the everyday, never-ending pressures of life.

The famous investor Bernard Baruch wisely says, "No general keeps his troops fighting all the time."

God knows that lesson better than anyone. God's Word teaches that this body of flesh and bones has been designed to work six days, but the body then needs to recharge itself with a day or period of rest.

Rest means rest! It doesn't mean stress. It doesn't mean pressure. It means rest!

Verse eight says, "Remember the Sabbath day." The word "sabbath" means "rest." Therefore, we could translate the verse, "Remember the day of rest."

"Keep the day of rest holy or sanctified. Set the day of rest apart from the other six days. Don't treat it the same as the other days."

God was so insistent on this lesson that He imposed the death penalty on the people who ignored His words (Exodus 31:15). That penalty may sound draconian to us, but it sent the signal to everyone both small and great that the body needs rest.

Does this Code apply to you? Do you need a day of rest? I sure do. I have been in the ministry for more than forty years. I was a part-time pastor for more than twenty-five of those years. In other words, I worked a full-time job (forty hours a week) for a business plus a part-time job (a minimum of twenty hours per week) pastoring a church. It was a grueling schedule!

My hardest day was always Sunday. Sunday was a physical nightmare for me. Some people treat Sunday as their day of rest but not so for the pastor!

I also served as a full-time pastor for nine years. During that time, my only job was taking care of more than two hundred members; it was the hardest job, but also the most enjoyable job, I've ever had. Would you like to guess what my hardest day was? My hardest day was still Sunday.

Fortunately, I am now retired from the Monday—Friday grind of secular work. The days of Medicare have finally arrived. Hurrah for me! But I still pastor one of God's churches. Would you like to guess what my hardest day is now? It is still Sunday! Sunday has *never* been my day of rest. It has actually been my hardest day of work. Thus, my time of rest has always been on a day other than Sunday.

What about you? What is your hardest day? What, also, is your easiest day? I encourage you to write down in the margin of this book a block of time—maybe a full day or parts of a couple of days, which you can set aside to just rest! Goof off, have a good time, unwind, relax!

You'll then be surprised how fresh your mind will be, how fresh your body will be, and how much better your outlook on life will be!

5. VALUE MY PARENTS AND FAMILY.

This instruction begins a new section. As noted earlier, the commandments are both vertical (1-4) and horizontal (5-10). The first four dealt with our relationship with God, whereas the next six deal with our relationship with others.

Verse twelve says, "Honor your father and your mother, that your days may be long in the land that the Lord your God is giving you" (Exodus 20:12, ESV). (Note: A parent-honoring nation will also be a God-blessed nation.)

Many years ago, a story came across my desk about a boy named Charles. His story should serve as a warning to all of us.

> One day in the latter part of November, Charles (who was in the seventh grade) was getting ready for school. As he was attempting to leave the bathroom, his old father (age sixty-two) was shaving at the sink and blocking the doorway. Charles said, 'Get out of my way, stupid.' The father did not say anything; he just allowed his son to pass by.
>
> As he was riding the school bus, Charles' conscience began to hurt him terribly. Before he reached school, he had decided what he would do. As soon as he got home, he was going to apologize to his dad.
>
> When he got home, though, his mother met him with the news that his father had suffered a heart attack that afternoon. Charles did not get too concerned because his father had been in and out of the hospital with heart problems several times before. He decided that as soon as his father got home, he would apologize to him.
>
> Then the telephone rang. It was a short conversation. Charles' mother came into his room and said, 'Your daddy had another heart attack. He died a little while ago.'
>
> How do I know this story is true? The Charles in the story is me. My daddy was buried on Thanksgiving Day. It has been about twenty years now, and still, I think about the last words I ever said to my daddy, 'Get out of my way, stupid.' I've asked God to forgive me, but I wish I could ask my daddy.

Honor your father and your mother and, may I also add, honor your family, too.

6. VALUE THE LIVES OF PEOPLE.

One of the most famous commandments is found in verse thirteen. It is only three words in length. Verse thirteen says, "Do not murder."

Have you ever met a murderer? I have. One of my church members was cruelly murdered. This member was one of the nicest people you have ever met . . . that is, when he was sober. Sadly, Jack had a life-long drinking problem. I knew Jack as a recovering alcoholic. He had a beautiful granddaughter; that little girl had given him a reason to fight for his recovery.

But one night, Jack slipped back into his old habits. Jack and his drinking buddy became so drunk they did not know what they were doing. Something happened. No one ever knew what that something was. Jack's buddy took a knife and stabbed Jack more than twenty times. He then passed out while Jack bled to death.

Jack was found the next morning. His buddy was arrested for the crime. The buddy told the police, "I do not remember anything about this. Jack was my friend. I would not have done this if I had been sober."

I remember attending the court proceedings with the family and looking into the face of a murderer. It was a very sad time.

God says in verse thirteen, "You have no right to take away someone's life. Furthermore, you have no right to *ruin* someone's life. Vengeance is mine. I will repay." Rest assured, God will repay better than you or I could.

That is the first reason Jesus teaches us to love people instead of murdering them or getting even with them. The second reason is that we will also hurt ourselves. We will inadvertently lower ourselves to a level from which we may never recover. In so doing, the inward scar in our hearts may become more problematic than the outward scar in our skin.

The apostle Paul instructs us, "Inasmuch, as is possible *within* you (you cannot control what others will do *to* you), live peaceably with all men" (Romans 12:18). The Christian's goal should always be one of peace: bringing people together rather than driving people apart. Are there exceptions? Of course, but they will be few if we express the right attitude. (Note: Jesus identified the Pharisees as whited sepulchers or whitewashed tombs in Matthew 23:27.)

There is an old saying: "I've never seen anybody happy who enjoyed making someone else miserable." How true! Yet some still try.

Jesus says, "You have heard that it was said to those of old, 'You shall not murder; and whoever murders will be liable to judgment.' But I say to you that everyone who is angry with his brother will be liable to judgment; whoever insults his brother will be liable to the council; and whoever says, 'You fool!' will be liable to the hell of fire" (Matthew 5:21-22, ESV).

When we plot to do evil—to get even—we not only destroy the other person, but we also destroy ourselves.

Let's remind ourselves that a critical spirit destroys people. A gossiping spirit destroys people. An egotistical spirit destroys people. A vengeful spirit destroys people. A hostile spirit destroys people. A selfish, ambitious spirit destroys people. An immoral spirit destroys people. A rebellious spirit destroys people. A lying spirit destroys people.

Surely, all of us know it is easier to destroy or harm people than to edify people. A house can be demolished in one day, but the same house would take months to build. Quite simply, the building ministry takes much more time, effort, and resources than a destructive ministry. That is why the edifiers or encouragers stand out from the rest of humanity. They tend to be the exception rather than the rule. And they seem to be much happier, too!

Contrary to public thinking, a person's value is not tied to his or her contribution to society. *Instead, a person's value is tied to being a created being!* Each person has been made in the image of an infinite Deity. This means if we destroy someone (including that person's influence), we are destroying someone who was made in God's image. Such destruction is not something to be done lightly!

It is true you can assign a dollar value to my human body. For example, my skin may be worth four dollars if it is sold at the price of a comparable product like cowhide. Other parts of my body can be sold, too. But no one can ever place a correct value on *me* as a human being.

My own Code includes this statement, "Prize each individual as someone for whom Christ died." Then again, "Treasure the individual above the organization." These values are based upon God's sixth commandment. Indeed, I have not hit the target 100% of the time, but I have done well most of the time.

I remember meeting a little boy at McDonald's during my years in Chattanooga (1976-1979). His t-shirt said, "I'm little and I'm good cos God don't make junk!" I was so impressed by the slogan that I wrote it down. Sometimes I get down on myself. I then repeat that slogan. "I'm now big and I'm still good cos God don't make junk!" I have value to myself, my family, and my God. And so do you.

Above all, don't let a spirit of murder, anger, or hatred take root in your heart. It will destroy who you are . . . and who you want to be.

7. HONOR MY MARRIAGE VOW.

Verse fourteen says, "Do not commit adultery." The New Testament equivalent reads, "Let marriage be held in honor among all, and let the marriage bed be undefiled, for God will judge the sexually immoral and adulterous" (Hebrews 13:4, ESV). In other words, sex outside of marriage is an abomination to God and is severely punished by God in ways we cannot always measure. But sex inside of marriage is a beautiful thing. The Bible even goes so far as to say,

> Now in response to the matters you wrote about: 'It is good for a man not to use a woman for sex.' But because sexual immorality is so common, each man should have sexual relations with his own wife, and each woman should have sexual relations with her own husband. A husband should fulfill his marital duty to his wife, and likewise a wife to her husband. A wife does not

have the right over her own body, but her husband does. In the same way, a husband does not have the right over his own body, but his wife does. Do not deprive one another—except when you agree for a time, to devote yourselves to prayer. Then come together again; otherwise, Satan may tempt you because of your lack of self-control. (1 Corinthians 7:1-5, CSB)

Let me share with you a little secret. Do you know why people commit adultery? It is because they believe—they may be wrong, but at the time, they honestly believe—the grass is greener on the other side of the fence.

I read about a testimony night at the local church. A lady testified, "We are living in a wicked land with sin on every hand. I have had a terrible fight with the old devil all week."

Her husband immediately shouted, "It's not all my fault; she's tough to get along with."

Sometimes the grass is indeed greener on the other side of the fence. That means a husband or wife has failed to make their marital grass the best grass it can be. The failure may be in the bedroom, time together, raising the children, the finances, or supporting one another.

Every husband and wife need to jointly grow the greenest grass possible in their marriage because the devil will eventually knock on their front door. The devil is an expert in knowing our weaknesses. Sometimes he knows our weaknesses better than we do. The devil will drive a wedge as deep as he can!

Therefore, we should heed the old admonition: "To be forewarned is to be forearmed!" The original warning was written to alert the settlers to the dangers of the frontier. But our foe is much more powerful than any human. No right-thinking spouse should give the devil an opening to destroy his or her marriage.

May I quote again from my own Code of Conduct? The preface explains that I am to be committed to Jesus Christ. The rest of my Code develops the many ways in which that commitment can be fulfilled.

What comes first in my list? "Esteem my wife as my companion for life, my truest friend, and my best advisor."

My wife and I are celebrating our forty-third anniversary on this very day (only God can arrange for this chapter to be written on our anniversary). Both of us have worked hard at growing green, green grass in our marriage. Neither one of us has strayed. We have both devoted our marriage and lives to God's work. I pray it will continue until God calls us home.

This Code means you honor your marriage vow in the bedroom, conversations with the opposite sex, internet sites, reading material, jokes, and overall attitude.

Two men in my church were talking about their respective marriages. One said, "I have been married thirty-two years and have not run around on my wife even once."

The second man said, "I have run around on my wife, and everyone I know has done the same. My wife and I play cards with a group, and all of our card players have done it, too."

The first man had the perfect response. He said, "You're spending time with the wrong people!"

Those adulterous card players were corrupting the second man; as a result, he brought corruption into his marriage and home. It was no wonder the children wanted out of the house!

What kind of grass does God recommend for our marriage?

> *Drink water from your own cistern, water flowing from your own well. Should your springs flow in the streets, streams of water in the public squares? They should be for you alone and not for you to share with strangers. Let your fountain be blessed, and take pleasure in the wife of your youth. A loving doe, a graceful fawn—let her breasts always satisfy you; be lost in her love forever. Why, my son, would you be infatuated with a forbidden woman or embrace the breast of a stranger? For a man's ways are before the Lord's eyes, and He considers all his paths. A wicked man's iniquities entrap him; he is entangled in the ropes of his own sin. He will*

die because there is no discipline, and be lost because of his great stupidity. (Proverbs 5:15-23, HCSB)

Make the grass in your own marriage as green as it can possibly be!

A similar statement ought to be included in every code of conduct.

8. RESPECT THE PROPERTY OF OTHERS.

"Do not steal."

Someone said, "Mail this commandment to Wall Street." Someone else added, "Be sure to mail this commandment to Main Street, also."

Our American society has become a thieving society. We steal the property of others. We steal through insurance fraud. We steal through raiding the pension funds. We steal at tax reporting time. Unfortunately, I have even known church members who stole from the church treasury.

Many of you remember the day someone shot President Ronald Reagan. Reagan was wearing some special cuff links which were shaped like the golden bear of California. The hospital staff removed Reagan's clothes and took him to surgery. A short time later, someone realized that one of the cuff links was missing.

The Secret Service agent asked, "Do you mean to tell me the President's cuff link was stolen as he lay bleeding on the gurney?" The answer was yes. (In case you're wondering, they never found the missing cuff link.)

My Code of Conduct includes this simple but poignant goal: "Be honest in all of my dealings." In other words, set your standards high and build the fence even higher! Make it very difficult for you to climb over that fence and violate your Code.

My wife once found an error on our bank statement. The error was not in our favor. The deposit receipt showed our deposit was $80 *less* than the amount shown on the bank statement. We did not hesitate in our response because we had already pledged ourselves to respect the property of others.

We concluded, "How can we teach our children to do right if we, as the parents, don't do right?"

We called the bank and said, "We believe we have $80 of your money."

We later learned the bank teller was out of balance by $80 on that day. Guess what we lost? We lost $80. Guess what we gained? The honor of doing what was right.

Remember these words: "Do right until the stars fall."

Always do right and respect the property of others.

9. ALWAYS TELL THE TRUTH AND DO NOT LIE.

The ninth commandment says, "Do not give false testimony against your neighbor" (Exodus 20:16, HCSB). That means we are never to lie when we provide testimony about anyone, whether it is in a court of law or in the court of public opinion. Has anyone ever lied about you? It's hard to fight a lie, isn't it?

David testified, "Mine enemies speak evil of me, When shall he die, and his name perish? All that hate me whisper together against me: against me do they devise my hurt" (Psalm 41:5, 7, KJV).

We might paraphrase the passage in this manner: "If you're alive, someone *will* lie about you. Guaranteed! If you're dead, someone *may* still lie about you." None of us can change this fact of life.

Guess what? I can't change what other people say about me, but I can change what I say about other people. The Bible says in Proverbs chapter six, "I, the Lord, hate seven things," and item #2 on that list is a lying tongue. That's why God hates gossip. Most gossip has a lie mixed with the truth, and it is difficult to separate the two.

The believer's adversary is called the *devil* for a reason. The word "devil" means "slanderer." He is also described as "the accuser of the brethren" (Revelation 12:10). In other words, the person who slanders others is the devil's right-hand man!

Lehman Strauss says, "It was a false witness against God that plunged the whole human race into sin and judgment . . . 'Ye shall not surely die' (Gen. 3:4). Because of man's disobedience instigated by a lie, all were made sinners, and many have gone into eternal condemnation." (*The Eleven Commandments*, p. 144)

The devil's right-hand men have slandered the Savior, the cross, the Bible, God's church, God's preachers and teachers, common-sense morality, the institutions of government and home, and even the work ethic "if you don't work, you don't eat."

The maliciousness that originates in the human heart is an awful thing!

The Mosaic Law states, "Thou shalt not go up and down as a talebearer among thy people" (Leviticus 19:16, KJV). The word "talebearer" means "one who bears tales about other people, that is, one who carries tales like other people carry groceries."

The Bible has a solemn warning for this type of person. Revelation 21:6 says, "All liars (including slanderers) shall have their part in the lake which burns with fire and brimstone which is the second death." Why? It is because the lake of fire is the place of final punishment for the father of lies (the worst slanderer of all time). "The Devil who deceived them was thrown into the lake of fire and sulfur where the beast and the false prophet are, and they will be tormented day and night forever and ever" (Revelation 20:10, HCSB). It is only proper that all of the slanderers spend eternity together.

It has been said that a dog has many friends because the wag is in his tail and not in his tongue! I need that to be true of me, how about you?

Someone said, "I don't gossip anymore about other people because I learned that what goes around comes around." Not surprisingly, if people will gossip *to* you, they will also gossip *about* you!

Unfortunately, there are no such things as *idle* rumors. Rumors are always busy! Everyone knows how to make a mountain out of a molehill: We only need to add a little more dirt. Due to our sin nature, dirt sells very well in today's society. Dirt about others is always in great demand.

William Boetcker writes, "Here are the names of seven 'Mischievous Misses' who are responsible for most of our troubles: misinformation, misquotation, misrepresentation, misinterpretation, misconstruction, misconception, and misunderstanding."

The ninth commandment helps preserve society by preserving the reputations of the people who make it up. *No one should invent a falsehood to injure anyone.* Quite honestly, the truth is usually bad enough to accomplish that same goal.

> "Guard well thy tongue—It stretches far;
> For what you say Tells what you are."

10. BE CONTENT TO LIVE WITHIN MY MEANS.

The final commandment deals with the downfall of many, many good people. It may be the final commandment, but it is certainly not the least commandment. It deals with an issue that is hidden within the privacy of one's own heart.

"You shall not covet your neighbor's house; you shall not covet your neighbor's wife or his male servant or his female servant or his ox or his donkey or anything that belongs to your neighbor" (Exodus 20:17, NASB).

Coveting anything that one does not possess is a very serious issue of the human heart. Coveting is more than a person simply saying, "I wish I had that." By contrast, coveting rises to a level where we set our entire being upon the treasured object. A covetous person may even say, "I feel like I will die if I don't get this. I must have it even if it is wrong, even if I cannot afford it, even if it costs me dearly."

King David thought those very words when he spied Bathsheba for the first time. David longed to have Bathsheba for himself even though she was already married to Uriah the Hittite. In the end, David did indeed get her. But God punished him severely for his horrible, uncontrolled desire. From that time on, the sword of violence never departed from David's house. What a tragedy for *all* of them!

Achan (Joshua 7) coveted the forbidden clothing, silver, and gold of Jericho. Achan's life proves the Bible is right when it says, "The love of money is a *root* of all evil" (1 Timothy 6:10). That root was, no doubt, unseen by others, but it had anchored itself in the very depths of his heart. Achan's downfall brought ruin not only upon himself but also upon his family.

Eve lusted for the forbidden fruit in Genesis chapter three. We know how that turned out. Not good! The coveting resulted in a worldwide curse.

The mother of James and John coveted thronelike power for her sons (Matthew 20:21). Jesus rejected her request. I doubt they were "man enough" to handle the responsibility.

Simon the Sorcerer coveted control of the miraculous, omnipotent Holy Spirit (Acts 8:19). He mistakenly believed the Holy Spirit could be bought and dispensed for money. His hoped-for racket never got off the ground.

The false apostle Judas coveted a great sum of money but sold his soul for a measly thirty pieces of silver (Matthew 26:15).

Lot coveted the lights and glamour of the big city Sodom—he wanted to be important—but he overlooked the immense, open sinfulness of Sodom and lost everything precious to him (Genesis 19).

Herodias, the mother of the dancing girl Salome, coveted the head of John the Baptist on a platter (Matthew 14:8).

All of these examples run contrary to the biblical teaching, "Be content with whatever God has given you" (Philippians 4:11). "Lay not up for yourselves treasures upon earth, where moth and rust doth corrupt, and where thieves break through and steal: But lay up for yourselves treasures in heaven, where neither moth nor rust doth corrupt, and where thieves do not break through nor steal: *For where your treasure is, there will your heart be also"* (Matthew 6:19-21, KJV).

Let's do some difficult soul-searching. Who is on the throne of your heart? Is it God, or is it your wants? It is one thing to have an "I *must* have these items" list, but it is another thing entirely to have an "I'd *like* these items, but I can live without them" list.

"For where your treasure is, there will your heart be also."

What is the number one sin in most marriages? It is coveting. How do I know? Survey after survey shows that money is the number one problem for most couples; people *want* more than they can afford, so they *spend* more than they can afford.

Most people would be happier if they cut out half of their wants and stayed with all of their needs. Jesus cautioned, "Take care, and be on your guard against all covetousness, for one's life does not consist in the abundance of his possessions" (Luke 12:15, ESV).

One woman correctly said, "The only difference between my husband and my son is the cost of their toys. And it's not my son that's going to bankrupt us!"

The Bible says we are to live within our means but also live within God's rules. Then we will realize that,

> *Godliness with contentment is great gain. For we brought nothing into this world, and it is certain we can carry nothing out. And having food and raiment let us be therewith content. But they that will be rich fall into temptation and a snare, and into many foolish and hurtful lusts, which drown men in destruction and perdition. For the love of money is the root of all evil: which while some **coveted** after, they have erred from the faith, and pierced themselves through with many sorrows. But thou, O man of God, flee these things; and follow after righteousness, godliness, faith, love, patience, meekness. (1 Timothy 6:6-11, KJV)*

Think of it like this. A salesman tried to convince a store owner to carry a new line of product. The store owner refused. He said, "You must remember that in this part of the country, *every want ain't a need.*"

A good life doesn't depend upon the things on the outside: our possessions. It always depends upon the most important item of all: our heart.

Let's review:

The Ten Commandments

"Above all else love God alone;
Bow down to neither wood nor stone,
God's name refuse to take in vain,
The Sabbath rest with care maintain,
Respect your parents all your days;
Hold sacred human life always,
Be loyal to your chosen mate;
Steal nothing, neither small nor great,
Report with truth your neighbor's deed;
And rid your mind of selfish greed."

Author unknown

9

GROWING THROUGH RIGHTEOUS THINKING

During the days of the Old West, a band of Apache Indians raided an army outpost and captured the paymaster's safe. The Apaches had no prior experience with safes, but they reasoned it contained something of great value.

The Indians pounded on the steel safe with large rocks, but this effort accomplished nothing. Then they used their tomahawks until they ruined them. Still not to be outdone, they built a great fire and roasted the safe in the fire. Unfortunately, that idea did not work either.

Someone came up with a new idea! They carried the big safe up a hill and rolled it off a cliff. The safe bounced off the rocks, but that action only broke one of the safe's wheels.

Then the Indians got some gunpowder and tried to blow open the safe. The only damage was to themselves! (Some of them were too close to the explosion.)

Finally, the Indians became so frustrated they rolled the safe into a ravine and left it there to rot. Sometime later, the army found the safe. Surprisingly, the army paymaster was able to open the safe despite everything the Indians had done.

That's the way it ought to be with each one of God's children, too. *The devil tries every day to break into our hearts*—to ruin our lives by causing us to think like him. He uses every trick in the book to persuade us to think like an unbelieving, faithless world. "The whole world lies in wickedness" (1 John 5:19); what kind of thinking can come from such a world but ruinous thinking?

My mind is very similar to that safe. The door to my mind can be either open or closed. If I so wish, I can lock my mind to outside intruders. Or I can allow any outside force (whether living or non-living) to feast upon my mind. The key that opens the safe (the safe contains my mind) is in my own hands.

The next verse is a very important verse for a growing saint to master: "For as he thinks within himself, so he is. He says to you, 'Eat and drink!' But his heart is not with you" (Proverbs 23:7, NASB).

"For as he thinks within himself, so he is." Look closely at the last three words. *"So he is!"* That's the real "he." But how do we identify the real "he"? It is not in his speech, but in his thoughts or in his mind. In other words,

- What we think is who we really are,
- How we think ultimately determines what we become.

Quite honestly, how we think is usually determined by what we value. We think upon certain things for a reason. Sometimes they are unpleasant things; we move on from those things as quickly as we can. Sometimes they are pleasant things; we allow those things to linger in our minds like sweet perfume for as long as possible.

There are two basic approaches to how we should think. The first approach is the positive thinking approach. Its primary proponent was

Norman Vincent Peale. He wrote *The Power of Positive Thinking* in 1952. Was it popular? Oh, yes! It urged the reader to think on something good rather than on something bad; its basic premise was the old saying, "Optimism is the only realism." *The Power of Positive Thinking* had such appeal that it stayed on the *New York Times* bestsellers' list for 185 weeks. During the last sixty years, it has sold more than five million copies.

There is much good to be said about positive thinking. The average American would be much happier if he emphasized positive thinking over negative thinking. But the average American lives in a stressed-out mind. No one can measure the amount of aspirin, coffee, tranquilizers, sleeping pills, uppers and downers that are necessary for the average American to function on a routine day.

It is estimated that 50-70% of doctor's patients are not physically sick but mentally or emotionally sick. In addition, some believe that as many as twenty percent of all fatal accidents are actually successful suicides.

Positive thinking would help considerably in so many cases. Focusing one's mind on positive events in our background or positive goals in our future would re-orient our disturbed minds to a much higher plane of living.

However, positive thinking is not biblical thinking. Though quite popular, it will lead a person astray at certain points. Positive thinking tends to emphasize the positive to such an extent that it ignores and even overlooks the negative, though the negative is often truer. For example, positive thinking ignores the depravity or sinfulness of man, so how can it understand man or the world of man? Positive thinking imagines a cyclical economy can somehow become an ever-growing economy, so how can it invest wisely? Positive thinking has no answer for the overall purpose of man's existence nor of man's ultimate destiny (positive thinking tends to overlook man's relationship with his Creator). No amount of positive thinking will help a man if he jumps from an airplane without a parachute either! Many other weaknesses could also be noted.

The second approach, though, is the more biblical approach. The righteous thinking approach is an accurate approach that sees life through the eyes of a righteous God, as revealed in the righteous Word of God: the Bible.

The difference between these two approaches is enormous. Being *rightly* adjusted to the truth is more important than being *positively* adjusted to one's ideals only to learn later, those ideals are incorrect or not attainable.

The process of sanctification is one of moving believers from that which is wrong to that which is right. God's process is to move believers to a life of righteousness. Paul writes regarding our body, "do not offer any parts of it to sin as weapons for unrighteousness. But as those who are alive from the dead, offer yourselves to God, and all the parts of yourselves to God as weapons for righteousness" (Romans 6:13, CSB). The word "righteous" simply means "doing what is right." Who, though, defines what is truly right? It is the righteous God of heaven who also does all things both right and well.

In my case, I would much rather be right than wrong. I would much rather be right than happy or sad. I would much rather be right than rich or poor. I would much rather be right than educated or dumb. I would much rather be right than employed or unemployed. *Quite simply, I want to be right in how I live my life!*

Key: Living right begins with <u>thinking</u> right! Living right always begins in the mind with righteous thinking. As a believer, I establish righteous values within my mind, and, over time, those righteous values become ingrained in me!

What does this lesson mean specifically? Let's do an in-depth look at how righteous thinking changes the way we *think* and *live*.

1. WE NEED A PURE MIND.

Jesus says in the Sermon on the Mount, "Blessed are the pure in heart (mind) for they shall see God" (Matthew 5:8). Peter says, "Stir up your pure minds" (2 Peter 3:1). Wuest defines the Greek word *eilikrines* (translated "pure") as "unmixed, free from falsehoods." (*In These Last Days*, p. 301) This word sets a very high standard for the child of God. This standard indicates a mind that is unmixed with the thinking of this corrupt world system.

I happened across an article by a so-called Christian who encouraged believers to indulge in trashy literature, trashy jokes, and trashy movies. The writer's objective was to acquaint believers with the reality of this world system.

Such a philosophy runs contrary to the above scriptures. Suffice it to say, every believer will, even by accident, get more than enough exposure to this world. In so doing, the believer will get a clear understanding of why he should live a life that is separated from this world's values and conduct.

A pure mind is the opposite of a trashy or impure mind. The man whose mind is on trash will ultimately become trash himself. The garbage truck may someday haul him away, too! But the man who seeks a pure mind and maintains a pure mind will ultimately *deal purely* with all the issues of life.

The world should never be allowed to set the morality standards for God's people! Righteousness, and righteousness alone, should set the morality standards for the children of God!

May I share the Swartzwelder parable of the day? "Trash in produces trash out." Why? It is because "as a man thinks in his heart, so he is continually in the act of becoming!"

Paul instructed young Timothy, "Keep yourself pure or free from sin" (1 Timothy 5:22). No one likes to drink from a dirty glass nor drink from a glass that has an insect doing backflips in his drink! Likewise, God has problems stomaching the impure Christian because he is not a sanctified Christian.

We can deduce from this scripture that purity of heart, soul, and action requires an act of the will. Paul says, "Keep yourself!" The English word "keep" is translated from the Greek word *tereo,* which expresses the idea of "alert or watchful care, to guard or protect." (Note: *Tereo* will be treated more fully in chapter fifteen.) The spiritual will of the new creation must overrule the fleshly will of the old creation.

Notice how that righteous will is expressed. "Finally, brothers, whatever is true, whatever is honorable, whatever is just, whatever is pure, whatever is lovely, whatever is commendable, if there is any excellence, if there is anything worthy of praise, think about these things" (Philippians 4:8, ESV). The key word is THINK! Not "do" but "think." The whole process begins with how we think. The believer must deliberately choose to think upon items that meet these six qualities: true in character (such a beginning quality is not easily found in a world such as ours, but it is a great description of Jesus), honorable or reverenced, just or righteous, pure as the just-fallen snow, lovely or pleasing to the soul, and, sixth, commendable or admirable.

How powerful is the human mind? R. G. Lee writes in his typical eloquent way,

> Looking upon this urge as a commandment we are wiser than when we accept the physicist's truth about corpuscles, the astronomer's truth about the movements of the satellites of Uranus and Neptune, the mathematician's truth about the numbers, the painter's truth about colors . . . For thought is a wonderful power.
>
> By means of thought you can travel to the uttermost parts in time and space . . . By means of thought we march with Caesar's armies, join Napoleon's campaigns, sit in the councils of the world, paint with Raphael . . . stand near Beethoven as he 'makes surging seas of tone subservient to his rod.'
>
> By means of thought, we can go with Columbus as he touches the shores of a new world, with Magellan as he circles the globe . . . with Galileo among the gardens of the stars, with

Faraday along the roadways of molecules and atoms . . . By means of thought we can view the kingdoms of the world, their cradles and tombs, their glory, and their tragedy.

A poet has pictured a dweller in a drab village answering a visitor's question: 'How can you live in Goshen—a wretched little place, where people talk about tawdry things and plant cabbages in the moonlight?' And the answer was: 'But I do not live in Goshen, but in Greece where Plato taught and Phidias carved—in Rome, where Cicero penned immortal lines, and Michelangelo dreamed things of beauty.'

Mind is as a ship at sea—and it needs a pilot.

Lee's last line is priceless: "Mind is as a ship at sea—and it needs a pilot." Guess what? The pilot's name is "Righteousness." Righteousness will steer us where we need to go in right thinking, and right thinking will result in right living.

Yes, "blessed are the pure in heart for they shall see God!"

2. WE NEED A PROTECTED MIND.

Motivational speaker Jim Rohn says, "You are the average of the five people you spend the most time with." That means we need to be careful with whom we spend the most time. It also means we need to be careful with what our mind spends the most time.

In his Ephesians commentary (p. 348), John F. MacArthur writes,

Satan attacks believers by leading them to disobey God's Word. Because God wants us to act faithfully, the enemy encourages us to act unfaithfully. Because God wants us to live morally, the enemy solicits us to live immorally. Because God wants us to speak the truth, the enemy tempts us to lie. Because God wants us to love, the enemy tempts us to hate. Because God wants us to be content with what we have, the enemy tempts us to covet. Because God wants us to live by faith, the enemy tempts us to live by sight. And so with every command and standard of scripture.

Where does that attack usually begin? In the mind! That's why we need a protected mind. Thank God, the Christian's armor includes the special "helmet of salvation" to protect our minds (Ephesians 6:17).

Paul writes, "Don't worry about anything, but in everything, through prayer and petition with thanksgiving, present your requests to God. And the peace of God, which surpasses all understanding, will guard your hearts and minds in Christ Jesus" (Philippians 4:6-7, CSB). We might paraphrase the scripture like this, "Don't worry, but let God do the worrying! His peace patrols like a sentinel before the door to our heart, continually keeping worry away."

One of my favorite Old Testament scriptures is, "Thou wilt keep him in perfect peace whose mind is stayed—or focused—on Thee" (Isaiah 26:3).

I remember meeting Bucky. He taught me the principle behind Isaiah 26:3. Bucky came to church one Sunday, and I visited him a few days later. Bucky had no television or radio and did not want either. Calming, soothing music played during my entire visit.

Bucky explained that he was a recovering alcoholic. He was a regular attendee of the Alcoholics Anonymous meetings. He explained that he was doing everything possible to keep his mind away from anything that might ensnare him again. He did not want to see or hear any temptations that might cause him to take even one drop of alcohol.

I then realized that I was seated in Bucky's fortress! He had carefully constructed a mind-protecting fortress to keep himself safe from temptation. Bucky would reinforce his mindset many times daily by repeating the AA pledge.

Bucky was not a Christian. (Note: The god of AA is not the God of the Bible but a god of man's imagination. It is true that AA encourages the recovering alcoholic to seek the power of a higher being, but that being can be anything or anyone. AA provides a very important tool for an alcoholic's reformation; however, AA does not promote regeneration through accepting Jesus Christ as *the one and only* Lord and Savior.) But Bucky taught me the power of a focused mind and a fortressed mindset!

Jesus offers the greatest protection of all. He says, "Come to me, all who labor and are heavy laden, and I will give you rest. Take my yoke upon you, and learn from me, for I am gentle and lowly in heart, and you will find rest for your souls. For my yoke is easy, and my burden is light" (Matthew 11:28-30, ESV).

"Commit your way to the Lord, Trust also in Him, and He will do it" (Psalm 37:5, NASB).

The believer's greatest protection is in the Lord and His righteousness. "The name of Jehovah is a strong or fortified tower, the righteous run into it and are safe" (Proverbs 18:10). That safety or security begins in our minds. It begins in the knowledge that our God shall do "all things after the counsel of His (not man's) will" (Ephesians 1:11). Furthermore, "shall not the Judge of all the earth do right?" (Genesis 18:25). Therefore, I feel compelled to commit my way unto Jehovah! He has never made a single mistake; He will not make His first mistake with me either.

Martin Luther came home one day with a very sad and distressed demeanor. A maid met him at the front door. She also appeared to be very sad, even more distressed than Luther. As a matter of fact, she looked as if a close friend had died!

Luther noticed her despair and asked, "What has happened?"

The maid answered, "He's dead," and began weeping.

"Who's dead?"

"He's dead."

Luther became frantic. He had experienced a long, tiring day. His emotions were at rock bottom. He had now come home only to be greeted with the news that someone was dead. He asked again, "Who's dead?"

The maid sobbed and said, "Martin Luther knows who died."

Luther thundered, "No, I don't! Who died?"

"Oh, God died."

The maid received a lecture for the next thirty minutes about God's eternal nature. Luther explained that God cannot die. The maid listened closely. When Luther finished, she stopped crying, looked up at Luther, and said, "Well, then start acting like it. God is alive! He is real! He's active! Quit acting like He's dead."

The lesson is clear: We would be much happier if we would only transfer our attention from the world to Christ. Instead of saying, "It can't be done," we would say, "By the grace of God, it can be done!" Instead of saying, "Woe is me," we would say, "Of all men, I am most richly blessed." Instead of saying, "There is no hope," we would say, "Our hope is in the Lord who made heaven and earth."

What is the difference? "As a man thinks in his heart, so is he!"

3. WE NEED A PATTERNED MIND.

My wife made her own wedding dress. But she didn't make it on her own. She used a pattern from McCall's. That pattern covered all the details. I recall thinking, "It's like a blueprint. All she has to do is follow the pattern." (Of course, that was easier said than done!) That pattern (we still have it) guided her in making a gorgeous dress for, what I still believe, an even more gorgeous lady.

Likewise, the Christian needs a pattern for thinking about everything! "Let this mind or attitude be in you—the attitude or mind that was in Christ Jesus" (Philippians 2:5).

God the Father says to each one of us, "I've given you a new mind. It's called the mind of Christ. This new mind will help you think in a right or righteous way about everything in your life. If you're not thinking right, you must be thinking with the wrong mind (Adam's). Your mission in life is to allow the mind of Christ to control you. His mind is to control your goals, interactions, worship, finances, marriage, home, employment, romance, politics, literally everything about you. Furthermore, even when you don't feel right, you can at least think right. Therefore, let this mind be in you which was also in My Son, Christ Jesus!"

Throughout His ministry, Christ Jesus demonstrated the attitude of a servant. Christ said, 'I seek not My own glory' (John 8:50). Instead, He came to be the servant of all. It is true He only once washed the disciples' feet, but He served them and others continually. He existed to lift the fallen, the unfortunate, the sick, and the uneducated; He fulfilled that mission in a way that no one else ever has.

"The blind receive their sight, and the lame walk, the lepers are cleansed, and the deaf hear, the dead are raised up, and the poor have the gospel preached to them" (Matthew 11:5). Jesus was willing to help anyone in any way.

On one occasion He said, "I must needs go through Samaria" (John 4:4). This was a strange statement because Samaria was miles out of His way. In addition, the Samaritans were deeply hated by the Jews; however, Jesus was not an average Jew. He continually put other people in front of Himself, so much so, that He often became exhausted from ministering to the masses that came to Him.

Simon Sinek teaches us, "Working hard for something we don't care about is called stress. Working hard for something we love is called passion." Is there any doubt that Jesus loved humanity, including you and me?

His pattern of thinking and living should be duplicated by every disciple.

4. WE NEED A PERCEPTIVE MIND.

The word "perceptive" expresses the idea of being able to see through things, to discern or understand, to have insight so that one is not easily fooled.

The devil, though, is a master trickster. He is a skilled illusionist. He is a smooth-talking deceiver. He is the best false advertiser in the business world. Many have been hypnotized by his various skills.

The book of 1 John captures this subject quite well.

"Do not love the world or the things in the world. If anyone loves the world, the love of the Father is not in him. For all that is in the world—the desires of the flesh and the desires of the eyes and pride of life—is not from the Father but is from the world. And the world is passing away along with its desires, but whoever does the will of God abides forever" (1 John 2:15-17, ESV).

"We know that we are from God, and the whole world lies in the power of the evil one" (1 John 5:19, ESV).

Contrary to how some people think, the world is not a disorganized mess with nothing holding it together. The Bible teaches there is a real devil organizing the world into an anti-God system whose purpose is to keep people from knowing the one true God. I don't like the devil one bit, but I must acknowledge he is a master in his art.

History records times of great revival in the world. But why are those times limited to only certain periods? Why isn't revival constantly occurring? There is widespread opposition to those movements of God.

There is an old saying, "The devil doesn't hit you over the head with a board. He changes your thinking."

There is a direct connection between what Christians watch on television and what they eventually accept as the norm. In time that new norm becomes the norm in their homes, and they, in turn, introduce the new norm into God's church. Who among us would dare say that our churches have the same power of God that they did in prior generations?

The Christian needs to understand what is happening around him. Think for a moment about the frog analogy. It has often been said that a frog will immediately hop out of a pot of boiling water. But put the frog in a pot of cold water, and it will stay. Slowly increase the temperature, and the frog will still stay. The frog will be gradually conditioned to remain in the pot until it dies. The frog will not perceive what is happening around it and to it.

The only hope for the child of God is the perceiving mind of Christ! "He that is spiritual judges or perceives all things" (1 Corinthians 2:15).

The battle is lost if the devil controls the believer's mind, but the battle can be won if the Lord controls the believer's mind.

A fine Christian woman told her church, "I lived as a young newlywed in a community in which many of the ladies spent their time in social affairs. Those social affairs were not necessarily evil, but they had no lasting, eternal value either. Before I realized it, I was involved in an endless round of social functions. I found myself neglecting my home, prayer, and personal devotions. I knew I had to make a choice between the world and Christ. I made the decision to follow Him and how I praise Him for it!" This lady had a perceptive mind.

"As a woman thinks in her heart, so she really and truly is."

5. WE NEED A PURPOSED MIND.

Robert Browning says, "Man was made to grow, not stop." A flower emerges from the soil and reaches for the sun. Likewise, a Christian emerges from new life and reaches for his Savior.

In so doing, the believer finds a new purpose for living. As he becomes more and more a disciple/follower, his thinking evolves into spiritual thinking. That spiritual thinking matures into a clearly defined purpose for living. In time, that purpose becomes fully integrated throughout his entire life.

There are many scriptures which express the purpose of God's saints *in their own words*. What you are about to read is very personal. You are getting a glimpse into their protected minds. As you read these scriptures, contrast each passage with how the non-believer thinks. In so doing, you'll get a new appreciation of the enormous gulf between those two perspectives!

"I have set the Lord always before me: because he is at my right hand, I shall not be moved" (Psalm 16:8, KJV).

"For although we live in the flesh, we do not wage war according to the flesh, since the weapons of our warfare are not worldly, but are powerful through God for the demolition of strongholds. We demolish arguments and every high-minded thing that is raised up against the knowledge of God, taking every thought captive to obey Christ" (2 Corinthians 10:3-5, HCSB).

"One thing have I asked of the LORD, that will I seek after: that I may dwell in the house of the LORD all the days of my life, to gaze upon the beauty of the LORD and to inquire in his temple" (Psalm 27:4, ESV).

"Brothers, I do not consider myself to have taken hold of it. But one thing I do: Forgetting what is behind and reaching forward to what is ahead" (Philippians 3:13, HCSB).

"Seek first the kingdom of God and His righteousness" (Matthew 6:33).

"Be constantly growing in the grace and knowledge of our Lord Jesus Christ" (2 Peter 3:18).

"Lay up for yourselves treasures in heaven" (Matthew 6:20).

"Set your affection on things above, not on the things of this earth" (Colossians 3:1).

"I was not disobedient to the heavenly vision" (Acts 26:19).

"As for me and my house, we will serve the Lord" (Joshua 24:15).

"These people gave to God out of their abundance but this woman gave out of her poverty" (Luke 21:4).

Would those statements of purpose be described as righteous thinking? Yes! But how sanctified are you in your thought processes? Here is a good test:

"Mirror, mirror on the wall,

Do you see Christ in me at all?"

Most likely, that depends upon how we think.

"As a man thinks in his heart, so he is becoming."

10

GROWING THROUGH FAILURE

Connie Mack managed the Philadelphia Athletics baseball team from 1900 to 1950. As of this date, he is the longest-serving manager in baseball history. He did not retire from coaching until he reached the incredible age of eighty-seven!

It is a truism to say that Connie saw it all during those fifty years. He saw many successes, but he also saw many failures, too. Connie said, "I've seen boys on my baseball team go into a batting slump and never come out of it. I've seen others snap right out of it and come back better than ever. *I guess more players lick themselves than are ever licked by an opposing team.*"

But some encounter the same degree of failure and yet keep growing. For example, one day, a six-year-old boy came home from school with a note from his teacher. The teacher recommended that the boy be taken out of school because he was "too stupid to learn." The boy's name was Thomas Alva Edison.

Obviously, the teacher was wrong! The teacher had not considered Edison's propensity to grow through failure. Of course, Thomas Edison went on to invent such items as the incandescent light bulb. But he faced many failing experiments along the way. At one point, he famously declared, "I have not failed. I have just found 10,000 ways that won't work." But eventually, one way worked! And that invention changed American life!

It has been said that the artist Vincent van Gogh sold only *one* painting in his entire lifetime. If I had been in his shoes, I would have found another line of work. But his paintings are now considered nearly priceless to the world of collectors.

History tells us about one man who dropped out of Harvard. Imagine how some family members must have viewed that decision! They probably said, "You're throwing your life away!" The dropout's name was Bill Gates. He set up shop in a small garage in Albuquerque with his partner Paul Allen. Thus, began the behemoth known as Microsoft— currently valued by investors at more than one *trillion* dollars.

The vacuum inventor James Dyson supposedly experimented with 5,126 failed prototypes—and his entire life savings—before developing the vacuum cleaner that made him a very rich man.

What do these people have in common? Simply this: It would have been so very easy for them to quit! But each one grew *through* his failures and into a better life.

The same principle applies in the Christian life. Contrary to how it is sometimes portrayed in Christian circles (especially television), the Christian life is not one of onward, upward to glorious success. It is instead a life of "Onward Christian soldiers, Marching as to WAR!" Sometimes that war occurs in our own soul, especially in dealing with failure.

Sadly, failure happens to all of us! Even more sadly, failure can ruin us *if* we do not grow *past* failure and grow *into* better, stronger Christians.

John chapter twenty-one records the failure and resignation of the same man who later rebounded and wrote, "Keep growing in the grace and knowledge of our Lord Jesus Christ." Poor Peter! Hot one moment, cold as ice the next moment! So excitable and yet so down! His cycles were volatile and swift.

Let's back up one chapter and get our bearings. John chapter twenty focuses on the resurrection of Jesus Christ and effectively concludes John's book. Many scholars describe chapter twenty-one as an epilogue because it stands apart from the previous twenty chapters.

Chapter twenty-one could be appropriately titled "Jesus and Peter" because the entire chapter concerns the relationship of these two people. It makes sense that such a chapter would be included in at least one gospel. After all, Peter's colossal failure on the eve of the crucifixion leaves us with many loose ends.

- "Lord, though these other apostles forsake you, yet never me!" (Matthew 26:33).
- "Peter, before the rooster crows in the morning, you will disown me three times" (Matthews 26:34).
- "Peter again disowned Jesus, even denied this time with an oath, 'I swear that I do not know this man named Jesus'" (Matthew 26:72).
- "The Lord turned and looked upon Peter. And Peter remembered the words of Jesus, 'Before the rooster crows, you will deny Me three times'" (Luke 22:61).
- "Peter then left the courtyard and wept bitterly. Pitiful tears and wailing!" (Luke 22:62).

Where do those events leave us with Peter and his catastrophic failure? It is true Peter failed the Lord. But we must never forget that Peter failed himself, too. Which would be harder for Peter to handle? It does not matter. But weeping bitterly indicates Peter had become a basket case.

Is Peter finished as an apostle? Can Peter really be "converted and later strengthen the brethren" (Luke 22:32)? Is there a way for Peter to emerge from the pit? His self-respect is gone. The necessary confidence to do the work of the ministry is likewise gone. Furthermore, the other apostles will evaluate him with a wary eye from this point forward.

Peter's failure has reduced him to nothing more than a shell. He needs major repair before he can ever be a blessing to others.

Then comes the resurrection of our Lord and Peter's Lord! Peter probably wonders, "Jesus is alive! But how will He treat me when we meet again? What savage words will He send my way for disowning Him? Will He send me home and brand me a misfit, a coward, a waste of His time?"

Mark 16:7 provides the only clue as to how that future meeting will transpire. The angel said to the women, "Go and tell His disciples **and Peter** that Jesus is going ahead of you into Galilee." It is significant that this message appears in Mark because many Bible scholars believe that much of Mark's first-hand information comes from Peter. If that is so, one can imagine Peter urging Mark to include his name in verse seven. It is as if Peter is saying to all of us, "Jesus had not given up on me! Though I failed Him, He was not about to fail me!"

Luke 24:34 indicates that such a meeting did indeed take place *prior to* Jesus meeting with the other apostles. Indeed, Paul lists Peter's meeting as occurring first in the six appearances by Jesus (1 Corinthians 15:5). Where did this meeting occur? We do not know. What was said in that meeting? We do not know. We can only assume it was a healing meeting for Peter—a healing of the soul!

1. FAILURE IS A HARD THING TO HANDLE, BUT IT *CAN* BE HANDLED.

Someone commented, "I am glad my God is the God of the second chance." I said, "As for me, I am glad my God is the God of the second chance *and* the third chance *and* the fourth chance *and* as many chances as I need."

Peter needed that kind of God. So do I. So do you.

A few weeks passed. It's time to turn the page from the resurrection chapter to the epilogue of John chapter twenty-one. (Note: John 20:31 indicates John's original purpose for writing is now complete. It is for that reason John chapter twenty-one is considered an epilogue by many scholars. What a wonderful epilogue it is!) As we begin John chapter twenty-one, Simon Peter is probably at the bottom of his typical roller coaster cycle. Such an evaluation is likely true for two reasons. First, notice the name that is used throughout this chapter. We are convinced that "All scripture is inspired by God." Thus, details matter because each detail is inspired and accurate; quite often, those details are revealed via the specific personal names that appear in scripture. In this case, the name Simon appears *eight times* in John chapter twenty-one. Eight times cannot be construed as an accident or mere filler.

Scholars mutually accept that Simon was Peter's *fleshly* name by physical birth. By contrast, Peter was his *spiritual* name. Jesus distinguished the two names when he said, "You are Simon, the son of Jonah, but someday you shall be known as Peter" (*petros* means "a stone") (John 1:42). Thus, we can surmise that we are looking closely at Peter's *unspiritual* side in John chapter twenty-one. *Jesus is addressing Peter more as a sinner in need of repair than a saint ready to repair others* (Galatians 6:1).

Second, John 21:3 suggests Peter has decided to quit the ministry. The phrase, "I go fishing," actually suggests much more than an afternoon fishing trip.

J. Allen Blair writes, "Most of these men had been fishermen when Christ found them. But He saved them out of this life to be His disciples. He gave them a new calling. 'I will make you to become fishers of men.' Their present action suggests retrogression. They were reverting to the old way of life. They had lost sight of God's plan for their lives" *(John: Devotional Studies on Living Eternally*, page 309).

John MacArthur agrees. He writes about Peter, "He was saying to the other disciples that he was going back to the fishing business—returning to what he used to do." (*Keys to Spiritual Growth*, p. 96) It was not a return to recreational fishing but to a secular occupation.

Though scholars disagree on the depth of Peter's decision, it seems prudent to consider the words of Moody Bible Institute's Greek scholar, Kenneth Wuest. Wuest writes,

> The words, 'I go' are the translation of *hupago*, which is used to denote the final departure of one who ceases to be another's companion or attendant. This was Peter's formal announcement . . . that he was abandoning his preaching commission. The words 'a fishing' are the translation of the present infinitive of the verb *halieuo*. The action is durative, progressive, action going on constantly. The tense refers to the habitual action of fishing . . . Thus, by using this word, John reports Peter as announcing the fact that he is going back to his fishing business permanently . . . When we remember that this decision was made by such a one as the unpredictable, vacillating, impetuous Peter, one can understand the possibility of such a thing. (*Great Truths to Live By*, p. 115)

The story continues with Peter fishing all night and catching nothing. He earned the wages of his rebellion: Not a single cent! Not one single fish found the net! But then Jesus arrived. Jesus was disguised and, therefore, not recognizable by Peter and the others. This stranger (Jesus) instructed Peter to drop the net on the right side of the boat. Peter accepted the stranger's recommendation and did so. In this instance, the right side proved to be the right side! *One hundred fifty-three* fish miraculously found the net!

The point is clear: With Jesus we can do much, but without Jesus, we can do nothing. The Peter who failed and denied his Lord, who failed in not even being present at the crucifixion, who failed in apparently resigning the ministry—that same Peter learns *153* times that Jesus can still use failures. *Each fish was a lesson in what God can do with failures that try again!*

Jesus says, "Without Me you can do nothing. But the one who abides in Me and I in Him will bring forth much fruit" (John 15:5).

Did that advice work for Peter? Yes! Consider what God did with Peter just a few weeks later. Acts 2:14 says, "Peter stood with the eleven apostles, lifted up his voice, and said, 'You men of Judaea and Jerusalem, listen!'" Peter preached his sermon, then God did what only God can do: God added three thousand converts to their number in one of the largest mass conversions of all time.

Failure does indeed put us in the pits. Most importantly, failure wants to *keep* us in the pits, too. But may I paraphrase? "Where failures abounded, God's grace did much more abound."

Peter's example is clearly pictured for us and is often repeated by us. Peter's life, though, proves that failure should never be a *stopping* point; it should only be a *single* point in the growing process.

Failure is a hard thing to handle, but it *can* be handled!

2. EVERYONE ENCOUNTERS MULTIPLE FAILURES AND IS PROVIDED WITH MULTIPLE REASONS TO QUIT.

I once announced that next Sunday's sermon would be for Christians that had failed at some point in their ministry. I then added, "There is no reason to attend if you have never failed." Guess who attended next Sunday's service. The same group as the previous Sunday! All of us had the same thing in common: We had failed at some point in our ministry.

Former New York City mayor Michael Bloomberg says, "You must first be willing to fail—and you must have the courage to go for it anyway. Life is too short to spend your time avoiding failure."

J. Vernon McGee evaluates the list of names in John 21:2 in this manner,

> This is the convention of the problem children. Here is Simon Peter, fervent but failing, warm-hearted, yet walking afar off; he is impulsive and impetuous and affectionate. Then here is Thomas, that magnificent skeptic, who has a question mark for a brain; Nathaniel, the wisecracker, who was also a doubter at the beginning; the sons of thunder, James and John; and two others

who are not named. Perhaps, since this is a crowd of problem children, they represent you and me. *(Thru the Bible with J. Vernon McGee Volume IV*, p.500)

My younger brother and I made a bad mistake when my father began preaching. I was perhaps thirteen years of age; my brother was four years younger. Dad would preach and then drive home. Like most children, we sat in the back seat. As Dad drove, we would point out his mistakes. I can still recall Dad preaching about the prodigal son in Luke chapter fifteen and saying, "His shoes were sticking out his feet!" Our comments deflated Dad. We did not understand at the time the damage we caused.

But then it became my turn. I grew up, and I began to preach. I invented some new mistakes never yet done by mortal man! I can still remember some of my early failures. Thank God, I wasn't live on television.

Unfortunately, some people fail in the area of a moral transgression—a sin that leaves a deep scar. But there is a solution for that failure, too! "Whoever conceals his transgressions will not prosper, but he who confesses and forsakes them will obtain mercy" (Proverbs 28:13, ESV).

Maurice Horn says, "Some people confess a sin a thousand times. I tell them to confess it once, then thank God a thousand times for forgiving them."

God is willing to move on. That means it is right for us to move on, too.

3. ANYONE CAN FIND AN EXCUSE TO STOP GROWING.

One psychologist says, "There are five common forms for 'excusitis' in the business world." Amazingly, those same five excuses are heard in churches, too. For example, "Pastor, my health isn't good. I am not well, so I cannot do certain things." That means someone else has to do double duty, or something does not get done.

Excuse #2— "I am not well. I cannot go to church today." But not being well doesn't stop some church people from doing everything else. They still go to work on Monday, and they still take a vacation.

Excuse #3— "You need brains to succeed. I don't know enough to do it." It is interesting to note that the apostles did not have much in the way of brains either. Most were common fishermen by trade, not educated surgeons! But they succeeded in what God had called them to do.

Excuse #4— "I attract bad luck. I just can't get ahead." The Word of God responds, "What does luck have to do with it? This is your moment. Perhaps you, Queen Esther, were made queen for such a time as this" (Esther 4:14).

Excuse #5— "I'm too young" or "I'm too old." The Bible encourages the young, "Let no man look down upon you because of your youthfulness but persist in being an example of the Christian lifestyle to all ages" (1 Timothy 4:12).

What, though, about the old? One person's testimony should suffice to show the folly about old age being an issue.

James D. Price served as the Old Testament Executive Editor and Chairman of the Executive Review Committee of the New King James Version. He also served as a translator on the Holman Christian Standard Bible. He has been kind enough to converse with me regarding some of my Greek questions. *James Price is now past ninety years of age.* Is he still growing and contributing to the cause of Christ? Yes! He recently wrote to me, "I keep busy with research and writing." Amazing! Still at it! Still learning, growing, contributing, and answering questions of want-to-grow people like me!

By contrast, some older Christians run the race for fifty, even sixty years only to then falter and fail to finish their race! For some reason, they lose their thirst for Christ. Perhaps John had them in mind when he writes, "Watch yourselves, so that you may not lose what we have worked for, but may win a full reward" (2 John 8, ESV).

I remember attending a chapel service at Tennessee Temple in the 1970s. Chancellor Lee Roberson began the service by playing a record (yes, there was life before CDs and DVDs) from a well-known Christian soloist. My wife and I owned that soloist's albums. Lee Roberson played the record then gave words of warning to all of us which I have never forgotten. He identified the soloist by name and said, "He was a wonderful Christian in his day. But he had a problem. He began drinking. He lost his ministry. He died a drunk."

The Bible has eleven words for that soloist and many others like him, "You were running well; who hindered you from obeying the truth?" (Galatians 5:7, NASB). No excuse should stop a child of God from serving the living God!

4. FAILURE IS A BETTER TEACHER THAN SUCCESS.

Failure stretches us in ways we may not want to be stretched but yet need to be stretched. Success, particularly easy success, tends to make us fat and lazy. Failure, though, rips away our feeling of invincibility. David, the greatest king in the history of Israel, sang, "My flesh and my heart may fail, but God is the strength of my heart and my portion forever" (Psalm 73:26, ESV).

The story may be old, but it must be told! A young preacher graduated from seminary and prepared the grandest sermon ever preached. Upon being introduced as the guest speaker, he stepped proudly, straight-backed into the pulpit area, read his text, opened his mouth to begin his sermon, but not a single word came out. His mind was totally blank, and, worst of all, he had not prepared any notes for guidance.

He read the text a second time, opened his mouth to preach, but not a single word came out. In despair, he repeated the process only to obtain the same result.

He thought to himself, "What can I do? Only one thing!"

He quietly closed his Bible, slunk away from the pulpit like a whipped pup, and slipped down the steps to the congregation. Someone reached out his hand in comfort and said, "Laddie, if you had gone up the way you came down, you might have come down the way you went up!"

But sometimes we have to learn the hard way, don't we? How many sermons and lessons have been rewritten on Monday morning! And on and on the list goes. What have we learned? We have learned what Thomas Edison meant when he said, "I have not failed. I have just found 10,000 ways that won't work."

But by God's grace, there will be a next time! So don't allow failure to stop you!

5. FAILURE IS AN EVERY-HUMAN QUALITY, NOT MERELY A PERSONAL QUALITY.

If I want to grow *through and past* failure, it would be good to understand that I am not alone in failing. You and I are part of a very large club of failures. A casual look around us will reveal that every person has a membership card in this club. Whatever is wrong with me must also be wrong with all of us!

We are human, and it is a human characteristic to fail. Regrettably, humans do not like to admit or face our failures. Instead, we prefer to ignore them or even run from them! We fail to realize that every person will encounter at least one meaningful failure in his past, present, or future. Something *will*, not may, happen that we wish could be blotted forever from the record. If we live long enough, it will come!

Jeremiah felt like a total failure when he wrote, "Oh that my head were waters, and mine eyes a fountain of tears. If only I owned a motel in the wilderness, I would abandon my people! They are nothing but adulterers, so very treacherous" (Jeremiah 9:1-2). In other words, "Good riddance!"

We can take special consolation by understanding that being human (along with its associated failures) is *not* a disqualification for Christian service.

James Boice writes about the list of names in John 21:2,

Can we miss that the church is made up of those who were doubters, deniers, and sinners of many varieties, but who have been brought to faith by Christ and have had their sins forgiven? These are the ones who do Christian work—normal people, with all the failings we are heir to, not fictitious characters of superhuman faith and fortitude . . . If John is showing that the five (disciples) of chapter one are here at the end also, then this is a testimony to God's perseverance with those who are His own. (*The Gospel of John*, p. 1449)

God started with these five men in John chapter one. God persevered with them for twenty chapters. Because of God's grace, they are still here in chapter twenty-one.

Do you know why you can make it to John chapter twenty-one in your own life? It is because God will persevere with you, too!

6. FAILURE TESTS OUR CHARACTER AND COMMITMENT.

What will it take to stop us from serving Christ? For some people, anything! For other people, nothing.

Vivian Greene teaches, "Life is not about waiting for the storms to pass. It's about learning how to dance in the rain."

Who are the most important people in our churches? *It is the people who finish what they begin!* They may not be flashy, but they get the job done. They face the same obstacles as anyone else, but they're dependable, and they somehow overcome. They may not be the best qualified, either, but they keep sowing Jesus; God rewards them with a bountiful harvest over a lifetime of ministry.

Failure often causes us to ask some very difficult questions. The most primary question of all is, "How much do I believe in the Christian ministry, and, in particular, my own ministry?" Many people enter the ministry without a firm conviction that ministry is truly worthwhile. Then something misfires, and they head for the exit.

Perhaps it is a case of mismatched expectations as in, "This isn't what I signed up for, Lord!" Perhaps it is a case of mismatched ministries as in, "I am a round peg, but this ministry is a square hole." Perhaps it is a case of mismatched loyalties as in, "Do you mean Jesus really wants *all of me?* Who does He think He is?" What about mismatched philosophies? The person begins the ministry only then to learn the Bible teaches a much different philosophy (for example, the principles of giving rather than receiving, serving rather than being served) and has very high standards.

I have more than a dozen biographies of Christian leaders on my shelf. All of those people failed and failed more than once. But the one common thread that unites them all is that *each one grew through his failures!* Each one possessed sufficient character and commitment to fight his way through the failure and move on in his ministry.

But none of those books would have been written if the person's character or commitment were lacking, nor would any of those lives be known by any of us.

I marvel at the success of a young man in the New Testament named John Mark. Mark joined Paul on his first missionary journey. But he lacked character, courage, and commitment. I have often said that Mark missed his momma's home cooking! He left Paul and ran home to Momma. Mark totally abandoned the missionary commitment.

But John Mark *grew through and past* the embarrassment of that particular failure. Mark allowed the experience to refine and develop his character. In time he tried again. And this time, he succeeded!

Paul later described Mark as "profitable to me for the ministry" (2 Timothy 4:11). Peter referred to Mark as "his son," apparently in reference to Mark becoming Peter's apprentice in the ministry. Sometime later, Mark recorded the Gospel of Mark, too! *That's not bad for a failure!* Mark succeeded because he believed in ministry.

The apostle Paul faced more obstacles than any man in our current day, but he says, "Woe is me if I do not preach the gospel! If I preach with a willing heart, I have a reward. If I preach against my will, I still have a commission that this is what I must do!" (1 Corinthians 9:16-17).

A young pastor once complained to C. H. Spurgeon that he did not have as big a church as he deserved. Spurgeon asked, "How many people do you preach to on Sunday morning?"

The young pastor replied, "Oh, about fifty."

Spurgeon solemnly said, "That will be enough to give account for on the day of judgment."

God help us to bloom where He has planted us!

7. FAILURE MAY NOT ALWAYS BE FAILURE.

Everyone needs a proper perspective on failure. Did you fail? Maybe so, but are you certain? *What we perceive to be a failure may actually be a success in the eyes of God or at least achieved God's purpose.*

Noah preached for more than one hundred years and won only his family to Christ. Noah would be considered a failure when compared to our modern-day televangelists. Elijah confronted Ahab and Jezebel about their sin of idolatry. He was soon on the run and was likely a laughingstock in the palace! John the Baptist rebuked King Herod for adultery. He was soon dead. Stephen promoted Jesus and the stones promptly fell. The apostle John was sentenced to the Isle of Patmos for the witness of Christ. The Bible records still another case where the crowd jeered, "He saved others, but He is powerless to save Himself." Who was "He"? Jesus. "He bore the *jeers* and sins of many."

On the surface, each one of these men was viewed by the secular masses as a failure. So did the religious establishment. But the serious Bible student knows they were anything but failures.

It could be said of each one that they served God in their generation (Acts 13:36). What more could be asked of them? Nothing! They served God as well as they knew how, and they left the consequences up to God.

As I have grown older in the ministry, my attention has been drawn more and more to Paul's admonition: "Therefore don't judge anything prematurely, before the Lord comes, who will both bring to light what is hidden in darkness and reveal the intentions of the hearts. And then praise will come to each one from God" (1 Corinthians 4:5, HCSB).

"Judge nothing before the time" is an appropriate philosophy for dealing with the failures of life. Many a pastor has "failed" in church power struggles and been terminated. But does that mean the pastor is a failure and should leave the ministry?

If that "failure" was the sole criteria, what do we do with Isaiah's rejection, "Is there anyone out there who believes our report? To whom is the arm of the Lord revealed?" (Isaiah 53:1). What about Jesus' instructions to "leave the Bible-rejecting town and shake the dust off your feet"? (Luke 9:5). Or poor Paul mentioning that "no man stood with me at my first trial"? (2 Timothy 4:16).

The truth is none of us fully understand what God will do with the seed we have sown (Matthew 13). God has assured us, though, that He will give the increase. Some seed will even yield a hundredfold result. *I believe with all my heart that some so-called failures on earth will be given a much better hearing in heaven.*

My wife and neighbor child planted a very small tree in our side yard. The neighbor child came back one month later and said, "The tree is dead." My wife said, "Let's wait and see." Four years have now passed. The tree, considered by one to be dead, is healthy and growing!

Are you discouraged with the results of your own ministry? Have you been slighted for someone with more charisma or ability or money or power? Did one of your efforts prove to be less effective than expected? Was the effort unappreciated? Rest assured, judgment day has not yet occurred!

Let's continue to give what we are able to give to our Lord and wait on the judgment day to reveal the final results.

8. EVERYONE, SUCCESSFUL PEOPLE AND FAILING PEOPLE, FACE THE SAME OBSTACLES.

Man has not changed since the beginning of time. There will always be some people that believe, while there will be other people who do not. There will always be some that stand alongside us in battle while there will be others whom we must face in battle. The devil has not changed since the beginning of time. Sin and its partner death have not changed since Adam's sin. Men continue to "love darkness rather than light." Depravity still reigns in the heart of man.

What does that mean? Let me mention three items of importance. First, our obstacles are no different than the world conditions which existed in Bible times. Second, our purpose is no different than existed in Bible times. Third, the power to accomplish God's ministry is no weaker than that experienced in the early church. Quite clearly, nothing has changed!

That means we can persevere just like the Bible characters persevered. **And so we must!** For how can we abandon those who have persisted since the beginning of time? We cannot fail them; furthermore, we must not fail them, for that would be a most horrible tragedy.

Dyson Hague served as a chaplain in an English hospital during the Great War. One day Dyson visited a ward of dying soldiers. A soldier asked Dyson to write his Sunday School teacher—to tell her that he would die as a believer in Jesus Christ because of her teaching. The chaplain wrote the letter. He received a reply a few weeks later. The reply said:

> "Just a month ago, I resigned my class of young men which I had been teaching for years. I felt that my teaching was going nowhere. Then came your letter telling how that my teaching helped win this boy to Christ. I have asked for my class back. May God have mercy on me!"

Failure comes to all of us, but let us never forget God's promise that, "We shall—not may but shall—reap if we faint not . . . if we do not lose heart and hope" (Galatians 5:9).

A small girl had often seen her older brother go to the top of a nearby hill and play. She yearned to go with him and enjoy the same experience. One day the mother finally relented and said, "Go ahead."

Off they went! They soon came to the steep, rough path that winded up the hill. The small girl stopped in fear. She said, "There isn't a smooth spot anywhere. The whole path is bumpy and covered with rocks."

The more experienced brother said, "Yes, it is. But how else could we climb to the top if it weren't? The bumps and rocks are what we climb on to get to the top."

Failures are what we climb on to be more like Him. God grant us the strength to climb on, over, and above our failures to be more like Him!

I urge you: Keep growing *through* your failures and don't stop until you find success on the other side!

11

GROWING THROUGH PERSONAL, INTIMATE PRAYER WITH THE ALMIGHTY

"Prayer is so simple;
It is like quietly opening a door
And slipping into the very presence of God,
There in the stillness
To listen to His voice;
Perhaps to petition,
Or only to listen;
It matters not.
Just to be there
In His presence
Is prayer."

        Author Unknown

"**O** thou that hearest prayer, unto thee shall all flesh come" (Psalm 65:2, KJV).

J. H. George wisely says, "I would rather teach one man to pray than teach ten men to preach." Wonder why?

The evangelist B. R. Lakin was called to hold a revival meeting in the mountains of Appalachia. This meeting occurred in the days when revival meetings often extended over multiple weeks. It was customary to spend the first week preaching to the church (getting the membership cleansed of its sin and re-focused on its mission) and the later weeks evangelizing the unsaved.

Lakin preached the first few nights but got nowhere with the congregation. The meeting was well attended, but the Spirit of God was strangely absent from the revival. Lakin felt as if the meeting was in a straitjacket. Something was obviously hindering the work of the Holy Spirit.

After a few nights of "struggling without the anointing," God reminded Lakin of a man who had extraordinary success in prayer. This man was known for walking with the Almighty. When he prayed, well, things happened!

Lakin called the man. Lakin said, "Brother, I know you live many miles away, but I need your help. This meeting is going nowhere. Something is holding back this meeting from accomplishing God's work. I need you to come and *pray this meeting open!*"

The man did not hesitate. He said, "I will be there." He traveled to the church, got down upon his knees, and interceded for the meeting. It was as if heaven then opened, and the Holy Spirit became free to do His work in the hearts of people. The meeting became a true revival, the church became re-focused on its mission, and many people accepted Jesus Christ as their Lord and Savior.

And it all began with a man *"coming and praying this meeting open."*

Lakin shared that testimony with us when I was around ten years of age. I have never forgotten his words. It was one of the ways God not only taught me about the importance of prayer but also about the personal, intimate nature of prayer.

The Bible says, "Thus the LORD used to speak to Moses face to face, just as a man speaks to his friend" (Exodus 33:11, NASB). Face to face! You can't get any closer than that—as one speaks to his friend! You can't be any more open, personal, or intimate than that. This three-word phrase "face to face" speaks volumes about the blessedness of talking with God in prayer. That is why this chapter is titled, *"Growing through Personal, Intimate Prayer with the Almighty."*

1. THE UNIVERSALITY OF PRAYER

Let's back up for a moment and consider the universality of prayer. Have you noticed that prayer to some form of deity is the one common link among practically all of the world's religions? Christians pray, Jews pray, Mormons pray, Jehovah's Witnesses pray, Muslims pray, Buddhists pray, recently discovered tribes in deepest Africa pray, along with many different religions mentioned long ago in both the Old and New Testaments.

The Old Testament records Elijah's challenge to the prophets of the Old Testament god named Baal. Elijah said, "You talk to your god Baal, and I'll talk to my God Jehovah. Then we'll find out whose God is really the Lord" (1 Kings 18). What an exciting contest that turned out to be!

The New Testament includes Paul's message in the multi-religious center of Athens, Greece. Paul said, "I know you Athenians are very religious. You have idols for every god recognized by man. As a matter of fact, you even have an altar to the Unknown God in case you have missed one. You're covering all the bases!" (Acts 17:23).

There can be no question that man is very religious even though he so often decries religion. The philosopher George Santayana once described prayer as merely, "painting your wishes against the clouds. When they come true, you call it answered prayer. When they don't, you call it submission to the Almighty." One must wonder, though, if George himself ever ignored his own words and prayed to the Almighty.

Just ask the man who has ever fought in a serious battle where lives were lost, and bodies were maimed. Why? It is said that even atheists begin to pray when the artillery falls!

Prayer remains the one common denominator that links all religions. Man may pray to different gods, but the point remains that man is a praying creature. Why? It is because *man has a need to pray.* Man has a need to be reunited with his Creator.

Saint Augustine teaches us, "Thou, God, hast made us for Thyself and our souls are restless until they find their rest in Thee." Not in religion but in Thee!

The emptiness or the void in man is so broad and so deep that man cannot escape the need to be reunited with His Creator. Thus, man devises some sort of religion in pursuit of that goal. Based upon the Word of God, we Christians believe that any non-Christian religion is a counterfeit, Satanic religion (1 Corinthians 10:20), but, even so, one must be impressed with the overwhelming urge to pray that exists in practically all religions. The need to pray is truly a universal need!

Therefore, we should not be surprised to identify prayer as one of the key components in our Christian faith. Some religions/denominations have written their own prayer books. By contrast, the Bible itself qualifies as the Christian's prayer book. Many Christians do not know the Bible is full of prayers (for every occasion) from its earliest chapters to its closing prayer of, "Even so, I ask you to come, Lord Jesus" (Revelation 22:20).

Many of the psalms were written in the form of a prayer. That is why some pastors urge their people to finish the day by reading one of the psalms *to God.* These prayers include Psalm 30, 51, 54-57, 59-61, 63-65, 69-71, 77, etc. Those psalms will work for any of us because they express universal needs. They can also be your prayer. All you must do is read it (and mean it) to God!

John 11:42 records Jesus going to the tomb of Lazarus and praying, "Father, I know that You *always* hear Me." WOW! Those words can be said about no one on earth, not even my own loving wife. She loves me deeply, but she does not always hear me.

John chapter seventeen is properly recognized as the actual Lord's Prayer . . . of God the Son talking to God the Father on a level which is beyond anyone's understanding. It is my humble opinion that John chapter seventeen is a passage that is better enjoyed than explained.

(Note: The sinless Son of God could never have prayed what is traditionally called the Lord's Prayer because it includes the phrase, "Forgive us our sins" (Matthew 6:12). It would be more appropriate to refer to the Matthew prayer as the Believer's Prayer or the Model Prayer. That prayer establishes a pattern for our prayers.)

The apostle Paul's letters include several tremendous, intimate prayers to the Father. For example, the book of Ephesians contains two prayers devoted to the growth of the Ephesian believers. It may surprise you to know Paul's prayers focus more upon spiritual growth than financial or material growth. Paul did not pray for us to prosper in the *world* but rather to prosper in the *Lord!* Even Paul's oft-used closing, "May the grace of our Lord Jesus Christ be with all of you," is a prayer.

One of the most popular passages on prayer is Matthew 7:7-8. Our Lord and Savior teaches us, "Keep on asking (present tense) and it will be given to you; keep on seeking and you will find; keep on knocking and it will be opened to you. For the asking one receives, the seeking one finds, and the knocking one will have the door opened." Jesus repeated that basic thought in Luke 18:1 when He says, "Men ought to keep on praying; men should never lose courage and, therefore, stop praying."

A. J. Gordon says, "There is more you can do AFTER you pray, but there is nothing you can do UNTIL you pray."

W. A. Criswell shares, "Every time I am given a new Bible, I write a sentence on the flyleaf at the front: 'He stands best who kneels most; he stands strongest who kneels weakest; he stands longest who kneels longest.'"

Charles Spurgeon explains, "Prayer pulls the rope below and the great bell rings above in the ears of God. Some scarcely stir the bell for they pray so languidly; others give but an occasional pluck at the rope, but he who wins with heaven is the man who grasps the rope boldly and pulls continuously with all his might."

The apostles knew the words of Gordon, Criswell, and Spurgeon by personal experience. One day they failed miserably in their Christian effort. They asked Jesus, "Why did we fail?" Jesus said, "This kind of problem is solved only by prayer and fasting" (Matthew 17:21). That's why they later came to Jesus and said, "Lord, teach us to pray as John the Baptist taught his disciples" (Luke 11:1).

They said, "Lord, teach us to pray! Teach us how to have personal, intimate prayer with Your Father! To talk to Him just like we now talk with You!"

I, and hopefully you, say, "Ditto for me, too!"

Let me suggest some ideas that will help you grow into a deeper, more complete prayer life. These ideas will help you transition from simply talking (and no one listening except yourself) to one of having a personal, intimate conversation with the Father.

Based upon the Bible and my own experience, I can assure you that such a relationship with the Almighty is possible; indeed, *God already seeks such a relationship with you,* and you, in turn, should seek such a relationship with Him.

2. WHAT EXACTLY IS PRAYER?

In its most basic definition, *prayer is simply having a conversation with God.* Have you ever had a conversation with anyone? Of course, you have. That means you already know the essential substance of prayer. Prayer is simply talking to God about anything *and* everything. William D. Longstaff speaks of such a sacred time when he writes, "Take time to be holy, Speak oft with the Lord."

Prayer is not some mystical experience that is purposely elusive to the many but experienced by only the privileged few. Rather, prayer is designed to be a common, easily attainable conversation with Almighty God.

That's the primary reason we object to written prayers. It is because written prayers are usually unnecessary. For instance, you would not conduct a conversation with your friend by reading a script. You would simply talk . . . and talk and talk some more. You would talk about anything and everything. The process is so simple that we don't even think much about it. We just call them on the phone and talk. Or we just talk by texting or email. Or we just talk with them face to face. And we do it without a script!

The Bible *urges* us to come to the Almighty for such a conversation! "For we do not have a high priest who is unable to sympathize with our weaknesses, but one who in every respect has been tempted as we are, yet without sin. Let us then with confidence draw near to the throne of grace, that we may receive mercy and find grace to help in time of need" (Hebrews 4:15-16, ESV). "Therefore, brothers, since we have confidence to enter the holy places by the blood of Jesus" (Hebrews 10:19, ESV).

Both passages say we can approach God with *confidence!* Not with fear and trepidation, not with trembling and doubt, not with uncertainty and timidity. But with absolute, 100% confidence that *we belong* in the throne room of heaven.

3. HOW CAN I PRAY IN CONFIDENCE?

Many Christians do not pray effectively because they lack confidence. They reason, "Surely the Almighty is not interested in what I have to say. Why should He listen to someone as lowly as me?" Those Christians do not doubt God, but they doubt themselves. They doubt their worthiness to enter God's throne room. They regard God as credible, but they do not regard themselves as credible.

But the Bible has good news for all of us! The reason that every believer can approach God with *confidence* is because of the blood of Jesus Christ. *His* death (not anything associated with us) has opened the door into the presence of the previously unapproachable God the Father. The Bible teaches that God "alone has immortality, who dwells in unapproachable light, whom no one has ever seen or can see. To him be honor and eternal dominion. Amen." (1 Timothy 6:16, ESV) "God, in His essence, is light and in Him there is no darkness or sin at all" (1 John 1:5).

The blood of Jesus, though, is the critical ingredient that turns an unapproachable God into an approachable God. Our previous studies have concluded that man is a sinner with a capital "S". Man's nature and output are even described as "darkness" in Ephesians 5:8. Based on that verse, we can conclude that our birth actually *increased* the amount of darkness in this world, because that darkness represents the character of our spiritual nature. Thus, the holy God of heaven was unapproachable by dark, sinful man.

The Old Testament prophet Isaiah states the dilemma quite clearly when he writes,

> *"Indeed, the Lord's hand is not too short to save, and His ear is not too deaf to hear. But your iniquities have built barriers between you and your God, and your sins have made Him hide His face from you so that He does not listen. For your hands are defiled with blood and your fingers, with iniquity; your lips have spoken lies, and your tongues mutter injustice" (Isaiah 59:1-3, HCSB).*

What a description! Built barriers . . . hide . . . does not listen.

What changed the situation? Jesus Christ settled the sin issue on the cross of Calvary. He died as a sacrifice to pay the penalty for my sin. As a result, I am now covered in the blood of Jesus Christ. When God the Father examines me, He now sees the blood of Jesus applied to my soul. God the Father has promised me (and you), "When I see the blood, I will pass over you!" (Exodus 12). That is what the Hebrews author meant when he writes, "Therefore, brothers, since we have confidence to enter the holy places by the blood of Jesus" (Hebrews 10:19, ESV).

The blood or sacrificial death of Jesus turns the unapproachable God into an approachable God because it satisfies His just demands. Someone had to die for my sin and, in my case, that Person was Jesus Christ. That's why God the Father now says, "Come, Tom, and let's talk!"

> *The biblically instructed Christian does not approach God through an intermediary such as a priest or Mary. He instead approaches God Himself with boldness!*

The Christian knows he will be welcomed into God's presence because he approaches God through the blood of Jesus. The blood is his ticket into God's throne room.

It is wonderful to realize our God is not hiding behind a curtain like the Wizard of Oz. Our God has instead opened the curtain and invited us to come into His presence. He even urges us to come whenever we want and as often as we want. His invitation is, "Come! Come at any hour of any day! You can even come when everyone else is asleep because I am the God who never sleeps" (Psalm 121:4).

That is why I come to God the HOLY Father in prayer. *I know I am welcome to approach Him* and have an intimate conversation with Him about even my deepest secrets!

And Who is Him? One Hollywood actor, a Scientologist, said, "I pray to the not yet fully understood God concept." What a tragedy!

I must disagree with his "leap into the dark" philosophy! The Bible reveals enough about my God that I can pray in confidence. I don't pray to an abstract Being any more than I am married to an abstract wife.

I know my God through the scriptures *as well as* through personal experience. Who is my God? He is the infinite Almighty! Omnipresent, Omniscient, Omnipotent! The Creator and Sustainer of all things! Holy beyond description, even thrice holy! Beside Him and beyond Him, there is no one greater or no one equal. "I am the LORD, and there is none else, there is no God beside me" (Isaiah 45:5).

I have the wonderful privilege to talk to Him and know that He listens!

4. How should I pray?

Three preachers sat at a table discussing the best way to pray while a telephone repairman worked nearby. One preacher said, "Kneeling is definitely best."

Another contended, "No. I get the best results standing."

The third preacher insisted, "You're both wrong. The most effective position is lying prostrate."

The repairman interrupted them and said, "Hey, fellows. The best prayin' I ever did was hanging upside down from a telephone pole!"

How should I pray? The answer should be clear. Pray wherever you are, whenever you want, and about whatever subject you wish. Must you have a specific location to have a conversation with your friend or spouse? No. That means one's location should not be a factor. Is your friend only available certain days of the year or even certain minutes of the day? Not if he is really a good friend. That means the time of day should not be a factor. Must your friend be told everything that happened in the last twenty-four hours? No. But he's still there as a resource to discuss anything because he is your friend.

How does God match up with "wherever, whenever, and whatever"? It's bragging time about our God because He is not limited by space, time, or knowledge. That means He can be even more special than our dearest friend on Planet Earth.

But sometimes, it is hard to begin our prayer. Speaking for myself, I often need time to empty my mind of worldly thoughts—to become focused. Heaven help me, but my first few minutes of prayer are often like priming a pump. Nothing of value gets done! *It takes time for me to settle down, clear my mind, and collect my thoughts.* There is nothing wrong with that. God wants my attention. Sometimes it takes time before I can do that.

That's why I occasionally begin my prayer by praying, "Lord, settle me into *my* spirit so I can commune with *Your* Spirit. Settle me down!" You might try that formula, too, if you have a rushing, anxious spirit like mine.

I also need quiet. Jesus advised, "But when you pray, go into your private room, shut your door, and pray to your Father who is in secret. And your Father who sees in secret will reward you" (Matthew 6:6, HCSB). Some people may succeed in praying during commercial breaks with the television blaring in the background, but that procedure does not work for me.

It reminds me of the husband and wife who reached a point of exasperation in their marriage relationship. The wife threw up her hands and said, "I just wish we could have a conversation."

The husband replied, "We talk all the time."

The wife explained, "But I'd like to have your undivided attention when we talk instead of your divided attention."

God views prayer in the same way. That's why Jesus says, "Go into your private room." Other translations express it as "your inner room" or "inner chamber" or even "closet." Such a room is isolated from the noise, confusion, excitement, and other distractions of ordinary life.

Then isolate yourself further by shutting or closing the door of your mind. Shut the world out and shut yourself in with God!

My wife has given me orders to avoid our bedroom after breakfast if *both* of the bedroom doors are closed. The closed doors signal Personal Time with God. I have been trained even to answer the telemarketing calls during her morning devotional time.

Time is also an important factor in effective prayer. A survey was recently taken of America's pastors. The survey asked the pastors to think about their greatest difficulties in the ministry. Would you like to guess which difficulty was ranked first? It was the issue of finding *time* to pray. The #1 struggle for most pastors is simply finding time to pray.

Unfortunately, the pastors had so many things to do that they could not focus on the most important thing to do—spend time with God.

Guess what? It is not just pastors that experience that problem. We are so busy with items we consider to be important, or that other people believe to be important. *We are so busy that we don't have the time to pray.*

But this problem can't be so because our current days are not any shorter than the days of the twentieth century or any century before it. I checked the clock a few seconds ago and realized the hands rotate through the entire cycle at the rate of once every twelve hours . . . and twice every twenty-four hours. Amazingly, every day in my life has been the same length: 1,440 minutes.

Quantity of time is not the problem; we have as much time as anyone in any age, including the Son of God during His earthly ministry.

Therefore, the answer is actually within us. We must *make* the time to pray. I must make the time to pray. You must make the time to pray.

If we have children at home, we must make the time to be with them. If we want a healthy marriage, we must make the time to be with our spouse. If we wish to keep our job, we must make the time to be at work. It is critically important that we deliberately and willfully *force* such an event into our schedule.

The same principle happens in prayer. Each one of us needs to make time to "cast my anxieties, concerns and cares upon the Lord because He cares for me" (1 Peter 5:7).

5. MY ROUTINE

Everyone needs a routine or a pattern for their prayer life. King David's routine was, "Morning, noon, and evening—those are the times I pray and cry out in my anguish of soul" (Psalm 55:17). Daniel's routine was to "open his windows toward Jerusalem, fall upon his knees three times a day, and pray" (Daniel 6:10). Jesus often withdrew from the masses and the apostles to pray (Mark 1:35).

During my years in secular work, I devoted twenty-five minutes each weekday morning to talk to my Heavenly Father. My Sunday morning routine was different because I did not operate under the same time constraints. My Sunday morning schedule has always included a pre-arranged slot of around seventy-five minutes to talk to my Father.

You can think of my own prayer time in terms of a coffee break with someone I view as very special. It's just a time for me to talk about this and that, but mostly, I talk about people and their needs.

I will often begin in the same way that my grandfather began his prayers. Grandpa would begin, *"Lord, we thank You that things are as well with us as they are."* I will then do something similar to King David in the Psalms: I will praise God for His multiplied goodness to my family and me. Yes, I am truly blessed! I am indeed the apple of my God's eye (Deuteronomy 32:10). My praise time resets my perspective from, "Oh, woe is me!" to, "Oh, blessed is me!"

Of course, I pray for my wife. I don't pray generically, but I pray specifically. I pray for her roles as a wife, pastor's wife, mother, mother-in-law, daughter, daughter-in-law, sister, sister-in-law, children's church director, soul winner, pianist, piano teacher, Bible teacher, choir member, friend, neighbor, and counselor. I am happy to say my wife is deeply involved in the lives of many people. She both needs and deserves my prayers.

I also pray for my three daughters and their individual issues, as well as my sons-in-law and grandchildren. I also pray for individuals in our church. I don't pray, "Lord, bless all of our people today," but I try to pray for each person by name. (If the number of people is large, I divide the church into groups and rotate the groups in my prayers.) In so doing,

I do my best to pray for individuals rather than groups. I also call out the names of specific unsaved people, some of whom I have never met.

My Sunday morning prayer includes a list of preachers that are about to proclaim the most wonderful message in the world. Plus more. Sometimes seventy-five minutes is not enough, especially if I have problems getting settled in my prayer. Or if God talks back and lays something on my heart. I always keep paper and pen close by so I can write down those special thoughts which come from above.

One item, though, becomes very clear after my season of prayer: I am now ready to go forth and do what God has called me to do. I am prepared spiritually, mentally, psychologically, and emotionally. "If God be for us, who can be against us?" I am now able to capably serve as God's ambassador to the world of humanity.

6. A FEW EXAMPLES

One day Andrew Bonar was ministering with D. L. Moody in Northfield, Massachusetts. Moody was in charge of the service. He said, "Dr. Bonar, these people would like to know how you live this victorious Christian life about which you have been preaching. Please tell us your experience."

Bonar quietly replied, "I do not like to speak about myself, but for fifty years, I have had access to the Throne of Grace." In other words, he got to know God in a very real, personal, and intimate way!

Lee Roberson will be remembered forever as one of the greatest leaders in the independent Baptist movement of the twentieth century. He pastored the 50,000-member Highland Park Baptist Church in Chattanooga, Tennessee. The church averaged 10,000 in Sunday School during my time at HPBC. It was believed that HPBC was the second largest church in America then. I graduated from its school, Tennessee Temple University (3,700 students).

The size of the ministry meant Lee Roberson was revered by many, many people, including me. One Sunday night, he told us about preaching in a revival with the great evangelist John R. Rice. After the service, the two of them went to the same motel room to spend the night.

John R. Rice said, "Let's pray. I'll pray first, then you."

Rice knelt by his bed and began to pray. He really prayed! Roberson said, "I have never heard anyone pray like that. He prayed for this and that. He prayed from memory for at least a hundred names. He prayed from the depths of his soul; God came and met with us in that room. It was as if it was just the two of them. I thought to myself, 'How can anyone know God on such a *personal* level like he does?' He prayed for thirty minutes . . . forty minutes, pouring out his heart to God, and then he said, 'Amen.' He then turned to me and said, 'Lee, please go ahead and pray.'"

Lee Roberson paused for a moment then said, "I thought to myself I can't pray like he does. I felt intimidated. I then said, 'I don't feel good. I need to go on to bed.' And I climbed into bed and turned out the light."

John R. Rice later wrote *Prayer: Asking and Receiving.* It is one of the finest books ever written on the intimacy of prayer. (The book is available at swordofthelord.com.) I encourage you to get a copy for yourself. Yes, prayer can be very personal and very intimate!

I was blessed to have a father who also knew the Almighty on an intimate, personal basis. One of Dad's most remarkable stories concerned the selection of a revival evangelist for Dad's church. During 1976-1983, Dad pastored a wonderful country church, Leatherwood Missionary Baptist Church, in Getaway, Ohio. Dad was convinced that God wanted Glenn Mathews from Charleston, West Virginia, to be the evangelist. Dad had even reserved a week on the church calendar for the meeting.

My father called Glenn and said, "We want you to preach our revival on such-and-such a date."

Glenn replied, "I am sure I am already booked for that week. I have a very busy schedule for that part of the year."

Dad was so confident that he said, "I don't believe you are busy that week. I feel very certain about this matter. Check your schedule."

Glenn left the telephone to check his schedule. A few minutes passed. Glenn came back to the telephone and said, "This is amazing, but that week is somehow open. I will be there." And he was.

I remember when Sharon was saved at my wife's home church. (Dad was the pastor.) The church had prayed for Sharon's salvation for many months. It came time for the annual revival. I was working the evening shift at the motor bank and could not attend the service. But I prayed earnestly for the meeting to become a true revival.

One night I went to the quiet of the bathroom where I could pray to my Father. I asked God to bless evangelist John Hankins as he preached. I prayed for God's power to bring sinners to Christ in the "Just As I Am" invitation. I also prayed for Sharon to be saved. I did not know if Sharon was in attendance, but I still prayed for her salvation.

God spoke to me as I prayed. I knew in my heart the church was experiencing a great service. God was blessing my soul as if I were present. I knew! My heart was thrilled, but I did not know what was happening.

Sometime later, the telephone rang. It was my father. Dad said, "Someone was saved tonight. Would you like to guess who?"

I did not need two guesses! I was not there in person to experience Sharon's salvation, but somehow God allowed me to enjoy the blessing even before I knew! *God was present at the church and the motor bank at the same time!*

"Dear friends, if our conscience doesn't condemn us, we have confidence before God and can receive whatever we ask from Him because we keep His commands and do what is pleasing in His sight" (1 John 3:21-22, HCSB). Confidence!

I was saved at the age of nine on January 14, 1965. My mother was confident that I would be saved that night. She wanted to let everyone know! Unfortunately, the telephone company had not yet extended the telephone line to our house. While I was at grade school, my mother took the family car, drove to several houses, and told the people, "Be sure to come to the revival tonight. My son Tommy will be saved tonight!" And I was. Confidence!

I will never forget the night my good friend Charlie was saved. I had spent many hours sharing the gospel with Charlie in his home. But his answer had always been no. Until this particular night!

My wife and I carpooled with Deacon Clyde and Betty Moore on the way to the church service. As we traveled, I told Clyde that Charlie would be saved in that night's service. I was sure of it! Several of us met in the prayer room before the service. I promised our prayer warriors we would have a great service because souls would be saved. Those men of God sensed the same thing I did. Confidence!

I was so confident I selected "It Is Well With My Soul" as one of the congregational songs. As we sang, I thought, "Charlie, you will be able to sing this song, too, before the night is finished!" And he was saved! Confidence!

It was settled in my heart before the service even began.

And ninety minutes later it was settled in Charlie's heart, too!

Such confidence existed because I had been in the presence of the Almighty.

This depth of confidence does not grow out of rushed prayers. On the contrary, it requires, yea, even demands that we take the time to pray—to pray things through until the fog is lifted, God speaks, and the way is finally clear.

> "I got up early one morning;
> And rushed right into the day,
> I had so much to accomplish
> I didn't take time to pray.
>
> Problems just tumbled about me,
> And heavier grew each task.
> Why doesn't God help me? I wondered.
> He answered: 'Son, you did not ask.'
>
> I want to see joy and beauty,

But the day toiled on gray and bleak.
I wondered why God hid His beauty.
He answered: 'Son, you did not seek.'

I tried to come into His presence,
I used all my keys in the lock.
When I could not gain an audience,
He answered: 'Son, you did not knock.'

I woke up early this morning
And paused before entering the day.
I had so much to accomplish,
That I had to take time to pray."

Author Unknown

12

GROWING THROUGH LOSS

"I walked a mile with Pleasure,
She chattered all the way;
But left me none the wiser
For all she had to say.
I walked a mile with Sorrow,
And ne'er a word said she;
But, oh, the things I learned from her
When Sorrow walked with me."

    Lettie B. Cowman

When was the last time you thanked the Lord for saying, "No"? When was the last time you thanked the Lord for taking something precious away from you? How about the last time you willingly exchanged Pleasure for that one named Sorrow? Probably a long time ago because we humans do not handle loss very well.

There are times, though, when all of us suffer loss at the hands of our sovereign God. The easiest response to such a loss is to become bitter (Hebrews 12:15). *The hardest response is to grow through our loss.*

Interestingly, there is a generally accepted axiom that loss is a greater teacher than gain. That principle extends throughout all life situations; it encompasses all people, including believers and non-believers.

But the universality of loss does not mean we willingly embrace it! For instance, there is a well-established principle in the financial world that investors fear losing money twice as much as they enjoy making the same amount of money. As a result, the average investor tends to be too risk-averse with his or her investments.

Practically everyone in life has a risk-averse attitude. Our innate tendency is to run away from loss rather than toward it!

But loss is a part of life, too. As a matter of fact, *loss is a part of God's sanctifying process for His children.*

May I suggest that you review this chapter the next time you experience a significant loss? This chapter may help you clarify the loss, survive the loss, and, most importantly, *grow through the loss* into a more mature Christian.

1. LOSS IS INCLUDED IN GOD'S PLAN.

"If you were created for happiness, there would be no affliction. Since you were created for holiness, affliction serves its purpose."

I previously mentioned that Lee Roberson was our pastor in the late 1970s at Highland Park Baptist Church in Chattanooga, Tennessee. HPBC owned a summer camp for children known as Camp Joy. The camp was a remarkable place to gather inner-city children and teach them about Jesus. But it is important to know how the camp came into existence!

Some years earlier, Roberson held a revival in the First Baptist Church of Russellville, Alabama. He was hosted in the home of Pastor Thomas Beele. The telephone rang on a Saturday; the message came of the death of Lee Roberson's baby named Joy. Roberson writes of that experience:

I don't believe that I've ever endured nor had I ever known in this life anything as dark, dismal, perplexing, and troubling as that was. Without a word to anyone, I left the house, got into my car and started driving back to Chattanooga.

Russellville is about two hundred miles away, maybe a little more. As I drove back, one single word came rushing in, 'Why?' I could not understand it. I could not see it. I did not know why the baby had to die. There was no way of explaining it as far as I could see then.

My favorite verse up until that time had been 1 Peter 2:21: 'For even hereunto were ye called: because Christ also suffered for us, leaving us an example, that ye should follow his steps.'

As I rode along, I couldn't get away from one single verse that kept driving its way into my heart—Romans 8:28. 'And we know that all things work together for good to them that love God, to them who are the called according to his purpose.'

Before I reached Chattanooga, I changed my life text. I changed from 1 Peter 2:21 to Romans 8:28.

Christine Caine says, "Sometimes when you're in a dark place, you think you've been buried, but you've actually been planted." Sure enough, Camp Joy emerged from Lee Roberson's horrible experience. The camp's establishment provided even more proof that Romans 8:28 is somehow true.

There are times when one may not see God's hand at work; it will be in those times that we must exercise great faith. We must trust His heart, for in His essence, we know, "The Lord is good, tell it wherever you go!"

"Sing praises to the Lord, O you his saints, and give thanks to his holy name. For his anger is but for a moment, and his favor is for a lifetime. Weeping may tarry for the night, but joy comes with the morning" (Psalm 30:4-5, ESV).

Joy! Especially in a camp called Camp Joy!

2. GODLY SAINTS ARE NOT EXEMPT FROM LOSS.

We live in an age when much of Christianity has forgotten the lesson that all must encounter loss in this life. Some foolishly proclaim what is commonly called "the health and wealth gospel" or "the prosperity gospel." One well-known television preacher says, "God intends for His children to die healthy and wealthy." Pardon my ignorance, but that makes me wonder how one can die if he is healthy; however, that is what my ears heard him say, and some of the people believed it. Such a false gospel teaches that it is God's intention for every child of God to be healthy and wealthy in this life . . . to live in prosperity.

The health and wealth philosophy states, "Jesus lived in poverty so I can live in riches." Such a philosophy distorts passages like, "For you know the grace of our Lord Jesus Christ, that though he was rich, yet for your sake he became poor, so that you by his poverty might become rich" (2 Corinthians 8:9, ESV). This "prosperity philosophy" defines "rich" in terms of physical and material riches.

However, if that is so, why didn't the apostles live in riches? Why didn't the people of faith in Hebrews chapter eleven live in riches? But instead, "they went about in sheepskins, in goatskins, being destitute, afflicted, ill-treated (*men* of whom the world was not worthy), wandering in deserts and mountains and caves and holes in the ground" (Hebrews 11:37-38, NASB).

Suffice it to say, the Bible distinguishes spiritual prosperity from physical/material prosperity. *The true riches of God's grace are those most experienced by the heart.* One of the themes of Ephesians is the "believer's riches in Christ." A casual reading of the entire book will reveal that those riches pertain spiritually to the inner man and not physical/materially to the outer man. The richest man in the world is the man who is rich in Christ rather than material possessions!

The scriptures are very plain from Genesis to Revelation that godly saints often suffer loss . . . and sometimes significant loss.

"But whatever things were gain to me, those things I have counted as loss for the sake of Christ. More than that, I count all things to be loss in view of the surpassing value of knowing Christ Jesus my Lord, for whom I have suffered the loss of all things, and count them but rubbish so that I may gain Christ" (Philippians 3:7-8, NASB).

"After you have suffered for a little while, the God of all grace, who called you to His eternal glory in Christ, will Himself perfect, confirm, strengthen and establish you. To Him be dominion forever and ever. Amen" (1 Peter 5:10-11, NASB).

Jesus says, "Whoever finds his life will lose it, and whoever loses his life for my sake will find it" (Matthew 10:39, ESV).

The apostle Paul was born again in the early part of Acts chapter nine. But how does chapter nine end? God sent Ananias to Paul with the message, "I will show him how much he must suffer for My name's sake."

"All that express a will to live godly in Christ Jesus will suffer persecution" (2 Timothy 3:12).

The Old Testament prophet Ezekiel suffered, too.

> *Then the word of the Lord came to me: 'Son of man, I am about to take the delight of your eyes away from you with a fatal blow. But you must not lament or weep or let your tears flow. Groan quietly; do not observe mourning rites for the dead. Put on your turban and strap your sandals on your feet; do not cover your mustache or eat the bread of mourners.' I spoke to the people in the morning, and my wife died in the evening. The next morning I did just as I was commanded. (Ezekiel 24:15-18, CSB)*

Job suffered in ways that I pray I will never have to suffer.

> *Then Satan answered the Lord, 'Does Job fear God for nothing? Have You not made a hedge about him and his house and all that he has, on every side? You have blessed the work of his hands, and his possessions have increased in the land. But put forth Your hand now and touch all that he has; he will surely curse You to Your face.' Then the Lord said to Satan, 'Behold, all that he has is in your power, only do not put forth your hand on*

him.' So Satan departed from the presence of the Lord."
(Job 1:9-12, NASB)

God allowed Satan to take away Job's seven sons and three daughters along with most of his 7,000 sheep, 3,000 camels, 500 oxen, 500 donkeys, and many of his servants. Yet, despite his loss, Job did not blame God for being unrighteous or doing wrong. In so doing, God gave us a book of consolation for our times of loss!

Abraham, the father of Israel, suffered. "Now Sarah lived 127 years; these were all the years of her life. Sarah died in Kiriath-arba (that is, Hebron) in the land of Canaan, and Abraham went to mourn for Sarah and to weep for her" (Genesis 23:1-2, CSB).

Joseph suffered. "When Midianite traders passed by, his brothers pulled Joseph out of the pit and sold him for twenty pieces of silver to the Ishmaelites, who took Joseph to Egypt" (Genesis 37:28, CSB).

The greatest suffering of all, though, was the suffering experienced by our Lord. His suffering began in the Garden of Gethsemane! "Being in an agony he prayed more earnestly: and his sweat was as it were great drops of blood falling down to the ground" (Luke 22:44, KJV). Then came the agony of the cross! "Jesus cried with a loud voice, saying, *Eli, Eli, lama sabachthani*? that is to say, My God, my God, why hast thou forsaken me?" (Matthew 27:46, KJV).

I am a born-again child of God, heaven bought, and heaven destined, but am I any better than them? No, not in the least. Therefore, I must expect loss to come my way because loss is one of the ways that God prunes my character to be more like Christ.

"Every branch in Me that bears fruit, My Father prunes it that it may be clean and bear more fruit" (John 15:2). Pruning includes the removal of that which hinders. And removal can also be spelled L-O-S-S.

Who can ever forget Job's immortal statement? "Yet He knows the way I have taken; when He has tested me, I will emerge as pure gold" (Job 23:10, CSB). But sometimes much pruning must be done to leave us in a condition of purified gold.

Romans 8:17 presents the Christian's glorious hope in a balanced fashion, "and if children, heirs also, heirs of God and fellow heirs with Christ, if indeed we suffer with Him so that we may also be glorified with Him" (Romans 8:17, NASB).

3. THE RIGHT OF THE POTTER OVER THE CLAY

Take a moment to glance over the names which were mentioned in the previous section. Then ask this question, "Did any of them anticipate the depth of their own loss?" The answer is no. (Even Jesus quivered at taking the cup!) The same answer will likely be given by us when our own loss arrives.

Quite simply, our expectations are so much different than God's plan. We expect our children to live to old age. We set our hearts upon giving them a good future. Some are even able to provide funds for their children's education. We also expect to be blessed with our mate throughout our entire life. Furthermore, we anticipate living the American dream, then retiring and living happily ever after! On and on our plans go.

We think this way for so long that we believe we have the <u>right</u> to the fulfillment of our plans!

Then God sends loss our way and our frustrated, sometimes angry, response is, "Why? God, I have a right to expect this, not to lose this! So give it back!"

However, we need to remember that God has *never* given us such a right. Most certainly, He did not put such a right in writing either!

But what does God say? If we read the contract, we will find these words: "You are no longer your own. I have bought you with the price of the blood of Jesus. Therefore, glorify Me with everything you have!" (1 Corinthians 6:18-19).

Jesus offered these words of caution, "Is it not proper or lawful for Me to do whatever I wish with my own?" (Matthew 20:15).

The apostle Paul writes a masterpiece about man's resistance to God.

> *You will say to me, therefore, 'Why then does he still find fault? For who can resist his will?' But who are you, a mere man, to talk back to God? Will what is formed say to the one who formed it, 'Why did you make me like this?' Or has the potter no right over the clay, to make from the same lump one piece of pottery for honor and another for dishonor? (Romans 9:19-21, CSB)*

Who is represented by the Potter or the Sovereign in that passage? It is not man, but it is God. Who is represented by the clay? The clay represents man, the lowly creation of the Creator. The clay represents you and me in our fragile makeup and our even more fragile lifestyle.

Paul's words are quite harsh, that is, until you think them through. First, I must acknowledge that I belong to someone, either God or the devil. Both are more powerful than I am.

Second, to whom would I rather belong? Would I rather belong to him whose goal is to rebel against the Creator—to then end my existence with him in a devil's hell? Or would I rather belong to Him who is described as the "God of all grace", a "God of love", a "God of wisdom, righteousness, sanctification, and redemption", a "God who does all things after the counsel of His own will", a God who has promised that "all things will somehow work together for the ultimate good of those who love God"?

The choice is simple for me. I want to hitch my wagon to God!

> "All the way my Savior leads me;
> What have I to ask beside?
> Can I doubt His tender mercy,
> Who thro' life has been my guide?
> Heavenly peace, divinest comfort,

Here by faith in Him to dwell!
For I know what e'er befall me,
Jesus doeth all things well."

   Fanny Crosby

Such thinking became the foundation for Paul's approach to life. He writes from prison, "I know how to get along with humble means, and I also know how to live in prosperity; in any and every circumstance I have learned the secret of being filled and going hungry, both of having abundance and suffering need" (Philippians 4:12, NASB).

It has been correctly pointed out that, "Someone else is happier with less than what you have." Therefore, let us "be content with what we have," and what do we have? We have Him who has promised, "I will never leave you nor forsake you" (Hebrews 13:5).

The tests of life may be severe, may cause us to bend until we almost break. But the promises of God are sure! "I can do all things through Christ who strengthens me" (Philippians 4:13). "The Lord Himself stood at my side and gave me strength!" (2 Timothy 4:17). "My grace will be sufficient for you!" (2 Corinthians 12:9).

As the flower becomes more and more beautiful as it turns toward the sun, so may we become more like our wonderful Lord!

4. LOSS MAY OR MAY NOT BE THE RESULT OF PERSONAL SIN.

There will come a day when loss knocks on the door in the form of a lost job, health issue, family problem, etc. Quite often, our first response is to ask, "What did I do wrong?" The critic hears our bad news and says, "God must be punishing him. Wonder what he did wrong?"

Likewise, Job's friends asked, "Job, what did you do wrong? How have you angered the Almighty?" Eliphaz directed harsh words not only to Job but also at Job: "They that plow iniquity and sow wickedness, reap the same" (Job 4:8).

Job answered as honestly as he knew how when he said, "I will defend my ways before God" (Job 13:15). "I desire to reason with God" (Job 13:3).

The story of Job contains many spiritual lessons that have lifted our spirits from the pit of despair. *One of the most important lessons teaches that loss is not always connected to personal sin.* The first chapter teaches us about Job's remarkable character; those words make it plain that his loss was not because of personal sin.

The first verse of Job's book declares, "There was a man in the land of Uz whose name was Job; and that man was blameless, upright, fearing God and turning away from evil" (Job 1:1, NASB). The word "blameless" suggests "full of integrity." There is not the slightest hint in Job chapter one that Job was being punished for his sin.

On the contrary, the chapter indicates that his loss was due to Satan's testing of Job's character.

> *Then Satan answered the LORD and said, 'Does Job fear God for no reason? Have you not put a hedge around him and his house and all that he has, on every side? You have blessed the work of his hands, and his possessions have increased in the land. But stretch out your hand and touch all that he has, and he will curse you to your face.' And the LORD said to Satan, 'Behold, all that he has is in your hand. Only against him do not stretch out your hand.' (Job 1:9-12, ESV)*

A similar passage occurs in the New Testament. Jesus said to Peter, "Simon, Simon, behold, Satan has demanded permission to sift you like wheat; but I have prayed for you that your faith may not fail. And when you have turned again, strengthen your brothers" (Luke 22:31-32, ESV).

Both cases are similar to the test faced by Shadrach, Meshach, and Abednego. Their test was a life-or-death test. Those three saints could kneel in worship of the king (life), or they would be thrown into the furnace of fire (death). Once again, personal sin had nothing to do with their predicament.

These three cases illustrate that God sometimes allows loss to grow our character. Such tests should be viewed as a sifting process designed to separate the worthless chaff of man's kingdom from the worthwhile wheat of God's kingdom.

In such times, we should never despair, but we should pray for the strength to weather the storm. We should dedicate ourselves to being a Shadrach and let our faith soar to God! In so doing, we can grow through our loss.

But, on the other hand, *some loss is directly tied to personal sin.* Adam lost paradise for his posterity because of *his* one sin. Lot lost his house, job, and sons-in-law because of *his* sin. Samson lost his eyesight and even life due to *his* sin. Jonah ended up in the belly of the great fish because of *his* sin. Ananias and Sapphira died because of *their* sin. On and on the list goes.

I recall a dear saint in Dalton, Georgia. She had worked many years in a carpet mill. She testified to me, "Some years ago, I rebelled against God. One day a large spool of carpet hit me in the head. I ended up in the hospital for many weeks. I have now made things right with God. My heart is now right, but my body will never be right again. Let my story be a warning to others!" She was convinced that her loss was directly tied to her rebellion against God.

What should a believer do when loss comes? Psalm 139:23-24 says, "Search my heart, O God. Look deeply into the recesses of my heart and determine if there is any wicked way in my heart or my motives. Test me! Know everything I am thinking. Show me anything that is displeasing to you! Then lead me in Your way—the everlasting way!"

John Phillips explains Psalm 139:23-24 in his *Exploring Psalms* commentary,

> The Psalmist was no hypocrite. He knew that there were depths of wickedness lurking in his own heart. He knew its secret lusts. Like a sensible man, faced with the omniscience of God, he did not try to hide his inner thoughts. He opened them up to God's inspection. He pleaded that the Lord would lead him

in the way everlasting—that not only his inward life, but his outward life might be pleasing to the Lord he cannot escape (and, clearly, from whom he had no desire to escape).

Don't be afraid to pray, "Search me!" The searching process can result in our being renewed in "the Lord's way." What better way is there than the Lord's way? The Lord's way will enable us to grow *through* our loss.

5. LOSS TEACHES US THE VALUE OF EVERYONE AND EVERYTHING.

After losing a loved one, we tend to value that person more highly; we realize how much they meant to us and did for us. Their absence creates a hole which nothing else seems to fill.

After losing our health, we suddenly realize the value of good health. Some may have to carry oxygen on a shopping trip, use a walker or cane, surrender driving at night, and, perhaps saddest of all, no longer venture to church. We miss doing what we used to do; we pray for our youthful vigor and abilities to be restored.

It is a human trait that we value people, money, home, and relationships *more* after we lose them. "Who can find a wife of outstanding quality? She is far more valuable than jewels" (Proverbs 31:10). But how many husbands truly understand her value until she is lost? The husband works his entire life for that which can buy jewels, but yet he is blessed day after day with one who is worth more than all the jewels in the world.

King Nebuchadnezzar of Babylon learned this very lesson in the hardest way imaginable. Nebuchadnezzar had become the most powerful person in the ancient world. Daniel chapter two describes him as the head of gold on the statue that represents the four largest Gentile kingdoms in world history. Being the head of gold, Nebuchadnezzar represented the highest quality or the most superior king of all. The prophecy further explained that the next three kingdoms would be inferior to the head of gold.

What a man! A man who had it all! Of all men, he, and he alone, was on top of the world! A man, though, who also needed to learn how to suffer loss . . . and which God was really in charge.

That brings us to Daniel chapter four. In many ways, Daniel chapter four represents the king's obituary to the civilized world. He wrote the entire chapter just one year before his death. It was written *after* the most humbling experience of his life—a truly life-changing experience.

The experience began with Daniel prophesying to the king, "You will be driven away from people to live with the wild animals. You will feed on grass like cattle and be drenched with dew from the sky for seven periods of time, until you acknowledge that the Most High is ruler over human kingdoms, and he gives them to anyone he wants" (Daniel 4:25, CSB).

Twelve uneventful months passed but then one day, God fulfilled His promise. God took away everything that Nebuchadnezzar valued. The great king lost all of his possessions, including his palace, but most of all, he lost his ability to reason.

I once asked my church, "Which do you fear the most: The decline of the body or the decline of the mind?" The vote was unanimous in favor of the mind. Above all, we don't want to lose our ability to reason. But that is what happened to Nebuchadnezzar! God, in judgment, removed the mind of humanity from Nebuchadnezzar and replaced it with the mind of an animal or beast of the field. Nebuchadnezzar lived like a beast for "seven periods of time," thus indicating it was a lengthy judgment.

In time, God reversed the curse; Nebuchadnezzar's mind and kingdom were restored to him. But Nebuchadnezzar's attitude was much different than before. He then sat down and wrote Daniel chapter four. That chapter serves as his obituary. (Note: In my mind, it is one of the most important chapters in the Bible, because it contrasts our inferiority with God's superiority.)

The beginning three verses make it clear that he is sharing his greatest discovery with the world. What was that discovery?

Nebuchadnezzar writes about Daniel's God, "How great are His signs And how mighty are His wonders! His kingdom is an everlasting kingdom And His dominion is from generation to generation" (Daniel 4:3, NASB).

Many scholars believe (and I agree) Daniel chapter four marks the conversion or born-again experience of Nebuchadnezzar. How else can one account for his humble confession? Indeed, the obituary ends with these words, "Now I, Nebuchadnezzar, praise, exalt and honor the King of heaven, for all His works are true and His ways just, and He is able to humble those who walk in pride" (Daniel 4:37, NASB).

He had been humbled . . . but what he gained was of much greater value than anything he previously possessed!

Nebuchadnezzar's loss taught him the value of everyone and everything . . . including himself . . . including the true God of heaven, also!

Loss brought gain! Big loss brought even bigger gain! And his ending was worth more than all of his earlier years combined.

A building contractor placed a sign on a house that was being renovated. The sign was written in capital letters, and it said, "DO NOT PASS JUDGMENT ON THIS HOUSE UNTIL IT IS FINISHED." Such a house probably needed to lose a wall or two, maybe some flooring, maybe some windows, but, without a doubt, the final house was better than the beginning house. Loss made that possible!

Sometimes, though, we totally miss the point. A little girl was walking in a garden when she noticed a particularly beautiful flower. The child admired the flower's beauty and enjoyed its fragrance. She looked at the soil and said, "What a shame! This flower is too pretty to be planted in such dirt."

The little girl pulled up the plant by its roots and washed off the clinging soil. It wasn't long until the flower wilted, and the plant began to die.

The gardener saw what she had done and scolded her. He said, "You have destroyed my finest plant."

She protested, "But I did not like it in that dirt."

The gardener replied, "I chose that spot. I collected and mixed the soil because I knew that only there would it come to maturity."

God has prepared a place for each one of us to come to maturity. It may not be a place of our choosing. *But it is God's place.* It has been chosen by Him who is a God of love, grace, and mercy. It is a place where loss, as well as gain, will indeed come. Let's do our best to embrace God's place and *grow through our loss!*

13

GROWING THROUGH OPPOSITION AND PERSECUTION

You're a child of God on your way to heaven. But you're still here on earth. What is the number one problem with the Christian life for you personally? Our church people could give many answers. For example, some might lament the giving aspect. "We give and give and give of ourselves, and yet many spongy, selfish people still want more. Christian service is so frustrating."

Others might struggle with Jesus' commandment to, "Take up your cross daily and come and follow Me." The lackadaisical Christian says, "I don't want to act like a Christian seven days a week."

Still others might emphasize their failures in Christian service. "I tried, gave it my best effort, but my effort did not accomplish what I expected. No one appreciated my effort."

So many answers could be given! But I believe the number one response would be in the category discussed in this chapter: Opposition and Persecution.

We humans are programmed with a basic trait: We want to be loved, accepted, and appreciated. We don't like to be embarrassed, criticized, judged unfairly, insulted, rejected, or cast out.

As a result, the whole concept of facing opposition/persecution rubs us the wrong way. We are often dumbfounded when we learn people do not agree with our Christian beliefs. We often respond, "How dare they? Why don't they see the error of their ways?"

The purpose of this chapter is to help each one of us understand that we can actually grow *through* opposition/persecution and emerge stronger on the other side.

One illustration will suffice at this juncture. A sculptor brought a large rock to a city park and began to work. The morning walkers visited him and asked him what he intended to do. He said, "I am making a statue of one of our town heroes." He named a local hero of days past.

The walkers said, "It doesn't look like much now."

The sculptor said, "I have my tools. I will chip away everything I don't want. Come back in a few days, and you will see your hero in stone."

That's exactly what happened, too. The walkers saw the final product; they saw their hero in a very prestigious pose. They also noticed that some of the large rock remained, but some of the rock was totally gone. The unnecessary part had been removed. In so doing, something beautiful had emerged!

God does a similar work in our lives by using the hammer and chisel of opposition, even persecution, to remove those parts in our lives that are unnecessary. God purges the dross, the superfluous, the waste, the chaff, the sins that so easily hinder us, and He creates a statue that demonstrates the glory of Jesus Christ.

Someone has written, "We are never more like Christ than when we suffer like Christ."

The apostle Paul emphasized,

> *Just one thing: As citizens of heaven, live your life worthy of the gospel of Christ. Then, whether I come*

and see you or am absent, I will hear about you that you are standing firm in one spirit, in one accord, contending together for the faith of the gospel, not being frightened in any way by your opponents. This is a sign of destruction for them, but of your salvation—and this is from God. For it has been granted to you on Christ's behalf not only to believe in him, but also to suffer for him, since you are engaged in the same struggle that you saw I had and now hear that I have. (Philippians 1:27-30, CSB)

How can we live in a manner *worthy* of the gospel of Christ despite opposition and even persecution? As always, God has the answer *and* the strength to make it happen!

1. WHO ARE WE TO BE? WHAT IS OUR IDENTITY?

Adrian Rogers preaches, "If I please Jesus, it doesn't matter whom I displease. If I displease Jesus, it really doesn't matter whom I please."

God calls us to set our standards high—very high—versus a world that sets its standards low—very low. There is an old saying: "The man who stands for nothing will fall for anything." God does not want us to be that man.

Two sentences appear in bold type on the back cover of my first book, *God's Greenhouse:* "It's who we are. It's what we do." Is there any doubt that the United States Marines know who they are and what they are to do? No. We expect them to go into battle and bloody the enemy. Is there any doubt that the New York Yankees know who they are and what they are to do? No. We expect them to entertain us in a game called baseball, but not chess or basketball or curling.

We know what to expect from those two groups. The same can be said about our relationship to this world. We represent Jesus Christ; the world, therefore, expects us to represent Him. Representing Him also means representing His beliefs, His strategy, and His values, including standards.

We are to be salt. Jesus teaches in the Sermon on the Mount, "You are the salt of the earth. But if the salt should lose its taste, how can it be made salty? It's no longer good for anything but to be thrown out and trampled under people's feet" (Matthew 5:13, CSB). Salt, of course, has a preserving ability to keep food from deteriorating, but I am most thankful that salt makes food taste better! "Come, taste of the Lord!" is not only something the Christian should speak, but it is something the Christian should live! We are the only salt in a saltless society.

It has been said the best salesman is the one who has tried the product and found the product to work. His testimony is deemed believable. In the same manner, a salty Christian is the best salesman for Jesus because he has tried Jesus, and he knows that Jesus works.

We are to be light. "You are the light of the world. A city situated on a hill cannot be hidden. No one lights a lamp and puts it under a basket, but rather on a lampstand, and it gives light for all who are in the house. In the same way, let your light shine before others, so that they may see your good works and give glory to your Father in heaven" (Matthew 5:14-16, CSB). Our light illuminates a cross where all men can be reconciled to God.

We are to be a witness. Jesus says, "But you will receive power when the Holy Spirit has come upon you; and you shall be My witnesses both in Jerusalem, and in all Judea and Samaria, and even to the remotest part of the earth" (Acts 1:8, NASB). We are not only to live the gospel, but we are also to proclaim the gospel.

We are to accomplish the Great Commission. "Go therefore and make disciples of all nations, baptizing them in the name of the Father and of the Son and of the Holy Spirit, teaching them to observe all that I have commanded you. And behold, I am with you always, to the end of the age" (Matthew 28:19-20, ESV). This commission is labeled "great" because it is great in importance. It is labeled "co" because it is in partnership with the Almighty. It is labeled "mission" because it sets forth a very clear mission statement. This specific mission makes our churches different than the other organizations in our community. Our mission is to make disciples who then reproduce themselves into more disciples.

We are to be an ambassador. "Therefore, we are ambassadors for Christ, since God is making his appeal through us. We plead on Christ's behalf: 'Be reconciled to God'" (2 Corinthians 5:20, CSB). The United States has more than two hundred ambassadors representing our nation's interests. Such a position is high-level. It is also honored—a position of great respect.

The Bible indicates that every child of God holds such a high-level position in God's kingdom! We have the honor of representing our God before the kingdom of men. "There was an ambassador sent from God whose name was John" (John 1:6). It is also correct to say, "There was an ambassador sent from God whose name is _____." (Insert your name.)

We are to be holy. "But as the One who called you is holy, you also are to be holy in all your conduct; for it is written, Be holy, because I am holy" (1 Peter 1:15-16, HCSB).

We are to be separate in our lifestyle. It is said the law of Moses contains 613 commandments. This comprehensive list covers every aspect of human life, including religion, diet, clothing, finance, mortgages, capital punishment, worship, hygiene, immigration, health, etc. The letter of the Mosaic law does not extend into the church age, but the spirit of a separated lifestyle continues throughout the years. We can say with certainty that Christianity *is* a lifestyle. It is a lifestyle that is easily distinguishable from the lifestyle expressed in our current world system.

We are to proclaim the truth. The King of the Jews told Governor Pilate, "For this I have been born, and for this I have come into the world, to testify to the truth. Everyone who is of the truth hears My voice" (John 18:37, NASB). Thus, we, as His followers, "proclaim the truth in the spirit of love" (Ephesians 4:15) and "wear truth as a belt around our waist" (Ephesians 6:14).

We are to be faithful until death, not merely until difficulty comes! Jesus promised the church at Smyrna, "Do not fear what you are about to suffer. Behold, the devil is about to cast some of you into prison, so that you will be tested, and you will have tribulation for ten days. Be faithful until death, and I will give you the crown of life" (Revelation 2:10, NASB). Be faithful until death!

Is there any doubt we are different from an unbelieving world? The Marines have a distinguishing purpose, the Yankees have a distinguishing purpose, and God's children also have a distinguishing purpose. We're different from anything or anyone the world has ever produced!

2. DO NOT BE SURPRISED WHEN THE WORLD TREATS YOU DIFFERENTLY.

"All that express a will to live godly in Christ Jesus will suffer persecution" (2 Timothy 3:12). Please underline the words "will suffer" because those words indicate something that is certain to occur.

As a matter of fact, it occurs every day in our community. For example, we advocate our position for old-fashioned morality, and someone gets upset. We encourage people to avoid the vices of drugs, alcohol, gambling, premarital and extramarital sex, pornography, along with Hollywood's loose values, and what is the result? World War Three begins. We ask people to avoid profanity; they retaliate by using more. We point out there is only one way of salvation; we are branded extremists. We take a biblical position against same-sex marriages; more than one person accuses us of bigotry.

We then ask, "What have I done wrong? Why don't they like me?" We are bewildered by the fact that a clean living, biblical testimony has been rejected. It makes no sense!

We even go so far as to think, "It's just *natural* for me as a child of God to *advocate* these positions." The world counters, "Likewise, it is only *natural* for us to *oppose* your positions. We will use any means necessary to prevent your views from becoming the norm in our society."

Jesus made it plain that we should not be surprised when opposition, even persecution, comes. Consider His next words carefully!

> *Blessed are those who are persecuted for righteousness'*
> *sake, for theirs is the kingdom of heaven. Blessed are*
> *you when others revile you and persecute you and utter*
> *all kinds of evil against you falsely on my account.*
> *Rejoice and be glad, for your reward is great in heaven,*
> *for so they persecuted the prophets who were before you*
> *(Matthew 5:10-12, ESV).*

"But I say to you, Love your enemies and pray for those who persecute you" (Matthew 5:44, ESV).

"If the world hates you, know that it has hated me before it hated you. If you were of the world, the world would love you as its own; but because you are not of the world, but I chose you out of the world, therefore the world hates you" (John 15:18-19, ESV).

"I have said all these things to you to keep you from falling away. They will put you out of the synagogues. Indeed, the hour is coming when whoever kills you will think he is offering service to God" (John 16:1-2, ESV).

Indeed, Jesus said to the Pharisees, "Therefore I send you prophets and wise men and scribes, some of whom you will kill and crucify, and some you will flog in your synagogues and persecute from town to town" (Matthew 23:34, ESV).

Someone asks, "But why?" The response is given, "It's just the way it is." But there is far more to it than just that!

3. WHY SHOULD I BE OPPOSED FOR DOING GOOD?

Section One of this book clearly establishes that there is a difference of *nature* between the regenerated child of God and the unregenerated child of the devil. Someone illustrated the difference by saying,

"Christian, be careful who you marry because you don't want the devil as your father-in-law!"

We should never forget there is an enormous difference between God's people and the devil's people . . . between those in the kingdom of heaven and those in the kingdom of darkness. This vast difference is demonstrated in our much different approaches to life . . . and in our battle over which philosophy should prevail in society.

Jesus warned us there would be a backlash to Bible teachings—that "tribulation or persecution arises on account of the word" (Matthew 13:21, ESV). The Bible not only contains truth, but we believe it is truth! Absolute truth! Take-it-to-the bank truth! But the world does not like to be faced with such plain Bible teachings as heaven and hell, salvation through faith, the depravity of man, as well as the sovereignty of God.

Second, the devil hates the child of God. Not just a little either! The Bible teaches about the end-time, "So the dragon was furious with the woman and went off to wage war against the rest of her offspring—those who keep the commands of God and hold firmly to the testimony about Jesus" (Revelation 12:17, CSB). The devil declared war on God's people . . . for acting like God's people!

One preacher points out, "If God says, 'I love football,' the devil would counter, 'I hate football.'" Such hatred against God also extends to God's people.

Third, and perhaps somewhat surprisingly, God Himself has determined it is best for us to face opposition, even persecution. Paul testified, "For I think God has displayed us, the apostles, in last place, like men condemned to die: We have become a spectacle to the world, both to angels and to people" (1 Corinthians 4:9, CSB).

One of the rules of life states, "Easy times create easy men." Difficult times, though, separate the committed from the uncommitted. That is why Paul admonishes Timothy, "Don't be ashamed of the testimony about our Lord, or of me his prisoner. Instead, share in suffering for the gospel, relying on the power of God" (2 Timothy 1:8, CSB). Paul encourages Timothy (and us) to "Rise up and share my suffering! Such suffering will refine you into a better man of God."

Peter expresses the same theme when he writes, "Therefore, since Christ suffered in the flesh, arm yourselves also with the same understanding—because the one who suffers in the flesh is finished with sin—in order to live the remaining time in the flesh no longer for human desires, but for God's will" (1 Peter 4:1-2, CSB).

The end of Peter's life exemplified that very verse. Peter was crucified for the cause of Christ. However, he left us with these words, "The God of all grace, who called you to his eternal glory in Christ, will himself restore, establish, strengthen, and support you after you have suffered a little while. To him be dominion forever. Amen" (1 Peter 5:10-11, CSB).

Consider this expression again, "The dominion belongs to Him forever." Those words establish who the winners are and who the losers are. It also establishes that even "the fiery trials" are under His control. That's why He is able to slip alongside us *after* the suffering and "personally restore, establish, strengthen and support" us. Hallelujah for His being there with us!

Yes, God sometimes wants us to experience pain so that we may "experience the surpassing value" of knowing Jesus Christ, our Lord. I do not say it is easy, but God says it is sometimes necessary.

4. HOW SHOULD I RESPOND TO OPPOSITION, EVEN PERSECUTION?

Some of the loneliest words in the Bible are found in Ezekiel 1:1. The prophet writes, "I was among the captives by the river of Chebar." A crushed Ezekiel no longer lived in the Promised Land of Israel. He had been transported to the heathen land of Babylon, along with thousands of Hebrew captives. He was not a free man but rather a captive of the enemy. That enemy had pounded Israel to a pulp. His homeland was ruined. Though surrounded by many countrymen, he was still alone in spirit; his life would seemingly never again be the same.

But it is important to note that those words appear in the *first* half of verse one. The *rest* of verse one declares, "Then the heavens were opened and I, Ezekiel, saw visions of God." The defeated Ezekiel then became the victorious Ezekiel. He took his pen and wrote and wrote and kept writing . . . forty-eight remarkable chapters in all, which include the future restoration of Israel to the entire land promised to Abraham.

Though Ezekiel had been deported by the opposition, he was still in God's plan. Ezekiel did not stop living for Jehovah. Instead, he kept living for Jehovah. It may be trite to say, "When life gives you a lemon, make lemonade," but that is exactly what he did.

Opposition did not change Ezekiel. We should not allow opposition to change us, either.

Winston Churchill reminds us, "You will never reach your destination if you stop and throw stones at every dog that barks."

We must instead keep our eyes on the goal, and that goal is to honor Jesus Christ by promoting Him to the opposition. The only solution for Planet Earth is Jesus Christ! He alone is the Prince of Peace!

Therefore, we plant our flag in the soil, and we take our stand.

Edmund Burke correctly frames the issue when he writes, "The only thing necessary for evil to triumph is for good people to do nothing." Speaking for myself, I think I will do something, how about you?

> "Stand up, stand up for Jesus, Ye soldiers of the cross;
> Lift high His royal banner, It must not suffer loss."
>
> George Duffield, Jr.

Evangelist Glenn Mathews exhorts,

> Listen, you can be right with God and experience great difficulties. You need to remember that. Did Abel who was righteous deserve to be killed by his brother Cain? No, but he

was. Did Joseph deserve to be sold into slavery in Egypt? No, but he was. Did Shadrach, Meshach, and Abednego deserve to be thrown into a fiery furnace? No, but they were. Did Daniel deserve to be thrown into a den of lions? No, but he was. Did Joshua and Caleb deserve to wait forty years to go into the land of Canaan? No, but they did. Did the apostle Paul deserve the persecution that he encountered, afloat in the Mediterranean, three times beaten with rods, stoned and left for dead? Did Paul deserve that? No, and the list goes on and on. Yet the mentality of Christianity today is not Christ-focused but people-focused, and that's the wrong focus. (*Expositions That Matter*, p. 47)

The apostles became more and more Christ-focused as they matured. But have you ever considered what happened to the apostles? Each of them stood firmly against the tidal wave of this world system.

Andrew, the one who brought Peter to Jesus, led the wife of a governor to salvation in Christ. The enraged governor proceeded to crucify Andrew on an X-shaped cross. Andrew hung on the cross for two days. It is said that he preached Christ and encouraged the believers until the end.

Barnabas, the missionary companion of Paul, was stoned to death, perhaps in Cyprus. The "son of encouragement" met his end in a very discouraging manner.

Bartholomew, also known as Nathaniel, began his ministry by asking in bewilderment, "Jesus, how do you know me? We've never met." Jesus answered, "I saw you while you were still under the fig tree. I know all about you." Nathaniel obediently followed Jesus and was flayed to death in the end.

The apostle Matthew, author of the first gospel, was killed with the sword, supposedly in Ethiopia.

Matthias, the replacement for Judas, was stoned and beheaded.

Peter was crucified upside down. He elected that method of execution because he did not believe he was worthy of being executed upright like his Lord.

Paul was beheaded in Rome. As his head fell to the floor, God picked it up and placed a crown of righteousness upon it.

Phillip was known for bringing many people to Jesus. In the end, Phillip was hanged by the neck.

Simon the Zealot was sawn in two.

Doubting Thomas became Certain Thomas and died on his knees while praying. Someone thrust a spear through his body. He finished his prayer in heaven!

Always remember: *God's people have never been viewed as sacred* and, therefore, "not to be touched" by the devil or the world. We never have, and we never will. Nor have we ever truly been in the majority. . . and we never will be in this earthly life.

But here is what we can do! "Hold firmly to the message of life. Then I can boast in the day of Christ that I didn't run or labor for nothing" (Philippians 2:16, HCSB).

Thank God, we know how the story will end!

> *You are being protected by God's power through faith for a salvation that is ready to be revealed in the last time. You rejoice in this, though now for a short time you have had to struggle in various trials so that the genuineness of your faith—more valuable than gold, which perishes though refined by fire—may result in praise, glory, and honor at the revelation of Jesus Christ." (1 Peter 1:5-7, HCSB)*

How wonderful! Let us, therefore, grow *through* whatever opposition, even persecution, comes our way!

14

GROWING THROUGH HUMILITY

He also told this parable to some who trusted in themselves that they were righteous and looked down on everyone else: 'Two men went up to the temple to pray, one a Pharisee and the other a tax collector. The Pharisee was standing and praying like this about himself: 'God, I thank you that I'm not like other people—greedy, unrighteous, adulterers, or even like this tax collector. I fast twice a week; I give a tenth of everything I get.' But the tax collector, standing far off, would not even raise his eyes to heaven but kept striking his chest and saying, 'God, have mercy on me, a sinner!' I tell you, this one went down to his house justified rather than the other; because everyone who exalts himself will be humbled, but the one who humbles himself will be exalted.' (Luke 18:9-14, CSB)

"Growing through Humility" sounds contradictory because growing has the idea of *moving up*, whereas humility has the idea of *moving down*. But this chapter is not talking about the ways of the world. This chapter is talking about the ways of the living God.

In God's world, humility and pride cannot co-exist. God has always had a problem with those who want the throne for themselves. The Bible teaches that the devil was the first such being. The powerful angel Lucifer became Satan when he abandoned humility, choosing instead to exalt himself through pride and uttered his five "I will's" in Isaiah chapter fourteen. That one single act started a war that has ruined the entire universe.

The devil's error has become ingrained in the rest of God's creation. In so many ways, the creature has traded the Creator for the creation, most notably, for himself. As a result, we tend to forget the words of the author C. S. Lewis, "True humility is not thinking less of yourself; it is thinking of yourself less."

This chapter flies in the face of our world's philosophy. That shouldn't surprise us because God's philosophy is a complete reversal of the world's.

Never forget: The way up with God is always down for "everyone who exalts himself will be humbled, but the one who humbles himself will be exalted."

Let's explore seven questions that can refine our spirit into a humble spirit.

1. WHO AM I BEFORE GOD?

We begin with this question because it quickly establishes who *is* on the throne as well as who *is not* on the throne. It is hard to be humble, especially in a world that pushes competition and fame. Today's promoters emphasize branding yourself to get your name out there. "Declare yourself to be the expert and make certain everyone knows it!" "The fastest rat wins the rat race!"

Quite frankly, everything is messed up from the top to the bottom. For instance, how can it be true that "Nice guys finish last"? That should not be!

One supervisor told me, "If I don't promote myself, no one else will." He promoted himself to such an extent that he diminished his staff. Another associate advertised himself as an "Award-Winning Speaker" but exactly which award was open for discussion.

In my case, suppose next Tuesday (or any Tuesday) I sell five copies of this particular book on Amazon; those five sales would place this book in the Top Ten *in its category* on Amazon's best-selling list. I could then advertise my book as a "Bestseller!"

Ah, there is so much self-promotion in our world. "Hey, everyone! Look at me!" How foolish it is! Everyone is trying to out-do everyone else.

The one being, though, who is being overlooked in this personal emphasis is God. The apostle Paul places this entire issue in perspective when he writes,

> *For we don't dare classify or compare ourselves with some who commend themselves. But in measuring themselves by themselves and comparing themselves to themselves, they lack understanding. We, however, will not boast beyond measure but according to the measure of the area of ministry that God has assigned to us, which reaches even to you (2 Corinthians 10:12-13, CSB).*

Paul emphasizes two items worthy of our consideration. First, we should not compare ourselves to other people. In so doing, we're comparing ourselves with the wrong item. Second, we should be content with whatever ministry God has imparted to us. In other words, we should place our focus on the correct question: *Who am I before God?* In reality, our answer to that question will settle everything else in this discussion.

A successful businessman climbed up on his soapbox and announced to anyone who cared to listen, "I am a self-made man." Luke chapter twelve records that man's story. This man was so self-made that he built bigger barns for his bigger harvests. But one night God said to him, "Mr. Self-Made Businessman, you're just a teeny-weeny fool in My sight. I require your soul on this very night. You are going to die! Wonder who will inherit your bank account?"

I am stunned at the insolence of people saying, "I know more than anyone else." The audacity of the teenager who says, "I don't need any advice from the old man or the old woman." The presumption of the scientist who closes his mind to the opening words of Genesis. The insolence of the psychologist who ignores man's spiritual nature, for man, the Bible says, is a living soul or a living spirit.

In contrast, the humble child of God confesses, "I am not a self-made man, but I am His workmanship (we get our English word "poem" from this Greek word), created in Christ Jesus unto good works" (Ephesians 2:10). The humble Christian believes, "If God chooses to promote me like Daniel, so be it! And if not, so be it! I am the servant of the Most High."

Based upon God's greatness, one should not be surprised that "God opposes the proud but gives grace to the humble" (James 4:6, ESV).

---

*There is only one great Being in this universe
and that is our God.*

Job encountered that very God in a life-changing way, but it is important to realize that he did not encounter God until *after* he encountered his so-called friends. Job debated his wife, Eliphaz, Bildad, Zophar, and the youngster Elihu for more than thirty chapters. During those debates, Job managed to hold his own against his friends. On one occasion, Job even said, "I want to defend myself before God" (Job 13:3). "Job was righteous in his own eyes" (Job 32:1).

But Job's attitude changed when God arrived upon the scene. The man of many words became speechless!

God stirred up a whirlwind, maybe a miniature tornado, just to show Job that He could do something which Job could not do. Then God thundered out of the whirlwind,

> *Get ready to answer me like a man; when I question you, you will inform me. Where were you when I established the earth? Tell me, if you have understanding. Who fixed its dimensions? Certainly you know! Who stretched a measuring line across it? What supports its foundations? Or who laid its cornerstone while the morning stars sang together and all the sons of God shouted for joy? Who enclosed the sea behind doors when it burst from the womb, when I made the clouds its garment and total darkness its blanket, when I determined its boundaries and put its bars and doors in place, when I declared: 'You may come this far, but no farther; your proud waves stop here'? (Job 38:3-11, CSB)*

There are many, so many like me, but *there is only one like Him!* Therefore, like Job and any sensible person, "I respond properly to His greatness by repenting. I sit in the dust and ashes of my repentance" (Job 42:6).

The only intelligent course is to humble myself before the Almighty.

"A king's heart is like channeled water in the Lord's hand: He directs it wherever he chooses" (Proverbs 21:1). How can anyone dare to stand against a God with that much power?

> *What should we say then? Is there injustice with God? Absolutely not! For he tells Moses, I will show mercy to whom I will show mercy, and I will have compassion on whom I will have compassion. So then, it does not depend on human will or effort but on God who shows mercy. For the Scripture tells Pharaoh, I raised you up for this reason so that I may display my power in you*

and that my name may be proclaimed in the whole earth. So then, he has mercy on whom he wants to have mercy and he hardens whom he wants to harden. (Romans 9:14-18, CSB)

But who are you, a mere man, to talk back to God? Will what is formed say to the one who formed it, 'Why did you make me like this?' Or has the potter no right over the clay, to make from the same lump one piece of pottery for honor and another for dishonor? (Romans 9:20-21, CSB)

May I repeat what I wrote earlier? *The only intelligent course is to humble myself before the Almighty.* He is greater than the universe because He created the universe. He is greater than the greatest man because He is infinite, and man is finite. He is greater than any part of creation because He is the one true God!

Therefore, we should build our life upon this next verse and, in so doing, we will enjoy a very blessed life! "What does the LORD require of you but to do justice, and to love kindness, and to walk humbly with your God?" (Micah 6:8, ESV).

A right relationship with God will set the stage for a right relationship with everyone else.

2. WHO AM I BEFORE MYSELF?

Man, at his best, is still nothing but a man. I can compare myself with many things, including God and the other items in this chapter, but in many ways, the "Me Test" is the most disappointing evaluation of all.

The results in the "Me Test" prove I do not even measure up to my own expectations. I still make mistakes, even some mistakes that fall into the sin category. It is true that I have sinned and fallen short of the glory of God, but it is also true that I have sinned, made mistakes, and fallen short of my own expectations. This knowledge humbles me greatly.

Am I alone in this knowledge? I don't think so. I have failed, you have failed, and that means we both need to walk humbly, always cognizant of the Bible warning that "whoever thinks he stands must be careful not to fall" (1 Corinthians 10:12, CSB). The warning is appropriate because falling is very human.

Just a few hours ago, my wife and I discussed a famous artist. (We were in a home just recently which possessed some of the artist's works.) My wife researched the artist on the internet then reported that the artist died from alcohol intoxication. This one who was on top had come down . . . all the way down. The same cycle is repeated regularly in life. No matter how important we may be, we are still apt to fail.

Someone wrote, "To be humble is also to recognize that you're going to make mistakes, but that you can learn from those mistakes and do better. When you lose that humility, mistakes always become someone else's fault."

Life teaches all of us that there will always be someone who can do it better than we can. Hopefully, my church's next pastor will be better than I am. But at the same time, I am human, and I do not want my contribution to be forgotten.

How well do I deal with pride? Well, far too often, I don't.

During the 1980s, our church was invited to attend an organizational meeting to create a new association of churches. I was privileged to preach the first sermon in the new association's history (they obviously wanted us to join). I learned a lesson about myself on that day that still makes me groan.

I walked into the auditorium and seated myself behind a group of what appeared to be preachers. I introduced myself, and they introduced themselves. As I recall, there were four of them. One was the pastor; the other three were associate pastors of the same church. I only knew about the church by its name and possessed no other knowledge of it.

But there they were! Four preachers in one church! That meant they had to be in a much bigger church than mine! As a young pastor, I was intimidated by their presence. It was obvious from the way they conducted themselves that they were really important and must have a great church.

I found myself sinking down in the pew, wondering, "They probably look down their nose at my little church. We're only averaging forty people on Sunday morning."

I finally got the courage to ask, "How many does your church average?" Guess who then sunk in his pew? It was as if I had stuck a pin in their balloon. I immediately noticed something was wrong; indeed, perhaps my opinion of them was wrong.

Finally, the pastor said, "We average twenty in our church. But in our church, we emphasize quality rather than quantity."

And I could feel myself rising in my pew, fluffing my feathers, and thinking, "My forty beats your twenty!"

Isn't that comical? It's comical because *all five of us* had a problem with pride and humility.

Wonder, though, what God thought of that whole proceeding? Wonder if God thought we had lost our minds?

Guess what? I had failed the "Me Test" big-time. That's not the only time I have fallen short of my own expectations.

Recognizing my weaknesses, failures, and lack of ability has helped me walk more humbly before my fellow man. Quite honestly, it has been a lifetime journey. I have learned, "If I walk humbly, I won't have as far to fall." Plus, the pain at the bottom will be more manageable, too!

3. WHO AM I BEFORE OTHERS?

Let's move from the "Me Test" to the "Others Test." What is my relationship to others? Am I justified in seeing myself superior to others? And others inferior to me?

This stage of human conditioning begins to manifest itself in our hearts around the age of six or seven. We begin comparing ourselves with others and developing a sense of superiority or inferiority. The issue continues to magnify itself as we become older. If left unchecked, it manifests itself (in some people) in its most animalistic form in ethnic cleansing or genocide.

This issue cuts to the heart of how we truly see ourselves. Four Bible passages provide much-needed illumination for the modern man as well as the man of the future.

The first passage is from the beginning pages of Genesis. In other words, it establishes a principle that should continue throughout time. "Then the LORD said to Cain, 'Where is Abel your brother?' He said, 'I do not know; am I my brother's keeper?'" (Genesis 4:9, ESV). The Bible's answer is a loud unequivocal yes. No man is ever too high to become low—low enough to deal with the needs of his fellow man. Many wealthy people live in gated communities, but the worse situation of all is those who live in a gated heart.

God makes it plain in one of His earliest teachings that all of us have a responsibility to our fellow man. No one should ever see himself as being above that responsibility.

The second passage includes our Lord's example. Jesus told the apostles,

> *You know that the rulers of the Gentiles lord it over them, and those in high positions act as tyrants over them. It must not be like that among you. On the contrary, whoever wants to become great among you must be your servant, and whoever wants to be first among you must be your slave; just as the Son of Man did not come to be served, but to serve, and to give his life as a ransom for many. (Matthew 20:25-28, CSB)*

A man who is full of himself will do a lousy job serving others because good service always begins with a servant's attitude. Jesus described himself meeting a man who was full of himself:

For I was hungry and you gave Me nothing to eat; I was thirsty and you gave Me nothing to drink; I was a stranger and you didn't take Me in; I was naked and you didn't clothe Me, sick and in prison and you didn't take care of Me. (Matthew 25:42-43, CSB)

Samuel Johnson rightly says, "The true measure of a man is how he treats someone who can do him absolutely no good."

That principle is exemplified for us in the story of the Good Samaritan. One day a lawyer tried to justify himself before Jesus. The lawyer asked brashly, "Who is my neighbor?" It seems that he viewed himself as being superior to the common man.

Jesus replied, 'A man was going down from Jerusalem to Jericho, and he fell among robbers, who stripped him and beat him and departed, leaving him half dead. Now by chance a priest was going down that road, and when he saw him he passed by on the other side. So likewise a Levite, when he came to the place and saw him, passed by on the other side. But a Samaritan, as he journeyed, came to where he was, and when he saw him, he had compassion. He went to him and bound up his wounds, pouring on oil and wine. Then he set him on his own animal and brought him to an inn and took care of him. And the next day he took out two denarii and gave them to the innkeeper, saying, 'Take care of him, and whatever more you spend, I will repay you when I come back.' Which of these three, do you think, proved to be a neighbor to the man who fell among the robbers?' He said, 'The one who showed him mercy.' And Jesus said to him, 'You go, and do likewise.' (Luke 10:30-37, ESV)

The words, "You go and do likewise," indicates that we are not able to walk away from others. "Do likewise" like the Good Samaritan. "Do likewise" like the One who has been the Good Samaritan to all of us lowly humans: Jesus Christ.

I cannot treat others like Jesus unless I am humble like Jesus. I must recognize that all of us are in this world together.

4. WHO AM I BEFORE JESUS?

An old preacher recounted an experience in his early ministry. He had become deeply bothered because someone slandered him. The evil treatment put him in a sour mood for three days. Then the Lord visited him. The Lord asked, "What are you troubled about?"

He said, "My reputation, Lord. You know I am trying to live a blameless life. But I've been slandered and abused."

The Lord said, "You're worried about your reputation? I voluntarily laid My reputation aside when I came to the earth. And here you are crying over yours!"

Who am I before Jesus, who loved me and gave Himself for me?

The Bible says, "Then Pilate went back into the headquarters, summoned Jesus, and said to him, 'Are you the King of the Jews?'" (John 18:33, CSB). It is easy to picture the scene. Jesus stands (probably bound) before Pilate. The soldiers stand at attention on each side. Pilate is dressed in his legal robe. A bloodthirsty crowd behind Jesus both hurls insults and announces charges against Jesus. It is a very ugly scene.

Yes, Jesus stands before Pilate. But who is really standing before whom? *Isn't it more a case that Pilate is standing before Jesus?* Isn't it more of a case that the soldiers, the Jews, and all of humanity are standing before Jesus?

Jesus put the entire issue in its proper perspective when He said, "You would have no authority over Me unless it had been given you from above; for this reason he who delivered Me up to you has the greater sin" (John 19:11, NASB). Pilate was inferior to Jesus in ability, office, and authority!

What about the Jews? Jesus had previously said, "You may destroy the temple of My body, but in three days I will rise from the grave" (John 2:19). The Jews were inferior to Jesus in theology, origin, and power!

What about me? What about you? One preacher summarized it quite well when He said, "If the President entered this room, we would all stand. But if Jesus entered this room, we would all kneel."

Why? Because He is King of Kings and Lord of Lords (Revelation 19:16). "The next time you see me, I, the Son of Man, will be sitting at the right hand of power and coming on the clouds of heaven!" (Matthew 27:64). *Riding on the clouds!* Then, and only then, will all men finally know! And every knee shall indeed bow . . .

> "Crown him the Lord of Heaven,
> Enthroned in worlds above,
> Crown him the King to whom is given
> The wondrous name of Love.
> Crown him with many crowns,
> As thrones before him fall;
> Crown him, ye kings, with many crowns,
> For he is King of all.
>
> Crown him the Lord of years,
> The Potentate of time,
> Creator of the rolling spheres,
> Ineffably sublime.
> All hail, Redeemer, hail!
> For thou has died for me;
> Thy praise and glory shall not fail
> Throughout eternity."
>
> Matthew Bridges

He is my Lord. And to Him, I freely and gladly belong . . . and submit!

5. Who Am I Before the Cross?

It has been correctly said that all men are equal at the foot of the cross. We are equal despite our background, deeds, education, income, or century. We are also equal in our sin and our need for grace. We are equally helpless in the eyes of God. "For while we were still helpless, at the appointed moment, Christ died for the ungodly" (Romans 5:6, HCSB).

The gospel message includes a call for a very humble admission on the part of sinners. The three words, "I have sinned" are generally recognized as the three hardest-to-say words in the Bible. It is difficult for many people to acknowledge their innate sinfulness. *Such an acknowledgment also includes the principle that they are impotent to save themselves.* They can bring nothing to the cross except a broken, sinful life. They must come admitting that grace is the only means of salvation. The message of the cross is not, "Do and live," but rather, "I, Jesus, have done all that needs to be done. Believe in Me and live."

"For by grace you have been saved through faith, and that not of yourselves; it is the gift of God. Not as a result of works, that no one should boast" (Ephesians 2:8-9, NASB).

One of my favorite songs is "Rock of Ages." It includes the line, *"Nothing in my hands I bring, simply to Thy cross I cling."* Those words carry enormous weight. I felt the sense of those words when I received Christ as my Savior on January 14, 1965. I have accomplished many wonderful things in the years since that date. I have been blessed with a good career in secular business, as well as God's work. I have raised three beautiful children. So much could be mentioned! But even now, I still confess those same words, "Nothing in my hands I bring, simply to Thy cross I cling."

I have never attained a single accomplishment on my own which will earn salvation. Not a single one!

The cross humbles me.

6. WHO AM I BEFORE GOD'S CHURCH?

It is a great privilege to be a part of God's local church. My church membership requires me to deal with people. How should I view the people in God's church? Perhaps I know more Bible than they do, or perhaps I can give more money than they do. How do those items affect my relationship with them?

It is important to recognize the Bible uses specific titles to describe the people in God's church. These titles are not military titles such as general and private. They are not business titles like president and clerk.

The Bible uses titles like one would naturally expect in God's church. For example, the people are addressed as brothers and sisters. In other words, we are family. We are addressed as fellow laborers (1 Corinthians 3:9). We are addressed as sheep (1 Peter 5:2). We are part of the same fellowship or partnership (1 John 1:3). (Note: What is a fellowship? The most common definition is a bunch of fellows in the same ship!) It is a body (1 Corinthians 12). The parts of the body are very dependent upon the other parts. We are also living stones (1 Peter 2:5) in the sense that each one of us is a building block in God's church.

None of these titles suggests the superiority of any person or position within God's church. The apostles and prophets qualified to be part of the church's foundation (Ephesians 2:20), but they also furnished us with wonderful examples of true, selfless humility. Their lives were devoted to serving others rather than being served. It appears they died without a pension or a savings account. But what an impact!

Indeed, they taught us by their example that the way up with God is down with self. "God resists the proud but gives grace to the humble" (James 4:6, CSB).

Evangelist Fred Brown taught us in the 1970s, "Make much of Jesus, and He will make much of you." Fred's advice is confirmed throughout the Word of God.

That is why Matthew Henry asked, "Shall those take upon them the form of princes who call themselves followers of Him that took upon Him the form of a servant?"

That explains why the apostle John singled out Diotrephes as a power-hungry individual who needed to be curtailed.

I wrote something to the church, but Diotrephes, who loves to have first place among them, does not receive our authority. This is why, if I come, I will remind him of the works he is doing, slandering us with malicious words. And he is not satisfied with that! He not only refuses to welcome fellow believers, but he even stops those who want to do so and expels them from the church. (3 John 9-10, CSB)

President Abraham Lincoln said, "Nearly all men can stand adversity, but if you want to test a man's character, give him power." Diotrephes failed the test. Wonder, though, about us?

7. WHO AM I BEFORE TIME AND ETERNITY?

Time flies. Whoever said that was not joking.

Can I stop time? No. Time is too big for me. But eternity is actually much, much bigger than time. If I cannot stop time, what shall I do when faced with eternity? If time is like a tidal wave sweeping down upon a beach, eternity must be the universe itself sweeping down upon the same beach.

I am now sixty-five years of age. I freely confess life has moved much too swiftly for me. It seems as if my graduation from high school was only yesterday. I preached my first sermon at Leatherwood Missionary Baptist Church in 1976. (The title was, "Jesus Is My Friend.") Wasn't that just yesterday? My first child was born in 1982. Wasn't that just yesterday? After all, I can still see one-year-old Ashley sitting patiently on my desk, watching me work on my sermons.

I am no match for time and eternity. I dare not enter the boxing ring with time and his sidekick eternity. It would be a very short match indeed. I find myself agreeing more and more with the Neil Diamond song, "Done Too Soon." I look at the notebooks of sermon ideas on my shelf, and I realize (even after forty-four years of preaching) I have more sermon ideas than I will ever preach. I wonder if these ideas will die with me or if someone will be able to use these preliminary thoughts and outlines.

What about you? Are you any better than me? Are you ready to take on time and eternity? Or are we both in the same boat? It's rather humbling, isn't it?

"Lord, make me aware of my end and the number of my days so that I will know how short-lived I am. In fact, you have made my days just inches long, and my life span is as nothing to you. Yes, every human being stands as only a vapor. *Selah"* (Psalm 39:4-5, CSB).

The psalmist asked God to teach him to number his days. Why? Because there is a definite number to our days! "There is a time to be born, but, lest we forget, there is also a time to die." Life will quickly be "done too soon" from our human point of view.

The proud man will die. The rich man will die. The genius will die. The investor will die. The athlete will die. The president will die. My parents will die. My children will die. And I will die. But time will remain . . . until the day God folds time into the endless eons of eternity.

And then what will we have left?

Ebenezer Erskine writes about his conversion, "On that day I got my head out of *time* and into *eternity.*"

That is why Jesus urges us, "Do not lay up for yourselves treasures on earth, where moth and rust destroy and where thieves break in and steal, but lay up for yourselves treasures in heaven, where neither moth nor rust destroys and where thieves do not break in and steal. For where your treasure is, there your heart will be also" (Matthew 6:19-21, ESV).

Let us close this chapter by praying the prayer of a humble saint.

"Have Thine Own way,
Hold o'er my being absolute sway.
Fill with Thy Spirit, Till all shall see
Christ only always, living in me!"

Adelaide A. Pollard

15

GROWING THROUGH UNCONDITIONAL LOVE

Jesus says, "I am giving a new commandment, a new charge to you. Keep loving one another. Keep loving one another as I Myself have loved you" (John 13:34). The biblical standard for treating one another is very imposing: *"as I Myself have loved you."* Therefore, the standard is not a merely human standard, even a wonderful motherly standard, but the biblical standard operates on a much higher level. It is even higher than an angelic standard. In its purest form, it is no less than a heavenly standard, for it is a level that originates solely within God Himself.

The songwriter Fanny Crosby alludes to different levels of love in her words,

> "There are depths of love that I cannot know
> Till I cross the narrow sea.
> There are heights of joy that I may not reach,
> Till I rest in peace with Thee."

"As I have loved you" is a very impressive level of love. As if that is not enough, Jesus took the new commandment one step further in the very next verse, "By means of one single act, sinful mankind will know that you are truly disciples of Me: It is the act of loving one another" (John 13:35). In other words, this love operates on such a high level that it will cause the world to sit up and take notice! Chafer comments that this love is "the indisputable evidence to the world of what is Christian reality."

Such love is much more than loving emotionally because the world understands that degree of love. Such love is rather the love of God Himself: the ability to love unconditionally or willfully.

1. GOD IS LOVE.

The scriptures reveal three truths about the nature of God. First, God is Spirit (John 4:24). He is not merely *a* spirit (it is true there is no definite article in the Greek text), but He exists *as* Spirit in His very nature or essence. Theologians like to use the term "incorporeal" to indicate that God is immaterial, and therefore, invisible to the naked eye, unable to be comprehended by fleshly, one-dimensional humanity. Being pure Spirit, He is unlimited by natural things such as space.

Second, the Bible declares, "God is light" or the opposite of darkness (1 John 1:5). The Bible makes it clear, "there is not even one iota of darkness in Him." God has never sinned, nor is He a partner in anyone's sin.

The third description is the one most pertinent to this chapter, "God is love" (1 John 4:8). Children have memorized those three words for generations. They are important for us adults, too! My pastor father taught me in my early days, "Preaching on hell will get the people's attention, but preaching on the love of God will get their hearts." He was right!

The phrase, "God is love" contains three of the most beautiful words in the entire Bible. Driven by curiosity, I checked twenty-eight translations of 1 John 4:8; twenty-seven translations use the same three identical words, "God is love." The fourth (Douay-Rheims Bible used in Catholic churches) uses a synonymous expression, "God is charity." Charity, of course, is the old English word for love. The point is well taken: God is love.

Do we truly comprehend the meaning of those three words? No, despite all of our study, I fear we barely scratch the surface of their meaning.

Lewis Sperry Chafer explains,

> This does not mean that He has attained to love or that He maintains it by an effort. He is love by reason of His essential nature and the source of all the true love which is found in the universe. However, love means, among other things, capacity to be indignant and to react in judgment upon that which is opposed to it unlawfully.
>
> Even human love is not subject to control by the human will. An individual cannot make himself love what he does not love, nor can he by any ability lodged within himself cause whatever love he experiences to cease. Thus, it is demonstrated that the presence of divine compassion in the believer's heart is none other than the direct exercise by God Himself of His own love through the believer as a channel. When there is some failure to be adjusted or in right relation to God, the divine love will not flow freely; but when right relation is sustained the flow of divine love is unhindered. Divine love is the dynamic, the motivating force in the spiritual life. (*Systematic Theology, Volume VI*, p. 205)

A father and son stood on a hilltop. The father directed his son's attention to the different landscape which existed in all four directions. He then waved his arm, turned completely around as if indicating everything in every direction, and said, "Son, God's love is as big as all of that."

The son immediately replied, "Then, Father, we must be in the middle of it!"

Where else would you rather be than in the middle of God's love?

2. THREE GREEK WORDS WORTH KNOWING

The New Testament was written in what is often referred to as *koine* or common Greek. For lack of a better term, the common Greek language of Bible times was a more naturalized version of the older classical Greek. Greek is an ideal language for the New Testament because it contains a dynamism that is lacking in our own English language.

That dynamism includes three Greek words that expressed "love" in Bible times. The first word does not appear even once in the Bible, but it deserves to be mentioned for the sake of full disclosure. It is the Greek word *eros*. We derive our English word "erotic" from *eros*. The word "erotic" conveys a meaning of deep sensuality, something which is very sexual or fleshly in nature, usually in a sinful way. Strangely, the apostle Paul does not use this term even once in describing the behavior of sinful men.

The second word is *phileo*. We were taught in grade school that the city of Philadelphia is known as the city of "brotherly love." Its name is taken from the Greek language. *Phileo* means "love," and *adelphos* means "brother."

Kenneth Wuest writes in his book *Golden Nuggets From The Greek New Testament* (p. 62), "'*Phileo*' is a love which consists of the glow of the heart kindled by the perception of that in the object which affords us pleasure. It is the response of the human spirit to what appeals to us as pleasurable. The word was used to speak of a friendly affection." In other words, we *phileo* something or someone because that something or someone brings us a degree of pleasure.

John 16:27 expresses this relationship very well: "The Father '*phileos*' you *because* you '*phileo*' Me." The order is important. The saints take pleasure in Jesus; therefore, the Father takes pleasure in them. "You like my child; as a result, I like you." Thus, we can reasonably say that *phileo* has a cause-effect relationship.

There is *nothing* negative about *phileo*. It is a much superior word to *eros* because *phileo* treats the object with respect and dignity. By contrast, *eros* is often concerned solely for self; it uses *or uses up* the object for personal satisfaction.

The third Greek word expresses the highest degree of love. It is used in the famous John 3:16 passage, "For God so *loved* the world!" The third Greek word is known by Bible students everywhere as *agape*. *Agape* love is viewed in the Bible as the highest degree of love. The Bible emphasizes its usage as a *God* kind of love because such love rises *above* man's capability.

For example, a mother loves her child but not the entire world, especially a world that seeks the death of her child. Yet "God so loved the world." The act of "giving up His Son" proves the degree of God's love.

Wuest explains, "God's love for a sinful and lost race springs from His heart in response to the high value He placed upon each human soul. Every sinner is exceedingly precious in His sight." (*Golden Nuggets From The Greek New Testament*, p. 61) Precious! But who assigned the exceedingly precious value to my otherwise worthless soul? It was a God of mercy and grace.

(Note: God did not choose to duplicate or extend this same degree of love to the fallen angels. Following Wuest's concept, we could say that God did not place the same precious value on the fallen angels that He sovereignly and graciously placed upon fallen man.)

In essence, this agape degree of love is
expressed in the act of loving the unlovable.

Those last three words, *loving the unlovable*, are the key to unlocking the depths of *agape*. *Agape* love is best regarded as love which exceeds every imaginable reason to love; in other words, *it is unconditional love*.

3. WHAT KIND OF LOVE ORIGINATES WITHIN GOD?

God is God, and there is no one like Him. As a result, we should expect superior results with God in every area. Based on Bible teaching, we will not be disappointed with God in the quality of His love.

Pink writes in *Gleanings in the Godhead* (p. 72),

> The love which one creature has for another is because of something in them; but the love of God is free, spontaneous, uncaused. The only reason God loves any is found in His own sovereign will: 'The Lord did not set his love upon you, nor choose you, because ye were more in number than any people; for ye were the fewest of all people: but because the Lord loved you' (Deuteronomy 7:7-8).
>
> Had God loved us in return for ours, then it would not be spontaneous on His part; but because He loved us when we were loveless, it is clear that His love was uninfluenced. God's love for me, and for each of 'His own,' was entirely unmoved by anything in them. What was there in me to attract the heart of God? Absolutely nothing. But, to the contrary, everything to repel Him, everything calculated to make Him loathe me— sinful, depraved, a mass of corruption, with 'no good thing' in me.

Phillip Bliss asks,

> "What was there in me that could merit esteem,
> Or give the Creator delight?
> 'Twas even so, Father, I ever must sing,
> Because it seemed good in thy sight.'"

John 3:16 says, "For God so loved the world." What kind of world did God so incredibly love?

We have this idea that God loved us because we were so adoringly lovable. As a result, God could not keep Himself away from us.

We visualize God as being the young man who sees a beautiful young lady walking down the sidewalk. This young man immediately falls in love, because she is very attractive, looks like she would be a nice companion, and appears to be intelligent. Surely there is not a single thing wrong with her!

The young man then does everything to win her heart. He sends her flowers, takes her out to eat, and buys her jewelry.

We see ourselves as being the beautiful young woman that God is trying to win for Himself, but that illustration is not so according to the Bible.

When the Bible says, "For God so loved the world," it does not mean the world of wonderful, kind, generous people who deserve God's very best. It means instead, the world of rebellious, sinful, God-hating, Christ-crucifying people who deserve God's very worst!

We must begin by understanding what we are to God. The book of Romans chapter five gives us some much-needed clarity on this subject.

The first description is revealed in the word "helpless" in verse six. Romans 5:6 says, "In due time," which is another way of saying in God's time or at the perfectly appointed time, "when we were without strength"—powerless, weak, down on the mat, and unable to pick ourselves up.

We are described as helpless. It is the idea that we are *not able* to help ourselves. We're like the bedfast person who cannot feed himself, bathe himself, or go to the bathroom by himself. We're like the blind man who must be led every step of the way. We are utterly helpless when it comes to lifting ourselves to God so that we might meet His holy standards.

We're like a worm that can never rise to a man's level. That is why Isaac Watts writes:

> "Alas, and did my Savior bleed
> And did my Sovereign die,
> Would He devote that sacred head,
> For such a worm as I?"

John 3:16 says, "For God so loved the *worms*," and those worms are you and me. Would you die for a worm? Of course not, but that is what the plan of salvation truly is!

271

Based upon our identity as being nothing but worms, it would not be a surprise if John 3:16 read, "For God so *hated* the world that He condemned the world."

Let's move on. The second description is revealed in the word "ungodly" in this same verse. The word begins with the two letters "un." Those two letters negate the letters that follow. In other words, those two letters mean the opposite of the letters that follow.

For example, the word unattractive means the opposite of attractive. The word unknown means the opposite of known. Likewise, ungodly means we are just the opposite of godly. *We are the very opposite of everything God is.* Whatever God thinks, we think the opposite. If God says turn left, we turn right. Whatever God hates, we love. Whatever God loves, we hate.

Why? Because we are ungodly or the opposite of God in our nature!

I must ask myself, "Would I die for someone who is the very opposite of everything I am and everything I believe in?" But Jesus did!

One night a twenty-two-year-old man named Bob attended the Union Gospel Mission in downtown Chattanooga. One of my professors, Wymal Porter, shared the gospel during that night's church service. Bob responded and came forward for counseling.

Bob said, "I'm too bad to have salvation. I've been drunk for two solid years. I have done some terrible things. Your holy Christ could never die for someone as *ungodly* as me."

Bob repeatedly used the word "ungodly" in his discussion. Wymal caught hold of that word. He opened his Bible to Romans 5:6 and let Bob read the great news that Christ died for the ungodly. That verse was all it took. Bob accepted Christ. He drank no alcohol during his next six months at the city mission then moved on to begin a new chapter in his life. Yes, Christ died for the ungodly!

The third description is revealed in the word "sinners" in verse eight. The verse says, "God makes known His own love for us in that while we were still sinners Christ died for us." The English word "sin" comes to us from the Greek word *hamartia*. *Hamartia* has been defined as "missing the mark" as in missing the bull's-eye of God's righteousness.

God says, "If you want to know Me, you must hit the mark—the bull's-eye—of My righteousness or holiness." God's standard is a standard of 100% righteousness or holiness.

God is so perfect that there are no B's, C's, or D's in His grading scale. There are only two possible grades: A+ or F. Either 100% perfection or one has sinned and fallen short of the glory of God.

I remember convincing a teacher to change a grade on my report card from a B+ to an A-. I saw my B+ grade and did not like it one bit. I asked the teacher, "What was my average?"

She said, "It was a ninety-four."

I responded, "A ninety-four was an A- in last year's class."

She said, "A ninety-four is a B+ in my class."

Guess what she did? She decided that I was trying to do my best. She decided to encourage that behavior by changing my grade to an A-.

That is something no one will ever be able to do with God. God's grading scale is one of either perfect righteousness or zero righteousness. Either A+ or an F.

The angels in heaven have always hit 100% perfection. That is why they are allowed to live in heaven.

The demons and Satan were once the angels in heaven, *but they failed one time.* That one failure turned their grade from an A+ to an F. That was why God kicked them out of heaven. The Bible says, "God then created hell for the devil and his angels" (Matthew 25:41).

Here is man's problem: Not one person in the entire history of mankind has ever hit 100% perfection except the God-man Jesus Christ. That is why He and He alone could provide a perfect sacrifice for our sins.

Question: Would you die for a creation that is never, ever going to be worthy of you?

The fourth description is revealed in the word "enemies" in verse ten. The verse begins with the words, "For if while we were God's enemies."

An enemy is a person who is fighting you every inch of the way. An enemy is at war with you. An enemy is planning how to kill you and remove you as a threat.

We are inclined to love people who love us, but *God loved a people who hated Him!* God loved a people who were at war with Him and His Son, Jesus Christ. Who were those hateful people? It was people like you and me.

Governor Pilate asked at the trial of Jesus, "Why? What evil has this Jesus done?" But we cried out, "Crucify Him! He is worthy of death!" We then beat Him, spit upon Him, mocked Him, drove the nails, and then crucified Him!

Fathers, would you die for someone who raped and murdered your daughter? Mothers, would you die for someone who ruined your son's mind with drugs and alcohol? Children, would you die for someone who is currently abusing your dear, sweet mother in a nursing home? Our emotions would scream, "No!" Our emotions would not be full of love but of anger, hate, and revenge.

In other words, the love of God is so deep in its depth that it runs *contrary* to emotions. *God loved sinful man despite His emotion.* What was that emotion? "God said, 'My heart is grieved that I have made man'" (Genesis 6:6). "God is a righteous judge, and a God who feels indignation every day" (Psalm 7:11, ESV). The King James Version expresses the same verse as, "God is angry with the wicked every day." Grieved, indignation, angry. Not one of those words expresses a happy, pleasant emotion.

I am writing from a purely human perspective when I write that *God had to overpower His emotions with a greater will:* the will to love that which did not deserve to be loved.

That is exactly what God did when, "God so loved the world," because it was His own enemies that He loved! For God so loved a world which so hated Him! That is how much God loved us!

Jesus looked down from the cross, and He prayed, "Father, forgive them for they know not what they do." In other words, "Don't send a million angels and destroy them for what they have done."

In so doing, God fully demonstrated how much He could love. He loved His enemies in order to make them His friends. He then says to us, "If God so loved us, we ought also to love one another."

This kind of love originates within the heart of God. *Everyone that loves like God also loves the helpless, the ungodly, the sinners, even the enemies . . .* and "everyone that loves like God loves can know that he has been born again of God and knows God" (1 John 4:7).

4. "KEEP YOURSELF IN THE LOVE OF GOD."

My father's largest pastorate was not his largest church when he first arrived. It was a troubled church with low attendance and low morale. Many of the members were suspicious of one another. There was no outreach ministry. The services were quiet, and the fellowship restrained.

God led my father to an often-overlooked scripture. "Keep yourselves in the love of God, waiting expectantly for the mercy of our Lord Jesus Christ for eternal life" (Jude 21, CSB). "Keep yourself in the love of God" became Dad's motto for that church during his seven-year ministry. He preached it often but quoted it at the conclusion of practically *every* service.

Dad left the church in the early 1990s. Nearly thirty years have passed. Just recently, I talked with one of the old-timers from that church. He said, "Your father taught us how to love one another."

The formula in Jude 21 will work for anyone. Let's look closely at what it says.

The Greek word for "keep" is *tereo*. (Note: We previously examined *tereo* in chapter nine.) The word means to "preserve, guard, or watch over." Let's gain some background on *tereo* by examining how it is used elsewhere. Jesus used this same word when He prayed, "Holy Father, keep them in Your name, *the name* which You have given Me, that they may be one even as We *are*. While I was with them, I was keeping them in Your name which You have given Me; and I guarded them and not one of them perished but the son of perdition, so that the Scripture would be fulfilled" (John 17:11-12, NASB). We are informed twice that we are being kept, guarded, or preserved by God.

(Note: Some people erroneously believe they must keep themselves saved by some action on their part. The above scripture, though, makes it clear that it is God who does the keeping and not we ourselves. Any reasonable person would thank God for preserving his soul because a deep look within himself would reveal his utter inability to preserve himself. Even the *sarkikos* believer in chapter six is preserved by God.)

Let's look at another example. Jude uses *tereo* for the first time in his opening verse: "Jude, the servant of Jesus Christ, and brother of James, to them that are sanctified by God the Father, and preserved in Jesus Christ, and called." (KJV) On this occasion, the KJV uses "preserved" to translate *tereo*.

The verb *tereo* is a perfect tense verb in the opening verse of Jude. The perfect tense indicates a completed past action whose results continue into the present time. In theology, the perfect tense is often used by the Bible writer to express an action in the past which has created a permanent result. Based upon that reasoning, a literal translation of verse one reads, "we have been guarded and will continue to exist in a permanent state of being guarded." Greek scholar James D. Price wrote to me in personal correspondence that it is a "perfect passive participle, referring to Christ's continual preserving of the saints."

Jesus promised, "I *give* to them eternal life" (John 10:28). In addition, He promised "*eternal* life." And He finished His promise with "they shall *never* perish." Terence Peter Crosby read John 10:28, then said, "If the truly converted man can be lost, Jesus must have meant 'lend' when He said 'give,' 'temporary' when He said 'eternal' and 'perhaps' when He said 'never.' Uncertainty is the hallmark of man-made religion." Yes, we are kept, or preserved, by God's hand.

Then we come to Jude's words in verse twenty-one. On this occasion, Jude uses *tereo* in the aorist tense. James D. Price writes, "The aorist tense is the indefinite tense signifying nothing about completeness or duration. As an imperative, it just states *what must be done.* The emphasis is on the *necessity* of the deed, not on temporal relations."

The meaning is undoubtedly clear: The responsibility in verse twenty-one is in the hands of the believer. The ball is in the believer's court. *The believer and only the believer will decide where he chooses to live.* Will he live *in* the love of God or *outside* the love of God?

"Yourselves!" Jude's plea is addressed to more than the church leaders. It is addressed to all believers everywhere. This promise is available to everyone. It is addressed to those who have been hurt, injured, frightened, abused, cursed, persecuted, even horribly misused. Jude fearlessly declares, "There is no barrier too high, no river too wide, no valley too low for any believer to miss out on living in the love of God."

Some dear reader may be thinking, "But I have been so badly damaged in my life!" If that is so, you have my deepest sympathy! It may very well be that your greatest achievement of all will be one of moving from the hurt to the love. I say those words with all sincerity because "with God all things are possible."

"In" typically denotes "sphere" or "position." For example, I live *in* a house. However, I could live *in* the woods. Or I could live *in* a box on the beach. My childhood hero Tarzan lived *in* a treehouse. The cartoon character, Jerry the mouse, lived *inside* a wall.

The believer should choose his "house" carefully. He can choose to live in the house known as God's love or live in a house of lesser value, including even hate at the far extreme. The decision belongs to the believer and to the believer alone.

Suffice it to say, the believer's decision is a conscious decision. Such a decision is made by an act of the human will. We deliberately and intentionally choose the house. As we move through life, that house will permeate our thoughts, ambitions, and lifestyle.

"The love of God." Of the three words translated love (*agape, eros,* and *phileo*), which one appears in verse twenty-one? It is *agape. Agape* is the love of heaven, an unconditional love which loves even its enemies, the all-surpassing love of God Himself. John Calvin became so stirred by this concept that he writes, "He has made love as it were the guardian and the ruler of our life."

"The *agape* love of God." God invites all of His children to live in the house called Agape Love. There is only one of those houses in the entire universe. Just one full of agape love, though there are many which are full of phileo love or eros love. It is the one house where God Himself lives for, "God Himself is agape love."

What is agape love? As demonstrated above in Romans chapter five, *agape love is unconditional love!* The entire house is saturated with God's unconditional love from the front door to the back door, even from the basement to the attic. It is the house where we experience both *being* loved and *being able* to love on a level which far exceeds normal human living . . . a level of agape love that far exceeds phileo love.

Chafer writes, "It is the *normal* work of the Spirit to fill the one who is rightly adjusted to God." (*He That is Spiritual,* p. 67)

The entire process begins with our position (house), because, as indicated in chapter four, *position always precedes practice or lifestyle.* Position creates the opportunity and means to practice. As a believer, I must place myself in the sphere, position, or house of God's unconditional love. This act of progressive sanctification requires a conscious decision on my part. In which sphere do I wish to live today?

Chafer's words, "rightly adjusted to God," are the key to where we live. We can either be rightly adjusted or wrongly adjusted. Jesus says, "As the Father has loved me, I have also loved you. Remain in my love. If you keep my commands you will remain in my love, just as I have kept my Father's commands and remain in his love" (John 15:9-10, CSB).

How do I remain in God's Agape House? I must keep the commandments or the will of Jesus. That requires living in submission to Him. "Take My yoke upon you and learn of Me!"

What is the result of such a surrendered life? "But the fruit of the Spirit is love, joy, peace, patience, kindness, goodness, faithfulness, gentleness, self-control; against such things, there is no law" (Galatians 5:22-23, NASB). Living in God's house makes such fruit possible!

Living in God's house also makes unconditional love possible.

> *But a Samaritan on his journey came up to him, and when he saw the man, he had compassion. He went over to him and bandaged his wounds, pouring on olive oil and wine. Then he put him on his own animal, brought him to an inn, and took care of him. The next day he took out two denarii, gave them to the innkeeper, and said, 'Take care of him. When I come back I'll reimburse you for whatever extra you spend' (Luke 10:33-35, CSB)*

What a picture of unconditional love! Let me repeat Chafer's words,

---

"Thus, it is demonstrated that the presence of divine compassion in the believer's heart is none other than the divine exercise by God Himself of His own love through the believer as a channel."

H. A. Ironside writes,

It is as though I say to my child, 'Keep in the sunshine.' The sun shines whether we enjoy it or not. And so God's love abides unchanging. But we need to keep in the conscious enjoyment of it. Let nothing make the tried soul doubt that love. Circumstances cannot alter it. Difficulties cannot strain it, nor can our own failures. The soul needs to rely upon it, and thus be borne in triumph above the conflict and the discouraging episodes incident to the life of faith. (*Addresses on The Epistles of John and an Exposition of The Epistle of Jude*, p. 54)

An aged church member held a deep grudge against his pastor which eventually turned into hate. The church member became sick. The pastor determined within his heart that he would unconditionally love this irate man. He visited the man repeatedly.

During one visit, the pastor learned the man enjoyed the writings of the humorist Will Rogers. The pastor decided to bring a biography of Will Rogers on his future visits. It became the pastor's routine to read several pages from the biography, read a few verses of scripture, then have prayer.

In time the church member warmed up to the pastor's visits. The visits continued. Sometime later, the church member's health took a precipitous decline. He realized that death was near. He made his wife promise that she would have the pastor conduct his funeral.

He then said, "I love that man because he loved me when I hated him."

Unconditional love . . . it is possible because God has made it possible.

16

GROWING THROUGH GOD'S DISCIPLINE

One day Dagwood was taking a walk and happened across the neighborhood boy named Elmo. Elmo was holding his backside, crying crocodile tears, but still smiling. He said, "Mom just beat the living daylights out of me because I ate a piece of the cake that she baked for the church social."

Dagwood asked, "But why are you still smiling?"

Little Elmo smiled even bigger and said, "Because it proves she's my mother. She wouldn't have done that to a total stranger."

We live in an age when every man wants to do what is right in his own eyes, but that policy does not work very well for the child of God. Christians tend to forget that the child of God is *not* independent. The Bible teaches the child of God has "been bought with a price." That means God now *owns* the believer. God has become the believer's spiritual Father; therefore, He has the right, power, and responsibility to mold His child into what *He* wants the believer to be—not what the believer wants to be.

But what happens when I rebel against my Owner, and I insist upon having it my way? What does God then do?

God then intervenes with a Bible process known as "being disciplined" or "being chastened." (Note: The old translations use the word "chastisement" in place of "discipline.") In a nutshell, this Bible process closely parallels the discipline experience which occurs within our natural families.

What is the difference between punishment and discipline/chastisement? Charles Stanley writes, "Punishment is God executing His judgment upon the wicked. Discipline is God's correction of His children in order to protect them from further disobedience and harmful consequences."

Thus, discipline/chastisement is a "growing up" experience that brings the out-of-line Christian back inside the line. Quite naturally, we may find God's chastening to be painful, even grievous. King David, though, puts God's discipline in its proper perspective when he writes, "Before I was afflicted (chastened) I went astray, but now after being disciplined I have kept Your law" (Psalm 119:67).

The subject of God's discipline is not often preached. Perhaps that is because there is not as much joy in such preaching. However, discipline is as much a part of the Christian's *growing* experience as it was in my own growing experience under Dad's roof.

I can honestly testify that my father was very patriotic. Dad applied the stripes, and I saw the stars! Dad's discipline was often necessary to restore me to the narrow way. Unfortunately, sometimes my Heavenly Father must do the same.

The most complete Bible passage regarding God's discipline of the believer is found in Hebrews 12:5-11. The text reads:

> *And have you forgotten the exhortation that addresses you as sons? 'My son, do not regard lightly the discipline of the Lord, nor be weary when reproved by*

him. For the Lord disciplines the one he loves and chastises every son whom he receives.' It is for discipline that you have to endure. God is treating you as sons. For what son is there whom his father does not discipline? If you are left without discipline, in which all have participated, then you are illegitimate children and not sons. Besides this, we have had earthly fathers who disciplined us and we respected them. Shall we not much more be subject to the Father of spirits and live? For they disciplined us for a short time as it seemed best to them, but he disciplines us for our good, that we may share his holiness. For the moment all discipline seems painful rather than pleasant, but later it yields the peaceful fruit of righteousness to those who have been trained by it. (Hebrews 12:5-11, ESV)

A dear saint read this passage of scripture then said, "This means I can either go to heaven holding hands with God and having a good time, or I can go to heaven being dragged by God and being whipped every step of the way. Woe be to that rebellious church member who isn't being whipped all the way."

To be honest, those words summarize this entire passage very well. Nine questions deserve our attention.

1. WHAT IS DISCIPLINE OR CHASTISEMENT?

We begin with the most basic question of all. The Greek word for "discipline" or its equivalent appears nine times in these seven verses. John MacArthur points out in his *Hebrews* commentary that the word comes, ". . . from the Greek *paideia*, which, in turn, comes from *pais* ('child') and denotes the training of a child. The word is a broad term, signifying whatever parents and teachers do to train, correct, cultivate, and educate children to help them develop and mature as they ought."

In other words, *God's discipline is a training process or a process of discipline* that is designed to eliminate the evil and encourage the good so that we become more and more like the Master, Jesus Christ.

This same concept exists in the animal world, too. For example, have you ever seen a mother animal chastening or disciplining her young?

I've watched on television as a momma bear would break up a fight between her cubs. She used her giant paws to move them around, find the culprit, then she would let the culprit know that she'd had enough!

Have you ever seen a momma cow get upset with her young calf at feeding time? The young calf gets a little frisky and does something wrong in getting her milk. Ol' momma then jumps around—she may kick her calf or do something else, but she knows how to get her point across.

Thus, even the animals know how to discipline their young. I wonder, where did they learn that? Who taught them how to do that?

The evolutionist says they learned it through evolution. Momma learned it from her momma, who learned it from her momma, who learned it from her momma and on it goes. But any grownup with half a brain knows such thinking is foolishness because that would mean the first momma had to sit down and figure it out for herself!

Where did they learn it? Evidently, God planted that wisdom within them to behave with a mother's heart. B. R. Lakin often said, "It's not evolution but inherited wisdom from God Himself!"

Our Heavenly Father has established this principle throughout nature that discipline/chastisement should occur between a parent and its offspring. Therefore, we should not be surprised to learn that this principle is also true in the spiritual world between God and His children.

We can even say that discipline/chastisement is just as natural as baseball, hot dogs, apple pie, and Chevrolet!

The very desire to perform discipline begins with God, who is Himself a *Father*. In turn, He gives that same desire to His creation!

2. WHY DOES GOD DISCIPLINE?

What motivates God to become involved in our lives? Why does God take the time to discipline us? The same question can be asked about us as parents. Why do we, as parents, discipline our children?

For example, let's suppose that our child comes home with a straight-A report card. Would we then discipline that child? Of course not. We probably would do the same thing that God does in verse eleven. God says, "I give a reward called the fruit of peace and righteousness."

God's reward for right living is amazing! The whole world is looking for peace and righteousness, but the Bible says peace and righteousness are the <u>results</u> of God's discipline . . . and a disciplined lifestyle.

But it is a much different matter when our child comes home with all F's except for one F minus. Suddenly we need blood pressure medicine!

Why then do we correct our children? Is it because they are doing right? No. It is because they are doing wrong. We need to correct a wrong lifestyle or a wrong decision.

One of the biggest reasons God disciplines is because we are living wrong, and we *keep* living wrong. For whatever reason, we have embraced a sinful pattern of living. We are no longer enjoying the fruit of righteousness via right living (verse eleven), but we are now embracing the fruit of unrighteousness via wrong living.

We have grabbed hold of some sin—it may be a public sin which everyone knows, or it may be a private sin which only we know—but we want this sin so much we won't let it go.

We treat that sin like a treasure; we bury it deep in our hearts where no one else can get to it. We *know* that sin exists deep in our hearts because we put it there.

We've reached a point where we don't care what God has to say about it, either. As a result, God has no choice but to convince us through the discipline process to let go of that sin so we can be more like Jesus!

3. GOD DISCIPLINES BECAUSE HE LOVES.

Verse six begins with the very important words, "For whom the Lord loves." The greatest motive for discipline will always be the motive of love.

I recall a day in my childhood when I was playing with my neighbor friend. My friend was two years older than me. I began to complain that Dad spanked me too many times. My friend broke down and began to cry. He said, "I wish my daddy loved me enough to spank me." Guess what I did? I stopped complaining; I thanked God that Dad loved me enough to discipline me when I needed it.

Aren't you glad God loves you? If God didn't love you, you'd probably ruin your life in the cesspool of sin, and no one would care about your soul.

Thank God, He promises, "As many as I love I rebuke and chasten or discipline." Based upon that line of reasoning, God must love me a lot. How about you?

4. WHOM DOES GOD DISCIPLINE?

The chastening hand of God ought to make us feel very special because it is administered to only a select group of people. Verse five says, "And have you forgotten the exhortation that addresses you as sons? 'My son, do not regard lightly the discipline of the Lord, nor be weary when reproved by him'" (Hebrews 12:5, ESV). To whom is God speaking? There is only one possibility: The Bible says that He disciplines His sons (plural). He encourages His sons on the right path. In verse seven, He disciplines His sons (plural, thereby meaning more than one son needs discipline.)

Whom does God discipline or chasten? He disciplines His sons or His own born-again children!

The question must be raised, "Does it matter if a Christian sins?" God answers, "Yes, it matters to Me! I discipline My children. I don't let them run loose to live their own way. I am their Father, and I discipline My own!"

This is good news for all of us. If we have been born again into God's family, we have His promise, His very guarantee, that He will discipline us when we get out of line!

The key question is this: Do you truly belong to Him? Verse six says He chastens every son whom He *receives*. Thus, has God ever received you into His family?

Many people try to enlist in the armed forces of our country. Unfortunately, some of them are rejected. Some are too tall; others are too short. Some have heart problems or other health problems. *Despite their desire, they will still be rejected.*

But what about God? Will God receive everyone, or will He receive only the educated, the healthy, the rich, or the poor?

Thank God, the Bible declares this invitation is open to all. John 1:12 says, "But as many as received Him, to them God gave the right to become children of God." God receives us at the same moment that we receive Jesus Christ as our personal Lord and Savior. I did that on January 14, 1965, and it's still just as true today as it was then.

I am now one of God's children. That means I am now subject to God's discipline.

5. WHOM DOES GOD <u>NOT</u> DISCIPLINE?

This question may be a surprise, but I insist it is one of the most important questions of all. It is a question that is mostly overlooked by modern-day teaching!

Verse seven declares, "If you endure God's discipline, God deals with you as with sons; what son is there whom a father does not discipline?" As pointed out in the previous section, the writer is stating that God disciplines those who are in His family. *If that is the case, doesn't it then make sense that God leaves alone those who are outside His family?*

Verse eight says, "But if you are without discipline—which all receive—then you are illegitimate children and not sons" (Hebrews 12:8, HCSB). The King James Version uses the vernacular of its day, "bastard," rather than our more modern "illegitimate children." The term "bastard" denotes more than a tinge of ridicule, but it accurately denotes how such a child was viewed in times past.

The illegitimate child was usually placed at the bottom of the ladder because he had been born outside a lawful marriage. This child had not been born in a *holy*, God-approved relationship because his mother and father were not married. It was often insinuated that the mother must have been a tramp or a whore. In many cases, the father's identity was never known because he never accepted responsibility for his actions. But what people did know for certain was that *this child was the result of an unholy, ungodly union*—born outside the holy vows of marriage!

No father accepted the responsibility to either discipline or provide for the child. As a result, the child was *disowned*.

How does this condition apply in our current study? Simply this: It is one thing for a person to *look* like he is a part of the family of God; it is a much different thing to *be* a part of the family of God. God's family consists solely of those who have been born again into God's family through a Holy Spirit salvation experience, whereby we become a new creation in Christ Jesus!

But the illegitimate child has never been born of God! He is included in the religious crowd of Hebrews chapter twelve because he has encountered some sort of religious experience, but that religious experience did not include God in His regenerating work. The experience may have included tears, it may have included a profession of faith, it may have even included baptism and attending church, but it did not include God in His redeeming work.

It may have even included teaching a Sunday School class, singing in the choir, or working in the church office, but *it did not include God.*

As to what actually happened, I do not know. ***But I do know this person's religious experience stopped short of a genuine salvation experience.*** That is a very frightening proposition! That is why the writer gives such a strongly worded warning to every illegitimate, religious person. Why? ***It is because they may not know they are illegitimate!*** They may not yet understand that their religious experience is not a valid born-again experience.

Highland Park Baptist Church in Chattanooga had a daily radio broadcast called *Gospel Dynamite.* The broadcast featured gospel music, prayer requests and prayer, followed by a short message. During one broadcast, the doors opened and in walked a Methodist pastor! He said, "I have been listening to your broadcast for some time. I have come to the conclusion that I have never been born again. Would someone help me?" Sure enough, a pastor got saved!

Jesus finished the Sermon on the Mount with the fearful words,

> *Not everyone who says to Me, 'Lord, Lord,' will enter the kingdom of heaven, but he who does the will of My Father who is in heaven will enter. Many will say to Me on that day, 'Lord, Lord, did we not prophesy in Your name, and in Your name cast out demons, and in Your name perform many miracles?' And then I will declare to them, 'I never knew you; depart from Me, you who practice lawlessness' (Matthew 7:21-23, NASB).*

Here is the warning: God's discipline/chastisement is a *proof* of sonship—of being a part of God's family. If a "Christian" is living in disobedience *and God does not send discipline* to bring that "Christian" back into line, it can mean only one thing: It means that so-called "Christian" has never been born again into the family of God! It does not matter how many times that one comes to an altar, is baptized, sings in the choir, confesses his sins to a priest, or takes Communion—God says that person is not one of His children! He has never been saved by *faith* in Christ!

Such a person, even at his best, is nothing but a "whitewashed sepulcher full of dead men's bones" (Matthew 23:27).

Someone may say, "But I am an exception to the rule, or I know someone who is an exception."

But verse eight disagrees with that logic. Verse eight leaves no wiggle room because it says, "*all* are partakers or recipients of God's discipline." Back where I come from, all means all, and that's all all means. "All" includes "everyone."

This entire answer makes perfect sense, too, because *sanctification is God's process to turn us into saints!* Therefore, how could God ever overlook one of His rebellious children? To do so would suggest that God is a failing Father!

Speaking from personal experience, I learned many years ago that I could not enjoy anything—anything at all—while Dad was applying the belt to my backside. A whipping at our home was not a time of peace; it was a time of no peace. It was not a time of satisfaction and laughter; it was a time of no satisfaction and laughter. Nor was it a time of joy; it was instead a time of pain and suffering.

There have been times when I wandered away from God, but guess whom I always found waiting for me over the next hilltop? God! Sometimes He takes the counseling approach with me. "Come now, and let's reason together and get you back on the right track." Sometimes, though, He has a switch in His hand, and I wish He would try counseling again.

How far will God go to bring me back into line? Verse six says that sometimes God will even resort to scourging. The Greek word is *mastigoo,* and it refers to flogging with a whip. *Mastigoo* has the idea of a severe beating. The same word is used in Matthew 10:17, where Jesus says, "they will flog you in their synagogues." In other words, God may resort to an awful thrashing that will leave us wounded and scarred.

Why? Because God may have to break our will to bring us back into line!

The Bible says, "The Lord knows those that are His" (2 Timothy 2:19). Does God ever let you know that you are different from the world?

I remember visiting in the home of one of our church members. This man had come forward years before at the end of a church service. He had made a profession of faith, been baptized, came to church for a few weeks then dropped out. He had not attended church in many years. He told me he did not think about God. He did not care at all about the work of God. It was plain he worshiped a god, but that god was himself.

I went through this Hebrews passage with him. I told him God would not allow a truly born-again man to take long-lasting pleasure in sin. Though there is pleasure in sin for a season, God would turn that pleasure into disappointment and frustration. God would eventually try to bring him back into line.

I will never forget what the man said to me. He said, "Pastor, I don't know what you're talking about." I left that home shaking in my boots for that man.

6. GOD SOMETIMES DISCIPLINES TO PREVENT A FUTURE PROBLEM.

It is hard enough for me to live in the present. But God is always able to be one, two, three, and even more steps ahead of me. Rest assured, we may not know what we will do on this coming Thursday, but God already does. *God is doing things today that will prepare us for success on Thursday.*

The apostle Paul testifies,

> *Therefore, so that I would not exalt myself, a thorn in the flesh was given to me, a messenger of Satan to torment me so that I would not exalt myself. Concerning this, I pleaded with the Lord three times that it would leave me. But he said to me, 'My grace is sufficient for you, for my power is perfected in weakness.' Therefore,*

I will most gladly boast all the more about my weaknesses, so that Christ's power may reside in me (2 Corinthians 12:7-9, CSB).

God knows my life better than I know my own life. He absolutely and accurately <u>knows</u> how my current road will end. Let's suppose God knows my current road will end in misery and failure. Would a good parent try to stop me from continuing in that direction? The answer is yes, yes, yes!

Ditto for Paul, too! Please allow me to paraphrase Paul's testimony.

> God looked at the road I was on. God knew that eventually, I would think too highly of myself. After all, I had experienced a vision in which I was caught up into the third heaven (2 Corinthians 12:2). I could write books entitled, 'The Visions of the Apostle Paul.' I could appear on all the talk shows and talk about me. But if I had done that, the people would only have seen me and not Christ!
>
> So God did a work of *mercy* in my life. He gave me a thorn to puncture my balloon and bring me back down to the earth where He could still use me. In other words, God used <u>preventive</u> discipline to strip away my own glory so that I might be overshadowed by His glory and power!

Paul provides his conclusion in the next verse. "So I take pleasure in weaknesses, insults, hardships, persecutions, and in difficulties, for the sake of Christ. For when I am weak, then I am strong" (2 Corinthians 12:10, CSB).

Paul says, "God loves me so much He prevented my life from being ruined! I thank God for my thorn because my thorn proves one more time that God loves me."

We have a bad tendency to complain too much. Maybe I don't get the job I want, the spouse I want, the house I want, the healing I want, the money I want, the skill I want, the grades I want, the education I want, the good looks I want, the car I want, or the inheritance I want! Many preachers complain that we didn't get the big congregation we deserved.

"Hey, Billy Graham, move over and let me show those 50,000 people what real preaching is!"

But I believe when we get to heaven, we'll bow before God and thank God that we didn't always get our way!

Paul Moody was the son of the great preacher Dwight Moody. Paul was ten years old when his father ordered him to bed at an early hour. Paul said, "I misunderstood. I thought Dad said to go to bed when I finished playing. Sometime later, Dad came in and saw I was still playing. He became angry and ordered me to bed. I ran away frightened and in tears. But within moments—not minutes but rather moments— Dad appeared at my bedside. Dad explained he had disciplined me because I had disobeyed him, but that he still loved me. Then we knelt together beside my bed. I looked over and saw tears running down Dad's face."

Paul said, "That was fifty years ago, but I'll never forget that scene. No sermon on the love of God ever touched my heart as much as those tears which were shed over my bed on that dark night."

I am just wondering: Has the Lord ever stood over your bed?

For whom the Lord loves, He also disciplines.

7. HOW DOES GOD DISCIPLINE OR CHASTEN?

Verse twelve says, "no chastening seems to be joyful for the present, but *painful.*" No truer words have ever been written than those. How does God discipline His own? *First, God removes the joy of His salvation from our souls.* I do not say God will take away your salvation (He will never do that), but I do say He will take away the *joy* of being saved.

Psalm 51 describes a rebellious child of God named King David. David is described in another Bible passage as "a man after God's own heart," but, even so, such a man fell into sin. One day David saw a beautiful woman named Bathsheba taking a bath on a rooftop; David liked what he saw.

I recall as a child hearing my pastor warn, "Satan always tempts you with the best; Bathsheba was probably the best-looking woman in all of Israel!"

David decided he wanted Bathsheba for himself. That wrong decision led to the sin of adultery, which was soon followed by the sin of murdering Bathsheba's husband. In so doing, David made a deliberate choice to walk away from God. But God hunted down David; God eventually brought David to his knees in repentance.

David then made two statements that are very significant to this study. Statement #1: "Against You—You alone—I have sinned and done this evil in Your sight. So You are right when You pass sentence; You are blameless when You judge" (Psalm 51:4 CSB).

Statement #2: "Restore the joy of Your salvation to me, and sustain me by giving me a willing spirit" (Psalm 51:12 CSB). What is David missing in this verse? He is missing the *joy*. What happens when we lose the joy of being saved? Church just isn't the same anymore, is it? The music doesn't thrill our hearts like it did previously. We feel like every sermon is being preached directly at us. Then comes the invitation and that awful song, "I Surrender All." Our church experience has gone from being a blessed experience to being an awful, horrible experience. And that experience continues even after the last prayer is prayed!

I will never forget counseling a twelve-year-old boy at the end of a service. Tears were running down his face. This boy had been saved, baptized, and knew his Bible better than most adults. I asked, "Jeff, why have you come?"

Jeff was crying so much he could hardly talk. He finally said, "I have lost the joy of the Lord's salvation! I have lost the joy!"

Thank God, he knew where to go to get it back! His cure was the same as David's cure. David prayed, "Create or renew within me a <u>clean</u> heart, O Lord, and restore to me the joy of Your salvation." God answered that prayer for David. He will be faithful to answer that prayer for us, too.

Second, God uses the unsaved to expose our hypocrisy. This may be the most embarrassing form of God's discipline. There is an old proverb that says, "Oh, that we could see ourselves as others see us."

The Lord cannot stand hypocrisy—pretending to be something we are not! Strangely, the world cannot stand hypocrisy either. *And the one thing the hypocrite cannot stand is having the world point out his hypocrisy.*

Case in point: Abraham, the great man of faith. His story begins in Genesis chapter twelve, with God promising to make a great nation from Abraham. Abraham responds, "God, I have never heard of You blessing anyone like me, but I believe You. I will obey You by faith."

In Genesis 12:5 Abraham passes through the heathen land of Canaan; everyone in Canaan knows Abraham is living by faith. In verse six, Abraham passes through Bethel, Ha-i, and the Negev desert; everyone in that region knows Abraham is living by faith. Everything is going great until one day, *Abraham stops living by faith.* Abraham starts depending upon himself; as a result, he commits one of the worst sins any husband can ever commit. The Bible says,

> *When he was about to enter Egypt, he said to his wife Sarai, 'Look, I know what a beautiful woman you are. When the Egyptians see you, they will say, 'This is his wife.' They will kill me but let you live. Please say you're my sister so it will go well for me because of you, and my life will be spared on your account.' When Abram entered Egypt, the Egyptians saw that the woman was very beautiful. Pharaoh's officials saw her and praised her to Pharaoh, so the woman was taken to Pharaoh's household. He treated Abram well because of her, and Abram acquired flocks and herds, male and female donkeys, male and female slaves, and camels. But the Lord struck Pharaoh and his household with severe plagues because of Abram's wife Sarai. So Pharaoh sent for Abram and said, 'What have you done to me? Why didn't you tell me she was your wife? Why did you say, 'She's my sister,' so that I took her as my wife? Now,*

here is your wife. Take her and go!' (Genesis 12:11-19, CSB).

Pharaoh said, "You hypocrite! You claim to be a great man of faith. Don't you believe God can protect you here in Egypt? Or did you leave your God back in Canaan? What kind of Christian are you anyway?"

Can you picture Abraham's reaction? No doubt, Abraham was stunned that he, a man known for his faith, would have his pedigree read by an unsaved, idol worshipper!

One does not need to live long to realize the unsaved world will see through our hypocrisy much faster than we will. The world exposes our hypocrisy in so many ways. "If you're a Christian, why don't you act like one?" "Hey! Does your church know you do that? I'll bet your pastor doesn't know." "Do you mean to tell me you're a Christian? I'm sorry. I've worked with you these many years, but I never guessed." Then comes the granddaddy of them all: "Would you tell me why I need to be saved? I'm just as good as you."

Third, sometimes God removes whatever is hindering me from being in His will—sometimes things and sometimes people. Consider the strange case of Naomi and her daughter-in-law Ruth. The book of Ruth is recognized as one of the greatest short stories in the entire world of literature, but it is important to know it has a very sad beginning.

"'Don't call me Naomi. Call me Mara,' she answered, 'for the Almighty has made me very bitter. I went away full, but the Lord has brought me back empty. Why do you call me Naomi, since the Lord has opposed me, and the Almighty has afflicted me?'" (Ruth 1:20-21, CSB).

Naomi said, "I went away full. I had many things between me and God. God, though, removed every single one of those things. I am now coming home empty."

Her story begins with God chastening the entire nation with a famine. The crops withered in the field; there was nothing to eat. Surely the nation would turn back to God, but no, the people like Naomi and her husband kept doing that which was right in their own eyes.

Irony of ironies, do you know where Naomi and her husband lived? They lived in Bethlehem. The name Bethlehem means the "house of bread and praise." In other words, Bethlehem was supposed to be the house of God's blessings!

We pastors often say, "If the preaching rubs the fur the wrong way, well, turn the animal around!" The symbolism associated with Bethlehem makes it clear that Naomi and her husband should turn the animal around; in so doing, Bethlehem will once again become the house of bread and blessing!

But what do they do? They do the worse thing possible. They *leave* the house of bread and praise; they move to the God-cursed land of Moab. Pray, tell, what exactly are they doing there? But it gets even worse. Verse two indicates, "and they *continued* there . . ." Deliberately, intentionally doing that which was right in their own eyes rather than God's eyes.

But God did not leave them alone because they belonged to God! How, though, can God get them back to the Promised Land? *God decided to remove everything that hindered* . . . everything that came between them and God. What happened next is a warning to all of us because God resorted to "scourging."

First, God removed the person who led the family into Moab. Verse three says, "Then Elimelech, Naomi's husband, died; and she was left, and her two sons." Did they repent at that time and go back to Bethlehem? No. The next verse says, "Now they took wives of the women of Moab: the name of the one was Orpah, and the name of the other Ruth. And they dwelt there about <u>ten</u> years."

Quite obviously, they decided to stay in Moab. But the Bible says, "He who is often rebuked, and hardens his neck, will suddenly be destroyed, and that without remedy or any hope of recovery" (Proverbs 29:1).

Then comes verse five, "Then both sons also died." Their deaths meant that God had removed Naomi's last reason to stay in Moab.

That is why she comes back to the house of bread and says, "The Lord has dealt very bitterly with me. I went out full. I thought I had everything important in life: a husband, sons, and a future, but the Lord's chastening hand has now brought me home empty."

One of the songs from my childhood says, "Wasted years, wasted years, o how foolish!"

The rest of the book of Ruth is beautiful to read, but it is only beautiful because God comes first in chapters two, three, and four.

God wants all of His children to live in the house of bread and praise. He doesn't want any of us to live in rebellion and sin. That is why God sometimes has to remove that which hinders us from being in His will.

8. GOD MAY SEND PREMATURE DEATH TO ONE OF HIS CHILDREN.

I have personally known *only one* person who, in my view, may, and I stress may, have been disciplined in this way. She worked in Sunday School, worked in the Wednesday children's program along with the other church programs plus gave tens of thousands of dollars to the church. But she committed almost the same sin as Ananias in Acts chapter five, and the church buried a very healthy woman just a few weeks later.

Let me give you, though, a Bible example that I *know* is true. 1 Corinthians chapter five reveals the church had a case of two people living together who were not married. It actually was a case of incest, of a man living in immorality with his stepmother.

Paul instructs the church, "hand that one over to Satan for the destruction of the flesh, so that his spirit may be saved in the day of the Lord" (1 Corinthians 5:5, CSB). This phrase "destruction of the flesh" essentially means that God has signed the believer's death warrant or something even more hideous. This believer has decided to go his own way; God is making it plain that the believer will be allowed to go no further.

J. Harold Smith says, "It is a horrible thing to die in the devil's slaughterhouse."

Paul says the believer's spirit is still saved, but he is going to heaven prematurely. It is time for God to bring him home.

There is a story about two boys playing ball in the front yard. One of the boys lived at the house, but the other boy lived next door. Something happened, and the boys began to argue. Then they began to fight. The front door opened, and the first boy's mother came outside. She broke up the fight, then said, "I don't want this to happen again."

Her son replied, "Mom, I promise this won't happen again."

A few minutes later, the boys were fighting again. Once again, the mother separated the two boys. She said, "Billy, this is the second time. Are you going to behave, or do I have to take you inside?"

He said, "I will behave. I promise."

The mother returned inside. Five minutes later, a third fight broke out. Once again, the mother stopped the two boys. But this time she said, "Billy, come inside. The game is over."

"But, Mom—"

"No buts, Billy. You've had your chance. Now you'll come inside and *spend the rest of the day with me.*"

9. HOW CAN WE RESPOND TO GOD'S DISCIPLINE?

First, we can regard *the discipline of God lightly*. Verse five cautions, "My son, don't despise the discipline of the Lord." The word "despise" is a very interesting word. Its appearance in verse five is the only time this word appears in the entire Greek New Testament. (Note: It is a different Greek word than the word which appears in verse two.) This Greek word in verse five has the idea of "regarding lightly or taking lightly." In other words, do not regard lightly, brush aside, forget or treat as nothing the discipline which comes your way.

The child of God may defiantly say, "I can live with the guilt. Therefore, I'll stay away from church, and the guilt will go away." In so doing, he regards the rebuke of God lightly.

(Note: If staying away from church removes the guilt, that person has probably never been saved. After all, the Holy Spirit knows the believer's address!)

A young pastor went to visit a veteran pastor. He said, "I have made a terrible mistake. Last Sunday night, I resigned my church. I got mad at them. I told them what I think of them. Now they won't take me back."

The veteran pastor said, "God was using that church to improve your performance as a pastor. But you missed His will. God may put you on the shelf and let you wait a while."

The young pastor had regarded the discipline of the Lord lightly!

Second, I can lose heart as God disciplines me. Verse three teaches one can become weary and fainthearted; in other words, one can lose heart. The King James Version of verse twelve expresses, "your hands are now hanging down." The arms are so tired that they're just hanging there; the arms would be lying on the floor if they weren't attached to the body.

The person's life has become like quicksand. Even the simplest things have become a struggle. Nothing comes easy. The person resembles a train that has gone off the tracks and is making a big mess of things.

The wayward believer can try everything under the sun. King Solomon tried money, sex, wisdom, literature, pleasure, work, companionship, sports, politics, even recreation, but God's chastening hand did not allow him to find satisfaction anywhere! Eventually, he became weary, and he said, "Life is nothing but vanity, nothing but emptiness."

It's like the Bible says: The arms just hang there, and the knees are weak!

Third, I can confess my sin and be restored to the right way. "But if we walk in the light, as he is in the light, we have fellowship with one another, and the blood of Jesus his Son cleanses us from all sin. If we say we have no sin, we deceive ourselves, and the truth is not in us. *If we confess our sins, he is faithful and just to forgive us our sins* and to cleanse us from all unrighteousness." (1 John 1:7-9)

What exactly does it mean to confess our sins? First, it means more than simply saying, "I'm sorry." God wants more than an empty, "I'm sorry."

Let me illustrate. Did you ever get caught with your hand in the cookie jar? You looked up and guess who was coming through the door? Your momma and she wasn't happy at all. So you put on a show. What did you say? "Mom, I'm sorry," and you may have even cried a little! I don't know about you, but the only reason I was sorry was that I had been caught. Deep down, I still wanted the cookie!

Confession is more than saying I'm sorry I got caught. The Greek word *homologeo* literally means to say the same thing as another, to be in agreement with another. In other words, true confession is taking God's view of our sin. It is not saying, "God, I am sorry I was caught, but I'll do it again as soon as You walk out of the room." But rather, it is saying, "God, I admit I was wrong. I wish I could relive that moment so it would never happen, so I could make a different decision, so I could make the decision You Yourself would make. God, I forsake my sin, and I ask You to forgive me, clean me up, and put me on the right path again!"

God then does what He has promised to do: He forgives us of our sins, and He cleanses us from all unrighteousness. And it sure feels good to be clean again! The joy of the Lord is back! The music is music to our soul! The preaching and Bible study are food for spiritual growth! Prayer is real, and we know what it means to enter the holiest of holies!

I remember the Sunday afternoon that God confronted me about my sinful rebellion. (I was a rebellious teenager.) It was as if God walked physically through the bedroom door and asked, "When were you the happiest?"

I said, "It was when I was obeying you. I was singing in the choir for Your glory. I enjoyed being with Your people."

I went forward that night and confessed my sins to God. I said, "I have sinned. Father, forgive me and clean me up!"

Guess what happened? God did exactly what He promised to do! I walked out of the church a different teenager than I walked in. That's what verse nine means when it says, "Be in subjection." My new prayer became, "Your will be done on earth, even in my heart as it is now done in heaven."

I then became a "partaker of His holiness." It felt good to be clean again! The struggle was gone, the misery was gone, and I was right with God.

Verse eleven says, "Once the discipline is complete, there will be a peaceful harvest of right living for those who have been trained in God's discipline." I want you to know those words are indeed true.

There is one story that best explains this chapter. Two brothers were convicted of stealing sheep. Their penalty was very unusual. They were branded on the forehead with the two letters "S" and "T" for Sheep Thief.

One brother could not stand the embarrassment. He became bitter and moved away. Eventually, he died and was forgotten.

The other brother chose a different course. He said, "I can't run from what I did. I'll stay here and win back the respect of my neighbors."

Many years passed. The brother eventually built a solid reputation for honesty and integrity. One day a stranger passed through the town. He saw the brother and noticed those two letters on his forehead: "S" and "T". The stranger asked an old man, "What do those two letters mean?"

The old man said, "It happened so long ago I can't remember, but I think the two letters 'S' and 'T' are an abbreviation for the word saint."

What was the difference? He had responded in the right way to discipline.

"For whom the Lord loves, He also disciplines!"

17

GROWING THROUGH GOD'S LOCAL CHURCH

A dilapidated, old car drove up to a toll bridge and stopped at the gate. "Fifty cents!" cried the toll attendant.

"Sold!" immediately replied the driver.

We live in an era which tends to cheapen that which is priceless and to regard as priceless that which is cheap. Jesus posed the question, "How valuable is a man's soul? What will a man give in exchange for his soul?" (Matthew 16:26). Jesus made it clear that the human soul is the most valuable thing in the world. Therefore, the organization which cares for the human soul must be of great, even awesome, value, too!

What organization cares more for the human soul than God's local church? There is none, not a single one. God's church is like an island amid a broad but empty ocean. It stands alone, and it also stands apart. There is nothing else like God's church because there is nothing else that accomplishes what God's church accomplishes.

Most organizations, even good organizations, deal solely with temporal issues, but *only God's church* deals with both the temporal issues and the eternal issues regarding a man's soul.

In a nutshell, that is why the local church exists. It was said more than fifty years ago, "All the church needs to do is be the church. God never told the church to be an accompanist. He called the church to be a soloist. We have our own song to sing; we don't have to sing anybody else's song."

God's local church does what I, as an individual, cannot do. I can contribute my effort to the church, but I can never do all that my church does. At my best, I am merely one of the parts; I am not the whole or even a large part of the whole. But I am a part! I can contribute to care for the souls of men.

Interestingly, God has designed the church to bless me at the same time that I am blessing others. I contribute to them, and they, at the same time, contribute to me. I minister to them, and they minister to me. I help them to become saintlier in the sanctified life. Guess what? They help me to become saintlier in my own sanctified life . . . in my own pursuit of Him who loved me and gave Himself for me.

How should I think about my own church experience and whether it is a worthwhile experience? A complete answer would require a complete book beyond the scope of this book's purpose. But five questions are definitely worth exploring. Each of these questions must be answered biblically for us to grow in the way God intends.

1. AM I EXPECTING TO FIND A PERFECT CHURCH?

Of course, the answer is no. We're smarter than that! Surely, we reason, none of us would expect to find a perfect church. Okay, but what about an "almost perfect church"? That pursuit is much more likely. How do I know? It is because of the inverse question, "Would I join a bad church as defined in the sense of a troubled church or an unbiblical church?" No, I would not. Therefore, all of us are looking for something better . . . and the more perfect, the better!

But then comes the disappointment when we realize our choice (our church) falls short of our expectations.

As a new pastor, I had to learn the very same lesson. I was thrilled with the opportunity to pastor my first church and be out on my own. I was blessed with a willing church, and we did a lot of new things. (My exuberance covered a lot of my blemishes.) I was on cloud nine! One day I bragged to my father about the church. My father (a veteran pastor) listened, sighed, then said, "Son, it's still a church." I received his comment as a downer, but he proved to be right.

If it is true that a man at his best is still nothing more than a man, then it is also true that a church at its best is still nothing more than a church. *A church can be nothing but a church*—an imperfect church—because it is made up of people with all the issues encountered by ordinary people. A church is made up of old and young, the wise and the unwise, mature saints of God and babes in Christ, milk Christians and meat Christians, Spirit-filled Christians and worldly-minded Christians, even people of different political persuasions. Yikes!

I have pastored for nearly forty years, but I have never pastored a perfect church or an almost perfect church or even a halfway perfect church. I have only pastored imperfect churches. Like all pastors, I have received new members who thought our church was better than it turned out to be; in some cases, it was not long until they went searching for that more perfect church.

The old saying is true: "Don't bother looking for the perfect church. Because if you ever find it, and then join it, it won't be perfect anymore!"

A man phoned a pastor and said he wanted to join the church. He went on to explain that he did not want to worship every week, study the Bible, visit the sick, witness to non-Christians, or serve as a leader or teacher.

The pastor commended the man for his desire to join the church but told him that the better church for him was located in another section of town. The man wrote down the address of the better church then disconnected the call. When the man arrived at his version of the perfect church, he found an abandoned church building, boarded up and ready for demolition.

No, there are no perfect churches, but any church can become *more* perfect as *we* (not merely them) devote our becoming-*more*-sanctified lives in that becoming-*more*-sanctified church to God's *completely* sanctified purpose.

One of the old-time preachers left us with this advice:

> When you get saved, be sure to join a church. Join a live church. Join where the preacher loves the Word of God and the souls of men. Keep out of these ecclesiastical deep-freezers. A deep freeze is all right for a dead chicken, or a chunk of cheese, or a leg of lamb, but it is no place for a live baby. A baby must be fed and nourished and given a chance to exercise, vocalize, and grow. He couldn't do that in a refrigerator.

The most important question is not, "Is this a perfect church?" but, "Can I grow here? And, as I grow, can I help others to grow here?" Church is not only a getting experience; it is also a giving experience.

Interestingly, the church's size is not a realistic reflection of what happens within the fellowship. Many large churches are as spiritually dead as the church of Laodicea, while many small churches are spiritually alive; the reverse is also true.

Margaret Mead popularized the saying, "Never doubt that a small group of thoughtful, committed citizens can change the world; indeed, it is the only thing that ever has." Out of one man came the nation of Israel; out of twelve men came the New Testament church!

During the late 1970s, my wife taught a Sunday School class at little Hillview Baptist Church in the carpet capital of America: Dalton, Georgia. Our church was quite small; it was staffed by students from our

Bible college. Nevertheless, we had a significant ministry to those people in Dalton.

There was a little girl who splendidly summarized our effort. My wife taught her in the primary class. One day she went home after Sunday School and told her mother, "I don't care if we have a church of wood or brick. I'm just happy to have a church made up of Christians."

That little girl knew something very important. Size isn't the real issue. Furthermore, skill isn't the real issue. Perfection or almost perfection isn't the issue either. True, effective ministry always begins with imperfect people loving other imperfect people . . . with imperfect ministers dedicating themselves to imperfect people with great needs.

2. DO I LOVE THE CHURCH LIKE JESUS LOVES THE CHURCH?

Some people erroneously believe they can love God but not love God's church. As a result, they do not place a very high value on the local church. Indeed, from their perspective, the church does not deserve their devotion, effort, or finances. The Bible, though, suggests such an attitude is an utter impossibility for the person who is walking in the Spirit.

Two Bible passages prove there is a link between loving God and loving His church. The first passage states, "He who does not love his brother whom he has seen cannot love God whom he has not seen" (1 John 4:20, ESV). Of what does the local church consist? The Bible refers to us as brothers and sisters. The church is practically equivalent to the totality of brothers and sisters in a specific location.

Let's substitute the word "church" for the word "brother" in the above verse. "He who does not love God's church which he has seen cannot love God whom he has not seen." Logic suggests that whoever wishes to be like God *will,* and *must,* also love whatever God loves.

The second passage states, "Christ loved the church so much that He gave Himself up for her" (Ephesians 5:25).

Doug Parsons writes, "I had a professor who used to say in class, 'Make a list of all the things for which you are willing to be shot at five o'clock tomorrow morning. Generally, it will be a very short list; but when you have completed it, you will find in that list the things for which you ought to live—things that will produce the ultimate satisfaction in life.'"

What did Jesus put on His list? The church! As we become more sanctified, God's church moves higher and higher on our list, too. For as the Master is, so shall His servant be.

Based upon these two passages, it is always true to say, "Whoever loves God also loves God's church." However, it is not always true to say, "Whoever loves God's church also loves God." Unfortunately, some people have a genuine, deep-rooted love for their church that falls short of loving God. They love the church members, the church activities, or what the church does for them. But that does not necessarily mean they have a close relationship with the Almighty.

Nevertheless, there is a definite link between loving God and the result of loving God, which is loving His church.

The church enjoys many unique relationships with its Savior. The church is His bride (2 Corinthians 11:2), His body (1 Corinthians 12:13, 27), His sheep (John 10), His building (Ephesians 2:19-21), His new creation (Ephesians 2:15), His house (1 Timothy 3:15), His temple or dwelling place (1 Corinthians 3:16-17), His garden or greenhouse (1 Corinthians 3:9), plus more.

Therefore, how can anyone dare say, "I love God. I just don't care much for His church."? It's like saying, "I love you, but I can't stand your wife or your kids, and I won't have anything to do with them."

How can a person love God but not love what
God loves? It is impossible to do so.

Someone may object, "The church has too many hypocrites in it." Unfortunately, that is very true. But the same statement can be made about every organization. If we are to progress in life, we must deal with hypocrites at work, on the ball field, on Facebook, and even in our own family. We sometimes forget that a Judas kiss is associated with someone very close to Jesus.

One preacher advises, "Don't stay away from God's church because of the sick people attending it. After all, the church is a hospital for such sinners! We can't cure everyone, but we can cure some."

Jesus Christ died for the gospel-believing church that is across the street or over the hill from your current address. He died to purchase Himself a bride; that bride is His church. His ultimate goal for the church of born-again saints is to completely sanctify it, cleanse it, wash it, clothe it, and beautify it until it has zero blemishes and defects.

To be honest, I have not yet visited that church, have you? That is why we must keep working on the blemishes, wrinkles, and defects.

I wish all of you could know deacon Kenny Rice. Kenny is eighty-five years of age. He walks with a cane. He can hear what is said in a one-on-one conversation, but he cannot hear any word spoken from a pulpit in an auditorium. No hearing aid can solve his problem. It would be wonderful if we had closed caption capability, but we do not. But guess who attends every church service? Kenny is always there alongside his wife, Sue. If necessary, Sue helps Kenny find the right song in the hymnal and the right scripture passage. Sue explains anything unusual.

Kenny is always there on Sunday morning, Sunday night, Wednesday night, and any other time the church doors are open. He attends, even though he cannot hear much of what is happening!

Kenny attends because he loves God's church. He has loved God's church since he was a boy. Our church is the only church he knows. He greets the people with a smile, promotes Jesus Christ in the community, and has been one of our pillars for many years. How fascinating! He may not be able to hear, but he can be seen . . . and he makes sure everyone knows whose side he is on.

The English architect Sir Christopher Wren was supervising the construction of a cathedral in London, England. A journalist decided to interview three of the construction workers. The journalist asked, "What are you doing?"

The first worker replied, "I'm cutting stone for ten shillings a day."

The second worker answered, "I'm putting in ten hours a day on this job."

But the third worker said, "I'm helping Sir Christopher Wren construct one of London's greatest cathedrals."

What a difference! You have the opportunity to help Jesus Christ construct people in His blood-bought church. In so doing, don't be surprised if God builds you, too.

3. WHAT OTHER ORGANIZATION IS THE PILLAR AND FOUNDATION OF THE TRUTH?

The apostle Paul put the entire issue in perspective when he declared, "But if I should be delayed, I have written so that you will know how people ought to conduct themselves in God's household, which is the church of the living God, the pillar and foundation of the truth" (1 Timothy 3:15, CSB).

Adrian Rogers is undoubtedly correct when he says, "As goes the West, so goes the world; as goes America, so goes the West; as goes the church, so goes America." In other words, the future direction of the world rests with God's church.

A close study of history will reveal that Europe's decline began with the decline of the church. We are now witnessing the early stages of America's decline, too, and that decline is the direct result of the decline in our churches. Why? It is because the churches are the pillar and foundation of truth, and *all absolute truth is God's truth!*

America is rapidly moving to an environment where every man will do that which is right in his own eyes. Sadly, we already know how that story will end (Judges 21:25).

Man will not believe he needs a Savior if he does not believe he is a sinner. Man will not know what to believe with certainty if he does not accept the Bible as God's final authority. Man will not prepare for eternity if he does not believe in heaven or hell. The list of possibilities is endless.

The bottom line is that man needs the truth. Man needs God's truth! The church and the church alone is the pillar and foundation of that truth. As for me, I stand unapologetically with God's church, because I stand for the truth of God's Word!

Most people do not know that the scientist Albert Einstein was born a German Jew, but later renounced his citizenship in Germany and became a citizen of Switzerland. Einstein writes,

> Being a lover of freedom, when the Nazi revolution came, I looked to the universities to defend it, knowing that they had always boasted of their devotion to the cause of truth; but, no, the universities were immediately silenced. Then I looked to the great editors of the newspapers, whose flaming editorials in days gone by had proclaimed their love of freedom; but, they, like the universities, were silenced in a few short weeks.
>
> Only the church stood squarely across the path of Hitler's campaign for suppressing the truth. I never had any special interest in the church before, but now I felt a great affection and admiration for it because the Church alone has had the courage and persistence to stand for intellectual and moral freedom. I am forced to confess that what I once despised I now praise unreservedly.

4. IS THE CHURCH BUILT UPON STRONG BIBLE TEACHING?

A black church in Kansas City has as its slogan: "Wake up, sing up, preach up, pray up and pay up, but never give up or let up or back up or shut up until the cause of Christ in this church and in the world is built up." That slogan cannot be accomplished with weak or nonexistent Bible teaching but only with strong, unapologetic Bible teaching.

Take a moment to review the five questions in this chapter (including the next one). Notice that *not one* of those questions mentions the church's denominational status. It is true the name over the door ought to settle many issues regarding the church's doctrinal approach to scripture. For example, is the church Calvinistic, Arminian, charismatic, etc.? But the church's doctrine is *only the beginning* of our search because many, many churches are seriously lacking in strong Bible teaching. The church's statement of beliefs may say the people believe something, but you would never learn those beliefs from their diluted preaching or teaching.

Contrary to what is often promoted, there is no such animal as a non-denominational church. It has become today's latest fad to promote churches as being non-denominational to attract people that have been turned off by the mainline denominations. However, every church/pastor has a denominational or belief bias, which will neatly align with one of the major denominations. *It is absolutely false for anyone to claim to be non-denominational because* that person has to preach something and that "something" can be categorized doctrinally.

Jesus was not known for weak teaching but for strong teaching. The Sermon on the Mount is one of the strongest sermons ever preached! It comes at you from every direction. I urge you to take the time to read the entire sermon in one setting (Matthew 5-7); you will be surprised at how Jesus zeroes in on your own weaknesses. The Sermon finishes with this amazing verse: "Jesus taught them as one having authority and NOT as one of the scribes" (Matthew 7:29).

How different, though, were the words of the poor bishop: "Unless we repent as it were in a measure and believe to a certain extent, we may possibly be damned so to speak to a certain degree."

There is a tendency in many churches to take the Bible out of the preacher's hands, take the preacher out of the pulpit, and take the pulpit out of the church. But that does not create saints out of sinners! That is only a recipe for weak Christians to stay weak.

Such churches reason, "Let's not offend anyone." However, I would be careful about any such church, because the Bible says, "The preaching of the cross is offensive to humanity!" (Galatians 5:11). "For Christ did not send me to baptize but to preach the gospel, and not with words of eloquent wisdom, lest the cross of Christ be emptied of its power" (1 Corinthians 1:18, ESV).

Arnot is right when he proclaims, "Buy the truth whatever it may cost. Sell it not whatever may be offered."

Mark this down in your thinking and never let it go: *The sanctified believer must want what he doesn't want . . .* that is, doesn't want in the flesh. 2 Timothy 3:16 says, "All scripture is God-breathed or originates with God. It is profitable; that is, it makes someone better. It does so in four areas: Doctrine or instruction in knowing what to believe, reproof or rebuke or conviction, correction or setting things right, and instruction/training in righteousness to produce the sanctified life." A "feel-good" church environment may make us "feel good," but it will not result in "training in righteousness or the sanctified life."

A good church is similar to a grocery store, a seminar, and a doctor's office all in one. The first provides us with the necessary food to grow, the second provides us with the knowledge to grow, and the third provides us with the health to grow.

We must never minimize the words of Hebrews 4:12. "The Word of God (the Bible) is alive. It's energized. It's sharper than even a two-edged sword, going so deep as to divide the soul from the spirit, even the joints from the marrow. Furthermore, it exposes, discerns, and judges the deepest conceptions of the human heart." In other words, the Bible changes lives! That's what I need! That's what you need, too.

W. A. Criswell, pastor of First Baptist Church of Dallas, had a woman in his congregation who wanted her husband to join the church. At her request, Criswell visited the husband and urged him to become a part of the church. The man rebuffed Criswell's plea and said, "I will not join your church because I do not like to hear you preach."

Criswell said, "I would like to know the reason why."

The man said, "I have been to your church several times with my wife. You preached the Bible every one of those times. I have never heard you preach anything else."

Criswell responded, "That is true. What do you want me to preach?"

The man continued, "When I go to church, I would like the minister to enlarge my field of interest, expounding on the political scene, on our economic dilemma, on current events, or about the latest and finest literature. I get tired of listening to you just preach the Bible."

Criswell never succeeded with that man. He never joined the church because Criswell never quit preaching the Bible.

Criswell concluded,

> "It seems to me that once in a while *a man would like to know what God has to say.* If God does say anything, who else but the preacher—God's spokesman—will tell us what God says? I am convinced that this is the assignment of the preacher—to stand in the pulpit, to open the Word of the living Lord, and to tell us how our souls can be saved and how we can enjoy the blessings of God in our lives."

How much we need to hear, "Thus saith the Lord!"

5. IS THE CHURCH FULFILLING ITS GOD-GIVEN PURPOSE?

This question deserves much consideration because we cannot get the right answer if we don't ask the right question. First, notice what the question does *not* ask. The question is not, "Is the church fulfilling *its* purpose?" It is not, "Is the church fulfilling its *main* purpose?" Many churches have developed a purpose—their *own* purpose—which falls short of God's purpose for His church.

The God-given purpose, of course, is the Great Commission. Everyone knows about the death, burial, and resurrection of Jesus Christ. What is less known is Jesus' final instructions to His disciples prior to

His ascension back to heaven. We describe those instructions as "The Great Commission." Jesus provided those instructions in all four gospels (Matthew 28:18-20, Mark 16:15, Luke 24:46-49, John 20:21-23) and Acts 1:8.

Let me paraphrase the Matthew passage and relate it to the widely accepted five-fold purpose (singular) of God's church.

> All authority to rule absolutely in heaven and earth has been given to Me (worship Me as Lord of all). As you go daily into the world, educate the lost to the point of their receiving Me (evangelism resulting in a born-again experience), baptizing them (bringing them into the Christian fellowship) in the name of the Father, the Son and the Holy Spirit, and educating (discipleship or learning how to follow Me) them to obey (ministry through living out My will) everything I have commanded you. And surely, I am with you always, to the very end of the age.

God's five-fold purpose for every church is underlined in the above paragraph. The paragraph also expresses how the five steps are linked in one complete process. No purpose stands alone or apart from the other purposes because they are linked. *Thus, the definition for a complete church is a church that follows the complete process completely.*

It is worth noting that the process is repeatable from generation to generation. A disciple makes another disciple who makes another disciple, and the process never ends. That is why we still have New Testament churches in today's world. The same process has worked for two thousand years. We can have every confidence it will continue to work because it is God's process.

There is a cardinal rule that holds true in any church: If we want our church to be a God-blessed Great Commission church, we must first determine to be a Great Commission church.

For example, does the church take the good news of Jesus Christ outside its walls to the community? Does the church enthusiastically support missionaries? Does the church train its members in how to share Jesus with others? What is the church's record on baptisms? Are people being developed for ministry? Most importantly, is the church really active in Jesus' final instructions or just giving it lip service?

Many years ago, I accidentally stirred up a hornet's nest! We were concluding the highest attended Vacation Bible School in the church's history. Following our normal routine, I invited the parents of our VBS children to attend our closing game night and hot dog supper. The parents showed up in an exceedingly large number on this occasion. Some of the "saints" complained that we had too many people to feed. Oh, they were upset! Others, though, rejoiced in the opportunity to build bridges to so many unchurched people. (Those bridges paid wonderful dividends during the next five years.)

What problem did the supper unearth? Jesus says, "The field is the world," but, unfortunately, many of the so-called saints believed the field is only us (Matthew 13:38).

The bottom line is this: If you want your church to be a God-blessed Great Commission church, you must first determine to <u>be</u> a Great Commission church. *Then commit yourself to personal growth through that kind of church!*

18

GROWING THROUGH SHARING JESUS WITH OTHERS

From that time Jesus began to preach, and to say, Repent: for the kingdom of heaven is at hand. And Jesus, walking by the sea of Galilee, saw two brethren, Simon called Peter, and Andrew his brother, casting a net into the sea: for they were fishers. And he saith unto them, Follow me, and I will make you fishers of men. And they straightway left their nets, and followed him (Matthew 4:17-20, KJV).

I was taught as a little boy how to sing the children's chorus, "Fishers of Men." My wife taught that same chorus to our three daughters when they were very young. She is also teaching the same chorus to the students in her children's church. It is a chorus which is good for any generation because it expresses God's highest calling for all of His children: We have been called to bring souls to Jesus. That calling is known as evangelism or soul winning.

One can only wonder if God pre-ordained that Simon and Andrew be fishermen by trade. The skills required to fish effectively for fish neatly parallel the necessary skills to fish effectively for the souls of men. How would God have better explained evangelism if Simon and Andrew had been accountants or scientists? But the whole concept of fishing makes sense to common people like you and me.

Verse nineteen is about a personal growth experience for Simon and Andrew. Though simple, it presents some very powerful truths.

1. TWO WORDS CAN CHANGE ANYONE'S LIFE.

"Follow Me."

Both Simon and Andrew already had an occupation. They were both fishermen by trade. They were brothers in the flesh who had become brothers in the Spirit under the preaching of John the Baptist. Based upon our general knowledge of that era, it is unlikely that either man had much education. In many ways, they were common laborers with no aspirations for a job on Wall Street.

Sometimes they fished from a boat; at other times, they fished from the shore. On this occasion, they were fishing from the shore by casting a net into the Sea of Galilee.

Then along comes Jesus. Just casually walking by. That is the sense of the text to me. Of course, there is never any such thing as "just walking by" in the case of Jesus. He always has a reason to be wherever He is! Though He may appear to be simply walking by, we can rest assured He is there for a reason.

Jesus did not come merely to occupy His time or watch them work. He did not come to learn how to fish or give advice. But He was most certainly there on a mission; what happened next changed the lives of two ordinary fishermen.

"Follow Me." "To where?" "Follow Me." "What about the nets?" "Follow Me." "My wallet is empty." "Follow Me." "When can I return?" "Follow Me." "Are You sure You really want me?" "Follow Me."

The Bible says, "They left their nets immediately and followed Him."

The Lord's instruction to "follow Me" leads you to do things you would otherwise not do. It leads you to places you would otherwise not be. It leads you to circumstances you would otherwise not encounter. It leads you to people you would otherwise not meet. It leads you to challenges you would otherwise not face. Above all, it leads you to know Him, grow in Him, and exalt Him!

J. Vernon McGee says, "I have always felt that since He called imperfect men like the disciples were, He may be able to use me, and He may be able to use you. It is encouraging to know that we don't have to be super-duper saints to be used by Him."

How did Andrew's ministry begin? It began with Andrew meeting Jesus (John 1:40-42) then introducing his brother Simon Peter to Jesus.

What about Philip? Philip met Jesus, then went to Nathaniel and said, "Come and see!" Nothing dramatic, but it worked! Nathaniel came, saw, and was born again.

The demoniac of Gadara was delivered from his captivity and immediately "began to publish what great things Jesus had done for him. And the crowd was amazed!" (Mark 5:20).

The woman of Samaria met the spring of Living Water; she then, in her own imperfect way, introduced that same spring to the entire town (John 4).

"Follow Me." And so I, too, have done for more than fifty-five years. I wouldn't trade my experiences for the world. What I have gained in following Jesus is of much greater value than I would have gained in following anyone or anything else.

2. LEARN WHAT THE GREAT TEACHER WANTS YOU TO LEARN.

The first call was to follow. If I follow, I am now in the position to learn. I can hear wisdom that I otherwise would not hear, pose questions to the Teacher, mull things over in my mind until they begin to make sense, then integrate these great teachings into my life.

"Learn of Me" are three of the most important words ever spoken by Jesus (Matthew 11:29). No one ever becomes like Jesus unless he first learns from Jesus and then aligns himself with those same teachings.

Jesus says, "I want to teach you how to become fishers of men rather than mere fishers of fish. I want to teach you how to share Me with others. In so doing, you will grow into what I want you to be."

There are three ways that Jesus describes one-on-one evangelism to His students. First, He speaks of "fishing for the souls of men." Second, He speaks of "a shepherd looking for that one lost sheep" (Luke 15:1-7). Third, He talks about laborers working in a field at harvesting time (John 4:35).

In addition, Paul identifies believers as God's ambassadors to proclaim the message of reconciliation—how to be restored to God through the blood of the cross (2 Corinthians 5).

Jesus says, "I will *make* you." The Greek word is not some awesome word that causes us to say, "Wow!" Quite honestly, it is the same word one would use on an assembly line at General Motors such as, "I am making a car." The one critical concept in the word "make," though, is the concept that *the product has yet to be made.* If someone does not make it, it will not exist, because it does not already exist.

"Making" has the idea of taking raw material and turning it into a refined product. As seen in the context of Matthew chapter four, it indicates that Jesus is re-orienting the thinking of Andrew and Simon from selfish goals to evangelistic goals. Their priority in life will no longer be a product such as fish, but it will be people. That which is only temporal will be replaced by that which is eternal.

What does Jesus want me to learn, especially? The value of a human soul!

> "There are clocks to tell the time of day,
> Scales to tell the weight of hay,
> But what rule, sir, would you employ,

To tell the worth of a girl or boy?

Measures there are for silver and gold,
By carats the worth of diamonds are told,
But there is no measure in all the earth,
To tell what a boy or girl is worth."

Unknown Author

Every soul has eternal value because every soul will live forever. That cannot be said about my house, my money, my pets, or even the universe itself. But it can be said about the human soul. And the soul that dies without Christ is lost forever!

Mark 9:44 pictures a man's soul in a wormlike form and, in effect, says, "The worm of a man's soul never dies and the fire in hell is never quenched." Everything I see with the naked eye shall pass out of existence with only one exception: the people I see! They will live throughout eternity in either heaven or hell.

This lesson must be learned by Andrew, Simon, and the rest of us. "What will it profit a man if he gains the whole world and forfeits or loses his own soul? What will he give in exchange for his soul? What will a man give to reclaim his soul once he has lost it?" (Matthew 16:26). That verse teaches one soul—just one soul—is worth more than all the gold, silver, oil, diamonds, stocks, bonds, airlines, railroads, universities, churches, skyscrapers, amusement parks, and everything else in this entire world. *Just one soul is worth more than everything man craves!*

Have we learned the value of a human soul? If yes, we surely would do something about that soul's condition. But, for many Christians, the answer must be "no" because John MacArthur writes, "It has been estimated that 95% of all Christians have never led another person to Christ. If that is true, 95% of the world's spiritual violins have never been played." What a shame to have so much of the orchestra listening to the much smaller 5%!

One church was blessed with a tremendous soloist. He had a habit of closing his eyes whenever he sang a solo. It so happened he continued that habit every time the offering plate was passed, too. He would close his eyes to the offering plate and sing softly to himself. And deliberately never see the offering plate!

One day the offering plate reached his pew. He did his normal thing. He closed his eyes and dared to sing a missionary song such as, "Send the light, the blessed gospel light!"

A missionary-minded worshipper publicly rebuked the singer and said, "You hypocrite! Open your eyes and see the opportunity you have to send the gospel forth instead of just singing about it."

Jesus says, "Instead of closing your eyes, lift up your eyes and look on the fields. They are already white and ripe for harvest" (John 4:35).

Elton Trueblood says, "Evangelism is not a professional job for a few trained men but is instead the unrelenting responsibility of every person who belongs, even in the most modest way, to the company of Jesus."

The Bible scholar A. T. Pierson reminds us, "Witnessing is the whole work of the whole church for the whole age."

The apostle Paul says, "Learn this lesson well then pass this same lesson on to faithful men who will be able to teach others also" (2 Timothy 2:2).

I once had an old deacon who had never led a soul to Christ. Worst of all, he was the chairman of the deacons. As you may suspect, he wasn't motivating the other deacons to lead souls to Christ either. Many of us had been praying for the deacon's son-in-law. The son-in-law came to church every Sunday morning, but he was not born again.

One Sunday morning, the son-in-law sat on the third row with his father-in-law. I preached and gave the invitation. The son-in-law was bothered by the Holy Spirit, but he did not come forward. We dismissed the service. Immediately one of our soul winners went to the son-in-law, talked a brief moment, then the two of them came to the altar and knelt.

I went to the old deacon and said, "Go to the altar and lead your son-in-law to Christ." The deacon immediately obeyed. I stayed away and just watched it unfold. No one needed my help! The son-in-law was wonderfully saved.

But what I remember the most was the deacon rising from the altar and saying, "I led my first soul to Jesus today." I am happy to say it was not his last soul, either.

Charles Spurgeon says,

> I would rather be the means of saving a soul from death than to be the greatest orator on earth. I would rather bring the poorest woman in the world to the feet of Jesus than be made the Archbishop of Canterbury. I would sooner pluck one single brand from the burning than to explain all mysteries. One of my happiest thoughts is that when I die, it shall be my privilege to enter into rest in the bosom of Christ and to know that I shall not enter heaven alone.

Learn what the great Teacher wants you to know: the value of the people around you!

3. THE MOST VICTORIOUS CHRISTIAN IS A FISHING CHRISTIAN.

"He that wins souls is wise" (Proverbs 11:30).

"And those who are wise shall shine like the brightness of the sky above; and those who turn many to righteousness, like the stars forever and ever" (Daniel 12:3, ESV).

"He that goeth forth and weepeth, bearing precious seed, shall doubtless come again with rejoicing, bringing his sheaves *with him*" (Psalm 126:6, KJV).

"The seed that fell into the good ground brought forth fruit, some seed even brought forth a hundred times more than that one seed!" (Matthew 13:23).

"The shepherd found the one lost sheep, then called his neighbors and friends together and said, 'Rejoice with me for I have found my one lost sheep'" (Luke 15:6).

God's goal for my life is that I be sanctified like Jesus. Jesus has made it abundantly clear that I am most like him when I point people to His cross. Jesus says, "If I be lifted up from the earth, I will draw all men to Me" (John 12:32).

Andrew and Simon Peter left their nets, followed Jesus, and began to find lost sheep. They became fishing Christians through both vocal evangelism and lifestyle evangelism. Both approaches should exist in the life of the believer. Vance Havner says, "Too many Christians live their Christian lives inside their heads. It never gets out through hands and feet and lips." But Andrew and Simon Peter both *lived* and *talked* it.

May I share a blessing that is only forty-eight hours old? Like Andrew and Simon, I both *lived* and *talked* it with a man at my secular employment for at least seven years. I have now been retired for more than two years. The two of us talked on the telephone forty-eight hours ago. He told me that he had gotten everything right with the Lord and had just returned home from a Wednesday church service. What a blessing that was to me!

C.S. Lewis says,

> As Christians, we are tempted to make unnecessary concessions to those outside of the faith. We give in too much. Now, I don't mean that we should run the risk of making a nuisance of ourselves by witnessing at improper times, but there comes a time when we must show that we disagree. We must show our Christian colors, if we are to be free in Christ. We cannot remain silent or concede everything away.

There are many excellent training tools available in Christianity today. Through the years, my pastorates have taught many techniques including Evangelism Explosion, Romans Road, the Wordless Book, F.A.I.T.H., the NET, Discovering My Life Mission, plus one of my own design. I especially recommend a small book by Lee E. Thomas titled *Praying Effectively for the Lost*. That book can change the way you pray! Each technique has its own strengths and weaknesses.

But the best technique of all will always be your testimony. As a matter of fact, your testimony is even more important than your knowledge of the Bible. Why? First, you are an expert on your salvation testimony. No one knows your testimony like you. You were there when it happened, and you ought to know!

Second, your testimony is unique to you. No one else has a testimony which is exactly like yours. Not me, not Andrew, nor Simon Peter!

Third, people will usually listen to your testimony because you are similar to them. For example, you aren't the paid preacher; many people see the preacher as being in a different class than you because the preacher is paid to say certain things!

Fourth, it's easy to understand because it is so personal. You are simply sharing what has happened to you. Not to anyone else! Just you!

Fifth, people relate very well to stories; your testimony is indeed a very precious story. It does not need to be embellished; it just needs to be truthful and, if it is truthful, it will also be real.

And sixth, praise the Lord, this experience worked for you! Therefore, it has the potential to work for the listener, also.

These issues are critically important to your effectiveness because D. L. Moody says, "No man can win souls unless he is saved and *knows* it." Likewise, Spurgeon writes, "God will not use dead tools for working living miracles." *A good testimony begins with your knowing, first, that you are born again and, second, why and how you were born again!*

The missionary C. T. Studd said to a lady in England, "Salvation is like smallpox. When you have it, you give it to others." The lady was offended at first. In time, though, the Holy Spirit helped the woman to realize her spiritual condition. Sometime later, Studd received a telegram that read, "Have a bad case of smallpox. Praise God! Dolly."

What should my testimony include? Let me suggest five items that we include in every Sunday bulletin at my church. (Hint: these five items can be occasionally published on your social media account, too.)

How to Be Right with God

1. Admit you are a sinner (Romans 3:23).
2. Accept, as a sinner, that you owe an enormous sin debt (Romans 6:23).
3. Know God loves you, and Jesus Christ, the Son of God, has already paid your sin debt (Romans 5:8).
4. Trust in what Christ did for you on the cross to save you (Romans 10:9).
5. Call upon the name of the Lord (Romans 10:13) and receive Christ as your Savior by faith (John 1:12).

How powerful is anyone's witness? We know the answer to that question by personal experience! Warren Wiersbe writes, "You are a Christian today *because* somebody cared. Now it is your turn."

How should I begin? Jonathan Hayashi suggests seven bridge questions to open the door to a gospel conversation:

• Are you a religious person?
• How interested are you in spiritual things?
• What do you think it takes to get to heaven?
• In your opinion, what is a Christian?
• Anything you want me to pray?
• Do you believe in God?
• What do you believe about Jesus?

It is an easy transition from *any* one of those questions to asking, "May I share what Jesus has done for me?" Ninety percent of the responses will be, "Yes." That response will open the door to sharing your testimony. This type of humble approach will create an intelligent conversation in which your heart speaks to the other person's heart about why you have become a disciple of Jesus Christ. Your testimony may conclude with the individual wanting to receive Christ as Savior. The person may say, "I want what you have!"

Some Christians immediately lead the sinner in a prayer of repentance and faith in Christ. I suggest sharing two verses of scripture before that prayer. John 1:12 emphasizes the two concepts of, first, personally receiving, or appropriating, Christ and, second, believing, or faithing, in Christ for salvation. The second verse, Revelation 3:20, paints a vivid picture of the "receiving" part of salvation. It is easy to visualize Jesus knocking upon a person's door/heart and asking for admittance.

Ina Duley Ogden pictures the event in her invitation hymn,

> "There's a Savior who stands at the door of your heart,
> He is longing to enter why let Him depart?
> He has patiently called you so often before,
> But you must open the door."

The moment of salvation comes when the human will relents/repents and opens the door! "There will be more joy in heaven over one sinner who repents than over ninety-nine righteous people who don't need repentance" (Luke 15:7, HCSB).

(Note: It is true Revelation 3:20 is addressed to a church rather than an individual. However, the verse vividly pictures the salvation process, also. The rebellious human will is the most difficult component in salvation. Jesus identified that problem when He said, "You *will* not come to Me" (John 5:40). Opening the door is a beautiful picture of the will surrendering to Christ.)

The late preacher Sam Morris of Stamford, Texas, was recognized in my early days as a "booze buster par excellent." But it took an ordinary someone to get him from point A to point B, from sin to salvation, from hell to heaven. He wrote this remarkable story about one person—the person most responsible for his conversion to Christ:

> In the community where I was converted there lived an elderly man who always went to church and Sunday School. He was always talking 'religion' to everybody he met. If you went hunting with him or rode to town with him, you talked

'religion.' He was full of his subject and talked it all the time. He was always 'ding-donging' at me to come to church.

Others praised the old man's zeal, commended his conduct, and had confidence in his religion. I detested him. I wouldn't hunt or fish with him, and I loved both sports. I would walk to town (six miles) rather than ride with him. The few times I went to church were not enjoyed because I occupied the seat of the scornful and went home making caustic remarks about 'that old hypocrite who runs everything.'

During a revival meeting I got under conviction. I became burdened because of my sins. One night I could resist no longer. In a contrite spirit and with a repentant heart, I accepted Christ and started down the aisle of the little country schoolhouse to confess Christ publicly by giving the preacher my hand.

I never reached him. Standing by the old organ, trying to sing the best he knew how, was this old man. I landed on his shoulder with my arms around his neck. We put on the biggest 'necking party' I have ever experienced as we wept and rejoiced together in my new-found salvation.

From that day to this, he and I have had blessed fellowship in the Lord. We have sung together. We have wept together. We have prayed together. We have read the Bible together. We love each other beyond words. He didn't change. He is the same energetic, bold Christian, always bubbling over and 'talking religion.' But, friend, I changed. I know I have passed from death unto life because I love the brethren.

An unknown poet prayed a prayer that all of us can pray,

> "I'm not a John the Baptist, a Peter or a Paul.
> I'll never lead ten thousand to heed the Master's call.
> But please, God, won't You help me in some small way to be
> A little bit like Andrew who led his friends to Thee?"

(Note: Additional material can be found in 15 Spiritual Laws to Grow People.)

19

GROWING THROUGH MANAGING GOD'S MONEY GOD'S WAY

T he numbers are staggering. One recent survey shows 65% of Americans lose sleep over money. Some worry about making ends meet while others worry about how to safely invest what they have. Another survey shows that money is the number one problem for 35% of married couples; it should come as no surprise that money is the largest cause of divorce. Fully one-third of Americans report they received zero instructions about how to handle their money properly.

How does the average American solve his financial dilemma? The answers are as diverse as the number of financial problems. We worry, complain, cheat, steal, blame someone or something, give up, stop spending, go further into debt, sell a possession, become depressed, or hope someone will just give us the money we need.

Whoever said, "Money is a root of all evil," sure got it right. As a matter of fact, I just got off the telephone with someone whose family is in a dispute over the family inheritance. Each family member wants his "fair" share, but no one can agree on what is "fair." What a shame!

My eighty-six-year-old mother receives multiple mailings each day from firms asking for her charity. It is so bad that I am expecting a fundraiser any day from the "Increase the Height of the Little Green Men on Mars Foundation." My mother summarizes her mail quite succinctly by stating, "Everyone wants my money, but I have none to give!"

And yet money has no soul or ambition, never communicates, is neither good nor evil. But ask anyone, "How much money do you want?" and the answer will always be, "At least one dollar more!" "Money makes the world go around" is truer than, "Love makes the world go around."

Money has become a very integral part of our lives. Thus, it should surprise no one that *sanctification extends into our personal finances.* Why? It is because money can destroy us, or money can bless us. Money can control us or be controlled by us. Money can be a solution, or money can create problems in need of solutions.

Jesus recognized the incredible, tantalizing power associated with money when He warned us about the *deceitfulness of riches* or the seduction of wealth (Matthew 13:22). What a unique expression to describe our greenbacks, certificates of deposit, stocks, and bonds! Riches can deceive. Riches can seduce just like a woman can seduce a man or alcohol can seduce its next victim. Riches can be like "wine which sparkles in a cup, goes down smoothly, but then poisons like a viper snake" (Proverbs 23:31-32).

God's warning to our modern society is, "Let the buyer beware!" Indeed, Jesus even went so far as to instruct the rich young ruler to give away his riches, then come and follow Him (Matthew 19:21). If he had obeyed, the rich young ruler would have found Jesus to be much more precious than all of his riches. But, alas, he chose the riches over Jesus.

The Christian also needs to beware! "But those who want to be rich fall into temptation, a trap, and many foolish and harmful desires, which plunge people into ruin and destruction. For the love of money is a root of all kinds of evil, and by craving it, some have wandered away from the faith and pierced themselves with many griefs" (1 Timothy 6:9-10, CSB).

This difficulty is the reason that every Christian needs to be reminded of both the value and purpose of money. The songwriter challenges us as follows:

> "When you look at others with their lands and gold,
> Think that Christ has promised you His wealth untold;
> Count your many blessings—money cannot buy
> Your reward in heaven, nor your home on high."

> Johnson Oatman, Jr.

1. A BIBLICAL WORLDVIEW INCLUDES A BIBLICAL VIEW OF MONEY.

"But you shall remember the Lord your God, for it is He who is giving you power to make wealth" (Deuteronomy 8:18, NASB). I suggest that you circle the word "He" in the previous sentence. That sentence is supported by chapter fourteen ("Growing through Humility").

Man, including many Christians, has a sinful tendency to say, "Look at me. I am self-made." But a biblical worldview says, "Look at God. I amount to something because I am God-made." What did Paul say? "By the grace of God, I am what I am." This is true in every aspect of life, but it seems to be especially evident in the world of money.

So many are like the rich fool who said, "Look at me! I will tear down my old barns and build newer, bigger barns. I will store up my crops in those bigger barns. I will say, 'Self, you have everything you need for retirement. Take it easy. Content yourself. Eat, drink, and be merry.'" But God called him a fool in the very next verse.

There is an arrogant spirit in so many rich people, as well as those who are working their way up the ladder to riches. A billionaire was asked in a recent television interview, "Do you deserve all of that money?"

He brazenly answered, "Yes, I do. I worked hard for it."

The questioner responded, "I do not question that you worked hard, but I am sure your employees worked hard, too, so you can have all of that money." In other words, the billionaire would not have made his billions on his own!

The arrogant spirit says, "It's mine. I worked hard for it." But that person has clearly forgotten that it is the Lord who gave that person the power, ability, and brains to acquire that wealth. Mark this down as a faithful saying: *The Bible teaches that wealth—**all** wealth—is the result of God's grace.*

Some may counter, "But I am smarter, and I deserve more." Okay, but Who gave you the brain power? Who gave you the health that enabled you to succeed? Who put you in a place and a century where that skill could best manifest itself? We must remind ourselves that God could have disadvantaged us with congenital disabilities, such as blindness. Or a poor home environment or poor school environment.

But God, for His own purpose, *chose to advantage some of us* so that we might go further than others. Why? It's His business and not ours! "Does not the potter have a right over the clay, to make from the same lump one vessel for honorable use and another for common use?" (Romans 9:21, NASB).

Even though I often wish to be someone I am not, in the end, I am left with being me, including all of my limitations. As a result, looking *up* the ladder will likely result in disappointment at how little I have climbed. However, I only need to look *down* the ladder to realize that I owe much, even very much, to the grace of my loving God. I will then pray, "Thank You, Lord, that things are as well with us as they are."

That is why God says I have a responsibility to you, dear reader, because you are my brother, and I am my brother's keeper (Genesis 4:9). It is the underlying principle in the story of the Good Samaritan (Luke 10:30) as well as the story of Ruth.

Above all, I need a biblical worldview of what money is, where it originates, and how it is gained.

2. MONEY IS A TOOL TO BRING GLORY TO GOD.

"Whether you eat, drink or whatever you do, do all to the glory of God" (1 Corinthians 10:31). That goal is much different than the much-pursued goal of working for the weekend or working for that new car or new boat.

The Preacher emphasizes, "Sometimes a person who has toiled with wisdom and knowledge and skill must leave everything to be enjoyed by someone who did not toil for it. This also is vanity and a great evil" (Ecclesiastes 2:21, ESV). Rest assured, misuse of money results in vanity, but the proper use of money results in glory.

"Do all to the glory of God." That lofty and proper goal includes making money, investing money, donating money, and spending money.

We should see ourselves not in the role of a consumer but as a manager!

In the old days (and older translations), this manager role was described as a steward. A modern-day parallel would be that of a mutual fund manager—someone who has a responsibility to manage the funds of his client properly.

The manager/steward's responsibility is to manage money on behalf of someone else. The money does not belong to the steward. Who is the client? God! The Bible teaches that *all* of the Christian's possessions belong to God. "We are no longer our own, but we have been bought with a price. Therefore, our new goal is the goal of our Owner" (1 Corinthians 6:19).

That verse of scripture is more than just words—it contains a philosophy for everyday living. For many of us, it is an eye-opening revelation that can totally change the way we view money. *We are managing God's money on behalf of God.* What an awesome responsibility!

That is the underlying reason for God's anger toward so many of the rich. It is because the rich often think it is *their* money!

> *Come now, you rich people, weep and wail over the miseries that are coming on you. Your wealth has rotted and your clothes are moth-eaten. Your gold and silver are corroded, and their corrosion will be a witness against you and will eat your flesh like fire. You have stored up treasure in the last days. Look! The pay that you withheld from the workers who mowed your fields cries out, and the outcry of the harvesters has reached the ears of the Lord of Hosts. You have lived luxuriously on the earth and have indulged yourselves. You have fattened your hearts in a day of slaughter (James 5:1-5, HCSB).*

Everyone needs to pray like the man who prayed, "Lord, may every dime in today's offering be used for Your purpose called the Great Commission." The man recognized that every dollar comes *from* God and is to be used *for* God!

My pastor father often told his church about a fellow employee who continued working past his retirement age to increase the amount he was giving to the Lord's work. The employee shared, "I give over fifty percent of my paycheck to my church so we can do the Lord's work. I can't do that if I retire, so I'll keep working."

3. MY FIRST INVESTMENT IS TO GOD AND HIS WORK ON EARTH.

Where should I invest my money? Obviously, I need shelter or housing. I also need food and clothing. Healthcare is another obvious necessity. *But the biggest necessity of all originates within my soul.* It is the necessity of knowing my Creator, my God, my Savior, and living out His will in my life.

God says, "Now without faith it is impossible to please God, since the one who draws near to him must believe that he exists and that he rewards those who seek him" (Hebrews 11:6, CSB). God has called us to live a life of faith based upon His biblical teachings (not some fantasy or mystical experience). That means we are to spend/invest our money in accordance with our biblical faith. *Practicing our faith includes funding God's work on earth.*

How was this funding done in the Old Testament?

> *Will a man rob God? Yet you are robbing Me!' You ask: 'How do we rob You?' 'By not making the payments of the tenth and the contributions. You are suffering under a curse, yet you—the whole nation—are still robbing Me. Bring the full tenth into the storehouse so that there may be food in My house. Test Me in this way,' says the Lord of Hosts. 'See if I will not open the floodgates of heaven and pour out a blessing for you without measure (Malachi 3:8-10, HCSB).*

The Holman translation has an advantage over older translations in that it defines the word "tithe" rather than uses the word "tithe." The actual Hebrew word means, "tenth." God's standard in the Old Testament was for *everyone* to give a tithe or a tenth. The tithe provided "food in My house" or funds to carry on the work of God.

(Note: There were actually *three* tithes in the Old Testament. The first tithe was for worship, the second tithe was for the national festivals and might be thought of as a federal income tax, and the third tithe—taken every three years—was for the poor. Based upon those numbers, it appears the Jews gave an average of 23% annually, not just 10% as is commonly believed.)

There is much discussion about whether tithing or freewill giving (otherwise known as grace giving, faith giving, or giving as God has blessed you) is the standard for today. Such a discussion seems to be a straw man—a straining of gnats and swallowing the whole camel along with probably the whole herd. Such a discussion is frivolous, wastes time, and confuses everyone. It is best to follow the K.I.S.S. formula and

Keep It Simple, Stupid: If it walks like a duck, quacks like a duck, swims like a duck, and looks like a duck, it's probably a duck.

Can we ever give too much to the cause of world evangelism and world discipleship? Of course not. But can we give too little? The answer is yes. Those two questions clearly establish that we should assign a high priority to God's work.

Any reasonable person knows the importance of God's work, as expressed in the Great Commission (Matthew 28:18-20, Mark 16:15, Acts 1:8). Has the work of world evangelization diminished in these New Testament days? Not by one inch or one cent! Why then would anyone want to lower the standard and go below 10%? It makes no sense because the need has not diminished in the least. *Today's need is the same as yesterday's need.*

I do not recall a time in my life when I did not give *at least* ten percent of my income (payroll check *plus* investment income) to the Lord. That included my first paychecks as a teenager. My 1968 paychecks averaged $10 a week from Jim's Dairy Land . . . and I thought I was rich!

My pattern did not change in later life, even though there were times when money became tight. My wife and I have always been blessed with enough money to buy Christmas gifts for our children, but there was more than one Christmas when we could not afford to buy for each other. I can assure you that life went on! (We have always believed that gifts do not make a home.)

The Bible urges, "Honor the LORD from your wealth And from the first of all your produce" (Proverbs 3:9, NASB). From the first! That instruction might seem like gambling to a farmer because he is called to give his tenth at the *beginning* of the harvest rather than the end. It is important to know the obedient farmer gives even though there is no guarantee that the "end harvest" will match his estimates. The end harvest might be destroyed by weather or pestilence, but the farmer still trusts God to provide for his needs. He steps out by faith and invests in God's work even before he has the entire sum of money in his hands. That action requires faith!

In many ways, tithing *appears* to be a form of gambling. We commit ourselves through our tithes and offerings to "seek first the kingdom of God." We give financially to the Lord and trust God to keep His word that "all these things shall be added to you" (Matthew 6:33).

Will God keep His promise? He has with us. He has with people around you. And somehow, God will keep His promise with you, too. Thus, tithing is not a gamble because *tithing is backed by God's guarantee,* whereas gambling has zero backing at all. Indeed, gambling is nothing but a shot in the dark with very, very, very, very, very, very little chance of ever achieving gain.

The difference between tithing and gambling is monumental and is easily identifiable in the life of Abraham. Abraham answered God's call by leaving his homeland. The Bible expression is unique: "He went out, not knowing where he was going" (Hebrews 11:8). Did God take care of Abraham? Yes, He did!

I left southern Ohio in 1976 to follow God's call and begin pastoral studies at Tennessee Temple in Chattanooga. My wife and I were married on August 28, 1976, and arrived in Chattanooga on August 29. (We have always referred to Chattanooga as our three-year honeymoon.) It did not occur to me at the time that our move to Chattanooga was an act of stepping out on faith just like Abraham from centuries before.

Many things could have gone wrong, and some things *did* go wrong. (We burned up our car's engine on the way to church in Dalton, Georgia.) Nevertheless, we did what we believed God wanted us to do. Perhaps we were naïve, but we believed God had issued the call; furthermore, we believed God would provide the means to accomplish the call. To us, it did not sound like faith (that word was reserved for the great saints like Abraham), but rather it sounded like common sense! *It took some time for us to realize our action truly fell under the category of "living by faith."*

I remember someone telling me, "I believe my family's financial problems exist because we never learned how to tithe. Tithing would have taught us how to bring our finances under control."

Do you know what I asked him?

I asked, "Are you now willing to make that commitment?"

4. HARD WORK IS REWARDED WORK.

Sam Ewing teaches, "Hard work spotlights the character of people: some turn up their sleeves, some turn up their noses, and some don't turn up at all." Which outcome is best for you and me?

The basic purpose of the Bible from Genesis to Revelation is to present the way of salvation. Bible scholars like to identify that entire presentation as "the scarlet thread of redemption." Salvation is by faith in the scarlet blood of God's Substitute, Jesus Christ. Most of our Bible studies, therefore, focus on the many components of salvation, including justification, sanctification, glorification, inspiration, redemption, depravity, eternity, regeneration, etc.

But it needs to be recognized that the Bible ventures into other areas, also, including some of the basic principles in economics. People will always debate the extent to which the Bible promotes free-market capitalism, especially *unfettered* capitalism. We may not like *all* of the current aspects of capitalism, but it must be remembered that capitalism is the system we currently have. *Despite its shortfalls, capitalism has lifted more boats than any other system devised by man.*

One of the Bible's most basic economic principles states that hard work should be handsomely rewarded. "Let the elders who rule well be considered worthy of double honor, especially those who labor in preaching and teaching. For the Scripture says, 'You shall not muzzle an ox when it treads out the grain,' and, 'The laborer deserves his wages'" (1 Timothy 5:17-18, ESV).

"Complete your outdoor work, and prepare your field; afterward, build your house." (Proverbs 24:27, CSB).

"Idle hands make one poor, but diligent hands bring riches. The son who gathers during summer is prudent; the son who sleeps during harvest is disgraceful." (Proverbs 10:4-5, CSB).

"He who tills his land will have plenty of bread, but he who pursues worthless things lacks sense" (Proverbs 12:11, NASB).

"The soul of the sluggard craves and gets nothing, but the soul of the diligent is made fat" (Proverbs 13:4, NASB).

"The point is this: whoever sows sparingly will also reap sparingly, and whoever sows bountifully will also reap bountifully" (2 Corinthians 9:6, ESV).

The Bible clearly indicates that God honors hard work!

5. IT IS BIBLICAL TO MAKE MONEY *WITH* MONEY.

There is nothing ungodly about learning how to make money or grow money. The law of sowing then *reaping more than we sow* is more than a farming principle; it is also a financial principle.

People are often surprised to learn the source of one of the most famous quotes in the world of finance. Scientist Albert Einstein said, "Compound interest is the eighth wonder of the world. He who understands it, earns it . . . he who doesn't, pays it." In other words, smart money makes money *with* money!

The Parable of the Talents reveals how Jesus thought about making money with money.

> *A property owner went on a journey. He gave five bags of silver to one of his stewards and one bag of silver to another steward. The 'five bag steward' immediately went to work investing his master's money. The 'one bag steward' dug a hole in the ground and buried his master's money. The master eventually returned. The 'five bag steward' brought the original five bags plus five more to the master. The master (the master*

represents God) was thrilled. The master said, "Well done! I will invest more of my financial resources with you." The 'one bag steward' brought the original one bag but no more bags. He said, 'Master, I was afraid I would lose your money, so I buried it.' The master said, "You're a horrible, good-for-nothing steward. Why didn't you deposit my money in the bank? It would have accumulated at least a few cents of interest! You're fired!" (Matthew 25:14-30).

The first steward made money *with* the original money. The second steward made zero money with the original money. God commended the first steward but condemned the second steward. The old saying, "Nothing ventured, nothing gained," lines up perfectly with this Bible story.

Recent surveys show that nearly half of Americans have no retirement savings. However, many of those people make enough money to save something for their retirement. In far too many cases, though, the people have made a deliberate choice to spend now rather than save/invest now. In so doing, they're ignoring Einstein's rule, God's rule, as well as their own future.

The Bible encourages all of us to study the ant. "Ants are not a strong people, yet they store up their food in the summer" (Proverbs 30:25, CSB). Ants know how to save! Likewise, we need to know how to save!

6. A FINANCIAL PLAN IS AS IMPORTANT AS ANY OTHER PLAN.

Many people have plans for the house, the car, and vacation but no plan for their finances. They have neglected the basic premise that "He who aims at nothing, hits nothing!" It must be emphasized that life occurs one day at a time, and those days ultimately add up to a lifetime!

Many ministers have neglected God's instructions about preparing for their post-ministry years. As a result, they often enter retirement with very little for daily provision. Despite ministering, they're already headed for the poor house, and God pity the poor wife who may outlive her husband in abject poverty. They have forgotten the Bible warning, "the one who does not provide financially for his family has denied the faith and is worse than an infidel" (1 Timothy 5:8). Perhaps that warning is fair because God gave us our family before He gave us our pastorate!

The words of Jesus still make sense in even modern-day America: "For which of you, wanting to build a tower, doesn't first sit down and calculate the cost to see if he has enough to complete it?" (Luke 14:28, CSB). The tower, of course, represents a goal or project.

Is financial survival a worthy goal? Of course, it is. It is a simple procedure to make a reasonable financial plan. Of course, the success of such a plan will require the same self-discipline that is necessary in any other area of life. My personal self-discipline includes an annual reading of *Simple Wealth, Inevitable Wealth* by Nick Murray. This book steadies my nerves during uncertain times and keeps me on track!

It cannot be emphasized too much that a financial plan has the potential to relieve a person of stress. In so doing, the plan can free a person for other activities.

Solomon, the richest man in the world, counsels us throughout the Proverbs about the importance of work, assigning a *proper* value to money, and a righteous or right living lifestyle. But he also counsels us against being *consumed* in our pursuit of financial gain. Solomon writes, "Don't exhaust yourself trying to get rich. Be wise in your planning; trust your plan and give your plan the necessary time to run its course. If your heart flies speedily in pursuit of wealth, don't be surprised if wealth flies away even faster . . . as fast as an eagle" (Proverbs 23:4-5).

(Note: The entire context in Proverbs chapter twenty-three emphasizes restraint or balance such as not being a "big, overzealous eater at the king's banquet and ruining yourself in the king's eyes." It does *not* emphasize one should ignore saving money. Such a view would be contrary to Solomon's many proverbs as well as his own staggering riches.)

Plan to succeed, and you will have a much better likelihood of success!

7. IDENTIFY THE *MANY* ENEMIES OF YOUR FINANCES.

Most people have or make *enough* money. Unfortunately, many people have a flawed monetary philosophy that is based upon worldly materialism. Materialism has been defined as "the science of knowing the price of everything and the value of nothing." It is based upon an attitude of getting rather than giving. Materialism replaces God with money, and, in its deepest essence, trusts money to solve our problems rather than God. Solomon cautions, "Better is little with the fear of the Lord than great riches and trouble with those same riches" (Proverbs 15:16).

The spirit of coveting destroys many pocketbooks. The tenth commandment says, "Thou shalt not covet" (Exodus 20:17). The apostle Paul identifies coveting as a form of heathen idolatry in Colossians 3:5. Too many people believe in the materialistic philosophy, "He who dies with the most toys wins." That isn't quite so because the person is still dead.

Socrates cautions, "It is not the man who has too little, but the man who craves too much that is poor." We want such-and-such because someone else has such-and-such. Quite often, ownership of certain objects is tied to our status in life or place on the economic ladder. Who has the bigger car, the bigger house, the better clothes, the better vacation? Who owns a second house or even a third house?

"He who loves pleasure will become a poor man; he who loves wine and oil will not become rich" (Proverbs 21:17, NASB).

There is a bad tendency for the average person to be swallowed up by materialism; such an obsession leads to our second enemy, which is excessive debt or out-of-control debt. Debt can be a blessing if it is properly controlled, but it can be a killer if it is not. "The rich rules over the poor, and the borrower becomes the lender's slave" (Proverbs 22:7, NASB).

Never forget: The one who lends reigns, but the one who borrows serves. The one who lends is the head, but the one who borrows is the tail. The one who lends is above, but the one who borrows is beneath.

The Bible establishes a very high standard. "Pay to all what is owed to them: taxes to whom taxes are owed, revenue to whom revenue is owed, respect to whom respect is owed, honor to whom honor is owed" (Romans 13:7, ESV). "Pay to all what is owed to them" is the equivalent of, "pay your bills on time."

I know a man who now pays cash for everything. Everything! He even pays cash for gasoline. I asked him why.

He said, "Some years ago, my wife and I got in credit card debt. That debt almost ruined us. We decided to burn all of our credit cards. We adopted a new philosophy of 'pay as you go'."

Everyone has limitations, and that is especially true regarding finances. Therefore, it is only reasonable to identify those limitations and then determine a way to minimize the potential damage!

For example, gambling is rapidly becoming a great enemy to the creation of wealth. Gambling has a very tantalizing, "get something for nothing" appeal. P. T. Barnum reportedly said, "A fool and his money are soon parted." The gambling industry is built upon that very saying. It knows how to separate a fool from his money. And there are plenty of fools who fall into that trap!

I knew a husband and wife who never had a dime and even had to borrow lunch money from co-workers, despite having a combined annual income of $100,000. Their gambling addiction ate them alive. It consumed them.

The Christian, though, should never open the door to such an addiction. *The Bible teaches us to trust in God rather than chance.* It is better to trust in hard work rather than a one-in-a-billion lottery drawing. Indeed, gambling should be viewed as leading to a perpetual empty hole rather than a pot of gold.

Lack of self-discipline is an equally bad enemy. The apostle Paul says, "We exercise self-control or personal discipline in everything" (1 Corinthians 9:25).

One of my supervisors hurt his family by purchasing a car that he could not afford. He got the car fever, and the fever consumed him. He bought a beautiful car, but it was the wrong car. He soon sold the car and bought the car he should have bought originally! He was hurt financially because he lacked self-discipline.

I often think of the day when my accounting supervisor summoned me into his office for an unscheduled meeting. He closed the door. I wondered what I had done wrong. Thank God, the answer was nothing!

He then shared, "You don't make much money here. Your wife stays home to take care of three young children. But you have more money than most of the people that work on the top management floor of this building. Most of them live from paycheck to paycheck. You're in better shape than most of them because you are self-disciplined." His words helped reinforce my Bible-based philosophy!

I deeply believe in these words from my Lord, "Make money-bags for yourselves that won't grow old, an inexhaustible treasure in heaven, where no thief comes near and no moth destroys. For where your treasure is, there your heart will be also" (Luke 12:33-34, CSB).

The newspaper headline read *Buried Life Savings Just A Rotten Idea.* The Associated Press reported that an eighty-two-year-old man in Beijing, China suffered a devastating financial loss. This man would not trust the local banks with his money. He instead dug a hole and buried his life savings in the hole. Five years passed. One day the man needed some cash. He dug up the money. Or what was left of it! To his dismay, he discovered that the money was now moldy and almost beyond recognition. The story concluded that he was only able to salvage one-third of his savings.

What a loss! But let me tell you what will never be a loss!

The financier Roger Babson wrote many years ago, "One dollar spent for a lunch lasts five hours. One dollar spent for a necktie lasts five weeks. One dollar spent for an automobile lasts five years. One dollar spent in the service of God lasts for eternity."

Amen.

20

GROWING THROUGH SEPARATION

An infidel asked the famous preacher, D. L. Moody, "How do you account for the fact that Mohammed began his work six hundred years after Christ and yet he now has more disciples than Christ?"

Moody did not argue numbers with the man. He simply answered, "A man can be a disciple of Mohammed and not deny himself nor have any cross. He can live in the darkest, blackest, foulest sin. But if any man will become a disciple of Jesus Christ, he must come out from the world; he must take up his cross daily and follow Jesus."

But it seems as if Moody's words are falling on deaf ears in much of today's Christendom. The early church wanted to know, "What must I do to be saved?" Regrettably, today's church asks, "What can I do and *still* be saved?"

During the Civil War, a man lived on the border which separated the North from the South. This man did not want to choose sides, so he wore a Confederate army jacket and Union army pants. But that solution did not work, because the Union soldiers shot at his jacket and the Confederate soldiers shot at his pants!

Joshua says in the Old Testament, "Choose you this day whom you will serve" (Joshua 24:15). That Civil War soldier needed to make a choice. So do I. So do you.

1. BIBLICAL SEPARATION IS A CALLING.

One of the most important items regarding Christian growth is personal separation *from* something *to* something much different. Doesn't that sound like sanctification?

The apostle Paul provides his testimony in the opening verse of Romans. "*Paul, a servant of Jesus Christ, called to be an apostle, separated unto the gospel of God.*" Paul's separation was from an earthly calling to a heavenly calling, from earthly standards to heavenly standards, from living for here and now to living for eternity. It was an inward calling that led to transformed external living.

Is there a negative side to separation resulting in things we no longer do? Absolutely, but there is also a very positive side to separation and *things we now do*. Bless God, the positive side *far outweighs* the negative side.

One of the weaknesses in the modern church is we talk too much about cooperation and not enough about separation—about separation from this ungodly world of ours. We live in a world with an unbiblical philosophy, an unbiblical lifestyle, an unbiblical morality, unbiblical entertainment, and, above all, an unbiblical mindset. In brief, we live in an unbiblical world which is also an ungodly world—a world deliberately set against God.

The crowd cried out at the trial of Jesus, "We do not wish to have this man rule over us!" That cry actually began in the Garden of Eden when Adam chose to eat of the forbidden fruit. In so doing, Adam declared, "I do not care what God says. I do not wish to have the Creator rule over me."

Four thousand years later, the world crucified the Lord of glory. Two thousand more years have passed, but the world is still in the same state of rebellion. Think of it! Six thousand years have passed since the age of Adam, and nothing—absolutely nothing of spiritual significance—has changed.

There is an old saying, "God put the church in the world to change the world—to be salt and light in a godless society." But, unfortunately, that saying has been replaced by a question of horrendous implications, *"Is the church changing the world, or is the world changing the church?"*

One pastor says, "It is no longer the case of the wolf being at the door, but the wolf is now inside the door!"

A commitment to Christian values is declining—of all places—in God's church! A Southern Baptist leader reports, "The world is getting into the church faster than the church is getting into the world. It is leading to a compromise of Christians. Time will tell whether we can survive this kind of moral decay and demonic onslaught."

Far too many sinners can point their finger at a church member and say, "If he is good enough to make it to heaven, well, so am I." Such words should never be said, but they have been said about some of my own church members.

Separation from the world is a very biblical concept that is also an expected biblical practice.

Separation is not merely a suggestion; rather, separation is a commandment from the Lord God Almighty. Separation is a means of purifying our lives so that we actually serve as God's light and salt to this dark, decaying world.

God's plan for our life includes biblical separation. The concept is stated very well by evangelist Glenn Mathews.

> "The sons of Aaron were to separate from the other people of Israel to God. Separate them FROM. Separate them TO Me. Separate them FOR. That's sanctification—to separate from, to separate to, to separate for. We are sanctified from the world, to the Lord, for the purpose of serving." (*Expositions That Encourage*, p. 150)

Let me share two passages of scripture to support this concept. Many passages could be shared, but I have chosen one from the Old Testament and one from the New Testament.

"Now the Lord said to Abram, 'Go forth from your country, And from your relatives And from your father's house, To the land which I will show you; And I will make you a great nation, And I will bless you, And make your name great; And so you shall be a blessing'" (Genesis 12:1-2, NASB).

Abraham was told to separate himself from his father's family and move to a far country. Daddy Terah was an idol worshipper, but Abraham was a Jehovah worshipper. That meant Terah's philosophy, standards, speech, plans—literally everything was in contrast to how Abraham lived.

God wanted Abraham's full, undivided attention and loyalty, so God said, "Go forth and leave your family. Be separated from the world and be separated to Me." Imagine what would have happened if Abraham had said, "No! I am staying here." Imagine the implications of such disobedience because Abraham's obedience still has implications for us in the twenty-first century.

The New Testament passage is familiar to every Bible student.

> *Do not be mismatched with unbelievers. For what partnership is there between righteousness and lawlessness? Or what fellowship does light have with darkness? What agreement does Christ have with Belial? Or what does a believer have in common with an*

unbeliever? And what agreement does God's sanctuary have with idols? For we are the sanctuary of the living God, as God said: I will dwell among them and walk among them, and I will be their God, and they will be My people. Therefore, come out from among them and be separate, says the Lord; do not touch any unclean thing, and I will welcome you. I will be a Father to you, and you will be sons and daughters to Me, says the Lord Almighty (2 Corinthians 6:14-18, HCSB).

Please underline the above phrase, "Therefore, come out from among them and be separate," then write your initials between the words "therefore" and "come." In other words, make this statement personal to you, because it is addressed to you, too!

Robert Gardner raises the flag high when he declares, "Every Christian should practice separation, every church should stand for separation, and every pastor should preach separation."

That leads me to the most important statement in this chapter.

Christianity IS a lifestyle. It is not merely a religion, but it IS a lifestyle. Indeed, Christianity is its own unique lifestyle in terms of philosophy, goals, speech, entertainment, clothing, attitude, etc.

---

2. THREE STORIES

Let me share three stories to emphasize why this teaching is so important to our testimony.

Story #1: My father pastored for nearly thirty years. One day Dad met a man who said, "I work at such-and-such a place."

My father became excited and said, "Then you work with so-and-so. He is one of my finest church members."

The man responded, "You're kidding me. He's one of the filthiest men I know. If he's in your church, I'll never visit."

That story raises a very difficult question for each one of us: "What is the difference between a sinner and me outside of church attendance?"

Story #2: Fred Brown was one of the finest preachers I have ever heard. He blessed us often during my three years at Tennessee Temple in Chattanooga, Tennessee. Fred liked to share stories from his childhood. One day his mother looked outside and saw Fred doing some not-so-good things with the neighborhood boys. Fred never told us what he was doing, but he gave us every indication it was bad but not *that* bad!

His mother called Fred into the house and disciplined him. Fred complained, "Mom, why can't I be like the other boys?"

His mother replied, "Because you're a Brown, that's why!"

Guess what God says? "Because you're a Christian, and you belong to Me! That's why!"

Story #3: My grandfather Merlin was born again when Mom was ten years old. On the next morning, Merlin went to the factory and told all of the men (a foul-mouthed, sinful lot) that he had been born again and intended to live for the Lord. Some of those sinful men were actually happy for him.

Merlin had worked with one of those men for several years. That man went to Merlin and said, "That's great news! I've been saved for many years, and there's nothing like it!"

Some years later, Merlin related that story and said, "Unfortunately, I replied to that man before I thought. I spoke the man's name then added, 'I'm sorry, but *I did not know you were saved.*'" Merlin did not know and *could not know* because that man's life was no different than any other factory worker.

The principle is clear: We can never reach the world if we are like the world. The world needs *something* different; God expects us to be that *something* different.

Would Jesus qualify as something different? Yes! We are called to be like Him!

I have asked a grieving spouse before the mate's funeral, "Was your spouse saved? Did your spouse know Jesus as the Savior?"

On more than one occasion, the spouse has answered, "I don't know."

I would never add hurt to the grieving spouse, but I would always wonder, "How can't you know? Didn't you ever ask? Didn't your spouse ever show you by how he or she lived?"

God expects us to live a separated life so people will know we are different from them! It should not be viewed as a superiority contest, but it should be viewed as spiritual, eternal living versus fleshly, temporal living. Jesus described us as being *in* the world but not *of* the world (John 17:14-16). "In" suggests our physical location, but "of" suggests our spiritual character. In other words, we may live among them, but we are not like them.

3. HOW DIFFERENT AM I?

Every Christian has to decide about whether to be a separated Christian fit for the master's use or a dirty Christian which has very limited use!

> Now in a large house there are not only gold and silver vessels, but also those of wood and clay; some for honorable use and some for dishonorable. So if anyone purifies himself from anything dishonorable, he will be a special instrument, set apart, useful to the Master, prepared for every good work (2 Timothy 2:20-21, CSB).

> How blessed is the man who does not walk in the counsel of the wicked, Nor stand in the path of sinners, Nor sit in the seat of scoffers! But his delight is in the law of the Lord, And in His law he meditates day and night. He will be like a tree firmly planted by streams of water, Which yields its fruit in its season And its leaf does not wither; And in whatever he does, he prospers (Psalm 1:1-3, NASB).

Here is our checklist:

- ✓ If our beliefs are the world's beliefs, we are no different from the world.
- ✓ If our standards are the world's standards, we are no different from the world.
- ✓ If our jokes are the world's jokes, we are no different from the world.
- ✓ If our speech is the world's speech, we are no different from the world.
- ✓ If our goals are the world's goals, we are no different from the world.
- ✓ If our expectations are the world's expectations, we are no different from the world.

God expects His children to believe differently, talk differently, eat differently, behave differently, think differently, spend our money differently, and even look different from everyone else. Why? It is because He has saved us to be different! It begins with believing differently; we believe differently because we have a Bible that teaches us differently!

I read about some small boys that were marching in a parade to the band's music. One little fellow, though, was out of step with the others. The instructor inspected the young fellow and discovered he was listening to music from a hidden radio. That's why he was marching out of step with the others!

That story has an application to the child of God. We ought to march through life in step with the beat of heaven rather than the beat of this world. We should not be afraid to march out of step with the world.

Gilbert K. Chesterton reminds us, "The world has been moved most by men who contradicted it most."

The reality is I don't have to be like the world, and I don't gain anything of eternal value by being like the world. But I do lose something by being like the world!

We must recognize Christianity is more than attending church once a week. *Christianity is a complete lifestyle.* This lifestyle is so complete it touches our soul, our church, our recreation, our appearance, our wallet, our internet usage, our work, our marriage, our children, our very purpose in life! It even affects where we attend church because all churches do not teach the truth!

Christianity is a complete lifestyle that touches everything we do! What was Paul's philosophy? "Whatever you eat, drink, think, plan, buy, sell, or say—do everything, absolutely everything, to the glory of God" (1 Corinthians 10:31). If we enlarge that principle, we end up with the Ten Commandments. If we enlarge the Ten Commandments, we end up with the entire Law of Moses (613 commandments). That law provided a *complete lifestyle* for the entire nation of Israel.

"I heard another voice from heaven, saying, 'Come out of her, my people, so that you will not participate in her sins and receive of her plagues; for her sins have piled up as high as heaven, and God has remembered her iniquities'" (Revelation 18:4-5, NASB).

During the early 1970s, my father's employer sent him to the University of Michigan for management training. There was little to do in the evening. Most of the men sat in the lounge and boozed it up until many became drunk. My father would eat dinner with them, then return quickly to his room.

One of the non-Christian men brazenly asked Dad, "Do you know what I think of you?"

Dad said, "I didn't ask for your opinion, but go ahead."

The man said, "I think you're anti-social."

Dad said, "No, I'm just choosy about who I am around. I don't run around with drunks."

4. BIBLE EXAMPLES OF UNSEPARATED BELIEVERS

What happens if there is no personal separation from evil to godliness? From the world's standards to God's standards? The answer is revealed throughout the Word of God in tragedy after tragedy.

Let's begin with Noah, the builder of the ark. Unfortunately, Noah's story does not end on that high note. It ends, first, with Noah becoming drunk; second, with Noah losing his modesty and becoming a laughingstock; third, with Noah exacerbating the situation by placing a curse upon his own grandchild. This amazing man of God lost his testimony with his own family and community. What a way to end a life!

Lot, the nephew of Abraham, is cited in every major work on the topic of separation. Lot's life is set in contrast to the life of his uncle Abraham. Abraham looked for a city whose architect and builder is God, but Lot looked for personal gain in a sinful city called Sodom. Lot *deliberately* chose to place himself, his wife, and his daughters in the worst cesspool of that day. While Abraham walked with God, Lot walked in the path of sinners and followed the advice of the wicked.

God, of course, decided to rid the earth of the Sodom pestilence. Two angels rescued Lot just shortly before God's judgment fell. But Lot's sons-in-law refused to heed his warning; they perished in Sodom in a bath of fire and brimstone. Lot's house and bank accounts burned to a crisp. His wife was turned into a pillar of salt. Lot's story ends in an incestuous relationship with his two daughters.

But things would have been much different if Lot had remained separated from the world and separated to God like his uncle Abraham. We must never forget there is always a cost—usually a high cost—in not living a separated life.

Samson was known as a mighty man in the book of Judges. But he also strayed from the right path! He paid a horrible price, too! God delivered Samson to his enemies. Those enemies blinded Samson. His final act was one of revenge, but, even so, he died as part of that revenge. He died with the unrighteous because he had engaged in unrighteous behavior. (Samson's end might even be classified as "sin unto death." See 1 John 5:16)

What about David's horrible sin with Bathsheba? David committed adultery with Bathsheba then arranged the murder of Bathsheba's husband in an attempt to cover his sin. God came down very, very hard on David. God said, "The sword shall never depart from your house because you have despised Me and taken the wife of Uriah to be your wife" (2 Samuel 12:10).

Interestingly, David's first sin and, therefore, the subsequent sin should never have occurred because David should never have been exposed to this temptation.

God called David to be a separated king; a separated king would have been with his army at that time of the year. The Bible specifically says, "In the spring of the year, the time when kings go out to battle, David sent Joab, and his servants with him, and all Israel. And they ravaged the Ammonites and besieged Rabbah. But David remained at Jerusalem" (2 Samuel 11:1, ESV).

In other words, David's remaining at Jerusalem was the *first* mistake; the first mistake led to the second mistake, and so on. David should have been separated from the world, away from Jerusalem, and on the field of battle fighting for the Lord. But he instead stayed home to play with the world and ended up in the biggest mess imaginable.

The story comes to us from America's frontier days. A covered wagon entered a young town. The driver stopped his horses and called to a passing man, "Hey, are there any saloons in this place?"

The man proudly said, "Sure! We have four saloons in our new town!"

The driver shouted to his horses, "Giddyap!" and he urged his horses on.

The man shouted back, "Stop!"

The driver on the wagon said, "I can't stop here. I have four boys in this wagon."

The man said, "I don't understand. What is your business?"

357

The driver said, "My business is to raise these boys for God, and I can't do that in a town with four saloons." He hurried his horses onward and out of the town.

That man did not lower his godly standards, because he knew there was a cost to it.

"But as for you, dear reader, you have been taught the truth that is in Jesus. Therefore, take off and lay aside your previous worldly lifestyle, a lifestyle which is corrupt based upon deceitful desires; replace that lifestyle with the lifestyle of the new man from above, a lifestyle which is in accordance with God's standards and purity of the truth" (Ephesians 4:22-24).

It always feels good to be clean. It always feels good to go to bed at night with a clean conscience. It always feels good to look into the eyes of your children and know they have a Christian parent setting the right example in front of them. It always feels good knowing you are indeed light to a people living in darkness. Above all, it always feels good to know your life has not been lived in vain.

Yes, Christianity **IS** indeed a lifestyle.

SECTION THREE

PERFECT SANCTIFICATION

Harry Ironside was once asked by a stranger if he was saved. The famous pastor replied, "Yes, I have been, I am being, and I shall be." What did he mean? Properly viewed, God's salvation has past, present, and future components.

Our salvation will not be complete until all three stages are complete. Thank God, we have His Word that our salvation will someday be complete!

21

DEATH IS THE VERY LAST ENEMY

Samuel Johnson, the eighteenth-century father of the English dictionary, said near the end of his seventy-five years on earth, "I struggle hard for life. I take physic and take air. *But who can run the race with death?"* (The italics are his.) The answer, of course, is no one.

We can accurately establish one principle at the outset: God's primary purpose for death. Why does death exist? The answer is clear: Death is the penalty for *any* sin as well as the penalty for the *totality* of our sins. "The wages, or paycheck, of sin is death" (Romans 6:23). "But each person is tempted when he is drawn away and enticed by his own evil desire. Then after desire has conceived, it gives birth to sin, and when sin is fully grown, it gives birth to death" (James 1:14-15, CSB).

The Bible states that all men, with the one exception of Jesus Christ, are sinners and, therefore, headed for a meeting with death unless Jesus returns before the hour of our death.

"In Adam, all men die" (1 Corinthians 15:22).

"All are of the dust, and all turn to dust again" (Ecclesiastes 3:20).

"The death angel shall pass through the land" (Exodus 12).

"This very night your soul shall be required of you" (Luke 12:20).

"The soul that sinneth, it shall surely die" (Ezekiel 18:4).

"Sin entered the world through the first man, Adam, and that sin resulted in death. In this manner, death came to all people because all people sinned in their father Adam" (Romans 5:12).

"It is appointed unto man once to die" (Hebrews 9:27).

Genesis chapter five bears testimony that sinful man may live many years, but death is still patiently waiting. Death may not be handled by mere proxy—it is coming for each one of us. Adam's life lasted 930 years, but he died. Seth's life lasted 912 years, but he died, too. Enosh lived 905 years, but he also died. The same living and dying process continued throughout the Old Testament in every race, culture, nation, and continent without fail. It continued throughout the days of Jesus, the apostles, the Dark Ages, the Age of Enlightenment, the Industrial Revolution, even to this very day like so many other things since the fall of man.

The old saying is true: "Sin and death are Siamese twins—they always ride together."

It continues on and on from one generation to the next. Your family is not immune. Nor is my family, for at 10:47 p.m. on June 30, 2016, my father, Ted Swartzwelder, finished his life on earth, and he died, too.

Death is undoubtedly here. *But is it here to stay?* The answer is an emphatic no!

The apostle Paul declares, "The last enemy that shall be abolished, rendered null and void, totally defeated is death" (1 Corinthians 15:26). Paul says, "We can be confident that death shall be defeated!"

The psalmist says, "Though I walk through the valley of the shadow of death (the valley of the deepest darkness), I will fear no evil. For Thou art with me. Thy rod and Thy staff comfort me. Surely goodness and love shall follow me all the days of my life and I shall dwell in the house of the Lord forever" (Psalm 23:4, 6). The psalmist believed (and *still* believes) in hope after death!

God promises, "I shall ransom them from the power of Sheol; I shall redeem them from Death. O Death, where are your plagues? O Sheol, where is your sting? Compassion is hidden from my eyes" (Hosea 13:14, ESV).

Jesus announced boldly at the tomb of Lazarus, "'I am the resurrection and the life. Whoever believes in me, though he die, yet shall he live, and everyone who lives and believes in me shall never die. Do you believe this?'" (John 11:25-26, ESV).

Based upon those scriptures, the Christian has every right to say, "For me to live is Christ but to die is *gain*!" (Philippians 1:21).

J. R. Caldwell watched as a loved one was lowered into the ground. He muttered to himself, "What a dishonor!" But immediately, the thought came to his mind, "This is the last thing that sin and Satan can do!"

How does the triumphant book of Revelation begin? It begins with the glorified Son of God declaring to one and all, "I hold in My hands the keys of Death and Hades . . . of the grave and hell" (Revelation 1:18).

As a result, there should be no doubt in the mind of the believer about his future. The believer can honestly and victoriously proclaim to one and all, "O death, where is your victory? O grave, where is your sting?" (1 Corinthians 15:55).

The death of death is scheduled on God's calendar.

Someday death will be abolished and become a thing of the past. We know that will be so because the *first* thing mentioned about heaven is the absence of death in heaven (Revelation 21:4, Luke 20:36).

But the death of death has not yet occurred, because death is still serving God's purpose. As a result, men are still dying; things still occur at death that happen at no other point in life.

Most people do not understand there are actually *three* components to death. The first component is the separation of the spirit from the body. This will be discussed in great detail in the next few pages.

The second component is the separation of the immaterial nature from this *kosmos* (organized world system), including worldly activity and relationships. The Bible says, "Naked I entered the world and naked I shall depart the world" (Job 1:21). "We brought nothing into this world, and we will take *nothing* out of it" (1 Timothy 6:7).

Someone asked a companion at the rich man's funeral, "How much did he leave?"

The answer came, "He left it all." Yes, we leave it all! Through death, the immaterial is separated from the material.

The third component is the separation of the new nature from the old nature. As a result, the warfare between these two natures will finally end. This component will also be examined in the following pages.

If possible, proper study techniques would require me to delink these three components for individual study; however, I find all three components inseparably linked or, as in the proverbial saying, "joined at the hip." Due to their overlapping nature, certain sections will discuss more than one component.

1. WHAT IS DEATH?

The death of a loved one can be very difficult to accept. W. E. Channing often spoke of his friend Thoreau's passing as "Thoreau's loss" or "when I lost Mr. Thoreau." He never used the word "death" to describe Thoreau's passing.

One day a friend sat with Channing amongst a copse of trees. It was a perfect afternoon. During their conversation, Channing turned to his friend and said, "Half the world died for me when I lost Mr. Thoreau. None of it looks the same as when I looked at it with him."

Each one of us has lost far too many friends to the enemy known as death. I sometimes feel as if death is a robber or a thief. It has taken away people that I love so much! I would really enjoy having just one more conversation with them, perhaps share some of God's current day blessings with them. But they are no longer available, and I am much the poorer because of it.

It is no longer a case of them coming to me but of me going to them. That is indeed a blessed promise from my Lord.

"And I heard a voice from heaven, saying, 'Write, 'Blessed are the dead who die in the Lord from now on!'' 'Yes,' says the Spirit, 'so that they may rest from their labors, for their deeds follow with them'" (Revelation 14:13, NASB).

There are only two ways out of this life. The first way is the more pleasant way and is totally painless! It is the event we call the translation of the saints. Eschatology scholars have different opinions about this event, but the amillennialist, postmillennialist, and premillennialist generally believe in the translation or glorification of the *living* saints at some future time. Most scholars equate that time with the return of the Lord (often described as the Rapture) *or* the sudden, climactic end of earthly events caused by the return of Christ. The living saints will escape death (similar to Enoch and Elijah) and be instantly translated from mortality to immortality. That is why we sing, "O joy, o delight, should we go without dying!" Imagine such an event taking place today!

The second way out of this life is far less pleasant and may incur unwanted pain and suffering. It is the event we know as death.

What, though, is death? James P. Boyce states, "It is sometimes called 'natural,' or 'physical' death, to distinguish it from that which is 'spiritual;' the death 'of the body' as opposed to that 'of the soul;' and 'temporal' death, in contrast with that which is everlasting." (*Abstract of Systematic Theology*, p. 437)

Above all, it must be stressed that death is *more* than the cessation of the body. Death also includes the separation of the spiritual nature of man from the physical nature of man. It is generally accepted that those two natures have been married since the moment of conception, thereby indicating that the soul is as old as the body. (Note: A few believe the soul is created after conception but before the birth of the child. An opposite view advocates that all souls were created at the time of creation and await a future union with a physical body. Both discussions, however, are outside the scope of this book.)

Based upon the Bible, it appears the human body is the only part of man that truly experiences death in the sense of cessation of being. For example, the story in Luke chapter sixteen records the death, and, we assume, the subsequent burial of the *bodies* of the rich man and the beggar Lazarus. However, it also records that both men were still alive *spiritually*: one was in hell, and the other was in heaven. The rich man even conducted a conversation with Abraham. In so doing, he expressed that *memory still exists outside the human body.*

In addition, the apostle Paul mentions an experience of being "absent from the body but present with the Lord" (2 Corinthians 5:8).

Jesus tried to explain this distinction to the unbelieving Jews when He said, "And as for the dead being raised—haven't you read in the book of Moses, in the passage about the burning bush, how God said to him: I am the God of Abraham and the God of Isaac and the God of Jacob? He is not the God of the dead but of the living." (Mark 12:26-27, CSB). Notice that Jesus did not say, "I *was* the God of Abraham, Isaac and Jacob" but, "I currently *am*!" In other words, all three of those deceased Old Testament saints were still living or alive!

The testimony of Moses confirms this teaching, too. Moses' body was buried in the last chapter of Deuteronomy on the wrong side of Jordan . . . just outside the Promised Land. However, he was very much alive *inside* the Promised Land on the Mount of Transfiguration (Matthew chapter seventeen) even though his body was still *outside* the holy land.

We can conclude, therefore, that death should not be defined in terms of cessation but of *separation*. Death is not a *state* but an *act*.

Amos Tarver says, "Death is not a period but a comma in the story of life."

I once wrote a skit to illustrate this very truth. The skit included some angels, adult mother, adult daughter, and other family members. The adult daughter represented the mother's spirit. The mother was seated in a chair on the stage with the daughter hidden behind the mother. The family members were closest to the mother; the angels were hovering nearby.

During the skit, the mother pretended to die. The family members immediately began to weep. The angels took the "*spirit*" (the daughter) by the hand and escorted the "spirit" from the body to heaven. Heaven was represented by a door on one side of the auditorium.

As the spirit of the deceased passed through the door, several voices on the door's opposite (heaven) side shouted the person's name and said, "Welcome home! Welcome to heaven!" The heavenly crowd then sang the chorus of "Sweet By and By."

The skit was simple to present, but it was quite effective. It visualized in the natural world what takes place in the spiritual world.

Physical death is the event in which the immaterial part of man is separated from the material part of man. The material part—the body—goes to *"sleep"* and *unconsciously* awaits the day of the resurrection (1 Thessalonians 4:14). During this time, the body no longer sees, hears, tastes, interacts, or understands. It has ceased to function in any capacity.

It is clearly seen, therefore, that the doctrine of soul-sleeping as promoted by Seventh-day Adventists is a false doctrine through and through. The soul never sleeps. Only the body sleeps!

This "separation" definition holds true in every aspect of death, including physical death, spiritual death, and the second or eternal death. Chafer correctly distinguishes those three aspects in Volume VII of his *Systematic Theology* (p. 112), "Physical death is separation of soul and spirit from the body, spiritual death is the separation of soul and spirit from God, and second death is the final and permanent form of spiritual death if the individual has not been saved from that."

Lockyer adds, "There is an everlasting perpetual life to be lived forever *away* from God, and this is eternal death. There is an everlasting, perpetual life to be lived *with* God, and this is eternal life." (The italics are mine.) (*All the Doctrines of the Bible*, p. 270)

Jesus emphasizes the same principle in these words, "And these shall go *away* into everlasting punishment or torment" (Matthew 25:46). The bitter word "away" is another means of denoting separation.

We cannot escape the conclusion that the second death or eternal death is the worst death of all: separated eternally from God with no hope of future restoration. What an agonizing prospect! It is no wonder that John the Baptist preached, "Who has warned you to flee from the wrath to come?" (Matthew 3:7).

The conclusion is clear: Death brings separation for both the believer and the unbeliever.

The Greek Aristeides wrote a friend in A.D. 125 about this new religion called Christianity. He tried to explain why Christianity was becoming more successful by the day. Interestingly, his letter focused on the Christian interpretation of death.

Aristeides writes, "If any righteous man among the Christians passes from this world, they rejoice and offer thanks to God, and they escort his body with songs and thanksgiving *as if he were setting out from one place to another nearby.*"

There is a tombstone in Alabama which, though humorous, states the Bible principle quite well:

> "Here lies Solomon Peas
> Under the lilies and under the trees.

Peas is not here, only the pod,
Peas has shelled out and gone home to God."

The poem is correct because death is the separation of the spirit or soul from the flesh or the body. However, this act of separation is only one component of death. It is time to take up the issue which is most germane to this book's theme.

2. WHY IS DEATH THE LAST ENEMY FOR THE BELIEVER?

Imagine Paul's total confidence in this matter! "Death, you are the last enemy I will ever face! But I want you to know that you are already a conquered enemy. Through the revelation of the Holy Spirit, I can now say to one and all, 'The last enemy that shall be abolished, rendered null and void, totally defeated is death' (1 Corinthians 15:26). You are indeed my last enemy, but rest assured, you shall be defeated! As a result, I can confidently assert that you, death, will turn out to be a blessing rather than a curse."

Someone might think, "Paul is wrong. Satan is the last enemy!" But Paul says, "No, death is the last enemy."

Another person might argue, "But sin is the last enemy." Paul, though, still insists, "Death is the last enemy!"

In our frustration, we might even cry out in unison, "Why do you argue with us? Why do you say that death is the last enemy?"

Knowing Paul as I do, he would probably smile and say, "It is because death will forever separate the believer from Satan, sin, temptation, this evil world system along with anything else that corrupts or destroys. *Death marks the demarcation for the one who believes in Jesus Christ!*"

It seems obvious death must provide an important benefit to the believer. If that is not so, death is but a continuation of our anguish and groaning (Romans 8:23).

Let's examine the following question: *Of what good is death if we take the same Adamic nature with us to the other side of death?* Doing so would leave us unchanged, and it is change that we so desperately need.

The same apostle Paul who speaks so triumphantly in 1 Corinthians 15:26, also speaks from deep frustration in Romans 7:24. He says, "O who will *deliver* me from this body of sin?" The word "deliver" appears in fourteen (mostly older) translations. The equivalent word "rescue" appears in nine translations. Another phrase, "set free," appears in two translations. The principle is clear: The believer needs and yearns to be set free! On the other hand, *the unbeliever does not wish to be set free.* "Men loved darkness rather than light" is the driving emphasis of the unbeliever on both sides of death.

That brings us to the most important component of death for the believer: the separation of the new, born again nature from the old, Adamic nature.

It may be profitable to pause for a moment and take a brief review. First, we became sinners and received Adam's sinful nature (the Adamic nature) at our conception. Second, we received the holy nature when we were born again by the Holy Spirit of God. From that time until this time, we have possessed two opposing natures. Third, and this item is to be discussed now, we lose our sinful nature at the time of our physical death. Fourth, and still to be discussed, our remaining holy nature will be reunited with a glorified body raised in holiness on the day of our physical resurrection. We will then, *for the first time,* be completely holy through and through. Paul's prayer, "May the God of peace sanctify you *wholly,*" will finally be fulfilled (1 Thessalonians 5:23).

Preachers often overlook this component of death. Too much attention is placed upon "everybody will be happy over there," but not enough attention is placed upon "we shall be righteous and holy like Him." As stated before, God's goal for the believer is not happiness but holiness! *Happiness is the result of holiness and never the cause of holiness.*

We must think of death in terms of a demarcation. Death is God's means of separating the holy nature from the Adamic nature.

We learned in chapter six that the Adamic nature is tied to our physical conception, which resulted in a physical body (*psuchikos*). Thus, the Adamic nature is married or joined to what we are by physical birth or conception. The apostle Paul connects the Adamic nature with the flesh throughout his writings. (See Romans chapter eight for many examples.)

Paul was undoubtedly thinking of the believer's separation from the Adamic nature when he asked, "Who shall deliver or separate me from the body of this death?" (Romans 7:24, NASB) Though Paul lived in a "body of death," he knew that only death could set him free. Thus, Paul looked forward to a "crown of righteousness" on the other side of death (2 Timothy 4:8). He finished his last writings on earth with the expectation that the "Lord will preserve me into His heavenly kingdom" (2 Timothy 4:18).

There are six ways we know that the believer is set free or separated from the Adamic nature at death. First, the Bible describes the believer in heaven as possessing only one nature, not two. "You have come to Mount Zion, to the city of the living God (the heavenly Jerusalem), to myriads of angels in festive gathering, to the assembly of the firstborn whose names have been written in heaven, to God who is the Judge of all, to the spirits of righteous people made perfect" (Hebrews 12:22-23, HCSB). The spirits of those in heaven have been made perfect. They are now described as righteous. That implies the sin nature has been thoroughly removed, discarded, and tossed away. No defects remain.

Second, the nature of heaven itself requires the saint to be truly sanctified, or holy, when he enters heaven. The reasoning is simple: The Bible describes heaven as a place where there is no more death, neither sorrow, nor crying. Logically, if the believer is still tainted by sin, there will still be death, sorrow, and crying, for death, sorrow, and crying are the results of the believer's sin.

Third, the return of Christ includes this act of separation for the living saints. The apostle Paul testifies, "we wait for the blessed hope, the appearing of the glory of our great God and Savior, Jesus Christ. He gave himself for us to redeem us from all lawlessness and to cleanse for himself a people for his own possession, eager to do good works" (Titus 2:13-14, CSB). Jesus has deliberately purposed to "cleanse for Himself a people for His own possession." 100% cleansed: body, soul and spirit! *This cleansing is followed by the saints joining Jesus in the air.* Since this action applies to the living saints before their meeting Jesus, it should also apply to the deceased saints before their meeting Jesus in heaven.

Fourth, the presentation of a holy and blameless bride (the composite of believers) to Christ necessitates that the sin nature be removed first. "Husbands, love your wives, just as Christ loved the church and gave himself for her to make her holy, cleansing her with the washing of water by the word. He did this to present the church to himself in splendor, without spot or wrinkle or anything like that, but holy and blameless" (Ephesians 5:26-27, CSB). The phrase "holy and blameless" expresses the absence of a sin nature or any individual acts of sin.

Fifth, the holy nature of God requires complete holiness on our part. Our God is declared to be thrice holy! "Thou art of purer eyes than to behold evil, and canst not look on iniquity" (Habakkuk 1:13, KJV). The scriptures make it clear that, upon death, the believer enters heaven. However, the believer can only enter heaven because he now meets the just demands of a holy God.

For instance, God told Moses, "No *man* can look upon Me and live" (Exodus 33:20). But a mere *man* named Paul writes of a day when he would be "absent from the body and present with the Lord." In other words, at death, Paul would meet God's standards and could live in God's presence.

A similar verse, Psalm 11:4, describes God as "living in His holy temple." But Jesus promises, "I go to prepare a place for you. In My Father's house are many dwelling places" (John 14). In other words, every believer gets to live with God the Father! That which has been made holy gets to live with Him who is holy!

Sixth, there is no indication anywhere in scripture that sin is an issue for the believer on the other side of death. But the scriptures do indicate the opposite is true. "He that is righteous let him continue to be righteous. He that is holy let him continue to be holy" (Revelation 22:11).

Augustine visualizes it like this: "Join thyself to the eternal God, and thou shalt be eternal." Our holiness is His holiness, our righteousness is His righteousness, our goodness is totally His goodness. Praise God from whom all blessings flow!

An unknown author writes, "For a child of God, death is simply the angel waiting on the threshold of the unseen to disrobe the soul of its earthly garments, preparatory to its passing into the presence of the King." Yes, we will disrobe the Adamic sin nature along with worldly activities and relationships. For the first time in our existence, the spirit, which has been created in righteousness and true holiness, will be set free (Ephesians 4:24).

3. WHAT HAPPENS AT DEATH?

The death of God's child is regarded as "precious in the sight of the Lord" (Psalm 116:15). Precious expresses the idea of "exceedingly valuable." James P. Boyce writes in his *Abstract of Systematic Theology* (p. 438), "The death of the saint, instead of being accursed, is precious in the sight of the Lord."

The same, though, cannot be said about the death of the unbeliever. "Have I any pleasure in the death of the wicked, declares the Lord GOD, and not rather that he should turn from his way and live?" (Ezekiel 18:23, ESV). The prospect of the unbeliever suffering in hell is a scary prospect, but we must acknowledge it is a righteous prospect, nonetheless.

However, this book is devoted to the saint, and it is regarding the saint's death that God says, "Of *exceeding* value is the death of My saints."

We often wonder what will happen at death. Will it be a going to sleep experience? Will there be pain? Will I be confused? Will I face death faithful or faithless? Will I die alone or surrounded by friends?

Some fearfully ask, "Will I even be missed?" Have confidence, dear believer, because *we don't have to be important to everyone;* we just need to be important to God.

Luke 16:27 gives us a good idea of what will happen at our death. Is this passage a parable or a real-life story? We do not know for certain. I do not believe we need to know for certain. The principles, though, are certain. One of those principles concerns our dying experience.

"The time came when the beggar Lazarus died. The angels came and carried the beggar to Abraham's side—to Abraham's bosom." In my opinion, "Abraham's bosom" is another way of expressing heaven or something equivalent such as paradise. (Note: Luke describes Lazarus as being far away ("a long way off" and "a great chasm") from the rich man in Hades.) The context makes it clear that the beggar Lazarus is now in a place where there will be no more death, mourning, crying, pain, loss, or suffering of any kind. He has truly been delivered!

The old spiritual is probably right:

> "Swing low, sweet chariot,
> Comin' for to carry me home,
> I looked over Jordan, and what did I see?
> Comin' for to carry me home,
> A band of angels comin' after me,
> Comin' for to carry me home."

The beggar Lazarus was just an insignificant beggar in the eyes of the world, but one would think he was the most significant person in the entire world to God. Who was there when he died? The angels of God.

Who provided the transportation to heaven? The angels. Who knew the directions to heaven? The angels. This lowly beggar didn't know the way to heaven. But the angels knew because they had just come from heaven.

This line of thought is supported in the opening verses of the book of Hebrews. "Now to which of the angels has He ever said: Sit at My right hand until I make Your enemies Your footstool? Are they not all ministering spirits sent out to serve those who are going to inherit salvation?" (Hebrews 1:13-14, CSB). It is obvious the believer has a guardian (ministering) angel in life; therefore, it is to be expected the believer will have a guardian angel in death! (Perhaps we will be introduced to our guardian angel at death. Imagine how that meeting will occur!)

Indeed, the "voice of the archangel" will be an important component in the resurrection of the saints (1 Thessalonians 4:16).

Could the idea of a chariot be true? Yes, indeed! That is how Elijah went to heaven: in a chariot of fire (2 Kings 2:11). So perhaps God will use the same chariot for you and me, too!

In my "sanctified" imagination, I can see the angel reaching down from the chariot and saying, "Give me your hand." My spirit will reach up and take the angel's hand. As the last breath leaves my mortal body, I (my spirit) will take one giant step *out* of this body and leave my body behind. I'll take my seat in God's chariot called "Deliverance," and I'll go home to be with my God as well as the saints who have gone on before me.

On the way home, I will shout loud enough for all the demons of hell to hear, "O death, where is your victory *now*? O death, where is your sting *now*? Death has been swallowed up in *victory*!" (1 Corinthians 15:55).

I will never go to sleep; I will be awake to enjoy the entire event!

On the eve of His crucifixion, Jesus said, "I am going away." But He left us this promise, "Where I am, there shall My servant be (someday)."

We have His guarantee that *we shall be together with Him* in the Father's house!

Frank W. Boreham provides a wonderful illustration of death in his book *Wisps of Wildfire.*

A few weeks ago, in a small boat, I was making my way up one of the most picturesque of our Australian rivers. The forestry on both banks was magnificent beyond description . . . A canoe glided ahead of us. Presently, the waters seemed to come to an end. We watched the canoe, and to our astonishment, it simply vanished . . . when we came to the point at which the canoe had so mysteriously disappeared, we beheld a sudden twist in the river artfully concealed by the tangle of bush. The blind alley was no blind alley after all!

Boreham compared that event to believers entering death. He concludes, "They have gone on—like the canoe. It had turned a bend in the river; they have turned a bend in the road."

The great preacher D. L. Moody is buried in Northfield, Massachusetts. He left us, though, with these words of great encouragement:

Someday you will read in the papers that D. L. Moody is dead. Don't you believe a word of it. At that moment I shall have gone up higher, that is all: out of this old, clay tenement into a house that is immortal—a body that death cannot touch, that sin cannot taint; a body fashioned like unto His glorious body. I was born of the flesh in 1837. I was born of the Spirit in 1856. That which is born of the flesh may die. That which is born of the Spirit will live forever.

Anna Letitia Barbauld (1743-1825) continues to bless through these words:

> "Life! We have been long together
> Through pleasant and through cloudy weather;
> 'Tis hard to part when friends are dear,
> Perhaps 'twill cost a sigh, a tear;
> Then steal away, give little warning,
> Choose thine own time;
> Say not 'Good night,' but in some brighter clime

Bid me 'Good morning.'"

22

LIFE BETWEEN DEATH AND THE RESURRECTION

"**G**od has set eternity in the heart of man, but, even so, man is unable to fathom what God has done since the beginning of time" (Ecclesiastes 3:11). World history bears abundant testimony about man's infatuation, even curiosity, about eternity.

Herbert Lockyer writes about historical man as not only *having* ideas about the afterlife but also of man *needing* ideas about the afterlife.

> Pyramids built with chambers because of the belief that the dead still lived and revisited their tombs. Rites and incantations with food being placed at the graves for the sustenance of those who had died. In the Egyptian Book of the Dead there are prayers and formulae for the guidance and protection of the deceased in the After-World.
>
> The Hindu yearns for 'long life among the gods'—The Buddhist for his four-and-twenty heavens—The Babylonian for the 'Merciful One among the gods . . . who restores the dead to life.'—The Persian for the naked body to be 'clothed only with the light of Heaven'—The Grecian for survival. Socrates, who

believed in immortality, said as he died, 'Bury me if you can catch me.'—The African for a new abode out west, in the way of the setting sun. (*All the Doctrines of the Bible*, p. 271)

Is there such a state of being as life after death? The universe itself answers the question with a loud and resounding, "Yes!" Lockyer adds, "The law of nature is life out of death, production out of destruction. The annual miracle of spring, the caterpillar from a tiny egg, the marvelous transformation of the hard, unsightly chrysalis into the gorgeous butterfly are natural emblems of life's continuance." Lockyer then quotes the well-known axiom, "From dearth to plenty, from death to life, Is Nature's progress."

We can conclude *even without the Bible* that everything (including living beings) in this universe teaches the principle that there is indeed life after death. Therefore, we should not be surprised that man also has a yearning to answer the questions about his own future. Why? It is because God has set the principle of eternity in the hearts of men—God has created man with the innate knowledge that he will somehow live beyond this life.

This is an incredible concept and is difficult, nearly impossible to comprehend. Man, throughout all centuries, all races, all cultures, and all levels of education, has somehow believed that life is *more* than just the here and now—there is also a hereafter. How can that knowledge exist except it be a work of our God? "He has established a *sense of eternity* in the deepest part of man!" No system of unbelief nor any circumstance nor height nor depth has ever quenched that innermost sense.

The theme of sanctification is also linked to eternity because it is in eternity that the believer becomes completely or perfectly sanctified.

Most world religions comprehend the conflict between the unrighteousness of sinful man and the righteousness of holy Deity. Man's religions try to resolve that conflict in a variety of ways. It is beyond the scope of this book to explore the different solutions posed by the world's religions. But it is within the scope of this book to discuss the relationship of sanctification to the opening days of eternity.

1. PURGATORY: YES OR NO?

God's purpose for sanctification is to make the believer like Christ in the *totality* of his being. That, of course, includes transforming the believer from the opening stage of positional sanctification (Christ's holiness has been imputed to the believer) to the final stage of perfect sanctification (the believer becomes 100% holy). We have previously devoted many pages to substantiating that salvation is through Jesus Christ and Him alone. There is no other means of forgiveness except through His cross.

However, the Roman Catholic part of Christianity begs to disagree. Due to the nature of this book, it seems appropriate to explore the Roman Catholic view of sanctification.

Loraine Boettner's volume *Roman Catholicism* remains to this day one of the most authoritative books on this subject. *Roman Catholicism* includes discussions on the priesthood, traditions versus the scriptures, the roles of Peter and Mary, the infallibility of the pope, as well as the Mass. The book may be nearly fifty years old, but its thoroughness makes it a splendid addition to any library.

Boettner summarizes the Roman Catholic view of purgatory in his first two paragraphs.

> The Roman Catholic Church has developed a doctrine in which it is held that all who die at peace with the church, but who are not perfect, must undergo penal and purifying suffering in an intermediate realm known as purgatory. Only those believers who have attained a state of Christian perfection go

immediately to heaven. All unbaptized adults and those who after baptism have committed mortal sin go immediately to hell. The great mass of partially sanctified Christians dying in fellowship with the church, but who nevertheless are encumbered with some degree of sin, go to purgatory where, for a longer or shorter time, they suffer until all sin is purged away, after which they are translated to heaven.

The Roman Church holds that baptism removes all previous guilt, both original and actual, so that if a person were to die immediately after baptism he would go directly to heaven. All other believers, except the Christian martyrs but including even the highest clergy, must go to purgatory to pay the penalty for sins committed after baptism.

An evangelizing Catholic co-worker gave me a small booklet by Rev. Joseph A. Kenney, pastor of St. Clement's Roman Catholic Church. The booklet provides a lengthy defense of purgatory. Kenney writes,

> Purgatory is that intermediary state or condition in the next world where the souls of those who die in the state of grace, but are not yet free of all imperfection, are purified before they enter heaven . . . Nowhere in Scripture does the word, 'Purgatory,' occur. We believe however, that the doctrine is implicitly contained in the scriptures . . . the Catholic doctrine does not rest on any direct Scriptural proof but on tradition, increasingly clear and unmistakable . . . The dead were clearly in need of some help if they were to become ready for Heaven. Hence, the names of the dead were frequently inscribed on special lists to be read at liturgical services, and solemn ceremonies were held at burial places to pray for the dead . . . The term itself comes from the Latin '*purgare*' which means 'to cleanse,' 'to purify,' 'to purge' . . . Perhaps it would be well to remark that many of the pictures drawn by writers and preachers in the past of souls writhing in agony in fiery pits are pictures that belong to another era . . . the souls in Purgatory are at peace . . . Our liturgy repeats the words of 2 Maccabees: 'It is a holy and pious thought to pray for the dead that they may be released from their sins.'

Seven points can immediately be made. First, by Catholicism's own admission, the entire doctrine rests upon tradition rather than scripture.

Catholicism cannot even once refer to "Thus saith the Lord." That is always a dangerous path to follow.

Second, the reference to 2 Maccabees does not substantiate anything since non-Catholic Christianity, with ample cause, rejects the inspiration of both 1 and 2 Maccabees as well as the entire Apocrypha. The scholar F. F. Bruce contends that there "is no evidence that these books were ever regarded as canonical by any Jews, whether inside or outside Palestine, whether they read the Bible in Hebrew or in Greek." Nor are the books quoted by Jesus or the apostles. Catholicism seems to recognize this weakness. Perhaps that is the reason for the statement in the above quotation that purgatory "does not rest on any direct Scriptural truth but on tradition."

Third, the church's tradition regarding purgatory has changed over the years. It was taught for centuries that a soul in purgatory existed in a state of torment until it was, at last, purified through fire from its sins. The church, always desirous of money, apparently used this concept of torment to raise funds from the common people. Tetzel (1515 A.D.) is credited with saying, "As soon as a coin doth cling, a soul from purgatory doth spring." On what basis, though, did they change their tradition from one of suffering to one of bliss? Was it because Catholics viewed the torment concept as being too rash? If that is true, should we expect the tradition to be refined further in the future? How can there be any confidence within Catholicism that the current view is the correct view since it is, by their own admission, a revised view?

Boettner quotes Robert Ketchum (*Let Rome Speak for Herself*) on page 224 of his *Roman Catholicism*:

> 'How do you know, Mr. Priest, when to stop praying and taking money from your parishioners for a given case? How do you know when John Murphy is out of purgatory? His getting out is dependent upon the saying of masses paid for by his bereaved ones. If you stop one or two masses too soon, what then? If you keep on saying masses for the fellow after he is out, that is bad. It is bad either way you come at it. I ask seriously, Sir, Mr. Roman Catholic Priest, How do you know when to stop

saying masses for a given individual? Do you have some kind of a connection with the unseen world?'

Fourth, Catholicism does not view the cross of Jesus Christ as being sufficient for the soul's salvation. In its view, the believer must supplement the death of Christ through his own suffering. The logical reasoning within Catholicism is that Jesus was mistaken when He said, "It is finished. I have finished the work My Father gave me to do." Quite honestly, either Jesus finished the payment for salvation, or we have no hope! But as for me, and hopefully for you, "On Christ the solid rock I stand, all other ground is sinking sand!"

Fifth, the entire system is built upon a works philosophy of earning one's way to heaven. James P. Boyce concludes in his *Abstract of Systematic Theology* (p. 450), "This doctrine of purgatory is based upon the very unscriptural theory of salvation through personal works and sufferings, which the Church of Rome holds, in connection with sacramental grace, to be supplementary to the meritorious work of Christ."

Earning one's way to heaven, though, is refuted from Genesis to Revelation. "For by grace are you saved through faith and that not of yourselves; it is the gift of God. Not of works lest any man should boast!" (Ephesians 2:8-9).

"Now to the one who works, pay is not credited as a gift, but as something owed. But to the one who does not work, but believes on him who declares the ungodly to be righteous, his faith is credited for righteousness" (Romans 4:4-5, CSB).

Sixth, and perhaps most important of all, Roman Catholicism misses the point as to who actually does the purging necessary to procure salvation. Kenney states that "purgatory" comes from the Latin *purgare,* which means "to cleanse," "to purify," "to purge." But who does the cleansing? Who does the purifying? Who does the purging? The biblical answer is Jesus Christ! It is not the believer. That point is proven by the following scriptures:

a) God "hath in these last days spoken unto us by his Son, whom he hath appointed heir of all things, by whom also he made the worlds; Who being the brightness of his glory, and the express image of his person, and upholding all things by the word of his power, ***when he had by himself <u>purged</u> our sins,*** sat down on the right hand of the Majesty on high" (Hebrews 1:2-3, KJV).

b) "The blood of Jesus Christ, God's Son, cleanses us from all sin" (1 John 1:7).

c) "'Come now, and let us reason together,' Says the Lord, 'Though your sins are as scarlet, They will be as white as snow; Though they are red like crimson, They will be like wool'" (Isaiah 1:18, NASB).

d) "He gave Himself for us to redeem us from all lawlessness and to cleanse for Himself a people for His own possession, eager to do good works" (Titus 2:14, HCSB).

e) "To Him who loves us and has set us free from our sins by His blood" (Revelation 1:5, HCSB).

Seventh, the scriptures plainly teach there are only two places in eternity, not three. "These shall go away into everlasting punishment but the righteous will enter eternal life" (Matthew 25:46). Jesus did not leave any wiggle room for a third place called purgatory in either this text or any of His other sayings. I respectfully suggest we stay with Jesus instead of the Roman Catholic traditions developed by man!

Herbert Lockyer writes a fitting conclusion for this topic,

> Some there are, who, when they come to die, seek out the ministrations of preacher or priest, as if he had the power to enable them to die sinners and wake up saints. The mere act of removing from one house to another, in no way changes the person removing. Thus, we continue on the other side, as we depart from this. Life *here* determines *that*. (*All the Doctrines of the Bible*, p. 217)

Yes, "as the tree falls, so shall it lie" (Ecclesiastes 11:3).

2. THE INTERMEDIATE BODY

The Bible contains many mysteries yet to be fully understood. One of those mysteries concerns the intermediate body. The apostle Paul emphasizes there is such a condition for believers as being "absent from the body and present with the Lord" (2 Corinthians 5:8). That is why he yearns to "depart and be with Christ, because such a departure is much better" (Philippians 1:23).

Even though Jesus' death removed the sting of death for every believer, death will still come. At death, the believer's body (material part of man) will essentially go to sleep (1 Thessalonians 4:13) and cease to function, but the soul/spirit (immaterial part of man) will continue to be totally alive . . . perhaps expressing itself even more as it is freed from the limitations of the human body and moves on to be "present with the Lord."

The Bible is very clear there is no such reality as "soul-sleeping" (currently taught by Jehovah's Witnesses and the Seventh-day Adventists) for either the believer or the unbeliever. The physical body will sleep and cease operation (the five senses will no longer be active), but the soul or spirit will be alert, capable of joy or sorrow (Matthew 22:32, Revelation 20:13), possess knowledge and memory (Luke 16:25), and have the ability to communicate (Luke 16:19-31).

All of this is already happening for the deceased individual, and yet the resurrection has not occurred! The graveyards are still full. The bones still lie undisturbed. The material part (the body) is still separated from the immaterial part (soul and spirit). The permanent reunion of the material and immaterial parts of man is still in the future.

That leads us to the question of the current or intermediate state of the believer. (Note: The same principles in this subject apply to the unbeliever.) My father went to heaven at 10:47 p.m. on June 30, 2016. He left his body here on earth. But someday, perhaps soon, he will reclaim that body (1 Thessalonians 4:14). What, though, is his current status? And what will be my status when I am "absent from the body but present with the Lord"?

It appears from various scriptures that the believer receives an intermediate body to house the naked soul or spirit. *This intermediate body appears to be a preview or prototype of the permanent, glorified body.* Some believe, and I include myself among them, that the apostle Paul is describing this intermediate body when he writes,

> *For we know that if the earthly tent which is our house is torn down, we have a building from God, a house not made with hands, eternal in the heavens. For indeed in this house we groan, longing to be clothed with our dwelling from heaven, inasmuch as we, having put it on, will not be found naked. For indeed while we are in this tent, we groan, being burdened, because we do not want to be unclothed but to be clothed, so that what is mortal will be swallowed up by life. Now He who prepared us for this very purpose is God, who gave to us the Spirit as a pledge (2 Corinthians 5:1-5, NASB).*

John R. Rice suggests,

> Does Paul mean here that before the resurrection there will be some heavenly body prepared for us? It seems so. He expected to be clothed and 'not be found naked' (vs. 3). He says, 'not for that we would be unclothed, but clothed upon' (vs. 4).
>
> When the departed Samuel appeared to the witch of Endor, did he not have some kind of a body, although he had died and was not yet resurrected? Moses and Elijah appeared to the Lord Jesus and three apostles on the Mount of Transfiguration. Did they not have some bodies—visible and definite bodies? Elijah had been changed and had been taken to heaven without dying, but Moses died and God had buried him.
>
> So whatever that heavenly mystery shall prove to be, those who die now are not left as wandering spirits, without form, without recognition by other loved ones, without physical senses. (*The Church of God at Corinth*, p. 197)

Luke 16:19-31 contains a reference to both Father Abraham and the rich man *after* death and *before* their final resurrection. Both men are clearly identified. How could they be identified unless they possessed identifying features? And those features would need to be similar to how our brains identified them in their physical life!

H. A. Ironside and others, though, beg to differ with this view. Ironside counters, "It says this house not made with hands abides '*eternal* in the heavens.' Between death and resurrection we pass out of the body and our pure spirits enter into the presence of the Lord." (*Addresses on the Second Epistle to the Corinthians*, p. 122)

How, though, did the witch of Endor recognize Samuel? By what means were Moses and Elijah known on the Mount of Transfiguration? Or Abraham in Luke chapter sixteen? Was it done via name tags? Hardly. There must be something more than Ironside's view.

The Presbyterian scholar Charles Hodge struggled mightily with this passage. His view is an outlier but deserves mention because of his status. Hodge discards the view that the passage has something to do with the intermediate *body* and prefers instead to emphasize the intermediate *state* of the believer. He interprets the words "house not made with hands" to mean "a mansion in heaven into which believers enter as soon as their earthly tabernacle is dissolved." This view leaves much to be desired because it ignores the literal meaning and spiritualizes the entire passage.

Hodge, though, does concur that "The soul of the believer does not cease to exist at death. It does not sink into a state of unconsciousness. It does not go into purgatory; but, being made perfect in holiness, it goes immediately into glory. As soon as it is absent from the body, it is present with the Lord." (*An Exposition of the Second Epistle to the Corinthians*, pp. 112-113)

Regardless of the different opinions, though, there is one common thread in all three views: The "house not made with hands" must be a completely sanctified house. It must be a house that is pure from sin because it was *made in the heavens.* Its designer is obviously God Himself.

Lewis Sperry Chafer, founder of Dallas Theological Seminary, summarizes what I believe to be the correct view:

> ". . . the human spirit earnestly desires not to be unclothed or disembodied but to be clothed upon; and to this end a body 'from heaven,' eternal—with respect to its qualities as any body from heaven must be—awaits the believer who dies. He will thus not be unclothed or bodiless between death and the resurrection of that original body which will be from the grave. The body 'from heaven' could not be the body which is from the grave, nor could the body from the grave serve as an intermediate body before the resurrection. Apart from the divine provision of an intermediate body, the believer's desire that he should not be unclothed or bodiless could not be satisfied." (*Systematic Theology Volume IV*, p. 414)

Charles Hodge concludes Paul's brief statements on this entire subject by writing, "This is all that is revealed and this is enough." It is indeed enough to provide peace of mind and hope of soul because, "we know that in time the earthly tent of our current house will fail and be torn down, but God will rescue us with a building from God, a house not made with human hands, a house which is eternal and never perishable in the heavens."

Abraham has lived four thousand years in that house. Amazingly, he is still waiting on his first trip to the doctor or the dentist!

Thank God, we will not be disappointed!

Nor will we be disappointed in what occurs next: our arrival in the sanctified, glorified city known as heaven.

> "I'll not be a stranger when I get to that city.
> I'm acquainted with folks over there.
> There'll be friends there to greet me,
> There'll be loved ones to meet me
> At the gates of that city four square."
>
> James B. Singleton

Who will be there to welcome you?

23

I AM FINALLY LIKE HIM!

The promise has been given that *"We shall be like Him."* Not like we were on our best day, nor like some relative or personality we admire. But the day is coming, and hopefully will come soon, when we shall be like Him: our Lord and Savior, Redeemer and Friend, Constant Companion, Shield and Protector Jesus Christ.

"Beloved, we are now children of God. To this date it has not yet appeared what we shall eventually be, but we know He is coming and when He at last appears, He will make us to be like Him. How can we be sure we are like Him? It is because we shall see Him as He genuinely is" (1 John 3:1-2).

"Whom my own eyes shall behold and not the eyes of another" (Job 19:27).

We shall be in His likeness! An examination of His body will make it clear that we, who are so frail down here, are truly like Him up there!

Evangelist Glenn Mathews says with such confidence,

You may say, 'I just don't know what is going to happen.' Oh, yes, you do. The Lord is going to come. Suddenly, but certainly, and the dead in Christ are going to be raised. And we who remain will be called up together with them in the clouds to meet the Lord in the air, and we will forever be with the Lord.

If you think it is rough now, you wait until the Church of Jesus Christ is gone, and seven years of hell on earth begin. The Lord is going to come back. He is going to establish His Kingdom. We won't study war anymore; it will be peace. Not just peace in the valley, but peace on the mountaintop. Not just for the Jews but for the Gentiles as well. We are going to enter into that. God is sovereign. (*Expositions That Matter*, p. 29)

One of the precious memories from my childhood is how often we would sing about a happy reunion when God's saints are reunited in heaven. That will indeed be a wonderful day. One of my older members said recently, "I now have more friends on the other side than on this side." He was looking forward to meeting his dear departed friends! Well, so am I!

There is another reunion, though, which holds special meaning to the child of God. *It is the reunion of the soul to the body*—a body that has housed our soul since the day of our conception. This body of mine may not look like much to you, but it is home to me.

If the Lord Jesus does not return soon, my body shall inevitably go the way of my father and those before him. Someone may stand at my grave and read the age-old committal,

> We commit his body to the ground, earth to earth, ashes to ashes, dust to dust, looking for the resurrection and the life of the world to come through our Lord Jesus Christ: at whose second coming in glorious majesty to judge the world, the earth and the sea shall give up their dead; and the corruptible bodies of those who sleep in Him shall be changed, and made like unto His own glorious body; according to the mighty working whereby He is able to subdue all things unto Himself. (*Christian Minister's Manual*, p. 137)

That committal is not read at many funerals today, but it was read without fail in prior generations. *In so doing, the final words associated with that believer were words expressing the believer's hope of a future resurrection!*

The previous two chapters provide substantial proof that the immaterial, spiritual part of the deceased believer is currently very much alive in the presence of the Lord. The deceased believer is in a state or condition described as "absent from the body but present with the Lord."

However, the Bible also makes it clear that *God's salvation is a complete salvation that saves completely.* Christ died for *all* of our being: in other words, for the whole or entire man. Throughout this book, we have observed that our salvation includes three aspects: past, present, and future. Perhaps you recall this paragraph from the fourth chapter:

> Sanctification Stage 1 is a single, unrepeated act on the part of God setting apart the believer. Sanctification Stage 2 is a continuing, repeated process from the day of salvation to the day of our going to be with the Lord. Sanctification Stage 3 is a single, unrepeated act when God, once and for all, eradicates the sin nature, glorifies the fleshly body, and allows the new nature to assume total control. What a day that will be for the child of God, because it will be the day of complete deliverance!

God's salvation will not be complete in my life until God also sanctifies my fleshly, corruptible body through the act of a physical resurrection. "[W]ho will transform our lowly body to be like his glorious body, by the power that enables him even to subject all things to himself" (Philippians 3:21, ESV). Another translation says it this way. "[W]ho will transform the body of our humble state into conformity with the body of His glory, by the exertion of the power that He has even to subject all things to Himself" (Philippians 3:21, NASB).

Therefore, we can be certain that God will not finish with *any* of us until the totality of *each* one of us is just like Jesus! One hundred percent like Him!

1. THE BACKGROUND OF THE RESURRECTION

The concept of a bodily resurrection is unique to the three religions that have emerged from Abraham: Judaism (not all of Judaism), Christianity, and Islam. Most world religions believe in a hereafter, but not in a physical resurrection. Those non-resurrection religions emphasize the preeminence of the soul living forever rather than of the body living forever. Some religions, including Buddhism and Hinduism, believe in the concept of reincarnation but also stop far short of belief in a bodily resurrection. From their perspective, the body lacks importance, but from God's perspective, the body has great importance.

Ironically, we base our belief in the resurrection upon a Bible, which was written mostly by Jews, but yet the resurrection was a very divisive issue within Judaism during Paul's day. There was even an occasion when Paul used that division to his advantage:

> *Men and brethren, I am a Pharisee, the son of a Pharisee: of the hope and resurrection of the dead I am called in question. And when he had so said, there arose a dissension between the Pharisees and the Sadducees: and the multitude was divided. For the Sadducees say that there is no resurrection, neither angel, nor spirit: but the Pharisees confess both. (Acts 23:6-8, KJV). (Note: That is why the Sadducees were "sad, you see.")*

One wonders how the Sadducees could adopt such a conclusion because the concept of a bodily resurrection was clearly taught in the Old Testament. It is impossible to understand the depth of the Old Testament saint's comprehension, but there are many scriptures to indicate the teaching was known and accepted. But how much was knowable and taught? We do not know.

The Old Testament teachings begin with what is generally considered to be the oldest book in the Old Testament: Job. For example, how many times have I stood at the grave and read, "If a man die, shall he live again? All the days of my appointed time will I wait, till my change come. Thou shalt call, and I will answer thee" (Job 14:14-15, KJV).

The theology of Job may have been ancient, but it appears to have been thorough. Job says, "For I know that my Redeemer lives, and at the last he will stand upon the earth. And after my skin has been thus destroyed, yet in my flesh I shall see God, whom I shall see for myself, and my eyes shall behold, and not another. My heart faints within me!" (Job 19:25-27, ESV).

One of the most familiar Old Testament stories includes a picture or type of a bodily resurrection. Abraham ". . . bound his son Isaac and placed him on the altar on top of the wood. Then Abraham reached out and took the knife to slaughter his son" (Genesis 22:9-10, CSB). Why was Abraham willing to sacrifice his "one and only" son? "He considered God to be able even to raise someone from the dead; therefore, he received him back, figuratively speaking" (Hebrews 11:19, CSB).

There is an abundance of other Old Testament scriptures that indicate there was a common belief of a physical resurrection in the years before Christ. "Therefore my heart is glad and my spirit rejoices; my body also rests securely. For You will not abandon me to Sheol; You will not allow Your Faithful One to see decay" (Psalm 16:9-10, HCSB).

"Thy dead men shall live, together with my dead body shall they arise. Awake and sing, ye that dwell in dust" (Isaiah 16:19, KJV).

"I will ransom them from the power of Sheol. I will redeem them from death. Death, where are your barbs? Sheol, where is your sting? Compassion is hidden from My eyes" (Hosea 13:14, HCSB).

"And many of them that sleep in the dust of the earth shall awake, some to everlasting life, and some to shame and everlasting contempt" (Daniel 12:2, KJV).

In addition, the Old Testament records the resurrection of three people: the widow's son (1 Kings 17:21-22), the Shunamite's son (2 Kings 4:32-36), and the man who touched Elisha's bones (2 Kings 13:21).

Based on this abundant evidence, one must wonder about how much more can God can do It is fair to say that God has borne Himself abundant witness regarding the resurrection of the last days.

The bodily resurrection was taught by Jesus, too. "Do not be amazed at this, because a time is coming when all who are in the graves will hear his voice and come out—those who have done good things, to the resurrection of life, but those who have done wicked things, to the resurrection of condemnation" (John 5:28-29, CSB).

"Jesus said to her, 'I am the resurrection and the life. The one who believes in Me, even if he dies, will live'" (John 11:25, CSB).

Moreover, the foundational truth presented throughout the book of Acts is that "with wicked hands you have slain the Holy One, but God has raised this same Jesus from the dead."

". . . Jesus Christ, the faithful witness, the firstborn from the dead . . . When I saw him, I fell at his feet like a dead man. He laid his right hand on me and said, 'Don't be afraid. I am the First and the Last, and the Living One. I was dead, but look—I am alive forever and ever, and I hold the keys of Death and Hades'" (Revelation 1:5, 17-18, CSB).

The Bible makes it clear that Christ is regarded as the firstfruits of those that now sleep (1 Corinthians 15:23). In this case, the firstfruits represent God's guarantee that the second fruits (you and me) will someday follow!

We can safely conclude that one does not have to look far to see the doctrine of the resurrection in the Bible. Herbert Lockyer points out that the expression "resurrection from the dead" occurs thirty-four times of Christ's resurrection and fifteen times of our own resurrection. In other words, the belief in a physical resurrection is everywhere in scripture.

2. THE MEANING OF "RESURRECTION"

The English word "resurrection" comes from the compound Greek word *anastasis*. It is a unique word with a very powerful meaning. *Ana* means "up." *Stasis* (from *histemi*) means "to cause to stand." Thus, the compound word expresses the idea that one who is prone is now *caused* to stand up. Oh, my, such a brilliant concept! The dead body lies horizontal without strength in a casket until it is *made* to stand perpendicular by Someone of greater power.

It is as if the body is rising in obedience to the General's order of, "Attention!" Suddenly, that body of flesh has strength; furthermore, it demonstrates that strength by rising in anticipation of some future activity. It stands to attention! The body is no longer asleep but is fully awake. It is responsive. It is functioning. It is ready to participate again.

Perhaps soon my body will return to the dust. But I have God's guarantee that He will someday save this body, too. Sometime in the future, the trumpet of God shall sound, and this body of mine shall immediately stand up!

The resurrection of Lazarus presents a beautiful picture of our resurrection.

> *So they removed the stone. Then Jesus raised his eyes and said, 'Father, I thank you that you heard me. I know that you always hear me, but because of the crowd standing here I said this, so that they may believe you sent me.' After he said this, he shouted with a loud voice, 'Lazarus, come out!' The dead man came out bound hand and foot with linen strips and with his face wrapped in a cloth. Jesus said to them, 'Unwrap him and let him go' (John 11:41-44, CSB).*

"It is sown in weakness; it is raised in power" (1 Corinthians 15:43). We might paraphrase those words in this manner: "Sown *into* the earth in weakness but raised *out* of the earth in power!"

As it was with the Master, so it was with the servant. "Up from the grave, Lazarus arose! Like a mighty victor over sin, death, and the grave."

3. THE NATURE OF THE RESURRECTION BODY

So also is the resurrection of the dead. It is sown a perishable body, it is raised an imperishable body; it is sown in dishonor, it is raised in glory; it is sown in weakness, it is raised in power; it is sown a natural body, it is raised a spiritual body. If there is a natural body, there is also a spiritual body. So also it is written, 'The first man, Adam, became a living soul.' The last Adam became a life-giving spirit. However, the spiritual is not first, but the natural; then the spiritual. The first man is from the earth, earthy; the second man is from heaven. As is the earthy, so also are those who are earthy; and as is the heavenly, so also are those who are heavenly. Just as we have borne the image of the earthy, we will also bear the image of the heavenly. (1 Corinthians 15:42-49, NASB)

What is the composition of the fully sanctified resurrection body? George Ladd states,

> Paul's 'spiritual body' is a new body that stands in some kind of real continuity with the physical body, which will yet be different because it has been transformed by the Holy Spirit and made like the glorious body of the resurrected Jesus (Phil. 3:21). The physical body was of dust, like Adam's body; the spiritual body will be heavenly, like Christ's body; but it is still a body. (*A Theology of the New Testament*, p. 564)

If the new body were mere spirit, as some claim, one would be forced to conclude the resurrected believer would have *two* spirits: one spirit, which is our current life, and a second spirit received at the resurrection. Such a belief could not be further from the truth and would compound the discussion with more issues than we could comprehend. Furthermore, such a belief lacks any confirming scriptural support.

It is best to focus one's attention on the phrase, "it is sown a natural body, but it is raised a spiritual body." Robert G. Gromacki distinguishes the two bodies in *Called to Be Saints* (p. 194):

> The natural body is a 'soulish' body (*psychikon*), a body adapted to the soul of man and suited to present earthly life in all

of its aspects (sex, reproduction, social relationships; cf. the *psychikos* man, 2:14). On the other hand, the spiritual body is not immaterial or pure spirit. Rather, it is a body which is adapted to the spirit or that which corresponds to the image of God in man. Today, the spirit is hampered by a soulish body, but in eternity, the body will be dominated by the spirit . . . The real difference was between the natural body (corruptible) and the spiritual body (incorruptible and resurrection).

The Bible makes it clear that we will "be like Him" (1 John 3:2). "He will transform the body of our humble condition into the likeness of His glorious body" (Philippians 3:21, CSB). Thus, the body of our resurrected Lord serves as a prototype (also called the firstfruits). He is the first in the order of resurrection and glorification; His glorified, resurrected body will be the pattern for those to follow (including you and me).

God will finish the entire process of sanctification through the resurrection. The process began at our salvation. It will be completed at our resurrection. Through the means of becoming glorified in our resurrection, we will exist in 100% conformity to the pattern of Jesus Christ!

What do we know about His new body?

First, Jesus arose from the grave in a real, touchable *body* of flesh and bones. The resurrected Lord said, "'Look at My hands and My feet, that it is I Myself! Touch Me and see, because a ghost does not have flesh and bones as you can see I have'" (Luke 24:39, CSB). The word "ghost" (Greek *pneuma*) can also be translated "spirit." One cannot touch a spirit or a ghost, but one can touch a body. If a person denies the *physical* resurrection of believers, he also denies the *physical* resurrection of Jesus Christ.

It is noteworthy that Jesus did not include "blood" in describing His resurrection body. The scriptures teach, "flesh and blood cannot inherit the kingdom of God" (1 Corinthians 15:50). The term "flesh and blood" obviously refers to this decaying body of sin, but "flesh and bones" refers to the resurrection body. Apparently, blood is not necessary for the resurrection body even though blood is necessary for the physical body (Leviticus 17:11).

Based on Luke 24:39, we can easily accept Gromacki's conclusion that the new body will be termed a "spiritual" body even though it is not a *pure* body of spirit.

Second, Jesus arose in a spiritual body which was not limited by physical barriers. The Bible indicates that Jesus appeared in a room with locked doors (John 20:19-20). How did Jesus enter the room? He apparently passed through the walls or transported Himself inside the room from outside the room. How He did it is not known, but it is known that He did do it! Also, Jesus overcame the laws of gravity when He ascended to the Father in the opening verses of Acts.

Third, the resurrected Jesus was able to consume food just as He did before His death. Jesus employed such an action to prove to the apostles that He was not a ghost. ". . . He said to them, 'Have you anything here to eat?' They gave Him a piece of a broiled fish; and He took it and ate it before them" (Luke 24:41-43, NASB). Food is probably not necessary for the resurrection body, but food can be consumed for personal enjoyment. That appears to be the basis for the promise in Revelation 2:7. The overcomer is given the right to eat from the tree of life. The Master's invitation to, "Come and dine!" sounds good to today's hungry soul.

Fourth, Jesus was recognizable yet *not* recognizable. Case in point: Mary Magdalene did not immediately recognize him on the day of His resurrection. John 20:14 states, "Mary saw Jesus standing there but she did not know or recognize Him as Jesus." She thought He was only a gardener but, oh, the surprise that was soon hers!

Jesus first addressed her as "Woman" and received no response. He then addressed her as "Mary". Speaking her *name* changed the situation because "I call My sheep by their personal *name* . . . they hear My voice and they follow Me" (John 10:3, 27). Mary immediately turned around to face Jesus, apparently recognized Him, and said with deep emotion, "*Rabbouni,*" which means "Teacher" or "Rabbi." She now knew!

Perhaps Mary did not immediately recognize Jesus by sight because she had a preconceived idea in her head that there would be no resurrection. But she recognized the way He said her name. *That suggests the resurrection body will be familiar to our friends.*

Later that day, Jesus showed His crucifixion wounds to the apostles. "Then were the disciples glad when they *saw* the Lord" (John 20:20). Mary *heard,* but they *saw.* That simple summary indicates that two human senses identified our risen Lord. Also, doubting Thomas was invited to *touch*! That is a third human sense!

Paul testified to the Corinthians that this resurrected Jesus appeared to Peter, the twelve, to five hundred brethren in one setting, plus to James, all the apostles, and last of all to himself. They believed it was Him because they *recognized* Him! Otherwise, they would not have qualified as eyewitnesses.

One dear brother asked his pastor, "Will we recognize one another in heaven?"

The pastor answered, "I'd hate to think I'm dumber in heaven than I am down here."

There will obviously be a difference in our appearance, but we can be confident that it will be a *glorified* difference with no weaknesses or defects of any kind! "For now we know in part, but then shall we know fully even as we are now fully known" (1 Corinthians 13:12).

"Therefore, from now on we recognize no one according to the flesh; even though we have known Christ according to the flesh, yet now we know *Him in this way* no longer" (2 Corinthians 5:16, NASB). (The italics are mine.)

Imagine what the new *you* will be like! One of my female co-workers was impressed with the hairstyle of a new female employee. She told the new employee that she wished her hair was as straight as the new employee's hair. She then asked, "Would you like to trade?"

The new employee said, "No. I don't want your gray hair."

Imagine you without all the defects, weaknesses, limitations, insecurities, forgetfulness, and sicknesses. Even so, the half has not yet been told.

"For this perishable must put on the imperishable, and this mortal must put on immortality" (1 Corinthians 15:53, NASB). ***When God is finished, all that have died in Christ will be raised to die no more.*** There will be no more "hastening to the grave." The last taint of sin will be removed. The body will be a holy body forevermore; such a holy body will be an appropriate home for a holy soul.

4. RECONSTITUTING THE RESURRECTION BODY

What happens if the body no longer exists? The Bible teaches every single body will somehow be reconstituted. That may sound like a major problem because some bodies have been cremated, and the ashes scattered to the four winds. Other bodies were destroyed in a bomb blast; barely any DNA remains to identify the deceased. Some bodies were devoured by the fish of the sea or by animals. In turn, those fish or animals were consumed by other fish or animals. There are many possibilities to utterly destroy a human body.

But the solution to resurrecting a nonexistent body is very simple: The God that created the universe has declared that He intends to resurrect the dead. God said it will happen; therefore, it will indeed happen!

"Do not be amazed at this, because a time is coming when all who are in the graves will hear his voice and come out—those who have done good things, to the resurrection of life, but those who have done wicked things, to the resurrection of condemnation." (John 5:28-29, CSB)

Thus, the resurrection of every single body must be accepted by faith. After all, "Is anything too difficult for the Lord?" (Genesis 18:14). The obvious answer is, "No." It is *less* difficult to accept the resurrection of a nonexistent body than to accept the big teachings like Genesis 1:1. If God can create a universe, it is a simple thing for Him to re-create something as small as a human body!

That's why the Bible says, "The sea will give up its dead. As a matter of fact, Death and Hades will give up their dead, too" (Revelation 20:13). No stone will be left unturned. It may very well be that somewhere somehow, the basic elements of that body still exist. God's thorough search will locate every element.

That is why the Bible affirms that *both* the believer and the unbeliever will be resurrected: the first to eternal life and the second to eternal damnation.

5. THE REUNION OF THE IMMATERIAL TO THE MATERIAL

There is a problem that needs to be resolved: The soul of the deceased saint is currently in heaven, but the body lies in a grave. We know from many Bible passages that the body will be resurrected. Thus, we will have a body as well as a spirit.

Will there be two of us? Body and spirit? Material and immaterial? The simple answer is no. The scriptures indicate that God will reunite the soul and/or spirit of the deceased saint with that saint's body. In other words, the soul and/or spirit will be *repositioned inside* the resurrected body. In so doing, the saint will, for the first time in his existence, become perfectly sanctified or glorified *both* on the inside as well as the outside.

> *For if we believe that Jesus died and rose again, even so God will bring with Him those who have fallen asleep in Jesus. For this we say to you by the word of the Lord, that we who are alive and remain until the coming of the Lord, will not precede those who have fallen asleep. For the Lord Himself will descend from heaven with a shout,*

> *with the voice of the archangel and with the trumpet of*
> *God, and the dead in Christ will rise first. Then we who*
> *are alive and remain will be caught up together with*
> *them in the clouds to meet the Lord in the air, and so we*
> *shall always be with the Lord. (1 Thessalonians 4:14-*
> *17, NASB)*

The dispensational scholar Merrill Unger summarizes the biblical teaching in *Unger's Bible Handbook* (p. 706): "Since believers are united to the risen Lord, when they die physically, they fall asleep 'in Jesus.' When Christ returns, He will bring their souls and spirits with Him to be united with their risen bodies."

Several biblical terms should be defined before we investigate the reunion. First, "the dead in Christ" is the equivalent of "them that have fallen asleep." These two designations represent the same universe of people.

Second, the believers are classified as "asleep" but also "in Christ." In other words, death did not separate them from Christ (Romans 8:38). Thank God, "he that is joined to the Lord is (perhaps we should use the word "remains") one spirit with the Lord" (1 Corinthians 6:17).

Then comes the exciting part! *The dead will return from heaven with the Lord.* "God will bring with Him all of those who have fallen asleep in Jesus" (1 Thessalonians 4:14). This is yet one more verse to indicate that the deceased believers are *currently* present with the Lord in fulfillment of John 14:2-3. Their bodies are to be resurrected *upward* in 1 Thessalonians 4:16, but the spirits are returning with Jesus *downward* in verse fourteen.

Can you get a glimpse of the heavenly picture? Our deceased friends are now in God's presence. Heaven is full of their praise and worship. Then God the Father interrupts and says, "Son, go get their bodies, and while you are at it, get Our children who are still alive."

Jesus will then announce to those saints surrounding His throne, "Children, two thousand years ago, I promised that I would resurrect your bodies. It is time for us to go back to the earth and claim that body which belongs specifically to you."

Somehow unknown to me, Jesus will lead all of His blood-bought saints out of heaven. Can you imagine the number? Will it be numberless like the sand by the sea? The entire family will return to this earth. For a short time, heaven will be occupied by only those who occupied it at the time of Genesis 1:1.

The Lord Jesus shall give a shout, perhaps a shout similar to His words at Lazarus' tomb. My father would often preach, "It will need to be a *specific* shout. If Jesus gives a general call such as, 'Come forth,' *all* will come forth, both the bodies of believers and unbelievers."

Perhaps every single body will hear its own name called. That body which is now dead, will be made to "stand up." That body, which is now lifeless, will once again have life.

"And the dead in Christ shall rise first." The dead bodies will be resurrected and changed from bodies subject to corruption to incorruptible bodies, which can never again be subject to corruption; this change will occur just one moment before God immortalizes the bodies of the living saints (1 Corinthians 15:51-52). Why does God specify this particular order? The answer is unknown.

It has been suggested the dead rise first because they have farther to go! Maybe so. Perhaps Hodge's words, though, need to be repeated: "This is all that is revealed and this is enough."

Hiebert states,

> The raising of the Christian dead *first* does not, however, give them any advantage over the living saints. Those that are alive 'shall together with them,' the resurrected, 'be caught up in the clouds.' 'Together with them' denotes that the two groups will unitedly and as one company arise to meet the Lord. It implies the full association and equality of the two groups.

The verb *caught up* denotes a sudden and forcible seizure, an irresistible act of catching away, due to divine activity. It might also be rendered, 'snatch up, sweep up, carry off by force.' The Latin for the

Greek verb is *rapturo* from which we derive our English word 'rapture.' (*The Thessalonian Epistles,* p 201)

Where will the reunion of the departed saint's spirit and body occur? The Bible says the believers will meet the Lord "in the air" (1 Thessalonians 4:17). It does not, though, reveal specifically where the reunion of the spirit and body will occur.

However, perhaps a clue is contained in the phrase "shall not *precede* those who have fallen asleep." The glorification of the *living* saint will apparently occur on earth at the very moment that he *begins* to rise through the air. He will become 100% sanctified at that moment in time. All three parts: the body, soul, and spirit will be sanctified, consecrated, yes, even made holy through and through. That glorified condition will remain throughout the eons of eternity.

But that will not happen *until* the dead reach the same state. It, therefore, seems reasonable to assume the following order of events:

1. The Lord Jesus and the spirits of just men made holy return from heaven.
2. Jesus stops in the clouds.
3. The spirits continue to the earth.
4. The body in the grave is restored to resurrection life as the spirit re-enters the body.
5. The grave, though, could not hold Jesus, and the grave will not hold our deceased loved ones either!
6. Up from the grave, the combined soul, spirit, and body will rise in glory.
7. The reunited saint will then continue skyward to meet the Lord in the air. He will not loiter on the earth, because he has a meeting to attend! The living, not yet deceased, saint will undergo his own transformation/glorification as the resurrected saint rises from the grave. (The living will receive glorified bodies without ever passing through the valley of the shadow of death.)

8. Then together—not in waves but in *one* wave—all believers
    will rise skyward to meet the Lord in the air.

"Caught up together with them in the clouds." Where are the clouds?
They are in the space *between* earth and heaven. Not quite earth, not
quite heaven. Findlay describes the clouds as being "half of heaven and
half of earth." What better place could there be than in the clouds? To
experience with great joy what Paul means when he asks, "Who shall
deliver me from the body of this death? I thank God for the victory that I
will someday experience in Jesus Christ" (Romans 7:25).

"We currently groan within ourselves for the redemption of our
body" (Romans 8:23). But all groaning will cease when we meet the
Lord in the air. One can only imagine the joy of that moment!

H. A. Ironside writes, "Notice that word 'together.' We have had
fellowship *together* down here; we have been workers *together* under
our Lord's authority, and when He returns, we will be caught up
together to meet the Lord in the air." (*Addresses on the First and Second
Epistles of Thessalonians*, p. 51)

Unger's summary is excellent and to the point:

> 'The Lord Himself,' personally, bodily 'shall come down
> from heaven with a shout' . . . The 'shout' is the shout of
> triumph over death, manifested in the raising of the dead saints
> and in the instantaneous glorification of the living saints, who
> will never taste physical death. 'The voice of the archangel' is
> evidently that of Michael . . . The dead in Christ rise first, then
> immediately the saints who are living . . . shall be suddenly
> conveyed away in the 'clouds' to meet the Lord in the air. In this
> manner the saints will forever be with the Lord. (*Unger's Bible
> Handbook*, p. 706)

It does not yet appear what we shall be. But someday it will indeed
appear.

You can count on it.

Thank You, Jesus.

24

A FOREVER LIFE OF SANCTIFIED PERFECTION

"Sanctification is glory in the seed, and glory is sanctification in the flower."

Many years ago there was a young boy in England whose father died. This boy had to quit school to provide for his family. He sold newspapers every day then stopped by the toy store to look at the toy soldiers in the window. He imagined the thrill that would be his if he could play with those toy soldiers. But, unfortunately, there was a glass between the soldiers and him. All he could do was imagine what it would be like to play with those toy soldiers.

One day, though, the boy did not come. The shopkeeper went out into the street and asked, "Has anyone seen the little boy who would look in our window at the toy soldiers?"

Someone responded, "Haven't you heard? He was hit by an automobile early today and is now unconscious in the hospital."

The storekeeper immediately gathered all of the toy soldiers and took them to the hospital. He set the toy soldiers at the foot of the boy's bed then left.

The boy soon regained consciousness. His attention was drawn first to his mother's smiling face. His mother immediately pointed to the foot of the bed and the toy soldiers. The boy could not believe what he saw! He reached out his hands toward those toy soldiers, got closer and closer until, at last, the soldiers were in his hands.

He then turned to his mother and said, "Oh, Mother, look! Here are my soldiers, and now *there is no glass in between.*"

I now see heaven through a glass—I can't touch heaven at all. I know some people in heaven, but I cannot touch them. I am sure my friends are rejoicing in heaven, but I cannot hear them. I have every confidence my friends are walking on streets of gold, walking where holy angels have trod, but I cannot see them.

But someday God is going to take away the glass. I am going to personally experience what is on the other side.

> "Then we shall be where we would be,
> Then we shall be what we should be;
> Things that are not now, nor could be,
> Soon shall be our own."

> Thomas Kelly

You and I began life with an impossible assignment. Jesus says, "Be perfect like your Father in heaven is perfect." My sinfulness, though, was so great that I could never hope to attain such a holy standard. But through the never-ending, all-sufficient grace of God, I shall finish life in accordance with that holy standard. I shall indeed be perfect—absolutely perfect—like my Father in heaven is perfect.

"Now to him who is able to keep you from stumbling and to present you blameless before the presence of his glory with great joy, to the only God, our Savior, through Jesus Christ our Lord, be glory, majesty, dominion, and authority, before all time and now and forever. Amen" (Jude 24-25, ESV).

The psalmist said to the Lord God Almighty, "But I will see your face in righteousness; when I awake, I will be satisfied with your presence" (Psalm 17:15, CSB).

For the first time in our lives, it will now be said: *By God's grace, we've made it!* Truly made it! We're finally home! The journey is over. Faith has now become sight. Hope has now become reality. The unknown has now become known. The confusion has now become clear.

Fear is gone, hurt is gone, pain is gone, rejection is gone, illness is gone, death is gone, the devil is gone, temptation is gone, confession of sin is gone, confusion is gone, war is gone, lusting is gone, crying and tears are gone, wickedness is gone, separation of friends is gone, failure is gone, hunger and thirst are gone, criticism is gone, night is gone, lies are gone, being alone and standing alone are gone.

Instead, glory is here, peace is here, health is here, friends are here, the saints of old are here, Jesus Himself is here and is pleased to call us His brothers and sisters, holiness is here, rest for the soul is here, godliness is here, the fruit of the Spirit is here, Surely Goodness and Mercy are here, full obedience is here, the tree of life is here, unrestrained worship is here, a new name is here, everyone agreeing is here, the law of God reigns here, the truth is here, righteousness is here, life's answers are here, acceptance is here, victory is here, a new heaven and new earth in which dwelleth righteousness are here.

And we are now here, too, for after death there is indeed destiny. *The believer's destiny is to live a "forever life" of sanctified perfection with God.*

"What is your life on earth? For your life is like a fog, even a mist that appears for a little time and then quickly disappears" (James 4:14). The temporal life will end quickly; the eternal life, though, will never end because it is a "forever life." "So shall we *ever be* with the Lord!"

A Sunday School teacher asked her second-grade class, "What is heaven to you?"

One student raised his hand and said, "Heaven will be the happiest part of my dead life." He was indeed right on "the happiest part."

"In my Father's house are many rooms; if not, I would have told you. I am going away to prepare a place for you. If I go away and prepare a place for you, I will come again and receive you to myself, so that where I am you may be also" (John 14:2-3). With Him forever!

Our future home has numerous names. John 14:2 identifies it as the "Father's house." The King James Version of Luke 16:22 employs the term, "Abraham's bosom." Jesus promised a place called paradise to the dying thief (Luke 23:43).

But the most familiar name for our home is heaven. "Now I know that the LORD saves his anointed; he will answer him from his holy heaven with the saving might of his right hand" (Psalm 20:6, ESV).

"Our Father, who art in heaven" (Matthew 6:9).

"Lay up for yourselves treasures in heaven where moth and rust cannot destroy, a place where thieves cannot break in and steal your treasures" (Matthew 6:20).

"After this I looked and there in heaven was an open door" (Revelation 4:1, CSB). "And the voice said, 'Come up here!'"

There once lived a Christian woman who was confined to her bed because of illness. This woman lived on the fifth floor of an old rundown building. One of her friends decided to visit her. This friend brought along a woman of great wealth.

There was no elevator; these two distinguished ladies had to walk up five flights of stairs. When they reached the second floor, the wealthy woman looked at the filth and said, "Oh, what a dark and filthy place this is!"

The friend said, "I know, but it's better higher up."

They made it to the third floor. The third floor was in even worse shape than the second floor. The wealthy woman said, "Things look even worse here!"

The friend said, "I know, but it's better higher up!"

They made it to the apartment on the fifth floor. The bedfast saint greeted them with a smile that seemed to fill her heart.

The wealthy woman said, "It must be very difficult for you to live in a building like this!"

The bedfast saint said, "I know, but I also know it's better higher up."

1. SANCTIFIED PERFECTION: THE REQUIREMENT TO LIVE IN GOD'S HEAVEN

Herbert Lockyer writes, "There are wheat and tares; good fish and bad; sheep and goats; loyal and disloyal; saved and lost; those who do the will of God and those who do it not; children of God and children of the devil. Each soul goes to its place."

"Depart from Me, I never knew you," will be the fate of those who are in the negative categories in the above paragraph: tares, bad, goats, disloyal, lost, do not the will of God, children of the devil. Without a doubt, each soul must go to its own place. Such a place is the deliberate choice of those who go there.

The old saying is true:

> "Sow a thought, and reap an act;
> Sow an act, and reap a character;
> Sow a character, and reap a destiny."

The requirement to live in God's heaven is made clear in the last verse of Revelation chapter twenty-one. "Nothing profane will ever enter it: no one who does what is vile or false, but only those written in the Lamb's book of life" (Revelation 21:27, HCSB).

Heaven is identified as the Holy City because everything in it is holy. One of my acquaintances was so proud of his new house that he established a new rule: No shoes inside! But it did not work. Somehow dirt found its way inside. That, though, will never once happen in the Holy City. Not even a speck of dirt or sin will find its way inside.

"Nothing profane (impure, unclean) will ever enter it."

During World War Two, a French town was severely bombed, forcing the evacuation of the entire town. The bombing left only a few undamaged houses. One of those houses was the most luxurious house in town.

A few pigs somehow escaped death in the bombings. Those pigs rooted their way through a narrow gap in the wall and entered this marvelously furnished house. The pigs proceeded to walk with their muddy feet over the rich velvet carpet. They overturned the expensive furniture. They tore the beautiful draperies. They chewed anything and everything that might satisfy their hunger.

The house was indeed beautiful, but that meant nothing to the pigs. *The pigs had the nature of a mere beast.* They did not have the appreciation of the owner. The pigs proved they did not have a nature that was compatible with such a house.

In effect, the pigs needed a new nature—a different nature—before they could appreciate this luxurious house!

"Nothing profane, that is, no pig-like nature will ever enter the Holy City: *no one who does what is vile or false, but only those written in the Lamb's book of life.*"

It is important to recognize what *is* mentioned, as well as what is *not* mentioned in this verse. Three qualities are revealed about those who are excluded from God's heaven. "Profane" expresses the idea of unclean or defiled. "Vile" is synonymous with abominable, detestable, even shameful. "False!" The King James Bible substitutes the term "maketh a lie" for "false." Each of these evil words belongs in the category of spiritual darkness—the devil's kingdom. We can, therefore, conclude that no one in the devil's kingdom meets the requirement to live in God's heaven. They "have sinned and come short of the glory of God" (Romans 3:23).

Only one quality is revealed about those who are welcomed into God's heaven: Their names are written in the Lamb's book of life. The book of life records the names of the redeemed or born-again ones. Jesus says to His sheep, "Rejoice because your names are written in heaven" (Luke 10:20).

Strangely, nothing is said about the accomplishments of the redeemed during their time on earth. The verse includes nothing about their prayer life, witness, Bible study, consecration, giving, church attendance, reliability, or a host of other items.

What *is* said, though, is all that needs to be said. If one's name is written in the Lamb's book of life, it can be concluded that he is no longer profane, vile, or false. Why not? Surely each one of us has experienced momentary lapses in our earthly experience.

But let us remember that our "forever" salvation is not based upon what we do but upon what Christ has already done for us on the cross of Calvary. "For by a single offering he has perfected for all time those who are being sanctified" (Hebrews 10:14, ESV). It is impossible for a perfected person to lose his salvation because there is no reason to exclude that person.

We previously looked at Hebrews 10:14 in chapter four. We learned that "perfected" (Greek word *teleioo*) has the idea of "having attained a state of completeness." That completeness applies to every believer because *the sacrifice of Jesus fully satisfies the believer's imperfections before a perfect God.* Nothing more can be added to Christ's sacrifice. Through the blood of the cross, the sanctified or "set apart ones" have been perfected for all time.

The exclusion of Exodus 33:20 no longer applies to the believer. Moses prayed, "Lord, show me Your glory." God responded, "No man can see My glory and live." That exclusion applied to sinful man, but not to the glorified, sanctified believer who has been perfected in body, soul, and spirit by the blood of the cross.

The exclusion of 1 Samuel 6:19 no longer applies either. "God struck down the people of Beth-shemesh because they looked inside the ark of the LORD. He struck down seventy persons. The people mourned because the LORD struck them with a great slaughter" (1 Samuel 6:19, ESV). Unholiness cannot look upon that which is holy. But the glorified, sanctified saint in heaven is described as "blessed and holy" (Revelation 20:6). The Bible also describes the believer as "he that is righteous, let

413

him be righteous still: and he that is holy, let him be holy still" (Revelation 22:11, KJV). The 1 Samuel 6:19 exclusion applies to sinful man, but not to the glorified, sanctified believer who has been perfected in body, soul, and spirit by the blood of the cross.

We can conclude that the saint is in heaven, because he is <u>qualified</u> to live in heaven.

Revelation's twenty-second chapter possesses a similar statement. "Blessed are those who wash their robes, so that they may have the right to the tree of life, and may enter by the gates into the city. Outside are the dogs and the sorcerers and the immoral persons and the murderers and the idolaters, and everyone who loves and practices lying" (Revelation 22:14-15, NASB). "Wash their robes" is the equivalent expression of "written in the Lamb's book of life." The person who has appropriated Christ (John 1:12) is qualified to live in God's heaven.

Pilate asked, "What shall I do with Jesus who is called the Messiah?" (Matthew 27:22). The world answers, "Crucify him!" But the believer answers, "Receive Him!" *The answer determines which person is qualified to enter heaven.*

2. SANCTIFIED PERFECTION: GOD'S GOAL IS NOW FULFILLED.

Eighty-four-year-old Rowland Hill (1795–1879) was close to his meeting with death but did not know it. One Sunday night, he was seen walking the aisles in the church auditorium shortly after the lights had been extinguished. Hill was singing softly,

> "When I am to die, 'Receive me,' I'll cry,
> For Jesus has loved me, I cannot tell why;
> But this I do find, we two are so joined,
> He'll not be in Heaven and leave me behind."

God's goal in salvation is to "bring many sons to *glory*" (Hebrews 2:10). The depth and breadth of the "glory" is a mystery yet to be revealed, but the "how" is clear from Genesis to Revelation.

The Hebrews writer explains the "how" just a few words before exciting us with the "glory." Hebrews 2:9 explains, "Jesus tasted death for everyone." Based on Jesus' perfect sacrifice, God the Father can treat every believer as an adult son and bring that adult son into the innermost circle where he can enjoy both glory *around* him and glory *inside* him.

What is glory? It expresses the idea of absolute magnificence—the superlative of superlatives.

I was raised in old-fashioned Baptist churches where people were prone to shout when they became happy in the Lord. We didn't have many material possessions in those days. The people lived poor, sometimes "dirt poor." Therefore, people often become very excited when someone sang a song like "Mansion over the Hilltop." Many of our people would have been thrilled beyond measure just to enjoy heat in their bedrooms! The concepts of a mansion, a soft bed, and a heated house were overwhelming to our feeble minds.

I can still visualize those church services. The more vocal people would often give a loud, hearty "Amen" when they agreed with the preacher. Occasionally, someone would get really excited and shout, "Hallelujah!" or "Praise the Lord!" But then there were other times when the excitement soared to an even higher level; some dear soul would wave his hand or handkerchief and shout, "Well, Gloooooreeeey!"

It may not have been proper English, but it was the highest form of praise that our people knew. It may not seem logical, but it just sounded right! I find myself agreeing with the brother who said, "Glory is what you say when no other word will do."

The Bible agrees with that philosophy. In many ways, "glory" is undefinable, but it will definitely be a knowable experience. "Glory" is one of those words which is better felt than explained.

No death, no crying, no pain, streets of gold, an incorruptible body, an enormous gate consisting of a single pearl, a city illuminated not by a sun but by the Son, reunion after reunion, nothing to offend!

"Its gates will never close by day because it will never be night there" (Revelation 21:25, CSB).

And yet all of those blessings pale in significance to the "glory" which shall be revealed "*eis*" us—toward us, upon us, unto us, or in us (Romans 8:18). Indeed, perhaps our experience will consist of all four translations at the same time.

"If children, heirs also, heirs of God and fellow heirs with Christ, if indeed we suffer with Him so that we may also be glorified with Him" (Romans 8:17, NASB). Glorified together with Him!

"When Christ, who is our life, is revealed, then you also will be revealed with Him in glory" (Colossians 3:4, NASB).

> "When by His grace, I shall look on His face,
> That will be glory, be glory for me!"

> Charles Gabriel

3. SANCTIFIED PERFECTION IS AVAILABLE TO ALL.

The Bible concludes with the Sanctifier extending both arms toward the Unsanctified and calling them to Perfect Sanctification. "Both the Spirit and the bride say, 'Come!' Anyone who hears should say, 'Come!' And the one who is thirsty should come. Whoever desires should take the living water as a gift" (Revelation 22:17, HCSB).

God accomplishes His goal of complete sanctification following the principle that salvation is "not of yourselves, for not of works can any man boast" (Ephesians 2:8-9). Salvation is wholly a work of Him who has become God's wisdom, righteousness, sanctification, and redemption (1 Corinthians 1:30).

We will live in a city which John identified as the Holy City, the new Jerusalem, which will be the Jerusalem of all Jerusalems (Revelation 21:2). That is why the Bible says, "There will be no curse in that city"

(Revelation 22:3). Rather, it will be a city in which righteousness will dwell. In other words, all things will be done *right* in God's Holy City.

Right, not wrong! No mistakes! The number of people elected by God to salvation will equal the number of people who said, "I believe!" Both the Calvinist and Arminian will finally agree, "The elect are the whosoever wills, and the non-elect are the whosoever won'ts."

No errors of any kind! The number of dwelling places ("I go to prepare a place for you") will equal the number of the redeemed . . . not one empty room nor one person without a room. Everything will be in perfect balance. Not one believer will miss heaven.

Our eternity with God will begin . . . and never end!

As we think back upon these many pages, we must conclude, "God has done a wonderful, incredible, very thorough job in saving our sin-sick souls." It is something only God could have done. *I marvel that God freely chose to undertake such a responsibility for "a worm such as I."*

> *This is the word that came to Jeremiah from the Lord: 'Go down at once to the potter's house; there I will reveal my words to you.' So I went down to the potter's house, and there he was, working away at the wheel. But the jar that he was making from the clay became flawed in the potter's hand, so he made it into another jar, as it seemed right for him to do (Jeremiah 18:1-4, CSB).*

Chafer is undoubtedly correct when he says, "Failure is impossible with God."

God the Potter has taken us through the three stages of salvation called positional sanctification, progressive sanctification, and perfect sanctification. In this final stage, He is now "presenting us *faultless* to Himself."

"Who shall bring any accusation against God's elect? God is the Judge and it is God who justifies" (Romans 8:33).

"I am sure of this, that he who started a good work in you will carry it on to completion until the day of Christ Jesus" (Philippians 1:6, CSB).

Well, completion has now come. All glory goes to Him!

Evangelist B. R. Lakin of Cadle Tabernacle fame was preparing to preach in a revival. Just before the sermon, a man walked to the pulpit and sang, "If anyone makes it, well, surely I will."

Lakin walked immediately to the pulpit and said, "Well, surely you won't. The only reason anyone makes it to heaven is because 'Jesus paid it all, All to Him I owe, Sin had left a crimson stain, but, thank God, His blood was sufficient to wash it white as snow!'"

The blood of Jesus will allow us to someday be like Him! That is why we will sing throughout eternity, "You are worthy to take the scroll and to open its seals, because You were slaughtered, and You redeemed people for God by Your blood from every tribe and language and people and nation. You made them a kingdom and priests to our God, and they will reign on the earth" (Revelation 5:9-10, HCSB).

An author unknown to man but known to God has left us with this blessing:

> "The Light of Heaven is the face of Jesus;
> The Joy of Heaven is the presence of Jesus;
> The Melody of Heaven is the name of Jesus;
> The Harmony of Heaven is the praise of Jesus;
> The Theme of Heaven is the work of Jesus;
> The Employment of Heaven is the service of Jesus;
> The Fulness of Heaven is Jesus Himself."

Our young family attended a special Easter service at my father's pastorate in 1986. I can still remember the stage. Three crosses had been constructed to the left of the audience. A tomb had been constructed on the opposite side of the stage.

We had two daughters, Ashley and Lindsay, at the time. Both of them were entranced with those crosses. They intensely studied them as if preparing for a test.

They did not miss a single detail! They witnessed Jesus die as the auditorium became dark. They witnessed the burial of Jesus inside the tomb. They witnessed the sealing of the tomb with an enormous rock. They witnessed the placing of the guard. But they were not yet ready to go home. They expected more! Much more! They knew the first two events were not the complete story.

Then came the rumbling sound of a great earthquake! That huge rock came rolling off the stage and bounced against the first pew. The choir burst forth in song, "Up from the grave He arose, With a mighty triumph o'er His foes; He arose a victor from the dark domain, and He lives forever with His saints to reign!"

Every single one of us looked into that tomb. We could see the grave clothes, but we could not see the body of Jesus. Why? He was no longer in the tomb.

A thrill surged through that entire audience, but our little four-year-old Ashley was disappointed. She looked at me and said, *"But, Daddy, I didn't see Jesus! I didn't see Jesus come out of the tomb!"*

Do you know what she wanted?

Our four-year-old daughter actually expected to see Jesus!

She was not going to be satisfied until she finally saw Jesus!

I have good news: Someday every believer shall be satisfied. "But I will see your face in righteousness; when I awake, I will be satisfied with your presence" (Psalm 17:15, CSB).

And the most amazing truth of all is that *He will be satisfied with me.* Why?

For I shall be sanctified like Him.

Amen and Amen.

BIBLIOGRAPHY

Blackaby, Henry T. and Claude V. King. *Experiencing God.* Nashville: Broadman and Holman, 1994.

Blair, J. Allen. *John: Devotional Studies On Living Eternally.* Neptune, New Jersey: Loizeaux Brothers, 1978.

Boettner, Loraine. *Roman Catholicism.* Philadelphia: The Presbyterian and Reformed Publishing Company, 1962.

Boice, James. *The Gospel of John.* Grand Rapids: Zondervan Publishing House, 1985.

Bounds, E. M. *Power Through Prayer.* Grand Rapids: Baker Book House, 1972.

Boyce, James P. *Abstract of Systematic Theology.* Pompano Beach, Florida: Dulk Christian Foundation, 1887.

Chafer, Lewis Sperry. *He That is Spiritual.* Grand Rapids: Zondervan Publishing House, 1918.

Chafer, Lewis Sperry. *Major Bible Themes.* Grand Rapids: Zondervan Publishing House, 1974.

Chafer, Lewis Sperry. *Systematic Theology.* Dallas: Dallas Seminary Press, 1948.

Corlett, D. Shelby. *The Meaning of Holiness.* Kansas City: Beacon Hill Press, 1944.

Cowman, Lettie B. *Streams in the Desert.* Grand Rapids: Zondervan Publishing House, 2006.

Christian Minister's Manual. Cincinnati: Standard Publishing Company, 1965.

Criswell, W. A. *Great Doctrines of the Bible, Volume 6.* Grand Rapids: Zondervan, 1983.

Foster, Henry. *A Homiletic Commentary On The Epistles Of St. Paul The Apostle To The Corinthians.* New York: Funk and Wagnalls, 1896.

Gromacki, Robert G. *Called to Be Saints.* Grand Rapids: Baker Book House, 1977.

Hiebert, D. Edmond. *The Thessalonian Epistles.* Chicago: Moody Press, 1971.

Hodge, Charles. *An Exposition of the Second Epistle to the Corinthians.* Grand Rapids: Baker Book House, 1980.

Ironside, H. A. *Addresses on The Epistles of John and an Exposition of The Epistle of Jude.* Neptune, New Jersey: Loizeaux Brothers, 1931.

Ironside, H. A. *Addresses on the First and Second Epistles of Thessalonians.* Neptune, New Jersey: Loizeaux Brothers, 1947.

Ironside, H. A. *Addresses on the Second Epistle to the Corinthians.* Neptune, New Jersey: Loizeaux Brothers, 1939.

Ladd, George E. *A Theology of the New Testament.* Grand Rapids: William B. Eerdmans Publishing Company, 1974.

Lockyer, Herbert. *All The Doctrines Of The Bible.* Grand Rapids: Zondervan, 1964.

Mathews, Glenn. *Expositions that Encourage.* Bennett, North Carolina: Truth Publishing, 2018.

MacArthur, John F. *Keys To Spiritual Growth.* Old Tappan, New Jersey: Fleming H. Revell Company, 1976.

MacArthur, John F. *The MacArthur New Testament Commentary: Ephesians.* Chicago: Moody Bible Institute, 1986.

MacArthur, John F. *The MacArthur New Testament Commentary: Hebrews.* Chicago: Moody Bible Institute, 1983.

McGee, J. Vernon. *Thru the Bible with J. Vernon McGee.* Nashville: Thomas Nelson Publishers, 1983.

Packer, J. I. *Growing in Christ.* Wheaton: Crossway Books, 1994.

Phillips, John. *Exploring Psalms.* Grand Rapids: Kregel Publications, 1988.

Pink, A. W. *Gleanings in the Godhead.* Chicago: Moody Bible Institute, 1975.

Pink, A. W. *The Doctrine of Sanctification.* Swengle: Bible Truth Depot, 1955.

Rice, John R. *The Church of God at Corinth.* Murfreesboro: Sword of the Lord Publishers, 1973.

Ryrie, Charles C. *Biblical Theology of the New Testament.* Chicago: Moody Bible Institute, 1959.

Ryrie, Charles C. *The Ryrie Study Bible*. Chicago: Moody Press, 1976.

Showers, Renald E. *The New Nature*. Neptune, New Jersey: Loizeaux Brothers, 1986.

Strauss, Lehman. *The Eleven Commandments*. Neptune, New Jersey: Loizeaux Brothers, 1946.

The New Scofield Reference Bible. Oxford University Press, 1967.

Thiessen, Henry Clarence. *Introductory Lectures In Systematic Theology*. Grand Rapids: Wm. B. Eerdmans, 1949.

Torrey, Reuben A. *The Bible and Its Christ*. New York: Fleming H. Revell, 1906.

Unger, Merrill F. *Unger's Bible Dictionary*. Chicago: Moody Press, 1966.

Unger, Merrill F. *Unger's Bible Handbook*. Chicago: Moody Press, 1966.

Vine, W. E. *Vine's Expository Dictionary of New Testament Words*. McLean, Virginia: Mac Donald Publishing Company.

Walvoord, John F. *The Holy Spirit*. Findlay, Ohio: Dunham Publishing Company, 1958.

Wesley, John. *Plain Account of Christian Perfection*. Pantianos Classics, 1738.

Wilson, William. *Wilson's Old Testament Word Studies*. McLean, Virginia: Mac Donald Publishing Company.

Wuest, Kenneth. *First Peter in the Greek New Testament*. Grand Rapids: Wm. B. Eerdmans, 1942.

Wuest, Kenneth. *Golden Nuggets From The Greek New Testament*. Grand Rapids: Wm. B. Eerdmans, 1940.

Wuest, Kenneth. *Great Truths To Live By*. Grand Rapids: Wm. B. Eerdmans, 1952.

Wuest, Kenneth. *In These Last Days*. Grand Rapids: Wm. B. Eerdmans, 1954.

Wuest, Kenneth. *Romans*. Grand Rapids: Wm. B. Eerdmans, 1955.

Wuest, Kenneth. *Studies In The Vocabulary Of The Greek New Testament*. Grand Rapids: Wm. B. Eerdmans, 1945.

Wuest, Kenneth. *The New Testament: An Expanded Translation by Kenneth S. Wuest*. Grand Rapids: Wm. B. Eerdmans, 1961.

INDEX

N

P

R

T

ABOUT THE AUTHOR

Tom Swartzwelder received his B.A. in Bible from Tennessee Temple University in Chattanooga, Tennessee in 1979 and his Master of Divinity from Luther Rice Seminary in 1987. He has pastored Baptist churches for nearly forty years in both bi-vocational and full-time roles. Tom retired in 2018 from secular employment as Finance Director for a local HUD agency. He continues to pastor and write practical how-to-do-ministry resources for church leaders. His resources are available for free download at GodsGreenhouse.net. Tom married Ruth Ellen Wiseman on the eve of beginning his ministerial training at Tennessee Temple University. They are the proud parents of Ashley, Lindsay, and Elizabeth and are enjoying a growing number of grandchildren. They reside in South Point, Ohio.